GENRE AND OPENNESS
IN PROVERBS 10:1–22:16

ANCIENT ISRAEL AND ITS LITERATURE

Thomas C. Römer, General Editor

Editorial Board:
Susan Ackerman
Thomas B. Dozeman
Alphonso Groenewald
Shuichi Hasegawa
Konrad Schmid
Naomi A. Steinberg

Number 39

GENRE AND OPENNESS
IN PROVERBS 10:1–22:16

Suzanna R. Millar

Atlanta

Copyright © 2020 by Suzanna R. Millar

Library of Congress Cataloging-in-Publication Data

Names: Millar, Suzanna R., author.
Title: Genre and openness in Proverbs 10:1–22:16 / by Suzanna R. Millar.
Description: Atlanta : SBL Press, [2020] | Series: Ancient Israel and Its Literature ; 39 | Includes bibliographical references and index.
Identifiers: LCCN 2019059606 (print) | LCCN 2019059607 (ebook) | ISBN 9780884144335 (hardback) | ISBN 9781628372724 (paperback) | ISBN 9780884144342 (ebook)
Subjects: LCSH: Bible. Proverbs, X, 1–XXII, 16—Criticism, interpretation, etc. | Bible. Proverbs, X, 1–XXII, 16—Criticism, Textual.
Classification: LCC BS1465.52 .M555 2020 (print) | LCC BS1465.52 (ebook) | DDC 223/.7066—dc23
LC record available at https://lccn.loc.gov/2019059606
LC ebook record available at https://lccn.loc.gov/2019059607

For Nicholas James Millar

20/09/58–17/11/18

I hope I made you glad (Prov 23:22–25)

Contents

Acknowledgments

More people have contributed to this book than it is possible to list here. I am indebted to many friends, readers, and critics—I hope each of them knows how grateful I am. A particular thanks goes to SBL Press for their meticulous work editing this manuscript.

The bulk of the work on this project was undertaken in Cambridge, UK. The daily stimulation, inspiration, and caffeine I received from friends and colleagues there proved invaluable. Most of all, I am grateful to Katharine Dell, who helped to guide this project from its beginnings and without whom it would never have reached completion. Thanks also to James Aitken and Christopher Ansberry for thoroughly reading and incisively critiquing my work and for encouraging me to think more fully about areas I had missed. I also thank Pete Williams and Kim Phillips for years of consistent support and advice, as well as many others at the Divinity Faculty and Tyndale House. I must also mention my friends at Lyn's House—Debbie, Mel, Ian, Julie, Philip, David, James, Janette, Dan, Judith, Annie, Janice, Katharine, Sarah, and others. With them, I saw more wisdom than in any library.

My thanks must also go to colleagues at Leeds University and, most recently, at Edinburgh University. I am very grateful for the fantastic biblical studies team—Anja Klein, Helen Bond, Philippa Townsend, Paul Foster, Matt Novenson, Timothy Lim, and Alison Jack—and for the continual generosity and support of Linden Bicket and Jolyon Mitchell.

My largest thanks are owed to my family: to my three brilliant sisters—Abi, Becky, and Steph—for putting up with me; to Jill Jackson (though not a blood relative)—a true woman of valor and a fountain of gentle wisdom throughout my life; and most particularly to my mum and dad. I cannot express how thankful I am for their thoughtful advice, abundant generosity, and unwavering love. My dad passed away unexpectedly when this manuscript was in its final stages. It is dedicated to him.

January 2019

Abbreviations

AB	Anchor Bible
ABRL	Anchor Bible Reference Library
AcBib	Academia Biblica
AEL	Lichtheim, Miriam, ed. *Ancient Egyptian Literature: A Book of Readings.* 3 vols. Berkeley: University of California Press, 1975.
AIL	Ancient Israel and Its Literature
AnBib	Analecta Biblica
ANET	Pritchard, James B., ed. *Ancient Near Eastern Texts Relating to the Old Testament.* Princeton: Princeton University Press, 1950.
AOTC	Abingdon Old Testament Commentaries
ATD	Das Alte Testament Deutsch
BASOR	*Bulletin of the American Schools of Oriental Research*
BBB	Bonner biblische Beiträge
BBR	*Bulletin for Biblical Research*
BBRSup	Bulletin for Biblical Research Supplement
BDB	Brown, Francis, S. R. Driver, and Charles A. Briggs. *Enhanced Brown-Driver-Briggs Hebrew and English Lexicon.* Oxford: Clarendon, 1977.
BHQ	Schenker, Adrian, et al., eds. *Biblia Hebraica Quinta.* Stuttgart: Deutsche Bibelgesellschaft, 2004–
BHS	Elliger, Karl, and Wilhelm Rudolph, eds. *Biblia Hebraica Stuttgartensia.* Stuttgart: Deutsche Bibelgesellschaft, 1977.
BHT	Beiträge zur historischen Theologie
Bib	*Biblica*
BibInt	*Biblical Interpretation*
BKAT	Biblischer Kommentar, Altes Testament
BN	*Biblische Notizen*
BSac	*Bibliotheca Sacra*

BTB	*Biblical Theology Bulletin*
BZAW	Beihefte zur Zeitschrift für die alttestamentliche Wissenschaft
CBQ	*Catholic Biblical Quarterly*
ConBOT	Coniectanea Biblica: Old Testament Series
DJD	Discoveries in the Judaean Desert
ESV	English Standard Version
ETL	*Ephemerides Theologicae Lovanienses*
FAT	Forschungen zum Alten Testament
FRLANT	Forschungen zur Religion und Literatur des Alten und Neuen Testaments
GBS	Guides to Biblical Scholarship
GKC	Gesenius, Wilhelm, Emil Kautzsch, and Arther E. Cowley. *Gesenius' Hebrew Grammar: As Edited and Enlarged by the Late E. Kautzsch.* Oxford: Clarendon, 1910.
HALOT	Koehler, Ludwig, Walter Baumgartner, and Johann J. Stamm. *The Hebrew and Aramaic Lexicon of the Old Testament.* Translated and edited under the supervision of Mervyn E. J. Richardson. 4 vols. Leiden: Brill, 1994–1999.
HAT	Handbuch zum Alten Testament
HBAI	*Hebrew Bible and Ancient Israel*
HS	*Hebrew Studies*
HCSB	Holman Christian Standard Bible
HSM	Harvard Semitic Monographs
HUCA	*Hebrew Union College Annual*
HvTSt	*Hervormde Teologiese Studies*
IBC	Interpretation: A Bible Commentary for Teaching and Preaching
IBHS	Waltke, Bruce K., and Michael O'Connor. *An Introduction to Biblical Hebrew Syntax.* Winona Lake, IN: Eisenbrauns, 1990.
ICC	International Critical Commentary
IEJ	*Israel Exploration Journal*
Int	*Interpretation*
JAF	*Journal of American Folklore*
JANER	*Journal of Ancient Near Eastern Religions*
JANESCU	*Journal of the Ancient Near Eastern Society of Columbia University*
JAOS	*Journal of the American Oriental Society*

JBL	*Journal of Biblical Literature*
JETS	*Journal of the Evangelical Theological Society*
JJS	*Journal of Jewish Studies*
JNSL	*Journal of Northwest Semitic Languages*
Joüon	Joüon, Paul. *A Grammar of Biblical Hebrew.* Translated and revised by Takamitsu Muraoka. Rome: Pontificio Istituto Biblico, 2003.
JPS	*Tanakh: The Holy Scriptures; The New JPS Translation to the Traditional Hebrew Text.* Philadelphia: Jewish Publication Society, 1985.
JQR	*Jewish Quarterly Review*
JSJ	*Journal for the Study of Judaism*
JSJSup	Journal for the Study of Judaism Supplement
JSOT	*Journal for the Study of the Old Testament*
JSOTSup	Journal for the Study of Judaism Supplement
JTS	*Journal of Theological Studies*
KJV	Authorized King James Version
KTU	Dietrich, Manfried, Oswald Loretz, and Joaquín Sanmartín, eds. *Die keilalphabetischen Texte aus Ugarit: Einschließlich der keilalphabetischen Texte außerhalb Ugarits.* Alter Orient und Altes Testament 24. Kevelaer: Butzon & Bercher; Neukirchen-Vluyn: Neukirchen Verlag, 1976.
LAI	Library of Ancient Israel
LHBOTS	The Library of Hebrew Bible/Old Testament Studies
LUÅ	Lunds Universitets Årsskrift
LXX	Septuagint, according to Rahlfs, Alfred, ed. *Septuaginta: Id est Vetus Testamentum graece iuxta LXX interpretes.* Stuttgart: Deutsche Bibelgesellschaft, 2005.
MT	Masoretic Text, according to *BHS.*
NABRE	New American Bible (Revised Edition)
NASB	New American Standard Bible
NICOT	New International Commentary on the Old Testament
NIV	New International Version
NKJV	New King James Version
NRSV	New Revised Standard Version
NTL	New Testament Library
OBO	Orbis Biblicus et Orientalis
OTE	*Old Testament Essays*
OTESup	Old Testament Essays Supplement

OTL	Old Testament Library
OTS	Old Testament Studies
P.Ins.	Papyrus Insinger
PEJ	*Palestinian Exploration Journal*
Pesh.	Peshitta, according to di Lella, Alexander A., ed. *Proverbs, Wisdom, Qohelet, Song of Songs*. Part 2.5 of *The Old Testament in Syriac: According to the Peshitta Version*. Brill: Leiden, 1979.
PMLA	*Publications of the Modern Language Association*
RA	*Revue d'assyriologie et d'archéologie orientale*
RB	*Revue Biblique*
RC	*Religion Compass*
REB	Revised English Bible
RelEd	Religious Education
ResQ	*Restoration Quarterly*
RSV	Revised Standard Version
SB	Sources bibliques
SBLDS	Society of Biblical Literature Dissertation Series
SBLMS	Society of Biblical Literature Monograph Series
SBT	Studies in Biblical Theology
SJOT	*Scandinavian Journal of the Old Testament*
SJT	*Scottish Journal of Theology*
SOTSMS	Society for Old Testament Studies Monograph Series
SubBi	Subsidia Biblica
Symm.	Symmachus
Targ.	Targum, according to de Lagarde, Paul, ed. *Hagiographa chaldaice*. Leipzig: [s.n.], 1873.
TDOT	Botterweck, G. J., and Helmer Ringgren, eds. *Theological Dictionary of the Old Testament*. Translated by T. Willis et al. 8 vols. Grand Rapids, MI: Eerdmans, 1990.
Text	*Textus*
ThH	Théologie historique
Venet.	Codex Veneuts
VT	*Vetus Testamentum*
VTSup	Vetus Testamentum Supplement
Vulg.	Vulgate, according to Fischer, Bonifatio, and Robert Weber, ed. *Biblia sacra: Iuxta Vulgatam versionem*. Stuttgart: Württembergische Bibelanstalt, 1969.

WMANT   *Wissenschaftliche Monographien zum Alten und Neuen Testament*

ZAW   *Zeitschrift für die alttestamentliche Wissenschaft*

ZTK   *Zeitschrift für Theologie und Kirche*

Introduction

Epigrams and sentences ... do not circumscribe their range of possibilities of comprehension; they offer no defence even against bold interpretations.

— Gerhard von Rad, *Wisdom in Israel*

This pronouncement from Gerhard von Rad's *Wisdom in Israel* has replayed in my mind like an earworm, or a proverb of old, since the first time I read it. It sparked an ever-increasing fascination with the multiple possible interpretations and uses of sayings and maxims—such as those in the book of Proverbs. I came to see them not as banal, formulaic clichés, as some interpreters have it, but as rich and complex epigrams. When pondered, they open out and draw in their readers, who can become explorers through their possibilities. Von Rad implies that boldness in interpretation is a foe and that the lack of defense is troubling. But boldness may in fact be a companion for well-founded and fruitful explorations.

Of course, at some point boldness can become too bold—a proverb cannot simply mean whatever you want it to mean. Von Rad goes on to speak of limitations to interpretation. He stressed that we must understand each proverb in light of the "ideological and religious factors" that shaped the composition.[1] Important as these undoubtedly are, my focus will be slightly different. I will suggest that interpretation should be guided by the genre of these sayings (which I will call the *didactic proverb*) and by a close consideration of their literary features.

My aim here is threefold: (1) to suggest that the sayings in Prov 10:1–22:16 should be seen as didactic proverbs and to explain what I mean by this, (2) to analyze a textual feature I call *openness* and demonstrate how this facilitates the sayings' *didactic* and *proverbial* functions, and (3) to show how reading Proverbs in this way may influence some key issues

---

1. Gerhard von Rad, *Wisdom in Israel* (London: SCM, 1972), 32.

in scholarship. In so doing, I hope to contribute to the growing corner of Proverbs' studies sensitive to the intricacies and ambiguities of the text.[2] Before I begin, however, the notions of *didactic proverb* and *openness* require some explanation.

Didactic Proverbs

I am using the phrase *didactic proverbs* as a genre descriptor. In chapter 1, I will justify why this is appropriate for Prov 10:1–22:16. Here I will introduce the methodological debates on genre and their place in Proverbs scholarship.

Genre studies first entered biblical scholarship within the framework of form criticism, especially through the pioneering studies of Hermann Gunkel. Gunkel thought it important to reconstruct the short oral *Gattungen* ("genres") that he believed lay behind the Bible's (considerably more developed) literary texts.[3] These were primarily distinguishable by their *Form*—the essential structural commonalities between units, above and beyond their specific manifestations. The *Gattung* and *Form* of each unit were controlled by rigid conventions, stemming from that unit's particular *Sitz im Leben* ("setting in life"). Gunkel's first followers enthusiastically reconstructed these *Sitze*—the legal, cultic, or social institutions apparently discernible from the hypothesized oral precursors to the Bible.[4]

The idea of early oral forms, as distinct from their later literary manifestations, found traction in Proverbs scholarship. Otto Eißfeldt influentially suggested a development from single-lined *Volkssprich-*

---

2. Recently, for example, Peter Hatton, *Contradiction in the Book of Proverbs: The Deep Waters of Counsel*, SOTSMS (Aldershot: Ashgate, 2008); K. M. Heim, *Poetic Imagination in Proverbs: Variant Repetitions and the Nature of Proverbs*, BBRSup 4 (Winona Lake, IN: Eisenbrauns, 2013); Anne W. Stewart, *Poetic Ethics in Proverbs: Wisdom Literature and the Shaping of the Moral Self* (Cambridge: Cambridge University Press, 2016).

3. For example, Hermann Gunkel, *Genesis* (Göttingen: Vandenhoeck & Ruprecht, 1901); Gunkel, *Die Psalmen* (Göttingen: Vandenhoeck & Ruprecht, 1926). For an overview of Gunkel's views in historical and intellectual context, see Martin J. Buss, *Biblical Form Criticism in Its Context*, JSOTSup 274 (Sheffield: Sheffield Academic, 1999), 209–62.

4. For example, Albrecht Alt, "The Origins of Israelite Law," in *Essays on Old Testament History and Religion* (Oxford: Blackwell, 1966), 101–71; Sigmund Mowinckel, *The Psalms in Israel's Worship* (Oxford: Basil Blackwell, 1962).

wörter ("folk proverbs") to the two-lined *Kunstsprüche* ("artistic sayings") we find in the book of Proverbs.[5] W. O. E. Oesterley incorporated these ideas into a schema of development for the whole book, moving from oral one-line sayings, to literary distichs, to more elaborate instructions (such as those in Prov 1–9).[6] A similar development was also found from an original, observational *Aussagewort* ("saying") to an instructive *Mahnwort* ("admonition").[7] In each case the movement was in the text's increasingly instructional nature: from proverb to didactic.

Gunkel offered a number of important insights to biblical studies: form and genre are closely related, genres are frequently embedded in social realities, and genres bring particular functions and conventions. However, modern form criticism has moved a long way since his time (so far, in fact, that many scholars have become uneasy of this label).[8] The possibility of reconstructing oral antecedents has been questioned, both in Proverbs and across the Hebrew Bible. Even if the biblical proverbs did derive from one-lined precursors (which is itself questionable), these are impossible to recover.[9] Furthermore, in light of modern genre theory, it is unconvincing to propose a distinct and unified *Gattung* rigidly corresponding to a pure *Form* and *Sitz im Leben*.[10]

---

5. Otto Eißfeldt, *Der Maschal im Alten Testament: Eine wortgeschichtliche Untersuchung nebst einer literargeschichtlichen Untersuchung der genannten Gattungen "Volkssprichwort" und "Spottlied,"* BZAW 24 (Giessen: Töpelmann, 1913).

6. W. O. E. Oesterley, *The Book of Proverbs* (London: Methuen, 1929).

7. For example, Johannes Hempel, *Die althebräische Literatur in ihr hellenistisch-jüdisches Nachleben* (Wildpark-Potsdam: Athenaion, 1930), 175.

8. For example, Erhard Blum, "Formgeschichte—A Misleading Category? Some Critical Remarks," in *The Changing Face of Form Criticism for the Twenty-First Century*, ed. Marvin A. Sweeney and Ehud Ben Zvi (Grand Rapids: Eerdmans, 2003), 32–45; Stuart Weeks, "The Limits of Form Criticism in the Study of Literature, with Reflections of Psalm 34," in *Biblical Interpretation and Method: Essays in Honour of John Barton*, ed. Katharine J. Dell and Paul M. Joyce (Oxford: Oxford University Press, 2013), 15–25.

9. Such views were largely based on a developmental model of texts, in which longer must mean later. This was challenged on the basis of Egyptian parallels, where one-line sayings occur late in the tradition. See, e.g., Berend Gemser, "The Instructions of 'Onchsheshonqy and Biblical Wisdom Literature," in *Congress Volume: Oxford, 1959*, ed. G. W. Anderson et al. (Leiden: Brill, 1960), 127–28. Some scholars do try to recover them, though; see, e.g., Michael V. Fox, *Proverbs 10–31*, AB 18B (New Haven: Yale University Press, 2009), 485.

10. On the idea of a "pure" (*reine*) *Form* in Gunkel's thinking, see Buss, *Biblical Form Criticism*, 237, 251–53.

Within biblical studies, focus has shifted from hypothetical oral *Gattungen* to literary genres, and there has been increasing engagement with literary theory.[11] In the 1970s and 1980s, the Society of Biblical Literature Genres Project catalyzed interest and insights in the field.[12] Particularly in recent years, genre studies have become prevalent for the wisdom literature. Mark R. Sneed's 2015 volume on wisdom in this series, for example, devotes its whole first part to "Genre Theory and the Wisdom Tradition."[13] Most of the discussions there, and in scholarship more broadly, focus on whether wisdom itself constitutes a genre, and if so, how to characterize and delimit it.[14] There is an increasing recognition that genres are not discrete in-out categories but are often flexible, indistinct, and changing.

My focus will be not on the macrogenre of wisdom but on one of the many microgenres of which it consists. Diverse genres can coexist within a single work. Job, for example, has been seen as a dialogue of competing generic claims or as a parody, intentionally mimicking different genres.[15] In Proverbs, a major distinction can be drawn between instructions (Prov 1–9) and sentences (Prov 10–29), but scholars have also found, for example, wisdom sermons in chapters 1–9, a dialogue with a skeptic in 31:1–14, numerical sayings in 30:15–33, and a hymn in 31:10–31.[16]

---

11. For an overview of the trends of scholarship, see Carol A. Newsom, "Spying Out the Land: A Report from Genology," in *Seeking Out the Wisdom of the Ancients: Essays Offered to Honor Michael V. Fox on the Occasion of His Sixty-Fifth Birthday*, ed. Ronald L. Troxel, Kelvin G. Friebel, and Dennis R. Magary (Winona Lake, IN: Eisenbrauns, 2005), 437–50.

12. Published in editions of *Semeia* from 1978 to 1986.

13. Mark R. Sneed, ed., *Was There a Wisdom Tradition? New Prospects in Israelite Wisdom Studies*, AIL 23 (Atlanta: SBL Press, 2015), 11–177.

14. In Sneed, *Was There a Wisdom Tradition?*, see Katharine J. Dell, "Deciding the Boundaries of 'Wisdom': Applying the Concept of Family Resemblance," 145–60; Michael V. Fox, "Three Theses on Wisdom"; Will Kynes, "The Modern Scholarly Wisdom Tradition and the Threat of Pan-sapientialism: A Case Report," 11–38; and Mark R. Sneed, "'Grasping After the Wind': The Elusive Attempt to Define and Delimit Wisdom," 39–68.

15. See, respectively, Carol A. Newsom, *The Book of Job: A Contest of Moral Imaginations* (Oxford: Oxford University Press, 2003); Katharine J. Dell, *The Book of Job as Sceptical Literature*, BZAW 197 (Berlin: de Gruyter, 1991).

16. Prov 1–9: Bálint Károly Zabán, *The Pillar Function of the Speeches of Wisdom: Proverbs 1:20–33; 8:1–36 and 9:1–6 in the Structural Framework of Proverbs 1–9*, BZAW 429 (Berlin: de Gruyter, 2012), 205–29. Prov 31:1–14: R. B. Y. Scott, *Proverbs, Ecclesiastes*, AB 18 (New York: Doubleday, 1965), 22; James L. Crenshaw, "Clanging

Such classification is by no means absolute, for genres are more heuristic tools than ontological realities.[17] No text is a pure manifestation of a genre, and our constructed categories can have a good deal of overlap. Carol A. Newsom's comment should be taken seriously: "Texts do not 'belong' to genres so much as participate in them, invoke them, gesture to them, play in and out of them, and in so doing continually change them."[18] Accordingly, the genre I suggest for the sayings in 10:1–22:16 is a flexible hybrid. They are didactic proverbs, simultaneously participating in both didactic and proverbial genres. Justification for this claim will be given in chapter 1. Discerning these genres will offer us conventions for interpretation, as well as clues about the expected situations and functions of the sayings.

Scholarship on the didactic aims and strategies of Proverbs is a burgeoning field, which this study will help to cultivate. Work on the sayings as proverbs (in a technical sense) has, on the other hand, been surprisingly minimal. I hope to plug this gap by drawing insights from paremiology (the technical study of the proverb genre), a rich field yet to be fully plowed by biblical scholars.

Openness

By *openness* I mean, in short, a text's ability to offer multiple possibilities of interpretation and use. Scholars sporadically use the term with reference to Proverbs, and some have drawn more extensively on the notion.[19] I have chosen the term because it is broader, less technical, and more affirmative than comparative ideas, such as ambiguity, vagueness, or indeterminacy.[20] While these are literary phenomena, pertaining to

Symbols," in *Justice and the Holy: Essays in Honor of Walter Harrelson*, ed. Douglas A. Knight and Peter J. Paris (Atlanta: Scholars Press, 1989), 51–64. Crenshaw recognizes various genres even within the dialogue. Prov 30:15–33: Wolfgang M. W. Roth, ed., *Numerical Sayings in the Old Testament: A Form-Critical Study*, VTSup 13 (Leiden: Brill, 1965). Prov 31:10–31: Albert Wolters, "Proverbs XXXI 10–31 as Heroic Hymn: A Form-Critical Analysis," *VT* 38 (1988): 446–57.

17. Sneed, "Grasping after the Wind," 39–68; S. Weeks, "Wisdom, Form, and Genre," in Sneed, *Was There a Wisdom Tradition?*, 164.

18. Newsom, *Book of Job*, 12.

19. E.g. J. Hausmann, *Studien zum Menschenbild der älteren Weisheit (Spr 10ff.)*, FAT 7 (Tübingen: Mohr Siebeck, 1995), 348–51.

20. These terms are often given technical definitions in linguistic scholarship

interpretation alone, openness pertains also to *use*. An open text may be used and applied in many ways. This seems to be a generic hallmark of proverbs, which are "inherently capacious," offering general principles to be fleshed out by the circumstances of the hearers' own lives.[21] An open text also provides vistas for mental examination. The readers may climb in and explore, further opening up the proverb for themselves. Limits will always be encountered somewhere, however. Meaning may be expansive, but it is not inexhaustible.

This raises the vexed question of where such meaning lies. The basic alternatives, often noted by literary critics, are the author, the text itself, or the reader.[22] Most interpreters nowadays acknowledge an interaction between all three (though they may stress one above the others). Each of these loci gives a certain warrant for finding openness but also imposes limits.

One approach is to locate meaning in *the author's intention*: the text means whatever he or she meant by it.[23] This runs into problems in any text, for we cannot reconstruct the author's thought processes, and it is all the more problematic in a text like Proverbs, whose authorship is unknown and probably multilayered. Furthermore, the proverb genre suggests not the distinct authorship of specific individuals but the distilled communal wisdom of ages past. Even if coined by an individual, by casting it in the form of a proverb, she or he renounces ownership of it.[24] A proverb is by

---

(though these definitions often vary between scholars). See, e.g., Brendan S. Gillon, "Ambiguity, Indeterminacy, Deixis, and Vagueness," in *Semantics: A Reader*, ed. Steven Davis and Brendan S. Gillon (Oxford: Oxford University Press, 2004), 157–87; Christopher Kennedy, "Ambiguity and Vagueness: An Overview," in vol. 1 of *Semantics: An International Handbook of Natural Language Meaning*, ed. Claudia Maienborn, Klaus von Heusinger, and Paul Portner (Berlin: de Gruyter Mouton, 2011), 507–33; Qiao Zhang, "Fuzziness—Vagueness—Generality—Ambiguity," *Journal of Pragmatics* 29 (1998): 13–31.

21. Ellen F. Davis, "Surprised by Wisdom: Preaching Proverbs," *Int* 63 (2009): 266; cf. Carole R. Fontaine, *Traditional Sayings in the Old Testament* (Sheffield: Almond Press, 1982), 76; Susan Niditch, *Folklore and the Hebrew Bible*, GBS (Minneapolis: Fortress, 1993), 86.

22. For a more extended discussion, see Doug Ingram, *Ambiguity in Ecclesiastes*, LHBOTS 431 (New York: T&T Clark, 2006), 5–22.

23. E.g., E. D. Hirsch, *The Aims of Interpretation* (Chicago: University of Chicago Press, 1976).

24. It may be "the wit of one," but it is also "the wisdom of many" (so John Russell's famous dictum).

definition a truth in the public domain. By choosing this genre, part of the author's intention seems to be, paradoxically, to legitimize interpretations other than those first intended. This warrants a reading that anticipates openness. It does not, however, do away with the author entirely. Though proverbs are public truths, they are created within and presuppose certain experiential boundaries, cultural frameworks, and social realities. Interpretation should not contravene the base assumptions of the author's world.

A second possible locus for meaning is *the text itself*. This approach came to the fore particularly in the New Criticism of the 1940s–1970s. Meaning here is language-based and cannot be derived extralinguistically (e.g., from the author's intention).[25] The text of a proverb, I suggest, is distinctively open in comparison to that of other genres. Proverbs are terse and elliptical, condensed into the minimum number of words, and lacking in the grammatical markers that could clarify meaning (such as object markers and relative particles). No elucidation is offered at any of their ambiguity points. Within the collections, their lack of clear literary context means that no subsequent discourse can answer any questions that have been raised.[26] Furthermore, proverbs are replete with poetic devices, such as polysemy, parallelism, and imagery, which often create openness (see ch. 2). However, the text also offers important constraints. Any interpretation must be rooted in the genuine possibilities of the language, requiring careful linguistic analysis.

The third locus for meaning is *the reader*. In this school of thought, a text has no objective meaning independent of the interpretation process. Reading a text does not uncover its preexisting meaning but actively constructs a meaning. Reader-response criticism made its ascendency in literary theory in the 1960 and 1970s and in biblical studies shortly thereafter.[27] Versions of it continue to be prevalent. Most radically, it denies the text and author any real role in meaning. More moderately (and with wider acceptance), meaning emerges from the interaction between text and reader. We should distinguish here between the ideal readers

---

25. The "authorial intention" paradigm was famously challenged by W. K. Wimsatt and Monroe C. Beardsley, "The Intentional Fallacy," *Sewanee Review* 54 (1946): 468–88.

26. See §1.6 below for a discussion of literary context.

27. See overview in Brittany N. Melton and Heath A. Thomas, "Reader-Response Criticism and Recent Readers," in *The Biblical World*, ed. Katharine J. Dell (London: Taylor & Francis/Routeledge, forthcoming).

apparently presupposed by the text and the actual readers who engage with it, as well as between original and contemporary readers (and all the many readers in between). My main focus here will be on *actual, original readers*. They are, of course, difficult to reconstruct, given our ignorance about the composition and transmission of the book. But their possible reading strategies may be recoverable, in part, through analysis of the text's genre with its attendant conventions and contexts. This can offer some constraints in interpretation. What was the original readers' framework of expectations, and what meanings were possible within this framework? What social conventions and hermeneutical principles may have guided them?

The rise of reader-oriented approaches has gone together with increasing recognition of openness and ambiguity in biblical texts. Finding multiple meanings in the Bible is nothing new (think of the allegorizing tendency of early Christian interpreters, and the rabbinic tradition of דבר אחר ["another interpretation"]), but its scholarly study has been influenced by the reader response school. The influential literary critic Wolfgang Iser focused on indeterminacy as the most important ingredient in the interaction between text and reader.[28] The reader gets into the gaps in the text, as it were, and fleshes them out for himself. Iser's approach has been followed explicitly or implicitly by many in biblical studies.[29]

Many biblical texts have been examined for their ambiguities (e.g., extensively Samuel and Qoheleth).[30] In Proverbs scholarship, though

---

28. Wolfgang Iser, "Indeterminacy and the Reader's Response in Prose Fiction," in *Aspects of Narrative: Selected Papers from the English Institute*, ed. J. Hillis Miller (New York: Columbia University Press, 1971), 1–45.

29. See, e.g., Meir Sternberg, *The Poetics of Biblical Narrative: Ideological Literature and the Drama of Reading*, Indiana Literary Biblical Series (Bloomington: Indiana University Press, 1985), 185–90; Ingram, *Ambiguity in Ecclesiastes*. For a discussion of the (mis)appropriation of Iser in biblical scholarship, see Zoltán Schwab, "Mind the Gap: The Impact of Wolfgang Iser's Reader-Response Criticism on Biblical Studies—A Critical Assessment," *Literature and Theology* 17 (2003): 170–81.

30. For example, explorations of ambiguities in 2 Sam 11 alone have been undertaken in Keith Bodner, "Layers of Ambiguity in 2 Samuel 11,1," *ETL* 80 (2004): 102–11; George G. Nicol, "The Alleged Rape of Bathsheba: Some Observations on Ambiguity in Biblical Narrative," *JSOT* 73 (1997): 43–54; Sternberg, *Poetics of Biblical Narrative*, 190–219; and Gale A. Yee, "'Fraught with Background' Literary Ambiguity in II Samuel 11," *Int* 42 (1988): 240–53. For Qoheleth, see, e.g., Rick W. Byargeon, "The Significance of Ambiguity in Ecclesiastes 2,24–26," in *Qohelet in the Context of Wisdom,*

interpreters often note ambiguity, there has been no thorough or systematic study. I hope that, by exploring the gaps in the proverb texts, I may help to fill this gap in the scholarship.

The Corpus to Be Examined

I will consider here not the whole of the book of Proverbs but a distinct unit: the "proverbs of Solomon" (משלי שלמה) in Prov 10:1–22:16. This may be split into two subcollections (10:1–15:33 and 16:1–22:16), though the distinction is not essential for my purposes.[31] In the present form of the book, these are followed by two more sayings collections: the "sayings of the wise" in 22:17–24:34 and the "Hezekian collection" in chapters 25–29 (sometimes subdivided into 25–27 and 28–29). These collections within Prov 10–29 are widely held to be distinct subunits. Though their relative chronology is disputed, they may all stem from the monarchic period.[32]

---

ed. A. Schoors (Leuven: Leuven University Press, 1998), 367–72; Ingram, *Ambiguity in Ecclesiastes*; Thomas Krüger, "Meaningful Ambiguities in the Book of Qoheleth," in *The Language of Qohelet in Its Context: Essays in Honour of Prof. A. Schoors on the Occasion of His Seventieth Birthday*, ed. Angelika Berlejung and Pierre van Hecke (Leuven: Peeters, 2007), 63–74; Lindsay Wilson, "Artful Ambiguity in Ecclesiastes 1,1–11," in Schoors, *Qohelet in the Context of Wisdom*, 357–66.

31. No new title is given for 16:1–22:16, suggesting that in the final composition, the two halves are considered as a single collection. But the subcollections can be distinguished by form and content: the former is characterized by antithetical parallelisms pitting the wise and righteous against the foolish and wicked; the latter has greater diversity.

32. Udo Skladny suggested the chronological order 10–15; 28–29; 16:1–22:16; 25–27 (leaving out 22:17–24:34 as Egyptian influenced). Conversely, Hans Heinrich Schmid argued that 25–27 is the oldest section, while 10–15 is a late "*Anthropologisierung*" of wisdom (see below, §4.1.1). R. N. Whybray concluded that relative chronology is impossible to determine. See Skladny, *Die ältesten Spruchsammlungen in Israel* (Göttingen: Vandenhoeck & Ruprecht, 1962), 76–79; Hans Heinrich Schmid, *Wesen und Geschichte der Weisheit: Eine Untersuchung zur altorientalischen und israelitischen Weisheitsliteratur* (Berlin: Töpelmann, 1966), 144–68; Whybray, *The Composition of the Book of Proverbs* (Sheffield: JSOT Press, 1994). A dating to the monarchic period is suggested by their frequent references to the king (see chapter 6). Other evidence sometimes offered for a monarchic dating includes (1) the ascriptions to Solomon and Hezekiah (Carr; Dell; Waltke); (2) the time needed for a development from Prov 10–29 to Prov 1–9 and from Proverbs to Ecclesiastes and Job (Dell); (3) the presence of "early" linguistic features, showing the influence of, e.g., Canaanite (Albright), Ugaritic (Waltke, drawing on Dahood), Israelian Hebrew (Rendsburg), and Aramaic

Due to the sayings' openness and multiapplicability, they were retained after the exile, when a compiler seems to have added an introduction (Prov 1–9) and appendix (Prov 30–31).[33] Composition and dating will not

---

(Fox); and (4) apparent roots in an early oral tradition (many scholars). W. F. Albright, "Some Canaanite-Phoenician Sources of Hebrew Wisdom," in *Wisdom in Israel and in the Ancient Near East*, ed. Martin Noth and David Winton Thomas (Leiden: Brill, 1955), 1–15; David M. Carr, *The Formation of the Hebrew Bible* (Oxford: Oxford University Press, 2011), 410–13; Mitchell J. Dahood, *Proverbs and Northwest Semitic Philology*, Scripta Pontificii Instituti Biblici 113 (Rome: Pontifical Biblical Institute, 1963); Katharine J. Dell, "How Much Wisdom Literature Has Its Roots in the Pre-exilic Period?," in *In Search of Pre-exilic Israel: Proceedings of the Oxford Old Testament Seminar*, ed. John Day (London: T&T Clark, 2004), 251–71; Fox, *Proverbs 10–31*, 504–6; Gary A. Rendsburg, "Literary and Linguistic Matters in the Book of Proverbs," in *Perspectives on Israelite Wisdom: Proceedings of the Oxford Old Testament Seminar*, ed. John Jarick (Oxford: Bloomsbury T&T Clark, 2016), 111–47; Bruce K. Waltke, *The Book of Proverbs: Chapters 1–15*, NICOT (Grand Rapids: Eerdmans, 2004), 31–36.

33. Scholars have argued that these sections are postexilic because (1) they serve as a prologue and epilogue to the sayings and so must have been composed later (Fox); (2) they show a more developed theology than the sayings (many scholars); (3) they display late linguistic features (Yoder); and (4) they may reflect postexilic social and ideological debates, particularly the dispute about marriage with foreigners in the Persian period (Maier; Camp). See Claudia Camp, *Wisdom and the Feminine in the Book of Proverbs* (Sheffield: Almond Press, 1985), 239–43; Michael V. Fox, *Proverbs 1–9: A New Translation with Introduction and Commentary*, AB 18A (New York: Doubleday, 2000), 48–49; Christl M. Maier, *Die "fremde Frau" in Proverbien 1–9: Eine exegetische und sozialgeschichtliche Studie* (Göttingen: Vandenhoeck & Ruprecht, 1995); Christine Roy Yoder, *Wisdom as a Woman of Substance: A Socioeconomic Reading of Proverbs 1–9 and 31:10–31* (Berlin: de Gruyter, 2001), 15–38. A minority have argued, however, that Prov 1–9 may be preexilic, largely based on its borrowing from Egyptian materials: Carr, *Formation of the Hebrew Bible*, 408–10; Dell, "Pre-exilic Period"; Christa Kayatz, *Studien zu Proverbien 1–9: Eine form- und motivgeschichtliche Untersuchung unter Einbeziehung ägyptischen Vergleichsmaterials*, WMANT 22 (Neukirchen-Vluyn: Neukirchener Verlag, 1966); Waltke, *Book of Proverbs 1–15*, 31–36. There are numerous instances of intertextuality between Prov 1–9 and other texts (esp. Jeremiah, Deuteronomy, and Isaiah), but these can be used to support either Proverbs' priority (Carr; Dell) or posteriority (Robert; Camp; Fox; Schipper). See Carr, *Formation of the Hebrew Bible*, 413–28; Dell, "Pre-exilic Period"; Camp, *Wisdom and the Feminine*, 223–39; Fox, *Proverbs 1–9*, 48–49; André Robert, "Les attaches litteraires bibliques de Prov. I–IX," *RB* 43 (1934): 42–68; Robert, "Les attaches litteraires bibliques de Prov. I–IX (Suite)," *RB* 44 (1935): 344–65; Bernd U. Schipper, *Hermeneutik der Tora: Studien zur Traditionsgeschichte von Prov 2 und zur Komposition von Prov 1–9* (Berlin: de Gruyter, 2012).

form a major part of my discussion. By their very nature, the proverbs are open to use in many different places and times.

It is important to take account of the final form of the whole composition, but we should also study each section in its own right. My attention is on 10:1–22:16, first, for pragmatic reasons: it provides a corpus of manageable size. It may be possible to extrapolate some conclusions to other sections of Proverbs, but that is a separate project. Second, I am interested in the didactic proverb genre, which seems to be best exemplified by these texts (and also perhaps by 25–29).[34] Third, these chapters are often characterized as the most banal and boring in the book.[35] I hope to counter this assumption by showing some of the interest and complexity I have found there.

I will work from the MT of these chapters. The textual and versional situation of Proverbs is complex.[36] The Qumran evidence is minimal and fragmentary, preserving vestiges of chapters 1–2 (4Q102) and 13–15 (4Q103). Its text is close to the MT.[37] The LXX diverges quite considerably,

---

34. These chapters are formally similar to 10:1–22:16, particularly chapters 28–29, which return to the antithetical style of chapters 10–15.

35. See, e.g., Stuart Weeks, *An Introduction to the Study of Wisdom Literature*, T&T Clark Approaches to Biblical Studies (London: T&T Clark, 2010), 32: "The first collection is characterised by advice so general that it is almost worthless"; Henry McKeating, *Studying the Old Testament* (London: Epworth, 1979), 159: "We are bound to wonder why the collector bothered to set them down."

36. For a good overview, see Richard J. Clifford, "Observations on the Text and Versions of Proverbs," in *Wisdom, You Are My Sister: Studies in Honor of Roland E. Murphy, O.Carm., on the Occasion of His Eightieth Birthday*, ed. Michael L. Barré (Washington, DC: Catholic Biblical Association of America, 1997), 47–61. The best scholarly editions currently available are probably the following: for Dead Sea Scrolls, Patrick W. Skehan and Eugene Ulrich, "Proverbs," in *Qumran Cave 4: XI: Psalms to Chronicles*, ed. Eugene Ulrich, Frank Moore Cross, and Joseph A. Fitzmyer, DJD 16 (Oxford: Clarendon, 2000), 181–86; for the LXX, since the Göttingen edition has yet to be released, see instead Alfred Rahlfs, *Septuaginta: Id est Vetus Testamentum graece iuxta LXX interpretes* (Stuttgart: Deutsche Bibelgesellschaft, 2005); for Peshitta, Alexander A. di Lella, *Proverbs, Wisdom, Qohelet, Song of Songs*, part 2.5 of *The Old Testament in Syriac: According to the Peshitta Version* (Leiden: Brill, 1979); for targum, no critical edition exists, so it is probably still best to use Paul de Lagarde, *Hagiographa Chaldaice* (Leipzig: [s.n.], 1873); For Vulgate, Bonifatius Fischer and Robert Weber, *Biblia sacra: Iuxta Vulgatam versionem* (Stuttgart: Württembergische Bibelanstalt, 1969).

37. Jan de Waard, "4QProv and Textual Criticism," *Text* 19 (1998): 87–96.

with differences both in individual verses and in the overall arrangement of the chapters. Many of the variations may be creative reworkings of a proto-MT—for example, introducing doublets, heightening antithetical parallelisms, and making the text more theologically pious.[38] Some differences, however, may stem from a different Hebrew *Vorlage*.[39] The other witnesses are of limited value as text-critical resources, as they seem to have known the MT and the LXX. The Peshitta apparently negotiated between them in a rather complex way.[40] Unique among the targumim, Targum Proverbs seemingly knew Peshitta and followed it in most cases, refraining from midrashic exegesis.[41] The Vulgate appears to have translated mainly from the Hebrew but also shows knowledge of the LXX and the Peshitta.

---

38. For an overview of translation practices in the LXX proverbs, see Michael V. Fox, "A Profile of the Septuagint Proverbs," in *Wisdom for Life: Essays in Honour of Maurice Gilbert*, ed. Nuria Calduch-Benages (Berlin: de Gruyter, 2014), 3–17. Concerning doublets, sometimes these are thought to stem from the work of a Jewish "Revisor" (Paul de Lagarde, "Anmerkungen zur griechischen Übersetzung der Proverbien," in vol. 1 of *Mittheilungen* [Göttingen: Dieterich, 1884], 19–26), or to represent the incorporation of a Hexaplaric text (Charles T. Fritsch, "The Treatment of the Hexaplaric Signs in the Syro-Hexaplar of Proverbs," *JBL* 72 [1953]: 169–81). Lorenzo Cuppi reviews these theories and argues that the doublets are instead the work of the translator; see Cuppi, "Long Doublets in the Septuagint of the Book of Proverbs with a History of Research on the Greek Translations" (PhD diss., Durham University, 2011). For antithetical parallelisms, see Gerhard Tauberschmidt, *Secondary Parallelism: A Study of the Translation Technique in LXX Proverbs*, AcBib 15 (Atlanta: Society of Biblical Literature, 2004). On those making the text more theologically pious, see Johann A. Cook, *The Septuagint of Proverbs: Jewish and/or Hellenistic Proverbs; Concerning the Hellenistic Colouring of LXX Proverbs*, VTSup 69 (Leiden: Brill, 1997).

39. Michael V. Fox, "LXX-Proverbs as a Text-Critical Resource," *Text* 22 (2005): 95–128; E. Tov, "Recensional Differences between the Masoretic Text and the Septuagint of Proverbs," in *Of Scribes and Scrolls: Studies on the Hebrew Bible, Intertestamental Judaism, and Christian Origins Presented to John Strugnell on the Occasion of His Sixtieth Birthday*, ed. Harold W. Attridge, John J. Collins, and Thomas H. Tobin (Lanham, MD: University Press of America, 1990), 43–56.

40. Michael V. Fox, "How the Peshitta of Proverbs Uses the Septuagint," *JNSL* 39.2 (2013): 37–56.

41. First influentially Theodor Nöldeke, "Das Targum zu den Sprüchen von der Peschita abhängig," *Archiv für wissenschaftliches Erforschung des Alten Testaments* 2 (1871): 246–49. The debate is summarized in John F. Healey, "The Targum of Proverbs," in *The Targum of Job, the Targum of Proverbs, the Targum of Qohelet*, ed. Céline Mangan, John F. Healey, and Peter S. Knobel (Edinburgh: T&T Clark, 1991), 7–10.

My selection of the MT as a base text is not because I necessarily consider it earliest in every reading (though in many instances it seems to be). Textual variants apparently arose during even the Hebrew transmission of book, which sometimes preserves two variant proverbs.[42] Michael V. Fox suggests that a similar process may explain some of the divergences in the Greek text: proto-MT preserved one variant, proto-LXX preserved the other.[43] In this sense, the LXX and the MT may be different recensions/editions of the book.[44] I work from the MT as a legitimate and important variant collection. I will, however, acknowledge the occasional need for emendation where the MT seems corrupted through, for example, copyist errors. I will refer to the versions mainly where they seem to be working from a proto-MT, as evidence of how early translators negotiated the text's openness and selected from its multiple meanings in translation.

Brief Overview of the Structure

Part 1 of this book deals with theoretical and methodological issues, justifying the reading strategy that I will employ. Chapter 1 explains my reasoning behind the genre designation *didactic proverb*. This is based on generically related texts, probable social settings, media, self-presentation, and form. Chapter 2 catalogues and explains some literary and linguistic phenomena that give rise to openness: polysemy, parallelism, and imagery. Chapter 3 suggests some ways that openness may enhance the potential of the sayings when used as didactic proverbs.

Part 2 explores the sayings themselves and considers the implications of this way of reading for some wider debates in Proverbs scholarship. Chapter 4 discusses the use of character terms, viewing them through the lens of prototype theory and arguing that they are open terms, useful for the book's didactic goal of character development. In chapters 5–7, I examine various key proverbs in depth, exploring their openness and highlighting their contribution to some important scholarly issues. Chapter 5 considers

---

Targum's dependence on Peshitta has been questioned by, e.g., Daniel C. Snell, "The Relation between the Targum and the Peshitta of Proverbs," *ZAW* 110 (1998): 72–74.

42. Comprehensively surveyed by Daniel C. Snell, *Twice-Told Proverbs and the Composition of the Book of Proverbs* (Winona Lake, IN: Eisenbrauns, 1993), see also §1.3 below.

43. Fox, "LXX-Proverbs."

44. Fox, "LXX-Proverbs"; Tov, "Recensional Differences."

the theory of the act-consequence connection, chapter 6 the role of the king, and chapter 7 the way that wisdom is acquired. These chapters will also demonstrate how openness helps the sayings to function proverbially (especially in evaluating situations and directing behavior) and didactically (developing their readers' worldviews, training their intellects, and forming their characters).

I intend to explore some of the many "possibilities of comprehension" alluded to by von Rad and to show that multiple meanings are not only possible but even probable and functionally important for didactic proverbs. I hope that these interpretations will prove thought-provoking and illuminating, bold but not indefensibly so.

Part 1
The Openness of the Didactic Proverb

1

The Didactic Proverb

To understand and use a text properly, we must consider its genre(s). A genre functions as a culturally conditioned mediating framework, informing the reader how to approach the text.[1] It signals what expectations to have for a text's content and what interpretive strategies are appropriate (a fairytale is interpreted very differently from a scientific treatise). Genre determines what sorts of situations the text may be used in (spoken to a child at bedtime) and what functions it may take (to impart a moral lesson, to send them to sleep). A single text may invoke several generic categories at once, for genres are flexible and allow for hybrids. I suggest that the sayings in Prov 10:1–22:16 invoke both didactic and proverbial genres. Neither of these terms is new to Proverbs scholarship, but I use each in a quite specific sense, which should be explained.

---

1. Scholars have used various metaphors to express this. Anne Freadman likens a genre to a tennis match, where utterances are meaningful because they abide by the "rules of the game"; see Freadman, "Anyone for Tennis?," in *Genre and the New Rhetoric*, ed. Aviva Freedman and Peter Medway (Bristol: Taylor & Francis, 1994), 37–56. David Fishelov draws an analogy between a genre and a social institution, for they both "provide a network of norms through which our experience is made culturally meaningful"; see Fishelov, *Metaphors of Genre: The Role of Analogies in Genre Theory* (University Park: Pennsylvania State University Press, 1993), quote on 2. For Alastair Fowler, a genre is a "shared code" between text and interpreter; see Fowler, "Genre," in vol. 2 of *International Encyclopedia of Communications*, ed. Erik Barnouw et al. (Oxford: Oxford University Press, 1989), 215–17. And for Frederic Jameson, genre is a "social contract"—an agreement to interpret a certain way; see Jameson, "Magical Narratives: On the Dialectical Use of Genre Criticism," in *The Political Unconscious: Narrative as a Socially Symbolic Act* (New York: Cornell University Press, 1982), 103–50.

Particularly since the time of Hans-Jürgen Hermisson, didactic interpretations have been popular for Proverbs.[2] Didactic texts are generically
oriented to teach, particularly to teach moral lessons. The reader adopts
the subject position of a student, receptive to the text's wisdom. Within
this, didactic texts have three particularly important functions: first, they
instill a broad and general *worldview* in their student; second, they foster
his *character development*; third, they train his *intellect*. This last function
may be in tension with some modern usage of the term *didactic*, which
sometimes has pejorative connotations of a top-down imposition of
knowledge, requiring no participation from the student. This is not how I
use the term, however. I contend that Proverbs' moral education includes
training in how to think. The book employs a range of complex pedagogical techniques to this end.[3]

I also maintain that these texts operate as proverbs, a term that (to
state the obvious) is familiar in Proverbs scholarship. Few scholars, however, have allowed the term *proverb* its technical sense or drawn insights
from paremiology (the study of the proverb genre).[4] I suggest that these
verses do in fact invoke the generic conventions of true proverbs. In particular, proverbs speak to specific situations with specific purposes. While
didactic texts form general worldview and moral character, proverbs give
particular evaluation and direction. While the former prompt a ponderous
reading process to train the intellect, the latter exploit their immediacy,

------

2. Hans-Jürgen Hermisson, *Studien zur israelitischen Spruchweisheit*, WMANT
28 (Neukirchen-Vluyn: Neukirchener Verlag, 1968).

3. See, e.g., William P. Brown, "The Pedagogy of Proverbs 10:1–31:9," in *Character
and Scripture: Moral Formation, Community, and Biblical Interpretation*, ed. William,
P. Brown (Grand Rapids: Eerdmans, 2002), 150–82; Ellen F. Davis, *Proverbs, Ecclesiastes and the Song of Songs*, Westminster Bible Companion (Louisville: Westminster
John Knox, 2000), 18–24; Stewart, *Poetic Ethics*; C. R. Yoder, "Forming 'Fearers of
Yahweh': Repetition and Contradiction as Pedagogy in Proverbs," in Troxel, Friebel,
and Magary *Seeking Out the Wisdom of the Ancients*, 167–83.

4. Exceptions include Ted Hildebrandt, "The Proverb: An Interdisciplinary
Approach to a Biblical Genre" (2005): https://tinyurl.com/SBL2642a; Aulikki Nah-
kola, "Orality and the Sage: A Word (Proverb) to the Wise Suffices," in Jarick, *Perspec-
tives on Israelite Wisdom*, 56–82; Timothy J. Sandoval, *The Discourse of Wealth and
Poverty in the Book of Proverbs* (Leiden: Brill, 2006) 10–13; Théo R. Schneider, *The
Sharpening of Wisdom: Old Testament Proverbs in Translation*, OTESup 1 (Pretoria:
OTSSA, 1992), 83–103. Paremiology is also occasionally drawn on in studies of the
term משל (see §1.5), and of proverb context (§1.6).

cutting into situations and provoking action. While not belonging fully to either genre, Prov 10:1–22:16 plays into both, drawing on both sets of conventions. Moreover, both can work together. A saying can be spoken specifically and later contemplated or analyzed and then applied.

In what follows, I will explain why I think this double interpretation strategy is warranted. There are no hard and fast criteria for distinguishing a genre. A writer might signal it and a reader might recognize it through a great variety of different features. I will focus on the related genres that Prov 10:1–22:16 evokes (§1.1), its social settings (§1.2), its media (§1.3), its self-presentation (§1.4), and its forms (§1.5–6).

1.1. Generic Relations: Didactic Instructions and Folk Proverbs

No reader encounters a text in a vacuum. Her accumulated experience of other texts will have built up in her a set of expectations about genre. Any new text will be viewed through these lenses. Equally, no genre is isolated, but the reader understands it in relation to others, as a sort of genre family.[5] In the family's diachronic aspect, genres may have descendants. The family spreads through time and space as one gives birth to another. The newborn genres are united by a common ancestry and may, synchronically, exhibit family resemblances.[6] Two genres may share, for example, stylistic and substantive characteristics, interpretive expectations and principles, or situations and functions of use. Occasionally, genres that seem foreign to each other may intermarry and give birth to children of mixed complexion.

Thus I suggest that the sayings in Prov 10:1–22:16 are closely related to two of their contemporary genres: the folk proverb and the didactic instruction. Here, I will briefly present the evidence that these genres were accessible to the writers/compilers of Proverbs. My interest is not in the possible diachronic development from one genre to another but on the generic conventions that might be signaled by the likeness.

---

5. For a discussion and critique of this family analogy, see Fishelov, *Metaphors of Genre*, 53–84.

6. The notion of family resemblances originally comes from Ludwig Wittgenstein, *Philosophical Investigations* (Oxford: Blackwell, 1958). See further below. It has been applied to genre in wisdom literature by Dell in "Deciding the Boundaries of 'Wisdom,'" 145–60.

1.1.1. Folk Proverbs

First, the didactic proverb is generically related to the folk proverb. Pare-miologists have discerned several features central to this genre, many of which are also exhibited by the sayings in Proverbs.[7] Folk proverbs are short, self-contained, sentential, poetic, and pithy (§1.5 below). They are spoken (§1.3), usually among the everyday people (§1.2), and lay claim to a traditional authority. Proverbs give a *relative* truth, in need of contextual specification (§1.6). As such, they are applicable to many situations and can have many functions (chapter 3). Particularly, they function to evaluate situations and to direct behavior. Nonetheless, there remains a certain indefinability about the genre, a notorious "incommunicable quality."[8] We should allow the genre to be flexible: these features are not necessary and sufficient.

Folk proverbs in some manifestation recur almost universally across space and time. In Mesopotamia, proverbs were gathered into collections from as early as circa 2600 BCE and are quoted in narratives, hymns, and letters.[9] These seem to reflect an oral tradition of the people.[10] In Hebrew texts too, proverbs are cited in narrative and prophecy, distinguishable by generic criteria like those given above and sometimes marked by "Thus it is said" (עַל־כֵּן יֹאמַר) or similar.[11] Even if these particular folk sayings are not genuine (but rather creations of the biblical writers), they are evidence that sayings were deemed usual and unremarkable in Israelite discourse.

---

7. For an overview of recent discussion, see Neal R. Norrick, "Subject Area, Terminology, Proverb Definitions, Proverb Features," in *Introduction to Paremiology: A Comprehensive Guide to Proverb Studies*, ed. Hrisztalina Hrisztova-Gotthardt and Melita Aleksa Varga (Berlin: de Gruyter, 2015), 7–27.

8. Archer Taylor, *The Proverb* (Cambridge: Harvard University Press, 1931), 3.

9. Many of the collections are published in Edmund I. Gordon, *Sumerian Proverbs: Glimpses of Everyday Life in Ancient Mesopotamia* (Philadelphia: University Museum, University of Pennsylvania, 1959). See also J. Taylor, "The Sumerian Proverb Collections," *RA* 99 (2005): 13–38; see esp. 21–24.

10. Bendt Alster, "Proverbs from Ancient Mesopotamia: Their History and Social Implications," *Proverbium* 10 (1993): 9; Gordon, *Sumerian Proverbs*. However, Niek Veldhuis thinks this is a romanticized interpretation; see Veldhuis, "Sumerian Proverbs in Their Curricular Context," *JAOS* 120 (2000): 383–99.

11. For examples of cited proverbs, see Judg 8:2, 21; 1 Sam 10:12 // 19:24; 16:7; 24:14[13]; 1 Kgs 20:11; Ezek 12:22; 18:2 // Jer 31:29.

Their function and import were seminally analyzed by Carole R. Fontaine, and several scholars have fruitfully followed her trajectory.[12]

There is a long-recognized similarity between such folk proverbs and the sayings in the book of Proverbs. As noted in the introduction, a diachronic progression is often postulated from the single-lined folk saying to the two-lined wisdom saying, though we cannot trace such development securely.[13] More fruitfully, perhaps, Fontaine drew on the similarities of content, structure, function, and worldview to argue for the same "wisdom at work" in both folk tradition and wisdom books like Proverbs.[14] Indeed, some cross-influence seems likely. Significant for my purposes here, the features held in common between biblical and folk proverbs mean that the interpreter applies to both certain conventions and strategies of interpretation and use.

1.1.2. Didactic Instructions

Second, there are family resemblances between biblical proverbs and didactic instructions from Egypt, Mesopotamia, and Syria.[15] We prob-

---

12. Fontaine, *Traditional Sayings*; see further, e.g., Claudia Camp, "The Wise Women of 2 Samuel: A Role Model for Women in Early Israel?," *CBQ* 43 (1981): 14–29; Galit Hasan-Rokem, "And God Created the Proverb…: Inter-generic and Inter-textual Aspects of Biblical Paremiology—Or the Longest Way to the Shortest Text," in *Text and Tradition: The Hebrew Bible and Folklore*, ed. Susan Niditch (Atlanta: Society of Biblical Literature, 1990), 107–20; Niditch, *Folklore and the Hebrew Bible*; Willie van Heerden, "The Rhetoric of Using Proverbs in Conflict Situations: The Cases of a Biblical Text and an African Proverb," *OTE* 16 (2003): 731–44; Michael D. Lieber, "Analogic Ambiguity: A Paradox of Proverb Usage," *JAF* 97.386 (1984): 423–41.

13. Seminally Eißfeldt, *Der Maschal*; critiqued by Hermisson, *Studien zur israelitischen Spruchweisheit*.

14. Fontaine, *Traditional Sayings*, 168–70.

15. The terminology used to describe these texts is disputed. They are sometimes classified as wisdom literature, but this superimposes a category from biblical scholarship onto ancient Near Eastern material; see Miriam Lichtheim, *Moral Values in Ancient Egypt*, OBO 155 (Fribourg: Universitätsverlag; Göttingen: Vandenhoeck & Ruprecht, 1997), 1–8. The most important texts from Egypt include (chronologically) the Instruction of Hardjedef, Instruction of Ptahhotep, Instruction to Merikare, Instruction of Amenemhet, Instruction of Ani, Instruction of Amenemope, Instruction of Ankhsheshonq, and the instruction in Papyrus Insinger published in *AEL* 1, 2, 3. From Mesopotamia come the Instruction of Šuruppak (Sumerian and Akkadian versions), Counsels of Wisdom, Advice to a Prince, and Counsels of a Pessimist; see

ably cannot speak of an international wisdom tradition as such, but Israel certainly interacted with foreign ideas.[16] By the Hebrew Bible's account, Solomon's wisdom "surpassed the wisdom of all the people of the east and all of the wisdom of Egypt" (1 Kgs 5:10 [Eng. 4:30]), and Prov 31:1–9 is attributed to Lemuel, King of Massa (a North Arabian people group). Furthermore, the biblical text has literary connections with ancient Near Eastern materials. Most striking are the similarities between Prov 22:17–24:22 and the Instruction of Amenemope, and scholars have also noted verbal parallels with, for example, the Aramaic Instruction of Ahiqar.[17] There are formal parallels, too, discussed below (§1.6). We should be cautious of assuming that Israel had ready access to and understanding of a broad corpus of foreign texts, but the plausibility of an international connection is further undergirded by Ugaritic materials. In the libraries of Ugarit, Sumerian and Akkadian didactic texts have been found, showing their influence just north of Israel at the end of the second millennium.[18] It is likely that the authors of Proverbs drew upon this genre with its conventions and adapted it toward their own goals.

In particular, these texts seem to have been intended for ethical formation. Egypt's didactic literature, like Israel's, stresses the importance of

---

Wilfred G. Lambert, *Babylonian Wisdom Literature* (Oxford: Clarendon, 1960). From Syria is the much-copied Aramaic Instruction of Ahiqar; see J. M. Lindenberger, *The Aramaic Proverbs of Ahiqar* (Baltimore: Johns Hopkins University Press, 1983) (sayings only); for good bibliography of other publications and editions until 1994, see the appendix of Stuart Weeks, *Early Israelite Wisdom*, Oxford Theological Monographs (Oxford: Oxford University Press, 1994); for an overview of recent scholarship, Michael V. Fox, "Ancient Near Eastern Wisdom Literature (Didactic)," *RC* 5 (2011): 1–11.

16. The notion of a "wisdom tradition" has been challenged in particular by Mark R. Sneed, "Is the 'Wisdom Tradition' a Tradition?," *CBQ* 73 (2011): 50–71.

17. The similarity with Instruction of Amenemope was first recognized by Adolf Erman, "Eine ägyptische Quelle der 'Sprüche Salomos,'" in *Sitzungberichte der preussichen Akademie der Wissenschaften, Sitzung der philosophisch-historischen Klasse* (Berlin: de Gruyter, 1924), 86–93. See discussion of more recent debates in J. A. Emerton, "The Teaching of Amenemope and Proverbs XXII 17–XXIV 22: Further Reflections on a Long-Standing Problem," *VT* 51 (2001): 431–65. For similarities to the Aramaic Instruction of Ahiqar, see John Day, "Foreign Semitic Influence on the Wisdom of Israel and Its Appropriation in the Book of Proverbs," in *Wisdom in Israel: Essays in Honour of J. A. Emerton*, ed. John Day, Robert, P. Gordon, and H. G. M. Williamson (Cambridge: Cambridge University Press, 1998), 55–70.

18. Leo G. Perdue, *The Sword and the Stylus: An Introduction to Wisdom in the Age of Empires* (Grand Rapids: Eerdmans, 2008) 36–39.

developing moral character and makes use of character types and antitypes to emulate and avoid (see chapter 4 below). The texts educate their readers in virtues, principal among which were (according to Egyptologist Miriam Lichtheim) "honesty and truthfulness; justice, kindness, and generosity; temperance and patience; thoughtfulness, diligence, and competence; loyalty and reliability."[19] This is very similar to what we find in Proverbs.

As well as moral formation, such didactic texts encourage reflection on their own words. The desired reading strategy is one of thoughtful interpretation. In Egyptian literature, the reader is called on to "penetrate" or "open" (ʿḳ) the instructions.[20] Ani claims he will make his reader "a wise man who can penetrate words" and later advises the reader to "penetrate the writings, put them in your heart."[21] This reflects an advanced stage of learning: the student must go deep into the sayings and consider their intricacies. The tightly worded epigram is likened to a "knot" (ṯs) that must be "untied" (wḥʿ) through the interpretive process. According to the Instruction of Amenemope, it is not enough simply to listen to the sayings; you must "put them in your heart, and become a man who unties their knots, one who unties as a teacher" (27.13–15; cf. 3.10).[22] This hermeneutical principle of careful consideration for the sake of intellectual training is essential for Proverbs too.

1.2. Social Settings: Court and Family

Since the 1960s, literary theorists have shown a sustained awareness that genres are inextricably tied to their situations of use.[23] Genres necessarily

---

19. Miriam Lichtheim, "Didactic Literature," in *Ancient Egyptian Literature: History and Forms*, ed. Antonio Loprieno (Leiden: Brill, 1996), 261.

20. Michael V. Fox, "Wisdom and the Self-Presentation of Wisdom Literature," in *Reading From Right to Left: Essays on the Hebrew Bible in Honour of David J. A. Clines*, ed. Jo Cheryl Exum and H. G. M. Williamson (Sheffield: Sheffield Academic, 2003), 166–67.

21. These are 15.4 and 20.4–5, according to the numbering of J. F. Quack, *Die Lehren des Ani: Ein neuägyptischer Weisheitstext in seinem kulturellen Umfeld*, OBO 141 (Fribourg: Universitätsverlag; Göttingen: Vandenhoeck & Ruprecht, 1995). Translation from Fox, "Wisdom and the Self-Presentation," 167.

22. Nili Shupak, *Where Can Wisdom Be Found? The Sage's Language in the Bible and in Ancient Egyptian Literature*, OBO 130 (Fribourg: Universitätsverlag; Göttingen: Vandenhoeck & Ruprecht, 1993), 64.

23. See esp. Edwin Black, *Rhetorical Criticism: A Study in Method* (New York:

interact with the social, cultural, and physical features of their environment. They both are shaped by, and go toward shaping, that environment.
They are put to use in certain settings to answer to the needs and desires
of particular communities. Little has been conclusively decided about
Proverbs' original setting(s), but two options seem most likely: the school/
court or the family/folk.

1.2.1. A Setting in a School/Court?

A school would provide an obvious context for a didactic book.[24] Indeed,
this seems to have been the setting for many of the generically related
ancient Near Eastern texts. Proverb collections seem to have provided
an early stage in the Mesopotamian scribal curriculum, and Egyptian
instruction texts may have been used in schools ("houses of life") to train
the aristocracy.[25] The presence of comparable institutions in Israel may
be hinted at through epigraphic finds (primarily abecedaries, reflecting
early education) and some possible allusions in the Hebrew Bible.[26] How-

---

MacMillian, 1965); Lloyd Bitzer, "The Rhetorical Situation," *Philosophy and Rhetoric* 1
(1968): 1–14. In biblical studies, Gunkel considered social setting in terms of *Sitz im
Leben* ("setting in life"). For Gunkel, this referred to a typical social situation that gave
rise to an oral *Gattung*, and not to the historical situation of a particular literary text.
I prefer the broader terminology "social setting," which designates both typical genre
settings and specific text settings (see "Introduction" above).

24. This was first influentially argued for Proverbs by Hermisson, *Studien zur
israelitischen Spruchweisheit*. See also Bernhard Lang, "Schule und Unterricht im alten
Israel," in *La sagesse de l'Ancien Testament*, ed. Maurice Gilbert (Leuven: Leuven University Press, 1979), 186–201; André Lemaire, *Écoles et la formation de la Bible dans
l'ancient Israël*, OBO 39 (Fribourg: Universitätsverlag; Göttingen: Vandenhoeck &
Ruprecht, 1981); Perdue, *Sword and the Stylus*; Shupak, *Where Can Wisdom Be Found?*

25. Mesopotamian: Veldhuis, "Sumerian Proverbs"; Jeremy Black, et al., *The Literature of Ancient Sumer* (Oxford: Oxford University Press, 2006) xli–xlii; Egyptian:
Perdue, *Sword and the Stylus*, 76. This may pertain, however, to the texts' reuse in later
periods more than to their original provenance. Stuart Weeks, *Instruction and Imagery
in Proverbs 1–9* (Oxford: Oxford University Press, 2007), 16–25.

26. David M. Carr, *Writing on the Tablet of the Heart: Origins of Scripture and Literature* (Oxford: Oxford University Press, 2005), 122–26; Lemaire, *Écoles*, 7–33; James
L. Crenshaw, "Education in Ancient Israel," *JBL* 104 (1985): 603–4; August Klostermann, "Schulwesen im alten Israel," in *Theologische Studien: Theodor Zahn zum
10. Oktober 1908 dargebracht*, ed. Gottlieb Nathanael Bonwetsch and Theodor Zahn
(Leipzig: Deichert, 1908), 193–232.

ever, such evidence is scant, and the presence of formal schools in Israel remains uncertain.[27]

Regardless, an elite educational function may be possible even without this. Within the Israelite court, these texts may have been used to train would-be scribes, sages, and royal officials.[28] Many Egyptian, Mesopotamian, and Syrian texts present themselves as wisdom passed from a king/royal official to his successor, and similarly, the collections in Proverbs are ascribed (probably eponymously) to Kings Solomon (1:1; 10:1) and Hezekiah (25:1; and Arabian King Lemuel, 31:1). A number of sayings specifically refer to the king or seem to presume acquaintance with him (see chapter 6). This evidence suggest that the proverbs probably passed through the court at some point. At the very least, they came into the hands of the educated literati (for they were written down, see §1.3) and were connected with the court through these writers. Within this setting, the book might serve as a broad enculturation program to establish the ideological foundations of this social group.[29] This elite may have been more available, equipped, and inclined to study than the everyday folk. Indeed, "The wisdom of the scribe depends on the opportunity for leisure.... How can one become wise who handles the plow?" (Sir 38:24–25).[30]

1.2.2. A Setting among the Folk?

But the one who "handles the plow" may also lay claim to proverbs.[31] Indeed folk proverbs operate universally within nonelite family settings.

---

27. See the discussion in Weeks, *Early Israelite Wisdom*, 132–53.

28. C. B. Ansberry, *Be Wise, My Son, and Make My Heart Glad: An Exploration of the Courtly Nature of the Book of Proverbs*, BZAW 422 (Berlin: de Gruyter, 2011); Michael V. Fox, "The Social Location of the Book of Proverbs," in *Texts, Temples, and Traditions: A Tribute to Menahem Haran*, ed. Michael V. Fox et al. (Winona Lake, IN: Eisenbrauns, 1996), 227–39; Perdue, *Sword and the Stylus*; von Rad, *Wisdom in Israel*. For criticism of the court hypothesis, see Weeks, *Early Israelite Wisdom*, 41–56.

29. Ansberry, *Be Wise, My Son*.

30. NRSV. All biblical translations are my own unless otherwise stated.

31. Suggesting a folk origin for (at least some of) the sentence literature are André Barucq, "Proverbes (Livre des)," in *Supplement au dictionnaire de la Bible*, ed. L. Pirot et al. (Paris: Letouzey & Ané, 1972), 8.1415–19; Katharine J. Dell, *The Book of Proverbs in Social and Theological Context* (Cambridge: Cambridge University Press, 2006); Friedemann Golka, *The Leopard's Spots: Biblical and African Wisdom in Proverbs* (Edinburgh: T&T Clark, 1993); Laurent Naré, *Proverbes salomoniens et*

The sayings in Prov 10:1–22:16 show similarity to the proverb stocks of other peoples, with some tropes strikingly recurring across space and time.[32] Many sayings reflect an agrarian society, with the language of husbandry and harvests frequent and the importance of diligent work stressed. There is sometimes ambivalence about the ruling elite (see ch. 6) and a deep concern for the poor.[33] The book has a strong community ethos, commending behavior conducive to harmonious communal life (avoiding quarrels, soothing social tensions, etc.), not specific skills needed for royal administration.

At the very least, the sayings were retained into postmonarchic Israel and so must have been able to function away from the court. But in earlier periods too, wisdom seems to have been at home outside the royal precincts, perhaps epitomized in figures like the local wise woman (2 Sam 14:2; 20:16).[34] The most prevalent social circle in Proverbs is familial, with frequent references to the parents and son. Both mother and father are mentioned, suggesting that the latter is not (as some argue) simply a cipher

---

proverbes mossi: Etude comparative à partir d'une nouvelle analyse de Pr 25–29 (Bern: Lang, 1986); John Paterson, *The Book That Is Alive: Studies in Old Testament Life and Thought as Set Forth by the Hebrew Sages* (New York: Scribner's Sons, 1954); Harold C. Washington, *Wealth and Poverty in the Instruction of Amenemope and the Hebrew Proverbs*, SBLDS 142 (Atlanta: Scholars Press, 1994); Claus Westermann, *Roots of Wisdom: The Oldest Proverbs of Israel and Other Peoples* (Louisville: Westminster John Knox, 1995); R. N. Whybray, *Wealth and Poverty in the Book of Proverbs*, JSOTSup 99 (Sheffield: JSOT Press, 1990).

32. For example, the view of speech held by biblical and folk proverbs seems very similar (see §7.2.2). Even a theme seemingly so distinctive as the contrast of wise and foolish is attested in proverb collections universally; F. Černak, "Reason and Thought: Pillars of Intellectual Behaviour in Proverbs," in *Tenth Interdisciplinary Colloquium on Proverbs*, ed. Rui Soares and Outi Lauhakangas (Tavira: AIP-IAP, 2017), 149–60; Golka, *Leopard's Spots*, 49–50. Several scholars have compared biblical proverbs with those of other nations. See, e.g., Barucq, "Proverbes (Livre des)," cols. 1415–19 (African); Golka, *Leopard's Spots* (African); Lechion Peter Kimilike, *Poverty in the Book of Proverbs: An African Transformational Hermeneutic of Proverbs on Poverty*, Bible and Theology in Africa 7 (New York: Lang, 2008) (African); Naré, *Proverbes salomoniens et proverbes mossi* (Mossi); Westermann, *Roots of Wisdom* (African, Sumatran, Sumerian, Egyptian).

33. There is a debate about the socioeconomic perspective reflected. Westermann thinks the perspective is that of the "simple folk" (*Roots of Wisdom*); Whybray thinks those in a middle class who were neither rich nor poor (*Wealth and Poverty*); Fox thinks the higher echelons of society ("Social Location").

34. Camp, "Wise Women."

for "teacher."[35] Within such a context, the sayings may have been used akin to folk proverbs, spoken in relation to problem situations arising in the family's life.

1.2.3. More Than a Single Setting

In all likelihood, the didactic proverbs had links with both of these settings—court and folk.[36] The sentences reflect an array of social locations. It is misguided to search for one setting alone, for it is in the nature of a proverb to be passed through many hands. A rough distinction might be made between origin, collection, and use (though not in a simple linear progression). Many proverbs may have originated among the folk, before a complex collection process. At this stage, some may have been altered or created by the literati. Smaller collections might have circulated independently in oral or written form before being brought together. There is little reason to think that the proverbs then fell out of popular usage.

Such a double context suggests a twin interpretive strategy: didactic use in the court and proverbial use in the family. But these should not be distinguished too rigidly. Scribes and courtiers are real people too, with families of their own, and proverbs learned in the court may have entered their folk interactions. Equally, the family may have been a primary locus for social, moral, and religious training in Israel (e.g., Deut 4:9–10; 6:20–25), providing an environment eminently suitable for didactic use.[37] The two settings are related to, but not necessary for, these two different usages.

1.3. Media: Written and Oral

1.3.1. Written

In the form we have it, Prov 10:1–22:16 is, clearly, a written text. Indeed, the written nature of comparable proverb collections seems fundamental to their purpose: in Mesopotamia they seem to have taught writing skills

---

35. See, e.g., Lang, "Schule und Unterricht," 192–95.

36. Though emphasizing one setting in particular, most scholars cited above in n. 28 (court origin) and n. 31 (folk origin) acknowledge the possibility of the other setting.

37. Ansberry, *Be Wise, My Son*, 40–45; Carr, *Writing on the Tablet of the Heart Tablet*, 129–30; Crenshaw, "Education in Ancient Israel," 614.

to aspiring scribes.[38] However, alphabetic Hebrew is much simpler than Mesopotamian cuneiform, so this is unlikely to be the primary reason that Israel's proverbs were penned. The extent of literacy and the prevalence of scribal culture in ancient Israel are disputed. Some argue for literacy as a commonplace from early in the monarchic period.[39] But a more moderate reconstruction is safer: probably only by the late monarchic period had literacy spread, perhaps beyond scribes, but not beyond an elite minority.[40]

Writing Proverbs down has semiformalized it into what could be used as an enculturation program to develop a distinctive worldview in its students (whether or not in a school). Writing can become a symbolic activity, establishing the identity and values of a particular group.[41] It makes the text less malleable, circumscribes its limits, and presents its instructions as a definitive totality: "Beware of anything beyond these" (Qoh 12:12). It makes claims about the text's authority—only that of utmost importance is honored with this expensive, specialist medium. Furthermore, a written text is removed from situational contexts, ready to be unrolled no matter when or where. Its general advice transcends particularities. It becomes a ready stimulus for intellectual training, a physical object to be pored over and analyzed. This may be a personal, reflective activity, with no need for a third party beyond text and reader. Its unchanging form allows repeated autodidactic study to explore its intricacies.

---

38. Veldhuis, "Sumerian Proverbs."

39. See, e.g., William G. Dever, *What Did the Biblical Writers Know and When Did They Know It? What Archaeology Can Tell Us about the Reality of Ancient Israel* (Grand Rapids: Eerdmans, 2001) 202–4; Richard S. Hess, "Questions of Reading and Writing in Ancient Israel," *BBR* 19 (2009): 1–9; Alan Millard, "Writing, Writing Materials and Literacy in the Ancient Near East," in *Dictionary of the Old Testament: Historical Books*, ed. Bill T. Arnold and H. G. M. Williamson (Downers Green, IL: InterVarsity Press, 2005), 1003–11.

40. Carr, *Writing on the Tablet of the Heart*; Christopher A. Rollston, *Writing and Literacy in the World of Ancient Israel: Epigraphic Evidence From the Iron Age* (Atlanta: Society of Biblical Literature, 2010); Seth L. Sanders, *The Invention of Hebrew* (Chicago: University of Illinois Press, 2009); William M. Schniedewind, *How the Bible Became a Book: The Textualization of Ancient Israel* (Cambridge: Cambridge University Press, 2004).

41. Susan Niditch, *Oral World and Written Word: Ancient Israelite Literature*, LAI (Louisville: Westminster John Knox, 1996), 79.

1.3.2. Oral

However, Proverbs is not just a written text; it is oral, too. It is easy to forget, in our contemporary writing-infused culture, that Israel was essentially an oral society, even within its literate subsections. The two media cannot be dichotomized or placed in a simple diachronic progression. Even when texts were set down in writing, their essential orality did not cease. Susan Niditch has expressed this in terms of an "oral-literary continuum" in Israel, and David M. Carr proposes that both media were parts of a much larger matrix for textual transmission, whose aim was to inscribe the texts on the recipients' hearts (Prov 3:3; 7:3).[42] Memorization, oral performance, and written records were all aspects of this much grander enculturation.

This accords with the self-presentation of didactic texts across the ancient Near East. They often depict a spoken discourse between father and son, which is subsequently recorded for posterity in written form.[43] Similarly, Prov 22:17–21 describes its own instruction in both oral and written terms: "Incline your ear, and hear the words of the wise.... Have I not written for you thirty sayings of counsel and knowledge?" We might imagine court recitations of entire collections, functioning as an important didactic tool for enculturation.[44]

However, the oral nature of the texts means that a proverbial use also becomes possible. They can no longer be the secret property of the literati. Even if recited at court, they may have been heard and repeated by more than just courtiers. In a similar vein, Jeremy Black suggests that the oral nature of Sumerian proverb collections made them "accessible to the vast illiterate majority too."[45] Orality can fragment textual unity, permitting piece-by-piece transmission. Such a process may be attested by the presence of variant proverbs: dispersed throughout the collections are multiple versions of what are ostensibly the same saying. While they could be explained otherwise, it is possible that these arose through the gradual "Chinese-whispers" effect of the oral repetition of units.[46]

---

42. Niditch, *Oral World and Written Word*; Carr, *Writing on the Tablet of the Heart*.

43. See Fox, "Wisdom and the Self-Presentation," 160–65.

44. Carr, *Writing on the Tablet of the Heart*.

45. Black et al., *Literature of Ancient Sumer*, il.

46. Carr in particular argues that these are "memory variants" (*Formation of the Hebrew Bible*, 25–34). Other possibilities include scribal error, different literary

Individual units might be spoken into specific contexts. Proverbs' fictive interaction situation—father instructing son—frequently recurs throughout life. The memorized text becomes a mental proverb inventory, each unit ready to be deployed at an opportune moment. Removed from its literary encasing, the proverb is no longer an artifact for individual study but a tool that can be used within interaction. An oral unit can cut into a situation with an immediacy inaccessible to its written counterpart. Its aural features (such as sound patterning) not only help its memorization but bring it particular potency when spoken.[47] The hearer assumes that there is some specific reason for this speech, some pressing importance for her own circumstance. It becomes a matter of urgency to follow its direction. Thus the book is insistent in its imperative: "Listen!" (1:8; 4:1; 5:7; 7:24; 8:32, 33; 19:20; 22:17; 23:19, 22). The Hebrew here—שמע—implies not just passive hearing but active obedience. Thus the media of the book give it dual function, both didactic and proverbial, or as Fox has put it, both "study and understand" and "hear and do."[48]

1.4. Self-Presentation: חידה and משל

We have seen, then, that the sayings in Prov 10:1–22:16 may be used akin to didactic instructions, read in the royal court, or akin to folk proverbs, spoken in the family. But does this tally with what the book says about itself? Does the book indicate how it wants its sayings to be used, the expectations and conventions it wants its interpreter to bring to bear?

Clues may be present in its statement of purpose (1:2–7). Positioned as a prologue, this offers itself as a hermeneutical guide for what follows. Its addressees are specified in verse 4 as the "simple" (פתאים) and the "youth" (נער)—the same characters to whom the speakers of chapters 1–9 subsequently appeal.[49] With such recipients, the sayings must allow for straightforward interpretations, akin to folk proverbs. They offer basic advice on how to behave more wisely. Their surface meaning is evident, and they can be applied straightforwardly to the hearer's life.

---

sources, and editorial activity. See Heim, *Poetic Imagination*, 5–9; Snell, *Twice-Told Proverbs*.

47. On sound patterning, see Thomas, P. McCreesh, *Biblical Sound and Sense: Poetic Sound Patterns in Proverbs 10–29*, JSOTSup 128 (Sheffield: JSOT Press, 1991).

48. Fox, "Wisdom and the Self-Presentation."

49. The פתי is appealed to in 1:22; 8:5; 9:4, 16, paralleled with the נער in 7:7.

However, the prologue abruptly shifts the book's addressee in verse 5, with a jussive exclamation: "Let the wise [חכם] hear.… Let the discerning [נבון] get guidance." The book's advice must go beyond the basics. The task of the wise is delineated in verse 6: "To understand the proverb and the saying, the words of the wise and their riddles" (להבין משל ומליצה דברי חכמים וחידתם:). The implication: these are not always easy to understand. Four literary terms are listed here, apparently describing the contents of the book. The meaning of מליצה is too poorly understood to offer much insight.[50] The phrase "words of the wise" (דברי חכמים) characterizes the book's imagined speakers and endorses its educational value. The other two terms, משל ("proverb") and חידה ("riddle"), can be used as genre descriptors and so may offer us conventions for interpretation.

The proverb and the riddle are recognized cross-culturally as folk forms. Evidence for the former in Israel has been given above (§1.1). Evidence for the latter occurs particularly in Samson's obscure puzzle of Judg 14.[51] The forms are closely related, and the sayings in Proverbs have been explained as stemming from both.[52] All are short, pithy, oral expressions,

---

50. מליצה occurs twice in the Hebrew Bible: here and in Hab 2:6 (also Sir 47:17), each time associated with משל. Its etymology is disputed. It may be from √ליץ, "to scorn, mock," hence "mocking saying" (BDB, sv. "ליץ"; Oesterley, *Book of Proverbs*). As a *hiphil* participle, the root designates an "interpreter," so some have suggested "a saying in need of interpretation" (Berend Gemser, *Sprüche Salomos*, HAT 1.16 [Tübingen: Mohr Siebeck, 1963]), which would be supported by the parallelism with חידה, "riddle." Alternatively, the root may be √מלץ, "to be smooth, slippery"—either a slippery, allusive saying (H. Neil Richardson, "Some Notes on ליץ and Its Derivatives," *VT* 5 [1955]: 163–79), or a smooth, sweet saying (John Parkhurst, *Hebrew Lexicon and Grammar* [London: Sherwood, Neely & Jones, 1821]). The LXX translates it as σκοτεινὸν λόγον, a "dark saying."

51. Claudia Camp and Carole R. Fontaine use insights from folklore studies to interpret this riddle; see Camp and Fontaine, "The Words of the Wise and Their Riddles," in *Text and Tradition: The Bible and Folklore*, ed. Susan Niditch (Atlanta: Society of Biblical Literature, 1990), 127–52.

52. The origin of the sayings in folk proverbs was first influentially advocated by Eißfeldt (*Der Maschal*, see above). Some propose an origin in folk riddles, reconstituted so that question and answer are pushed together into a single saying. This has been suggested in particular for the numerical sayings in Prov 30:15–33; see, e.g., Harry Torcszyner, "The Riddle in the Bible," *HUCA* 1 (1924): 125–49. Some have suggested this for other sayings too; see, e.g., James L. Crenshaw, "Wisdom," in *Old Testament Form Criticism*, ed. John Haralson Hayes (San Antonio: Trinity University Press, 1974), 225–64; Torcszyner, משלי שלמה [Proverbs of Solomon] (Tel Aviv: Yavneh,

often employing figurative language.[53] However, proverb and riddle also have important differences. A proverb has a self-evident meaning, even to the simpleminded; a riddle requires wise interpretation. The former intends to clarify, the latter to obscure.

1.4.1. משל—Speech for the Simple

Elsewhere in the Hebrew Bible, the term משל designates apparent folk proverbs (e.g., 1 Sam 10:12; 24:14[13]; Ezek 12:22–23; 18:2–3). Two sayings in Proverbs speak self-referentially of משלים, perhaps also implying this meaning: "A proverb [משל] in the mouth of fools" is "like legs that dangled from a cripple" (26:7) and "like a thorn that went up into a drunkard's hand" (26:9). The fool uses the saying in a particular situation, expecting it to have an effect like a folk proverb. But it proves ineffective (26:7) or downright harmful (26:9). Most scholars believe that משל is etymologically derived from "to be like" (משל√).[54] This provides an immediately plausible semantic background, for folk proverbs often function as similitudes. They clarify for the simple the likeness between two situations or phenomena. In Proverbs, many sayings contain comparisons (esp. in Prov 25–26) and/or can be used as standards of comparison for situations in life.

Proverbs designates its contents as משלים in three titular verses (1:1; 10:1; 25:1). By giving itself this title, the book signals that the reader should bring to bear the expectations and principles of the proverb genre. Each saying can be pronounced as a comment on a particular situation, evaluating it and directing the hearer's subsequent behavior. Each provides straightforward clarification and guidance.

1947); Mordechai Zer Kavod, "חידות בספר משלי" [Riddles in the Book of Proverbs], *Beit Mikra* 64 (1975): 7–11.

53. On the structural similarities between the proverb and the riddle, see Alan Dundes, "On the Structure of the Proverb," *Proverbium* 25 (1975): 961–73; cf. Roger D. Abrahams, "Introductory Remarks to a Rhetorical Theory of Folklore," *JAF* 81.320 (1968): 143–58; Thomas Green and William Pepicello, "The Proverb and Riddle as Folk Enthymemes," *Proverbium* 3 (1986): 33–46.

54. BDB, s.v. "משל I." Some have suggested instead "to rule" (BDB, s.v. "משל II"), hence "sovereign word" or "word of power"; see, e.g., recently Leo G. Perdue, *Proverbs*, IBC (Louisville: John Knox, 2000), 27. This view has largely been discredited, however, mainly based on cognate languages; see discussion in William McKane, *Proverbs: A New Approach*, OLT (London: SCM, 1970), 24–26.

1.4.2. מָשָׁל—Perhaps Not So Simple?

However, the situation may not be quite so simple. The term מָשָׁל can be used for a variety of forms: taunt songs (Isa 14:4; Mic 2:4), allegories (Ezek 17:2; 21:5[20:49]), poems (Pss 49:5[4]; 78:2), discourses (Num 23:7; Job 27:1), even a person or nation who has become a byword (Ps 44:15[14]; Deut 28:37). Some scholars have tried to account for all these diverse uses within a single umbrella category, perhaps based around the idea of likeness.[55] Ezekiel's allegories, for example, are founded on comparisons, and bywords are exemplars. However, this will not work for all cases, and it is probably better not to look for a unifying genre but to recognize the flexibility of the term.

With the designation מְשָׁלִים, therefore, the introductory verses prime us for strategies of interpretation appropriate for folk proverbs, but they do not hem us in to such strategies. In form and substance, the sayings are not quite folk proverbs (see §1.5, below). Indeed, nothing much resembling folk proverbs appears until nine chapters later, in 10:1. The mismatch may prompt consideration of other ways the term can be used. מָשָׁל sometimes describes texts that are obscure and ambiguous, requiring much greater reflection.[56] Such strategies may also be appropriate here.

This is possibly the implication in Qoh 12:9: "He heard and investigated, composed many proverbs" (וְאָזֵן וְחִקֵּר תִּקֵּן מְשָׁלִים הַרְבֵּה).[57]

---

55. Arthur Stanley Herbert, "The 'Parable' (*Māšāl*) in the Old Testament," *SJT* 7 (1954): 180–96, esp. 181; Joachim Jeremias, *The Parables of Jesus*, NTL (London: SCM, 1963), 20; George M. Landes, "Jonah: A *Māšāl*?," in *Israelite Wisdom: Theological and Literary Essays in Honor of Samuel Terrien*, ed. John G. Gammie (New York: Scholars Press, 1978), 139; Niditch, *Folklore and the Hebrew Bible*, 67–91. See also Crenshaw, "Wisdom," 229–39; Eißfeldt, *Der Maschal*; Fox, *Proverbs 10–31*, 54–55; A. R. Johnson, "מָשָׁל," in *Wisdom in Israel and the Ancient Near East: Presented to Professor Harold Henry Rowley*, ed. Martin Noth and David Winton Thomas (Leiden: Brill, 1955), 162–69; McKane, *Proverbs*, 22–33; Timothy Polk, "Paradigms, Parables, and *Měšālîm*: On Reading the *Māšāl* in Scripture," *CBQ* 45 (1983): 563–84; David W. Suter, "*Māšāl* in the Similitudes of Enoch," *JBL* 100 (1981): 193–212.

56. See esp. the allegories in Ezekiel: Niditch, *Folklore and the Hebrew Bible*; Mark W. Hamilton, "Riddles and Parables, Traditions and Texts: Ezekielian Perspectives on Israelite Wisdom Tradition," in Sneed, *Was There a Wisdom Tradition?*, 241–64.

57. On the translation of אָזֵן and תִּקֵּן, see the discussion in C. L. Seow, *Ecclesiastes: A New Translation with Introduction and Commentary*, AB 18C (New York: Doubleday, 1994), 384–85.

may be the object of all three verbs. He "investigated … proverbs" (חקר
… משלים)—that is, penetrated beneath their surface and explored their
nuances.[58] Even if this parsing is rejected, Qoheleth's intellectual searching is closely linked with his proverb use. Equally, the "words of the wise"
(דברי חכמים; Qoh 12:11; cf. Prov 1:6) are "like goads" (כדרבנות)—perhaps
prompting deeper reflection.[59]

Later tradition describes the job of the wise interpreter. Sirach 39:2b–3
depicts him as engaging with the παραβολή ("parable/proverb") and the
παροιμία ("proverb"), both of which elsewhere translate משל.[60] These are
described as having turnings/subtleties (στροφή), secrets (ἀπόκρυφος),
and enigmas (αἴνιγμα). The interpreter must engage wisdom to explore
the language and discover what lies beneath its surface. In this sense, they
are akin to חידות ("riddles"), which Sirach can also translate as παραβολή
(47:17) or παροιμία (8:8) and which occur in Prov 1:6 as counterparts to
the משלים.

1.4.3. חידה—For Wise Interpretation

Nothing much like Samson's obscure puzzle occurs in Proverbs (despite
the recurring tropes of lions and honey!).[61] But to search for strict
examples of the folk riddle is, I think, to miss the point of the prologue's
pronouncement. Rather, it invokes this genre to offer principles for interpretation and expectations about content. Told that an item is a riddle,
we expect it to be obscure and enigmatic. So in Num 12:8, God spoke to
his prophets "in riddles" (בחידות)—not in pithy folk puzzles but in words
difficult to understand. By contrast, he spoke to Moses clearly, "face to
face" (פה אל־פה).

---

58. Fox, "Wisdom and the Self-Presentation," 169; Nili Shupak, "Learning Methods in Ancient Israel," *VT* 53 (2003): 416–26, esp. 422.

59. The precise significance of this simile is disputed. Related to this view is the
idea that they prompt readers to right action. See Craig G. Bartholomew, *Ecclesiastes*
(Grand Rapids: Baker Academic, 2009). Alternatively, they prick and hurt; Michael V.
Fox, *A Time to Tear Down and a Time to Build Up: A Rereading of Ecclesiastes* (Grand
Rapids: Eerdmans, 1999); Tremper Longman III, *The Book of Ecclesiastes*, NICOT
(Grand Rapids: Eerdmans, 1998).

60. The Hebrew text of these verses is lost. παραβολή is the LXX's usual translation
for משל. παροιμια translates משל in Sir 6:35; 47:17; and Prov 1:1.

61. Lions occur in Prov 19:12; 20:2; 22:13; 26:13; 28:1, 15; 30:30; honey in 5:3;
24:13; 25:16, 27; 27:7.

Riddles require wise interpretation—thus the queen of Sheba used them "to test" (לנסת) Solomon's famed wisdom (1 Kgs 10:1). They force their interpreters to think of their subject matter in new ways, compelling recategorizations and links between phenomena unconnected before.[62] They emphasize the enigmatic and paradoxical, the disorder in reality. This makes the reader contemplate and reflect. They serve as a jolt out of the ordinary, an upsetting of conventional categories, a disorientation. Through the interpretive process, order is restored, and resolution is found, making riddles eminently suited for the didactic wisdom enterprise.[63] This process has a psychological impact on the reader and may bring about his formation and growth.[64] This is what we should expect when the text tells us it contains חידות. The saying should be read reflectively, with an eye to what is beneath the surface.

The self-presentation of Prov 1:6, therefore, permits two different strategies for the sayings' interpretation and use. They can be understood as משלים, folk proverbs, applied straightforwardly to life, so as to direct the simple in their actions. Or they can be interpreted as though חידות, riddles, catching the wise up in their obscurities, provoking fresh reflection on reality and training the mind.

1.5. Form 1: Aphorism and Proverb

Central to most scholarly accounts of genre is form—the structural and stylistic features shared by the texts. This often directly impacts how a text can be interpreted and used. The distinctive form of the sayings in Prov 10:1–22:16 allows them to be used both proverbially and didactically (akin to aphorisms).

---

62. Don Handelman, "Traps of Trans-formation: Theoretical Convergences Between Riddle and Ritual," in *Untying the Knot: On Riddles and Other Enigmatic Modes*, ed. Galit Hasan-Rokem and David Shulman (Oxford: Oxford University Press, 1996), 37–61, esp. 44.

63. Galit Hasan-Rokem and David Shulman, introduction to Hasan-Rokem and Shulman, *Untying the Knot*, 3–9, esp. 4; Leo G. Perdue, "The Riddles of Psalm 49," *JBL* 93 (1974): 535.

64. Hasan-Rokem and Shulman, introduction, 5.

1.5.1. The Form of a Proverb

The sayings in Prov 10:1–22:16 have formal, structural, and stylistic features, similar to those of folk proverbs, which make them suitable for application to life situations.[65] Formally, a proverb is a self-contained unit, often short and pithy. It lacks a straightforward literary context to elucidate it, and its meaning can be filled out instead by social context (see §3.2.1 below). In its self-containedness, it sets itself aside from the discourse and announces itself as a summary remark.

Structurally, a proverb can often be represented as [topic—comment].[66] It is a simple, succinct description of a situation, spoken as an incisive comment on a topic relevant to the circumstances. Unlike folk proverbs, biblical proverbs often employ parallelism: [topic—comment] // [topic—comment]. They thus observe the situation from two similar or opposite perspectives. Frequently, the slots are filled with characters, acts, or consequences: [act—character], [act—consequence], or [character—consequence]. As we will see (§3.2.2), this makes them particularly useful for evaluating situations and directing behavior.

Stylistically, a proverb often uses heightened poetic language, with figures of speech, wordplay, or soundplay. This increases its memorability—it is added to the mental inventory, ready to be redeployed in an appropriate situation. The heightened form draws attention to it as a comment and gives it persuasiveness and power. Proverbs are indirect and observational, subtly persuading their hearers without abrupt imperatives.

1.5.2. The Form of an Aphorism

If one formal comparison is offered by folk proverbs; another is offered by literary aphorisms.[67] Great thinkers throughout the centuries—from Francis Bacon to Friedrich Nietzsche—have found short sayings effective

---

65. Though the form, structure, and style of folk proverbs have themselves provoked much paremiological dispute. See Norrick, "Subject Area."

66. Dundes, "Structure of the Proverb"; see also Raymond C. van Leeuwen, *Context and Meaning in Proverbs 25–27*, SBLDS 96 (Atlanta: Scholars Press, 1988), 47–51.

67. See esp. James G. Williams, "The Power of Form: A Study of Biblical Proverbs," *Semeia* 17 (1980): 35–58 and Williams, *Those Who Ponder Proverbs: Aphoristic Thinking and Biblical Literature* (Sheffield: Almond, 1981).

for conveying philosophical insights and provoking reflection.[68] Some of the very same formal features that make sentences suitable for immediate application can turn them into goads to extensive musings. Furthermore, the biblical sayings often go beyond their folk counterparts in their literary stylization, enhancing their contemplative capacity. Three characteristics are particularly significant for aphoristic function: compressed expression, poetic flavor, and stark language.

These qualities make aphorisms highly affective. The aphorism *feels* true and important. The intensity of poetic language gives it an incontrovertible air. It is a concise, unified thought, beautifully packaged and deposited before the reader. Its allure compels her to take it up and unpack it, to feel the weight of its unqualified assertion. The heavy, emphatic language, the polarities, the all-encompassing categories make this a statement of the utmost significance. As one scholar put it, aphorists "are stirred by the hope of economizing glimpses of eternity into single-worded statements."[69] There is much to explore here—the world in a phrase.[70]

The compressed form gives the aphorism the impression of being a moment of insight, a flash of comprehension of some universal truth. It appears, all of it, all at once. Its stark and unapologetic immediacy causes a momentary psychological disruption, demanding explanation. Rather than reflection leading to a conclusion, the conclusion comes first with an aphorism.[71] Discerning how it is true (for it *must* be true) is the task of future contemplation. The aphorism is often figurative or elliptical. Its precise implications are not always clear, and the reader must employ interpretive dexterity. Modern aphorisms are often veiled in paradox and are intentionally deconstructive and problematizing. While the prevailing

---

68. See, e.g., Francis Bacon, *The New Organon*, ed. Lisa Jardine and Michael Silverthorne, Cambridge Texts in the History of Philosophy (Cambridge: Cambridge University Press, 2000); Friedrich Nietzsche, *Beyond Good and Evil* (New York: Modern Library, 1917).

69. Harold E. Pagliaro, "Paradox in the Aphorisms of La Rochefoucauld and Some Representative English Followers," *PMLA* 79 (1964): 42.

70. Thus James Geary, *The World in a Phrase: A Brief History of the Aphorism* (New York: Bloomsbury, 2005).

71. So Roland Barthes: "The intellect perceives first of all the full essence, not the progressive flux of thought" ("L'intellect perçoit d'abord des substances pleines, non le flux progressif de la pensée"). Barthes, "La Rochefoucauld: Réflexions ou sentences et maximes," in *Le degré zero de l'écriture: Suivi de nouveaux essais critiques* (Paris: Éditions du Seuil, 1972), 69–88, quote at 71–72, my translation.

mode of biblical proverbs is constructive, moments of paradox occasionally disrupt their attempts at order.[72] They have endless nuances upon which the wise can reflect.

1.6. Form 2: Collection and Saying

The proverbs have come to us not one isolated saying at a time but as a written collection, bearing signs of literary craftsmanship. This may change how we read them: while it is still legitimate to take each proverb on its own terms, as a literary whole they take on a particular didactic flavor.

1.6.1. The Didactic Collection

If the proverbs are read together as a collection, then the connections between the parts become important: between the introduction and the sentence literature, between sentences in different parts of the collection, and between a sentence and its immediate literary context.

First, the sayings can be read in light of the introduction (chapters 1–9), which may offer a hermeneutical lens for the book, suggesting its purpose for general education and moral formation. Such prologues are very common in ancient Near Eastern didactic literature. They conventionally begin by giving the title, nature, and eponymous author of the text, followed by either a narrative account of when and how the instructions were spoken, or exhortations to listen and take heed.[73] Proverbs falls into the latter tradition.[74] Such introductions present a didactic setting: a royal father passes on instruction to his son. The reader is called upon to adopt

---

72. Williams considers Proverbs and Ben Sira to be "aphoristic wisdom of order," where paradox is recognized but not prevalent. By contrast, Qoheleth and the sayings of Jesus are "aphoristic wisdom of counterorder," where paradox abounds (*Those Who Ponder Proverbs*).

73. For the former, see, e.g., Instruction of Ankhsheshonq, Instruction of Ahiqar; for the latter, see, e.g., Instruction of Šuruppak, Instruction of Amenemhet, Instruction of Amenemope.

74. Kenneth A. Kitchen sees a development in the tradition from short hortatory introductions to longer narrative ones. He suggests that Proverbs' long hortatory introduction indicates that it is chronologically a transitional work. See Kitchen, "The Basic Literary Forms and Formulations of Ancient Instructional Writings in Egypt and Western Asia," in *Studien zu altägyptischen Lebenslehren*, ed. Erik Hornung and

the receptive, submissive posture expected from the latter and implicitly to retain it throughout the book. Furthermore, in Prov 1–9, the key theme wisdom is introduced and made to seem a great object of desire. This will serve as important motivation to embody the sentences' later advice.

Second, we may consider connections between sayings in different parts of the collection. Folk proverbs are met one piece at a time; a written collection is encountered as a whole and as such can inculcate a worldview into a student. Each proverb presents a single instance of a category or pattern. Though they are not arranged systematically, the reader may combine them into a fairly coherent system to make sense of the world. By dedicated study, he becomes aware of recurrent themes and important messages. His ethical vision is shaped and his character is formed. The combined weight of the sayings becomes for him an ideological foundation upon which to stand when observing and tackling the world.

However, when the sayings are combined, they do not neatly assemble into a watertight system. Proverbs often offset each other with slightly different messages or alternative stances on the same issue, even blatant contradictions (e.g., 26:4–5).[75] Peter Hatton has called Proverbs "heteroglossalic": different voices are allowed to speak without clear adjudication.[76] The student of the collection must learn how to resolve the tension, or, if not, how to bear it. Apparently contradictory sayings train the mind to confront apparently contradictory situations in life.

Some seemingly contradictory proverbs may be deliberately arranged to problematize the confident assurances of wisdom and to make the reader think (again, see 26:4–5).[77] This leads to the third type of connection between parts: between a saying and its immediate literary context. There is evidence of some literary ordering in Proverbs' use of alliteration, catchwords, and thematic links. By Stuart Weeks's analysis,

Othmar Keel (Fribourg: Universitätsverlag; Göttingen: Vandenhoeck & Ruprecht, 1979), 247.

75. Several scholars have examined apparent contradictions in Proverbs. See, e.g., Hatton, *Contradiction*; Raymond C. van Leeuwen, "Wealth and Poverty: System and Contradiction in Proverbs," *HS* 33 (1992): 25–36; Yoder, "Forming 'Fearers of Yahweh.'"

76. Hatton in *Contradiction* employs the term as part of his Bahktinian hermeneutic.

77. Hatton in *Contradiction* conceptualizes the arrangement of proverbs as a "stream" of wisdom, where certain sayings are dropped in provocatively to disrupt the flow and cause ripples.

58 percent of the proverbs in 10:1–22:16 are connected to their neighbor in some way.[78]

Knut M. Heim in particular finds interpretive significance in this and has developed a theory of proverb clusters.[79] Like eating a cluster of grapes, our experience of each individual item is enhanced by taking in the whole. As he explains, "This reading-together allows for inferences and cross-references which lead to a cross-fertilization and inter-animation of meaning."[80] The proverbs are, in the terms of Heim, "co-referential," referring to the same individual, whose character is fleshed out as the connections between the proverbs are explored.[81] The reader builds up a single multifaceted picture of the wise and righteous man, to whom he can assimilate himself for his own ethical formation. The connections also invite him to exercise his mind, to contemplate possible links with imagination and discernment.[82]

1.6.2. The Individual Saying

However, just because we *can* read proverbs with their literary surroundings does not mean we *have to*. There are also benefits to sampling each proverb individually and chewing it over. Ingesting the proverb in this slow, ponderous process can effect the reader's intellectual and moral development. Some scholars find this suggestion of reading proverb-by-proverb untenable. They object that a saying's brevity requires it to be elucidated in a context. The logic runs that the *social context* of a folk proverb (which allows it to be taken and applied individually) is here replaced with the *literary context* of a collection. I suggest, however, that the proverbs can indeed be taken individually. Social context is still possible, and literary context is not necessary.

---

78. Weeks, *Early Israelite Wisdom*, 24.

79. Knut M. Heim, *Like Grapes of Gold Set in Silver: An Interpretation of Proverbial Clusters in Proverbs 10:1–22:16*, BZAW 273 (Berlin: de Gruyter, 2001), 67–108.

80. Heim, *Like Grapes of Gold*, 107.

81. Heim, *Like Grapes of Gold*, 77–103. Heim's terminology has been followed by several scholars, e.g., Ansberry, *Be Wise, My Son*, 77, 84; Fox, *Proverbs 10–31*, 928; Lyu, *Righteousness*, 135. See further §§4.3.2 and 4.3.3 below.

82. Zoltán Schwab, "The Sayings Clusters in Proverbs: Towards an Associative Reading Strategy," *JSOT* 38 (2013): 59–79.

The possibility of a social context? It is important for the proverb genre that the text be applied to a social context, used and reused to comment on situations arising in life. Social context elucidates the proverb's otherwise underspecified sense. Such paremiological insights were first drawn into studies of the biblical book by Claudia Camp. In her words, proverbs, "by definition, *require* a performance context to be fully meaningful."[83] When gathered in a literary collection, proverbs are stripped of any such performance setting. Camp suggested that in the history of the sayings' development, this led to their loss of function and encalcification as dogma.[84] It further required that they be recontextualized into the literary brackets of Proverbs' introduction (Prov 1–9) and conclusion (Prov 31).[85]

However, the mere fact of collection cannot kill a proverb.[86] Hezekiah's men are not murderers, and paremiographers are not coroners. Collections have existed throughout the centuries, menageries of proverbs alive among the people.[87] But might this particular type of collection, with its specific purpose and addressees, prohibit social use? In this vein, Heim argues that readers of the book are probably seeking general guidance in faith and practice and are therefore unlikely to apply the proverbs to particular contexts.[88] But I would question how faith and practice are manifested other than through specific situations? Surely the reader may apply the guidance to his life. This simplest way to do this is through contextual application.

---

83. Camp, *Wisdom and the Feminine*, 166.

84. Camp, *Wisdom and the Feminine*, 151–78.

85. Camp, *Wisdom and the Feminine*, 179–208.

86. See Wolfgang Mieder's often-appropriated dictum "The proverb in a collection is dead" (Mieder, "The Essence of Literary Proverb Studies," *Proverbium* 23 [1974]: 892; cited in, e.g., Dave Bland, "A Rhetorical Perspective on the Sentence Sayings of the Book of Proverbs" [PhD diss., University of Washington, 1994], 6; Hatton, *Contradiction*, 47; Fontaine, *Traditional Sayings*, 54; Hildebrandt, "Proverb," 6).

87. On ancient Sumerian proverb collections, see, e.g., Bendt Alster, "Literary Aspects of Sumerian and Akkadian Proverbs," in *Mesopotamian Poetic Language: Sumerian and Akkadian*, ed. Marianna E. Vogelzang and H. L. J. Vanstiphout (Groningen: Styx, 1996), 1–21; on medieval collections, see, e.g., Barry Taylor, "Medieval Proverb Collections: The West European Tradition," *Journal of the Warburg and Courtauld Institutes* 55 (1992): 19–25; on contemporary collections, see, e.g., K. Tamás, "Paremiography: Proverb Collections," in Hrisztova-Gotthardt and Aleksa Varga, *Introduction to Paremiology*, 229–42.

88. Heim, *Like Grapes of Gold*, 72–74.

The necessity of a literary context? Heim further suggests that readers will instinctively and necessarily contextualize the proverbs in their literary setting. He notes that when a folk proverb is spoken in a social context, the hearer expects it to be contextually relevant. Correspondingly, when biblical proverbs are read, the reader expects them to be contextually related and so searches for the connections between them.[89] But this is a false equation. A spoken conversation is very different from a literary collection and brings very different conventions and expectations. While the former includes the expectation of contextual relevance, the latter need not.[90]

Indeed, such contextual links are often far from obvious, and those that do emerge may not be intentional: proverbs in *any* arrangement will generate some apparent links, purely by chance.[91] Even if intentional, perhaps they are not significant: the scribe may simply have ordered proverbs according to some simple associative principle, or in a manner to help the flow of reading.[92]

---

89. Heim, *Like Grapes of Gold*, 74.

90. See Herbert Paul Grice's conversational principles, which include the "maxim of relation"—"be relevant." Grice, "Logic and Conversation," in vol. 3 of *Syntax and Semantics*, ed. Peter Cole and Jerry L. Morgan (New York: Academic Press, 1975), 41–58, 46.

91. Fox, *Proverbs 10–31*, 479–80 experimented with Weeks's method (see above) on groups of sayings randomly jumbled. He found that 36–60 percent of them had links with their neighbors.

92. Arguing for significant arrangement in the sayings: Gustav Boström, *Paronomasi i den äldre hebreiska maschallitteraturen med särskild hänsyn till proverbia*, LUÅ 1.23.8 (Lund: Håkan Ohlssons Boktryckeri, 1928); Hatton, *Contradiction*; Ted Hildebrandt, "Proverbial Strings: Cohesion in Proverbs 10," *Grace Theological Journal* 11 (1990): 171–85; Ruth Scoralick, *Einzelspruch und Sammlung: Komposition im Buch der Sprichwörter Kapitel 10–15*, BZAW 232 (Berlin: de Gruyter, 1995); Patrick W. Skehan, "A Single Editor for the Whole Book of Proverbs," in *Studies in Ancient Israelite Wisdom*, ed. James Crenshaw (New York: Ktav, 1976), 329–40; Waltke, *Book of Proverbs 1–15*; R. N. Whybray, "Yahweh-Sayings and Their Context in Proverbs 10:1–22:16," in Gilbert, *Sagesse de l'Ancien Testament*, 153–65. Suggesting the arrangement is relatively insignificant: Fox, *Proverbs 10–31*; McKane, *Proverbs*; Scott, *Proverbs, Ecclesiastes*; Weeks, *Early Israelite Wisdom*; Weeks, *Introduction*; Westermann, *Roots of Wisdom*. Arguing for an associative principle is Fox (*Proverbs 10–31*, 480). Arguing arrangement to aid reading flow is Weeks (*Early Israelite Wisdom*, 33).

The reader's immediate impression is of random arrangement. Had the collector wanted to make a contextualized reading imperative, he could have offered much clearer groupings. Reading straight through the proverbs may be disorienting. As Don Quixote rebukes Sancho Panza (the incessant proverb-speaker): "To pile up and string together proverbs at random makes conversation dull and vulgar."[93] Sancho's lists of unconnected sayings make his argument hard to follow, and the relevance of each individual proverb is lost. Similarly perhaps with a contextualized reading of the biblical collections. But Don Quixote nuances his criticism: "Mind, Sancho, I do not say that a proverb aptly brought in is objectionable." We may take the biblical proverbs as a selection of different tools, each of which may be "aptly brought in" at an appropriate time. Each can be used purposefully to comment on a specific situation.

Proverbs 10:1–22:16 then presents itself as a didactic collection and may be interpreted as such—a manual for the reader's ideological, moral, and intellectual formation. However, the collection's apparent disorder offers us a second strategy: each proverb in its own right, as a tool for application to the world.

1.7. Conclusion

We have seen that the sayings in Prov 10:1–22:16 participate in two sets of generic conventions: didactic and proverbial. They are not fully fledged members of either genre, but invoking them raises certain expectations about content and encourages certain strategies of interpretation and use. On the one hand, they are didactic—general advice intended to inculcate a worldview, train the intellect, and bring about moral formation. They are akin to didactic instructions and may have had a setting among the educated elite. They present themselves as חידות ("riddles") and are formally similar to aphorisms. In their written form, they comprise a pedagogically oriented collection.

On the other hand, they are proverbs—incisive maxims to be applied to a specific situation with a particular purpose. They are generically related to folk proverbs and may have been spoken in a family setting. They present themselves as משלים and are formally akin to such proverbs,

_____

93. Miguel de Cervantes, *The History of Don Quixote De La Mancha*, Great Books of the Western World 29 (Chicago: University of Chicago Press, 1952), 334.

particularly suited to purposeful application. The apparent disorder in the collection allows us to take each in its own terms.

While these strategies of interpretation and use are distinct, the very same unit of text stimulates both: one and the same didactic proverb. Indeed, the strategies can work together, didactic reflection leading to situational application and vice versa. I suggest that both these strategies can be employed and indeed probably were employed by the original recipients of this book. In part 2, I will explore the sayings, using this double strategy. In particular, I will examine how the openness of the sayings contributes to both their didactic and their proverbial uses. This aspect of openness requires further examination, and I will turn to it in the next chapter.

2

Literary Openness

I suggest that the sayings in Prov 10:1–22:16 are particularly open to different interpretations and applications. As noted in the introduction, there has been much recent scholarship on openness and ambiguity in the Hebrew Bible, and some attention paid to its place in Proverbs.[1] According to Anne W. Stewart, "Many of the sayings in the book delight in ambiguity and multivalency," and Heim goes as far as to call ambiguity a "hermeneutical key to the entire book," with further studies "urgently needed."[2] This study will help to fulfill this need.

The openness of biblical proverbs is, paradoxically, often due to their constriction in form. With few exceptions, the proverb is only a single verse, usually just seven or eight words long. Often omitting clarifying elements such as object markers and relative pronouns, the parts of the proverb press tightly together without making obvious their interrelationships.[3] The compression cries out for elaboration and elucidation but without offering any itself. Terse text and intrigued reader interact, generating a superabundance of open meaning potential. Furthermore, the generic conventions of both didactic and proverbial texts prompt the reader to look for openness. Didactic texts are to be pondered and explored, their surface penetrated and their depths plumbed. Proverbial texts expect to be applied in many different ways to many different situations.

---

1. E.g. Bland, "Rhetorical Perspective," 1–2; James Alfred Loader, "The Problem of Money in the Hand of a Fool," *HvTSt* 68 (2012): 1–9; Roland E. Murphy, *Proverbs*, WBC (Nashville: T. Nelson, 1998); James G. Williams, "Proverbs and Ecclesiastes," in *The Literary Guide to the Bible*, ed. Robert Alter and Frank Kermode (London: Collins, 1987), 263–82.

2. Stewart, *Poetic Ethics*, 50; Heim, *Poetic Imagination*, 639, 640.

3. Robert Alter, *The Art of Biblical Poetry* (New York: Basic Books, 2011), 207; Philip J. Nel, "Juxtaposition and Logic in the Wisdom Sayings," *JNSL* 24 (1998): 115–27.

In this chapter, I will examine three phenomena that give rise to openness in proverbs—polysemy (§2.1), parallelism (§2.2), and imagery (§2.3)—before offering some important constraints (§2.4). Not every proverb employs these devices; not every one is an open enigma of poetic genius. But such phenomena are notably frequent. The discussion here is mainly theoretical. It catalogues the phenomena explored in later chapters and provides foundations for analyzing them.[4]

2.1. Openness through Polysemy

Polysemy here refers to the possible multiple meanings of a proverb caused by semantics (§2.1.1) or grammar (§2.1.2). I will survey its variations, illustrated with examples from proverbs not discussed elsewhere. In the footnotes, I will indicate where the phenomenon occurs in proverbs explored later (listed in the order they will occur). These are tabulated in the appendix.

2.1.1. Semantic Ambiguity

2.1.1.1. Conceptual Distance between Meanings

A word can have multiple possible meanings. For some words, the meanings are close together conceptually, such as the meanings of "to paint" (e.g., painting a picture or painting lines on the road). For other words, they are conceptually distant, like the meanings of "bank" (a financial institution or the side of a river).[5] Traditionally, this distinction has been explained in terms of polysemy and homonymy. Polysemy describes one semantic unit that can have different nuances of meaning; homonymy describes different semantic units that happen to take one form. This is a diachronic distinction: polysemes share a common root (all meanings of "paint" from Old French "peint"), whereas homonyms are etymologi-

---

4. My linguistic methodology falls within cognitive linguistics. This will be evident in my view of polysemy (§2.1, seeing meaning as flexible, without rigid boundaries) and imagery (§2.3, employing the idea of "encyclopedic knowledge" and cognitive theories of metaphor). In chapter 4 it will also undergird my discussion of character types (drawing on prototype theory).

5. These examples come from an influential article by David Tuggy, "Ambiguity, Polysemy, and Vagueness," *Cognitive Linguistics* 4 (1993): 273–90.

cally distinct (the financial institution from Old Italian "banca," the river edge from proto-Germanic "baṇkan").[6] This historical distinction does not always apply on a synchronic level, however. Words with the same etymology do not always remain conceptually connected, nor do words with different etymologies always remain distinct.[7]

Recognizing the problems of this historical approach, some scholars prefer to speak of a synchronic distinction between *ambiguity*, where a lexeme has multiple discrete meanings, and *vagueness*, where it has one meaning open to differences in interpretation. So "bank" is ambiguous, and "paint" is vague.[8] A number of linguistic tests have been proposed to help recognize the distinction, but these often yield contradictory results.[9] Meaning is a flexible phenomenon, and there is no absolute division between ambiguity and vagueness. We can, however, loosely speak of a spectrum between conceptually distant and conceptually close meanings. I will use the terms polysemy and ambiguity in a broad sense to cover this whole spectrum.

Conceptually Distant Meanings[10]

Sometimes in Proverbs, a word has two conceptually distant meanings, and it is unclear which is intended.

15:7: שפתי חכמים יזרו דעת ולב כסילים לא־כן:
The lips of the wise scatter knowledge, but the heart of fools—not כן.

כן may be a denominative adjective from כון ("to be firm"), meaning "steadfast, honest" (so JPS, NIV). Alternatively, it may be an adverb (so

---

6. T. F. Hoad, *The Concise Oxford Dictionary of English Etymology* (Oxford: Oxford University Press, 1996).

7. For examples, see Barbara Lewandowska-Tomaszczyk, "Polysemy, Prototypes, and Radial Categories," in *The Oxford Handbook of Cognitive Linguistics*, ed. Dirk Geeraerts and Hubert Cuyckens (Oxford: Oxford University Press, 2010), 142.

8. So Tuggy, "Ambiguity, Polysemy, and Vagueness."

9. See Lewandowska-Tomaszczyk, "Polysemy, Prototypes, and Radial Categories," 141–44.

10. In the proverbs explored below, some of the double meanings are conceptually quite distant (Prov 20:11 [התנכר]; 16:17; 13:2; 20:2 [נפש]), some conceptually closer (19:28 [און]; 20:8, 26 [מזרה]; 20:2 [חטא]; 16:14 [מלאכים]; 10:22 [עצב]), and some closer still (16:17 [נצר, שמר]; 16:10 [משפט]).

ESV, NASB), such as occurs frequently in the expression לֹא־כֵן "not so!" (e.g., Gen 48:18; Exod 10:11; Num 12:7). The possible interpretations are not only conceptually distant, but from different parts of speech. Either is possible in the context of the proverb.

Conceptually Close Meanings

Often a proverb may include a word with several conceptually close interpretations.

14:8a: חכמת ערום הבין דרכו

The wisdom of the shrewd הבין his way.

The *hiphil* of בין can have the two related senses: "to discern" (emphasizing the process of thought) and "to understand" (emphasizing the outcome of thought).[11] Either may be discerned and understood here. Sometimes meanings may be less distinct still, with interpretation varying on whether certain connotations are found.[12]

Vague and General Terms[13]

A term might be vague with regard to certain features.[14] "To paint" is vague concerning what the "paint" is and how and where it is applied. Thus its interpretation differs for Picasso, a makeup artist, and a road-marking machine. A term with few specifying features is general, allowing it many nuances. Some general terms have a *prototypical* interpretation, a phenomenon I will discuss further in chapter 4.

16:29b: והוליכו בדרך לא־טוב:

And he makes him walk in a way not good.

Not specified is *how* the way is "not good": ethically? in its material quality? in its destination?

---

11. BDB, s.v. "בין."

12. See below 10:14 (יצפנו); 11:16 (חן, ערוץ); 16:10 (קסם); 20:11 (מעללים).

13. Vagueness occurs in 11:24 (מפזר). Generality occurs in 10:16 (חטאת); 16:17; 14:22; 12:21 (רע); 21:1 (כל).

14. Also sometimes referred to as "indeterminacy," "lack of specification," or "contextual modulation."

Soundplay[15]

Though not polysemy proper, soundplay is an important related phenomenon. Two words, whose meanings may be conceptually distant, sound very similar. The proverb contains only one of them but may evoke both.

14:3a: בפי־אויל חטר גאוה

In the mouth of the fool is a rod of pride.

גאוה means "pride," but it sounds similar to גוה "back" (Job 20:25). Accordingly, the hearer might discern "a rod for his own back" in these words (cf. Prov 10:13; 26:3).[16]

2.1.1.2. Type of Relation between Meanings

We might consider not only the conceptual distance between meanings but the type of relationship between them. What sort of semantic extension has occurred? Two of the most common are metonymy and metaphor.

Metonymy[17]

In metonymy, the word no longer designates its usual referent but something associated with it. Thus Brits may bemoan the decisions not of "the government" but of "Westminster," Americans of "Washington," and Amos of "Damascus," "Gaza," and "Tyre" (Amos 1:3, 6, 9). A metonymy creates ambiguity when it is unclear whether the concrete term or its extension is intended. For example, בית means "house" but can be metonymically extended to the "household," including family, servants, cattle, and so on. Sometimes either interpretation is possible.

14:11a: בית רשעים ישמד

The house of the wicked will be destroyed

---

15. See below 13:5 (יבאיש); 11:6 (ברשעתו); 20:11 (מעלליו).

16. Some have suggested emending to גוה, "his back" (*BHS*; RSV; McKane, *Proverbs*). Others find an allusion to the back problematic because the word for "rod" here is the rare חטר (cf. Isa 11:1) rather than the שבט used elsewhere; see Waltke, *Book of Proverbs 1–15*.

17. See below 11:24 (ישר); 20:8 (רע); 21:1 (כל); 16:1 (מענה).

Will the physical building only, or all associated parties, succumb to this fate?

Metaphor[18]

Meaning can also be extended through metaphor. For example, in English and Hebrew, "fruit" (פְּרִי) does not necessarily refer to the physical "fruit of the tree" (פְּרִי הָעֵץ; Gen 3:2) but may stand figuratively for an outcome, the "fruit of deeds" (פְּרִי מַעַלְלֵיהֶם; Isa 3:10; cf. Prov 12:4; 13:2; 18:20). Usually it is clear whether a literal or metaphorical sense is intended, but sometimes there is ambiguity.

12:7b: וּבֵית צַדִּיקִים יַעֲמֹד

The house of the righteous will stand.

Both בַּיִת ("house") and יַעֲמֹד ("will stand") may be taken literally.[19] But if בַּיִת is a metonym for the whole household, יַעֲמֹד might take a metaphorical extension: "to be established, to endure."[20]

2.1.2. Grammatical and Syntactic Ambiguity

Sometimes, instead of ambiguity arising at the lexical level, it comes through syntax or grammar.

2.1.2.1. Ambiguous Modifier[21]

A *modifier* is an element in a sentence (typically an adjective or adverb) that modifies the meaning of another element. Sometimes it is ambiguous what it modifies.

13:10a: רַק־בְּזָדוֹן יִתֵּן מַצָּה

רַק by insolence comes strife

---

18. Both metaphorical and literal interpretations are possible in 10:16 (פְּעֻלָּה, תְּבוּאָה); 20:17 (לֶחֶם); 16:14 (מַלְאָכִים); and 21:31 (מִלְחָמָה, סוּס); as well as for the figure of the king (see chapter 6).

19. Though עמד usually refers to a human being "standing," it can also refer to a building (Job 8:15, cf. Ezr 2:68; Neh 3:1; 2 Chr 24:13; 25:14; 33:19).

20. BDB, s.v. "עמד III."

21. See below, 20:8 (בְּעֵינָיו); 20:11 (גַּם).

רק ("only") might qualify the immediately subsequent element (בזדון): "only by insolence" comes strife, not by any other factors. Or it might qualify the entire clause: "only this: by insolence comes strife." Implicitly, it then may apply to the most salient element, "strife," hence the common translation "by insolence comes only strife" (e.g., ESV, JPS, NASB).[22]

2.1.2.2. Subject-Object Ambiguities[23]

In Classical Hebrew prose, the subject and object of a verb are usually distinguished by word order (typically VSO) and the object marker את. However, the proverbs rarely conform.[24] Word order is variable, and את is almost always elided. Sometimes it is difficult to tell subject from object.

17:11a: אך־מרי יבקש־רע

Only the rebellious man seeks evil/the evil man seeks only rebellion.

What is the subject of יבקש ("seek"): מרי or רע? Facilitating the ambiguity is the possible metonymy in both terms (see above, §2.1.1.2). מרי can mean "rebellion" or stand metonymically for "the rebellious man." רע can mean "evil" or "evil man." So either "the rebellious man seeks evil" (מרי as subject; JPS, NASB) or "the evil man seeks rebellion" (רע as subject; ESV, NIV, RSV). Note also the ambiguous modifier אך ("only"). Does it qualify מרי alone, or the whole clause?

2.1.2.3. Juxtaposition of Terms[25]

Very often in Proverbs, two nouns or noun phrases are simply placed side by side, without an intervening verb. In this "blunt juxtaposition," it may be unclear what relationship holds between them.[26]

10:28a: תוחלת צדיקים שמחה

The hope of the righteous—joy.

---

22. Because of the word order, רק can probably not apply directly to מצה.

23. See below 16:17 (סור); 13:2 (יאכל); 16:10 (ימעל); 10:22 (יוסף).

24. Robert D. Holmstedt argues for a basic subject-verb word order in Proverbs. See Holmstedt, "Word Order in the Book of Proverbs," in Troxel, Friebel, and Magary Seeking Out the Wisdom of the Ancients, 135–54.

25. See below 14:22; 10:17; 13:2; 20:2; 18:4.

26. This terminology comes from Fox, Proverbs 10–31, 561.

Unclear here is the precise relation between the "hope" and the "joy." Do the righteous hope for joy? Is the process of hoping a joyful one? Or will their hope (whatever its content and manner) end in joy?[27]

2.1.2.4. Construct State[28]

The Hebrew construct state can express a number of different relationships between nouns, a range overlapping with (but not identical to) the English "of" construction.

רשע עשה פעלת־שקר וזרע צדקה שכר אמת׃ :11:18
A wicked man earns the wages of lies, and he who sows righteousness, a reward of truth.

It is possible here that the wicked man's wages are earned through lying practices and the righteous man's through truthful ones (genitive of means).[29] Alternatively (or additionally), the wages of the wicked will prove to be deceptive, and those of the righteous will be reliable (attributive genitive).[30]

2.1.2.5. Ambiguous Prepositions and Conjunctions[31]

Prepositions and conjunctions have little lexical definition but have an important grammatical function in a sentence. Hebrew has a limited selection of such words to convey a wide range of functions, and sometimes ambiguity can arise.

הון מהבל ימעט׃ :13:11a
Wealth מן vapor/vanity will decrease.

---

27. Similar ambiguities are found in the variant verses 11:23 and 12:5. Do the righteous desire good, or does their desire end in good (11:23)? Are their thoughts about justice, or do they end in justice (12:5)?

28. See below Prov 20:17 (לחם שקר); 20:2 (חוטא נפשו); 20:27 (נר יהוה).

29. Ronald J. Williams, *Williams' Hebrew Syntax*, rev. and exp. by John C. Beckman, 3rd ed. (Toronto: University of Toronto Press, 2007), §45b.

30. Williams, *William's Hebrew Syntax*, §41.

31. See below Prov 11:5; 20:8; 16:10 (ב); 11:24 (מן); 20:11 (אם); 21:30 (לנגד).

מִן "from" can be used comparatively: "Wealth will decrease to *less than* vapor." It could also denote the source of the wealth: "Wealth *derived from* vanity will decrease"—that is, from vain and deceptive economic practices. Here הבל takes on its metaphorical extension, from "vapor" to "vanity."[32] The resulting double interpretation, connecting deceptive practices and fleeting wealth, is close to that in 11:18 (above; see also 20:17, explored in chapter 5).

2.1.2.6. Ambiguous Function of the *Binyan*[33]

The *binyan* in which a verb occurs can change its meaning. Each of the *binyanim* has certain common functions, but there is no absolute uniformity, and sometimes ambiguity arises.

13:7: יש מתעשר ואין כל מתרושש והון רב:
There is one who מתעשר but with nothing, one who מתרושש but with abundant wealth.

In the *qal*, עשר means "to be rich," and it is unclear here how the *hithpael* is altering the sense.[34] It could be reflexive-factitive: "makes himself rich." The comment "with nothing" might then express a future scenario (he will have nothing in the end) or relativize wealth's value (he has nothing of true worth).[35] Or the *hithpael* could be reflexive-estimative: "thinks himself rich" or "pretends to be rich," tying in with the book's theme of deception (see §7.2.1).[36] The same possibilities arise for the *hithpolel* of רוש ("to be poor") in the *b* colon—he "makes himself," "thinks himself," or "pretends to be" poor.

---

32. The Greek translation of this verse adds a further complexity. It has ὕπαρξις ἐπισπουδαζομένη μετὰ ἀνομίας ἐλάσσων γίνεται ("property gathered hastily with illegality dwindles"). μετὰ ἀνομίας (with illegality) translates מהבל in the second sense given here ("from vanity"). ἐπισπουδαζομένη ("hastily") seems to offer a double translation, but with a metathesis in the Hebrew, to מבהל (*pual* participle from √בהל "to hasten").

33. See below 13:5 (ויחפיר יבאיש); 10:17 (מתעה).

34. As the *hithpael* of this verb is so rare, it is admittedly possible that the uncertainty stems from our lack of knowledge, rather than from genuine openness in the Hebrew text.

35. Williams, *William's Hebrew Syntax*, §154.

36. Williams, *William's Hebrew Syntax*, §155.

2.2. Openness through Parallelism

2.2.1. Introduction

The second way in which a proverb's meaning may be opened is through parallelism—that is, through the elusive relationships between the two lines. Parallelism was defined by Robert Lowth in the seminal work *De Sacra Poesie Hebraeorum* (1753) as "the correspondence of one verse, or line, with another."[37] He went on to make a now famous tripartite distinction: synonymous parallelism, "when the sentiment is repeated in different, but equivalent terms"; antithetical parallelism, "when a thing is illustrated by its contrary being opposed to it"; and synthetic parallelism, "in which the sentences answer to each other ... merely by the form of construction."[38] This analysis proved foundational for the subsequent centuries of scholarship, and Lowthian parallelism came to be seen as near-definitional for Hebrew poetry.

While not denying parallelism's prevalence and importance in Hebrew verse, more recent scholarship has disputed its designation as the *sine qua non*.[39] Lowth's approach has been challenged from a number of perspectives. The overriding theme of these criticisms is his failure to account for the openness of the phenomenon and the diversity of ways it can occur.

First, Lowth's categories prove problematic, as they are a somewhat artificial dissection. As we will see below, *synonymous* and *antithetical* are problematic terms. The *synthetic* category is an amorphous catch-all for many diverse relationships that can exist between lines. More finely delineated classifications have been offered, but while these can be heuristically useful, even they cannot do justice to the rich diversi-

---

37. Robert Lowth, *Lectures on the Sacred Poetry of the Hebrews* (Andover: Codman, 1829), 156, n. 9. Lowth was not the first scholar to examine this phenomenon, but he was certainly the most influential. For discussions of developments before and after Lowth, see James Kugel, *The Idea of Biblical Poetry: Parallelism and Its History* (New Haven: Yale University Press, 1981), 96–286; Roland Meynet, *Rhetorical Analysis: An Introduction to Biblical Rhetoric*, JSOTSup 256 (Sheffield: Sheffield Academic, 1998), 44–166.

38. Lowth, *Sacred Poetry*, 157, 161, 162.

39. See, e.g., F. W. Dobbs-Allsopp, *On Biblical Poetry* (New York: Oxford University Press, 2015), 56.

ty.[40] Second, parallelism occurs at different levels of language. Though he did recognize a grammatical element to parallelism, Lowth and his followers focused almost exclusively on semantics.[41] From the late 1970s, a group of scholars challenged this approach, studying parallelism from a linguistic perspective, some even seeing parallelism in purely grammatical terms.[42] Thus to Edward L. Greenstein, parallelism is simply "the repetition of a syntactic pattern."[43] Third, Lowth focused on parallelism between the two cola of a verse. But it can also occur within a verse and between verses, and it must find its place among other devices (such as chiasmus and refrain) that structure larger portions of texts.[44]

Overall, there has been an increasing recognition of openness and reader involvement in parallelism.[45] The verse's meaning is not exhausted

---

40. For examples, see esp. Wilfred G. E. Watson, *Classical Hebrew Poetry: A Guide to Its Techniques*, JSOTSup 26 (Sheffield: JSOT Press, 1984), 114–59; Watson, *Traditional Techniques in Classical Hebrew Verse* (Sheffield: JSOT Press, 1994), 104–261.

41. Lowth recognized grammatical parallelism occasionally, e.g., "When a proposition is delivered, and a second is subjoined to it, or drawn under it, equivalent, or contrasted with it in sense, *or similar to it in the form of grammatical construction*, these I call parallel lines." See Robert Lowth, *Isaiah: A New Translation: With a Preliminary Dissertation, and Notes, Critical, Philological, and Explanatory* (Boston: Hillard, 1834), 9, emphasis added.

42. See, e.g., Terence Collins, *Line-Forms in Hebrew Poetry: A Grammatical Approach to the Stylistic Study of the Hebrew Prophets*, Studia Pohl, Series Maior 7 (Rome: Biblical Institute Press, 1978); Stephen A. Geller, *Parallelism in Early Biblical Poetry*, HSM 20 (Missoula, MT: Scholars Press, 1979); Michael O'Connor, *Hebrew Verse Structure* (Winona Lake, IN: Eisenbrauns, 1980); each independently presented a method for analyzing the grammatical structure of a verse and its parallelism. The methods are compared in Dennis Pardee, *Ugaritic and Hebrew Poetic Parallelism: A Trial Cut (ʿnt 1 and Proverbs 2)*, VTSup 39 (Leiden: Brill, 1988), 23–46. Most influentially, in *The Dynamics of Biblical Parallelism*, Biblical Resource Series (Grand Rapids: Eerdmans, 2008), Adele Berlin systematically studied parallelism across different "aspects" of the language: morphological/syntactic, lexical-semantic, and phonological.

43. Edward L. Greenstein, "How Does Parallelism Mean?," in *A Sense of Text: The Art of Language in the Study of Biblical Literature*, ed. Stephen A. Geller (Winona Lake, IN: Eisenbrauns, 1982), 44.

44. So, e.g., Jan, P. Fokkelman, *Reading Biblical Poetry: An Introductory Guide* (London: Westminster John Knox, 2001); Meynet, *Rhetorical Analysis*. Heim distinguishes between semilinear, intralinear, interlinear, and translinear parallelism in Proverbs (*Poetic Imagination*, 29–32).

45. David J. A. Clines, "The Parallelism of Greater Precision," in *Directions in Biblical Hebrew Poetry*, ed. Elaine R. Follis (Sheffield: Sheffield Academic, 1987), 94–95;

in the first line; a parallelism "delays meaning in order to offer a heuristic quest for meaning."[46] The second line may offer some help in the quest but may also increase its challenges, for the relationship between lines may not be entirely clear.[47] The reader must decipher it for himself.

I will focus on two particular ways that the reader meets such diversity and openness in Proverbs' parallelisms. If a prototypical Lowthian parallelism contains two lines, balanced by their similarity or opposition, the proverbs often diverge in the following ways: first, it may be unclear whether synonymy or antithesis is intended; second, there may be a perceived imbalance between the lines, which the reader tries to fill out.

2.2.2. Synonymous or Antithetical?[48]

First, then, it may be unclear whether the proverb is characterized by (to use Lowth's terms) synonymy or antithesis. These may at first seem to be easily distinguishable, even opposite phenomena. But in language and thought, there is no true synonymy or true antithesis (not even between these very terms). From one perspective two things may be alike; from another they are necessarily unalike. Even opposites must be similar in some ways, or they would not be commensurable. Sameness and difference in meaning are fluid and cannot be confined by rigid categories.

The complex interplay of sameness and difference has proved central in many scholars' accounts of parallelism. For Adele Berlin, parallelism intertwines "equivalences and contrasts," not just in word meaning but in morphology and syntax.[49] For James Kugel, the lines display "integration

---

Geoffrey Payne, "Parallelism in Biblical Hebrew Verse," *SJOT* 8:1 (1994): 126–40; A. Wagner, "Der Parallelismus Membrorum zwischen poetischer Form und Denkfigur," in *Parallelismus Membrorum*, ed. A. Wagner (Göttingen: Vandenhoeck & Ruprecht, 2007), 1–28.

46. Payne, "Parallelism in Biblical Hebrew Verse," 136.

47. On the tension between "disambiguation and ambiguity" in parallelism, see Berlin, *Dynamics of Biblical Parallelism*, 96–99.

48. This ambiguity occurs in Prov 11:16; 19:12; 18:4; 16:1, 9; 21:31, commented on in later chapters. See the table in the appendix.

49. Berlin, *Dynamics of Biblical Parallelism*, 130. Drawing on Russian formalist Roman Jakobson, Berlin argues that parallelism "projects the principle of equivalence from the axis of selection into the axis of combination." That is, instead of surveying equivalent/similar terms and "selecting" only one, parallel lines "combine" two. This then shows them to be different (140).

and differentiation," saying "the same thing" and "something more."[50] For Heim, "The creative combination of repetition with variation is the very essence of Hebrew poetry," manifesting itself most fully in parallelism.[51] Opposing two similar ideas highlights their differences; apposing different ideas emphasizes their similarities.

The two cola of the proverbs' parallelisms are sometimes paired without a conjunction (parataxis), or (more often) with the basic conjunction *waw*. Depending on context, this might be translated as "and," "or," "namely," "moreover," "but," and so on.[52] The relationship between the lines is thus left to the discernment of the reader.

Sometimes it is unclear whether the similarities between the cola are paramount (rendering the parallelism loosely synonymous, "and") or the differences (antithetical, "but"). Consider, for example, Prov 17:17:

בכל־עת אהב הרע ואח לצרה יולד׃

	The friend	loves at all times;
and/but	a brother	is born for adversity.

The two main sets of parallels here are "friend" // "brother" and "at all times" // "for adversity." In some senses, the terms in each set are similar, and the proverb can be read synonymously. Friend and brother are alike in the support they show at various times. However, there are also differences that might render the proverb antithetical. Perhaps the friend is the better figure (cf. 18:24). He can be relied on "at all times," but the brother only at specific ones. Or maybe the preference is for the brother. He, and not the friend, should be turned to in "adversity." Indeed, Proverbs displays a

---

50. Kugel, *Idea of Biblical Poetry*. Kugel expresses this in three main ways. First (1, 53–54), a verse is read as _____/_____//, where / corresponds to a small pause, and // to a larger one. The reader integrates the half-lines (separated from surrounding discourse by the large pause) and distinguishes them (through the small pause). Second (16), paradoxically, the differentiation of the lines integrates them, for "it asserts A + B to be a *single statement*." Third (8), B at once looks back at A and beyond it. It is both equivalent and contrasting.

51. Heim, *Poetic Imagination*, 636 (italics original). Heim's discussion of parallelism occurs within a larger argument about "variant repetitions" in Proverbs—verses that occur in several places in the book, with some similarities and some differences.

52. Berlin, *Dynamics of Biblical Parallelism*, 91; K. Seybold, "Anmerkung zum Parallelismus Membrorum in der hebräische Poesie," in Wagner, *Parallelismus Membrorum*, 110.

general skepticism about the reliability of so-called friends (e.g., 19:4, 6, 7). Antithesis might then emerge in the verbs. The friend's apparent love is an ironic comment or a fleeting virtue, opposed to the prenatal vocation of support that the brother was "born for." The complex interaction of contrast and equivalence means that this proverb, along with others explored in later chapters, is open to being read as synonymous or antithetical.

2.2.3. Unbalanced Parallelisms[53]

A second type of openness can arise from parallelism if there is a perceived imbalance between the lines, an apparent gap that the reader tries to fill out.[54] This perception of imbalance rests upon an expectation of balance. In Proverbs (especially chapters 10–15), such is the proliferation of balanced antithetical parallelisms that this becomes the expected form. While elsewhere in the Hebrew Bible there is often a dynamic movement between the cola, here stasis often prevails.[55] This has led to some scholars devaluing parallelism in Proverbs. It is, according to Luis Alonso Schökel, "trivial and academic" and "easily forgotten" and, according to Joze Krašovec, "neither stimulating nor rewarding."[56] However, balanced proverbs have a value of their own, and they place in sharp relief the unbalanced examples.[57]

In an unbalanced or imprecise parallelism, the reader perceives that the two lines are in some sense parallel—for example, through a semantic antithesis in one pair of terms, or a matching of syntax between the cola. Other features, however, are not parallel. Contemplating the relationship

---

53. In the proverbs explored later, this occurs in 13:5; 10:8, 14, 16; 12:21; 13:2.

54. See Michael V. Fox, "The Rhetoric of Disjointed Proverbs," *JSOT* 29 (2004): 165–77; Heim, *Poetic Imagination*, 638–39; William E. Mouser, "Filling in the Blank: Asymmetrical Antithetical Parallelism," in *Learning From the Sages: Selected Studies of the Book of Proverbs*, ed. Roy B. Zuck (Grand Rapids, MI: Baker, 1995), 137–50.

55. Thus Alter, *Art of Biblical Poetry*, 206: "The general dynamic complexity of semantic parallelism in biblical verse has given way to a didactic and mnemonic neatness of smoothly matched statements clicking dutifully into place."

56. Luis Alonso Schökel, *A Manual of Hebrew Poetics*, SubBi 11 (Rome: Editrice Pontificio Instituto Biblico, 1988), 88; Joze Krašovec, *Antithetical Structure in Biblical Hebrew Poetry*, VTSup 35 (Leiden: Brill, 1984), 17.

57. Their value is seen, for example, in their didactic utility as simple and emphatic forms (Alter, *Art of Biblical Poetry*, 206) and their proverbial potential for motivation (Ted Hildebrandt, "Motivation and Antithetical Parallelism in Proverbs 10–15," *JETS* 35 [1992]: 433–44).

of the terms, the reader has different interpretive options. She may empha-size what is new in the second line and read the proverb as a progression, or she may level the difference and read it as an equilibrium. If the latter, further options of interpretation open up.

Let us take as an example one of Alonso Schökel's "trivial and aca-demic" proverbs, 15:6:

בית צדיק חסן רב ובתבואת רשע נעכרת:
In the house of the righteous[58] is abundant wealth,
but the produce of the wicked is troubled.

A progression may be seen in this proverb, from the quantity of the wealth in the first colon to its quality in the second.[59] The climax is the declara-tion that the wicked's produce is *troubled*. Its quantity is only of secondary significance. Whether it is substantial or not, the reader can rest assured that the wealth will do the wicked man no good.

Alternatively, the proverb may be an equilibrium. The righteous-wicked word pair signals balance in the proverb; what applies to one of them cannot apply to the other. If the righteous has abundant wealth, the wicked cannot; if the wicked has troubled produce, the righteous cannot. The interpretation strategy is to take the unbalanced term from each colon and to reverse it into the opposite colon. The full thought thus emerges as something like: "In the house of the righteous is abundant [*untroubled*] wealth; but the produce of the wicked is [*minimal and*] troubled." If they are reading hastily, interpreters may not consciously supply these rever-sals, but savoring the proverb, they are likely to.

However, the precise reversals are unclear and open up the proverb to further interpretations. Reversing a term may involve simply negating it or affirming its opposite. For example, take the phrase יפיח כזבים ("breathes out lies").[60] It occurs in 14:5, where its antithesis is given as a simple nega-tion לא יכזב ("does not lie"), but in 14:25 it is reversed by עד אמת ("true

---

58. Reading as בבית and ותבואת (so Pesh., Targ.). See discussion in Fox, *Eclectic Edition*, 231–32. The decision of whether to retain or emend the MT does not affect the overall interpretation of this proverb.
59. A "developmental" understanding of parallelism has been prevalent in much scholarship. See esp. Alter, *Art of Biblical Poetry*, 1–28.
60. Or "witness of lies"; see Dennis Pardee, "YPḤ 'Witness' in Hebrew and Uga-ritic," *VT* 28 (1978): 204–13.

witness"). Not only does he not lie; he is positively truthful. Equally, in 15:6, נעכרת ("troubled") might be reversed by negation ("untroubled") or by affirmation of the opposite. But the opposite is open to further inter- pretation, depending on the nature of the "trouble"; there is no absolute antithesis in language. Is the wealth of the righteous peaceful? depend- able? flourishing? רב ("abundant") may be reversed as "not abundant" or as "minimal," "absent," or "deficient."

Another point of ambiguity may arise if a phrase is being reversed (rather than a single term), for it may be unclear which term to reverse. In 28:12, ובקום רשעים ("when the wicked rise") is reversed by בעלץ צדיקים ("when the righteous exult")—that is, the character term is reversed, and a synonym is given for the verb. In 28:28, however, the same phrase is paralleled with באבדם ("when they perish"). The character term stays the same (just represented by a pronoun) and the direction of the verb is switched. Perhaps in 15:16 חסן רב should be leveled not by reversing רב, as above, but as an ironic "abundant poverty" (cf. 28:19). Overall, par- allelism is a flexible and diverse phenomenon, which may give rise to openness in a number of ways. Here, I have highlighted two particular phenomena, important for our later investigations. It may be unclear whether the two lines of a verse are intended to be synonymous or anti- thetical; there may be a perceived imbalance between the lines, which invites imaginative filling out.

2.3. Openness through Imagery

Having shown how openness emerges in Prov 10:1–22:16 through pol- ysemy and parallelism, I turn to its final main source, imagery. Much scholarly work on imagery in Proverbs focuses on chapters 1–9, with their vibrant personifications of Wisdom and Folly.[61] In the sentence lit- erature, imagery is not ubiquitous, but it does occur, and with increasing frequency from chapter 16 onward.[62] William McKane drew attention

---

61. See, e.g., Camp, *Wisdom and the Feminine*; Norman C. Habel, "The Symbolism of Wisdom in Proverbs 1–9," *Int* 26 (1972): 131–57; Weeks, *Instruction and Imagery*.

62. Notable studies include William, P. Brown, "The Didactic Power of Metaphor in the Aphoristic Sayings of Proverbs," *JSOT* 29 (2004): 133–54 (on food metaphors); Torva L. Forti, *Animal Imagery in the Book of Proverbs*, VTSup 118 (Leiden: Brill, 2008) (on animal imagery); Sandoval, *Discourse of Wealth and Poverty* (on imagery of wealth and poverty).

to concrete imagery as conferring a "hermeneutical openness" on true "proverbs" (משלים).[63] Of Mesopotamian examples, he noted an "openness to interpretation … and the quality of opaqueness, or even enigma, which may characterize the imagery."[64] McKane excluded the bulk of the sayings in Proverbs (which he did not see as genuine משלים) from any such open or enigmatic potential. But this is unwarranted. Indeed, their imagery is sometimes rich, and I suggest that it contributes to their openness in three main ways. First (§2.3.1), the image may invite the reader into an imaginary world to explore. Second (§2.3.2), it may interact and blend with its metaphorical referent in an open-ended manner. Third (§2.3.3), it may apply to the reader's life in various ways.

2.3.1. Imagining

Imagery can open up a world to be imagined and explored by the reader. The importance of the imagination in interpretation has been increasingly stressed in recent Proverbs scholarship.[65] The proverb does not pen in every detail of its images; these are left for the reader's mind. What are the precise dimensions of the "strong city" (קרית עזו) in 10:15/18:11? How do you imagine it? How thick are its walls? How dark is its stone? Are there soldiers manning the lookouts or merchants calling in the streets?

In imagining this city, I have brought to bear a whole set of related concepts—building materials and practices, inhabitants, warfare—a broad encyclopedic knowledge. When a word is read or heard, particularly when that word conjures up an image, our minds are not constrained to the dictionary definition. Each word may evoke related concepts, personal experiences, cultural perceptions, emotional responses, ingrained

---

63. McKane, *Proverbs*, 23.

64. McKane, *Proverbs*, 183.

65. See, e.g., Heim, *Poetic Imagination*; Perdue, *Proverbs*; Leo G. Perdue, *Wisdom Literature: A Theological History* (Louisville: Westminster John Knox, 2007); Stewart, *Poetic Ethics*. In addition, some have applied a Ricoeurian hermeneutic to Proverbs. Ricoeur suggested that poetic texts project a symbolic world "in front of the text," which the reader is called to imagine and inhabit. See, e.g., Bland, "Rhetorical Perspective"; Sandoval, *Discourse of Wealth and Poverty*; Anneke Viljoen, "An Exploration of the Symbolic World of Proverbs 10:1–15:33 with Specific Reference to 'the Fear of the Lord'" (PhD diss., University of Pretoria, 2013); and less explicitly Craig G. Bartholomew and Ryan, P. O'Dowd, *Old Testament Wisdom Literature: A Theological Introduction* (Downers Grove, IL: InterVarsity Press, 2011).

storylines, evaluations, patterns of reasoning, and the like. Each opens up a world to explore.

The world imagined varies from individual to individual, and from culture to culture. As much as possible, we should try to reconstruct the world accessible to the ancient Israelite. This is problematic, separated as we are by time and space, but an interdisciplinary approach can be fruitful. We may examine relevant biblical passages, comparative ancient Near Eastern literature, iconography and archaeology, sociological and anthropological research, and scientific fields like geography, zoology, and meteorology.[66]

Poetic texts often evoke imaginary worlds and flesh them out over the course of the text. In Proverbs' sentence literature, however, the image is confined to a single line, and any work of elaboration must be done in the reader's mind. The form is terse and elliptical, and the contextual information that could potentially direct interpretation is sparse. The proverbs are a small window into a world, but one that can be climbed through for extensive exploration.

2.3.2. Blending

The images in Proverbs tend not to be images only, but metaphors. This ushers in another level of openness.[67] In a metaphor, the image (or imagined world) serves as a *source domain*, which depicts something else, a *target domain*. When Prov 12:4 says "An excellent wife is the crown of her husband," the source domain is the "crown" (עטרה) with its associated world of rarity, esteem, and value. The target domain is "the excellent wife" (אשת חיל).

In Proverbs, metaphors are often expressed bluntly: "X (is) Y." The copula is usually lacking, so two images are simply juxtaposed: "An excellent wife—the crown of her husband." James G. Williams describes the

---

66. Several biblical scholars fruitfully adopt this approach. See, e.g., William, P. Brown, *Seeing the Psalms: A Theology of Metaphor* (Louisville: Westminster John Knox, 2002); Forti, *Animal Imagery*; Alison Ruth Gray, *Psalm 18 in Words and Pictures: A Reading through Metaphor*, BibInt 127 (Leiden: Brill, 2014); Ellen José Van Wolde, *Reframing Biblical Studies: When Language and Text Meet Culture, Cognition, and Context* (Winona Lake, IN: Eisenbrauns, 2009).

67. Bartholomew and O'Dowd, *Old Testament Wisdom Literature*, 65; Williams, "Power of Form."

impact of this form: the images "are projected stroboscopically" (imagine viewing them under a strobe light); "they are seen quickly side by side, then they are shut off."[68] The reader becomes puzzled by the juxtaposition and is drawn in to examine their relationship. Alternatively, the metaphor may be embedded into the syntax of the sentence. When the son's "lamp is put out" (יִדְעַךְ נֵרוֹ) in 20:20, the reader must infer that it refers to his death and destruction.

In the twentieth century, metaphor theory underwent great developments.[69] According to the early substitution theory, a metaphor is simply the substitution of one word (a literal term) with another (a figurative one), based on resemblance between them. It is an ornament, perhaps with emotional impact, but with no new cognitive content. It may be translated back into literal language without loss of meaning. However, this view is problematic and was influentially challenged by I. A. Richards (1936).[70] Rather than a substitution, he spoke of a metaphor as an *interaction*, between a tenor (the referent, or target domain) and a vehicle (the image, or source domain). The interaction creates meaning that would not be attainable otherwise.

Richards's theory was built upon by Max Black (1962).[71] He pointed out that the interaction is not between two words alone, but between two "systems of associated commonplaces": the shared knowledge and assumptions held by a speech community about the words (encyclopedic knowledge). In a metaphor, the system of commonplaces evoked by the source is projected onto the target, serving as a filter for how we view it.

However, it is probably not a case of direct projection but more a blend of ideas. Gilles Fauconnier and Mark Turner have proposed that the interaction between source and target takes place in a "blend space" in the mind.[72] They suggest three stages here, each giving scope for openness:

---

68. Williams, "Power of Form," 41.

69. For an overview, see Gray, *Psalm 18 in Words and Pictures*, 17–33.

70. I. A. Richards, *The Philosophy of Rhetoric*, Mary Flexner Lectures on the Humanities 3 (Oxford: Oxford University Press, 1936).

71. Max Black, *Models and Metaphors: Studies in Language and Philosophy* (New York: Cornell University Press, 1962).

72. Gilles Fauconnier and Mark Turner describe four "mental spaces"—small packets of conceptual structure dependent on larger domains of encyclopedic knowledge. Source and target are two "input spaces," what is common between them constitutes the "generic space," and they are imaginatively combined in the "blend space." Fauconnier and Turner, "Conceptual Integration Networks," *Cognitive Science* 22

composition, completion, and elaboration. In composition, the interpreter transfers information from the source and target domains into the blend space. She then completes the structure by bringing in broader encyclopedic knowledge and conceptual architecture. It is open to her which particular information and encyclopedic knowledge to select. Finally, she elaborates, running a mental simulation, imagining the new emergent structure. The story that she develops is open-ended: "We can 'run the blend' indefinitely."[73] Fauconnier and Turner provide a convincing theoretical description, drawing out the inherent openness of metaphors. While not drawing extensively on the technicalities, I will employ the basic procedures of imaginative blending in my explorations in part 2.

2.3.3. Applying

The interpretation process does not stop there, however. We are not dealing simply with metaphors, but with proverbs, which demand application (see §3.2.1). The imagery in folk proverbs relates figuratively to some situation in the hearer's own life. Drawing a parallel of genre between folk and biblical proverbs, Timothy J. Sandoval has suggested that this is true of the latter too, "because proverbs by their 'nature' … are concerned to say something metaphorically."[74] For some biblical proverbs, a figurative interpretation looks appealing: "he who gathers in the summer" (10:5a) may be metaphorically applied to someone who has never gathered in his life but who is diligent in his work.

However, most biblical proverbs cannot be taken as figures. A distinction should be made between biblical sayings that *contain* metaphors (e.g., "An excellent wife is the crown of her husband" [12:4]) and folk proverbs that *are* metaphors (e.g., "Birds of a feather flock together"). Put differently, a biblical proverb usually specifies its target (e.g., "an excellent wife"), but a folk proverb does not. This raises a problem for folk proverbs: how can we interpret a metaphor without a target domain?

Early paremiologists suggested that a general principle is abstracted from the proverb and applied to different situations in the world: the

---

(1998): 133–87. For more recent developments, see Gilles Fauconnier and George Lakoff, "On Metaphor and Blending," *Cognitive Semiotics* 5 (2009): 393–99; see also the bibliography compiled by Turner at https://tinyurl.com/SBL2642b.

73. Fauconnier and Turner, "Conceptual Integration Networks," 144.

74. Sandoval, *Discourse of Wealth and Poverty*, 11.

proverb's "abstraction idea," "philosophical meaning," or "general/maxim level."[75] Developments in metaphor theory, however, have nuanced these views. Just as a metaphor cannot be translated into literal terms, a proverb cannot be translated as a literal maxim. The process is much more complex and imaginative. Over the last decade, recent metaphor theories, particularly blend theory, have been applied to proverbs.[76] The situational context serves as the target domain and is blended imaginatively with information from the proverb itself. Similarly with biblical proverbs. In effect, they have two target domains: a textual target, stated in the proverb, and a situational target—the contextual application to the interpreter's life.

The two targets overlap but are distinct. For example, in Prov 19:13, "A wife's quarreling is a dripping of rain" (ודלף טרד מדיני אשה). Two related questions arise: "How is a wife's quarreling a dripping of rain?" (textual target) and "How is *my wife's* quarreling a dripping of rain?" (situational target).[77] Interpretation will depend on the reader's encyclopedic knowledge of wives and quarreling, and on his own specific circumstances. Accordingly, features may be reorganized, backgrounded, foregrounded, eliminated, and so on. For example, aural qualities may come to the fore if applied to a woman with a particularly distinctive voice: are your wife's tones dull and monotonous, or piercing and insistent? Both are plausible connotations of dripping rain. Application to a situational context directs

---

75. See, respectively, Heda Jason, "Proverbs in Society: The Problem of Meaning and Function," *Proverbium* 17 (1971): 620; Joyce Penfield and Mary Duru, "Proverbs: Metaphors That Teach," *Anthopological Quarterly* 61.3 (1988): 121; Nigel Barley, "A Structural Approach to the Proverb and the Maxim with Special Reference to the Anglo-Saxon Corpus," *Proverbium* 20 (1972): 738–41.

76. See, e.g., Erik Aasland, "Two Heads Are Better Than One: Using Conceptual Mapping to Analyze Proverb Meaning," *Proverbium* 26 (2009): 1–18; Daniel Andersson, "Understanding Figurative Proverbs: A Model Based on Conceptual Blending," *Folklore* 124:1 (2013): 28–44; Gabrijela Buljan and Tanja Gradečak-Erdeljić, "Where Cognitive Linguistics Meets Paremiology: A Cognitive-Contrastive View of Selected English and Croatian Proverbs," *Explorations in English Language and Linguistics* 1 (2013): 63–83; J. D. Johansen, "When the Cat's Away, the Mice Will Play: On Proverbs, Metaphors, and the Pragmatics of Blending," in *Semiotic Rotations: Modes of Meanings in Cultural Worlds*, ed. Sunhee Kim Gertz, Jaan Valsiner, and Jean-Paul Breaux (Greenwich, CT: Information Age, 2007), 61–76; Karen Sullivan and Eve Sweetser, "Is 'Generic Is Specific' a Metaphor," in *Meaning, Form, and Body*, ed. Fey Parrill, Vera Tobin, and Mark Turner (Stanford, CA: CSLI, 2010), 309–28.

77. Or, for modern female readers—how is my husband's?

and partially closes the interpretation of a proverb, but it may also open
the proverb to nuances not noticed before.

2.4. The Limits of Openness

Most sentences include some ambiguous elements, but these are not
always accepted or even perceived by interpreters. (I doubt, for example,
that you have just thought of a legal judgment against the shady characters of hydrogen and helium! The polysemies of "sentence," "ambiguous,"
and "elements" were not realized.) Theoretical openness is constrained by
certain interpretive boundaries. Proverbs itself recognizes the danger of
misinterpretation, of straying out of bounds. It establishes the need for
careful interpretation (1:6) and warns of a proverb misspoken "in the
mouth of fools" (26:7, 9).

The limits of openness are encountered at various levels. An ambiguous expression may have an entrenched interpretation (§2.4.1). It may be
clarified by the verse-level context (§2.4.2) or by a wider context (§2.4.3).

2.4.1. Entrenched Interpretations

Sometimes the ambiguous feature has a default interpretation—one
that has been entrenched in the reader's linguistic memory. It instantly
springs to mind and does not invite further pondering. This can occur at
different levels.

2.4.1.1. Entrenched Word Meanings

The different meanings of polysemous words have different levels of cognitive prominence. Prominent meanings are well-entrenched in the mental
lexicon, ready for instant access when the word is encountered. Less
entrenched alternatives must be searched for and may not be perceived.[78]
Meaning entrenchment may correlate with, for example, frequency within

---

78. Eye-tracking experiments show that interpreters read smoothly over an
ambiguous word if it has a prominent interpretation, instantly selecting it over less
prominent alternatives. If the alternatives have equal prominence, readers linger over
the word, unsure. See Matthew Traxler, *Introduction to Psycholinguistics: Understanding Language Science* (Chichester: Wiley-Blackwell, 2012), 117. For an explanation of
"entrenchment," see Hans-Jörg Schmid, "Entrenchment, Salience, and Basic Levels," in

the language, familiarity to the language user, conventionality within a speech community, and prototypicality/stereotypicality.[79] Frequency, being the most easily measurable, can serve as a rough-and-ready guide (even within a limited and idiosyncratic corpus like the Hebrew Bible). If a potential ambiguity rests upon an uncommon meaning, we ought to be careful, for it may not be empirically perceived.

Take Prov 13:16a:

כל־ערום יעשה בדעת

Every shrewd man יעשה in knowledge.

עשה might have two meanings: "to do, act" (extremely common) and "to take cover" (extremely rare).[80] Bruce K. Waltke suggests the latter for this verse, translating it as "Every shrewd person takes cover through knowledge." However, given its ubiquity, the former meaning probably springs to the reader's mind immediately, foreclosing the latter before it arises.[81]

2.4.1.2. Entrenched Constructions

Analogously, grammatical and syntactic constructions may have default construals, assumed by the reader unless there is strong suggestion otherwise. In the above verse, I (with most interpreters) have taken כל־ as qualifying ערום ("every shrewd man"). Heim, however, reanalyzes the syntax and interprets it as the object of יעשה: "A shrewd man does *everything* with

---

The Oxford Handbook of Cognitive Linguistics, ed. Dirk Geeraerts and Hubert Cuyckens (Oxford: Oxford University Press, 2007), 117–38.

79. For an overview of these, see Rachel Giora, *On Our Mind: Salience, Context, and Figurative Language* (Oxford: Oxford University Press, 2003), 15–18. For further explanation of linguistic "prototypes," see chapter 4 below.

80. The meaning "to take cover" is not certain (recognized by *HALOT* but not BDB). Evidence comes from the Arabic cognate ġašiya. It has also been proposed for Gen 6:14 and Ezek 17:17 (G. R. Driver, "Problems and Solutions," *VT* 4 [1954]: 243) and for the nominal form מעשה in Ps 104:13 (Joseph Reider, "Etymological Studies in Biblical Hebrew," *VT* 4 [1954]: 284).

81. Waltke, cites as evidence a connection with Prov 12:23a: דעת כסה ערום אדם ("A shrewd man covers knowledge") (*Book of Proverbs 1–15*). This is suggestive, though "covering knowledge" (12:23a) is not the same as "taking cover in knowledge" (13:16a) and is probably not strong enough to carry the case.

knowledge."[82] But the Masoretic punctuation connects כל and עָרוּם in a construct relationship, implying they are not object and subject respectively. Furthermore, the frequency of the construction כל + noun meaning "every" primes the reader to expect this meaning. The object-subject-verb alternative would probably not be empirically recognized.

2.4.1.3. Entrenched Metaphors/Metonymies

A special case of entrenchment can occur with metaphors and metonymies. Through repeated use, they are conventionalized and encoded within the mental lexicon, closing off the openness of their imagery. So we conventionally construe חטא as "to sin," without exploring the metaphor's extension from "to miss the mark"; we sometimes understand דרך as "conduct," without strolling the metaphorical "path" to get there.[83] In Proverbs, body parts often take a metonymic extension: לב ("heart") signals "mind, sense"; אפים ("nostrils") signals "anger"; שפתים ("lips"), לשון ("tongue"), and פה ("mouth") signal "speech." Metaphors and metonymies like these are sometimes seen as dead, their imaginative potential killed off and their openness closed (though we will later see how they can be resurrected and reopened).

2.4.2. Verse-Level Context

As well as level of entrenchment, the immediate linguistic context of an ambiguous word directs its interpretation.[84] Verbal cues prime the inter-

---

82. Heim, *Poetic Imagination*, 320, emphasis added; cf. Pesh. and Vulg.

83. See Joseph Lam, *Patterns of Sin in the Hebrew Bible: Metaphor, Culture, and the Making of a Religious Concept* (Oxford: Oxford University Press, 2015), 156–78. Though sometimes the imagery is used more imaginatively; see §5.3.1 below.

84. This has been verified empirically by, e.g., eye-tracking (Katherine S. Binder, "Sentential and Discourse Topic Effects on Lexical Ambiguity Processing: An Eye Movement Examination," *Memory and Cognition* 31 [2003]: 690–702; Keith Rayner et al., "Immediate Disambiguation of Lexically Ambiguous Words during Reading: Evidence from Eye Movements," *British Journal of Psychology* 97 [2006]: 467–82) and brain scanning (Robert A. Mason and Marcel Adam Just, "Lexical Ambiguity in Sentence Comprehension," *Brain Research* 1146 (2007): 115–27; M.-Z. Zempleni et al., "Semantic Ambiguity Processing in Sentence Contexts: Evidence From Event-Related Fmri," *NeuroImage* 34 [2007]: 1270–79). The relative importance of context and meaning entrenchment is disputed. According to the "exhaustive access" model, the full

preter, tuning her in to a particular understanding. Particularly important are the word's colocations and its relevance to the whole proverb.

2.4.2.1. Colocations and Constructions

Words have preferences about the company they keep, conventionally occurring in some combinations but not others. Each word might be polysemous in isolation, but its colocation with others constrains the interpretation. The most obvious case is the idiom—a conventional phrase whose meaning cannot be derived from its parts. For example, יד ליד ("hand to hand"? Prov 11:21; 16:5) probably means "be assured, certainly" (though given the dearth of occurrences, we cannot be assured). The potential polysemy of יד (hand, power, monument, beside) is not realized.

נפש is polysemous (soul, life, desire, throat, self), and its polysemy is sometimes exploited.[85] However, its meaning is closed down in conventional expressions. For example, נשא נפש (19:18) seems to mean "to direct one's *desire*," and הציל נפש (14:25; 23:14) seems to mean "to save a *life*." It is unlike that double meanings would be perceived. The expression יראת־ יהוה ("fear of the Lord") refers to fear felt *toward* God, not fear felt *by* him, though both are grammatically permissible. יראה is conventionally understood within this expression not as terror but as reverence. Heim suggests that, in light of the usual negative connotations of "fear," its designation as "good" (טוב) in Prov 15:16 is "puzzling and counterintuitive." However, this underestimates the strength of the conventional colocation.

2.4.2.2. Relevance and Parallelism

Beyond the specific construction, the whole verse must be considered. Readers expect it to be sensical and logical and search for the most relevant interpretation.

16:16a: קנה־חכמה מה־טוב מחרוץ
Acquiring wisdom, how much better than חרוץ.

---

range of meanings is always accessed. According to "selective access," only those that fit with context are. Many prefer an "ordered access" model, in which both play an important part (see Giora, *On Our Mind*).

85. See discussion of Prov 13:2 below.

חרוץ can mean "strict decision" (Joel 4:14[3:14]) or "moat" (Dan 9:25), but these do not logically fit the context (nor are they well entrenched in the mental lexicon). Two meanings seem relevant: wisdom is better than "diligence" (Prov 10:4 for this meaning) or better than "gold" (3:14; 8:10, 19).[86] The second colon can guide the interpretation: וקנות בינה נבחר מכסף: ("And acquiring understanding is more choice than silver"). The parallelism with silver supports the understanding of חרוץ as gold, and the theoretical ambiguity is clarified in context.

2.4.3. Wider Contexts

2.4.3.1. Contextualized by Surrounding Discourse

Beyond the individual verse, various wider contexts can impose limits on openness. Proverbs can operate both as individual units and as a wider collection (see §1.6 above). This wider discourse functions pedagogically to form a certain type of interpreter—one whose character and worldview are permeated with Proverbs' wisdom. She is shaped to discriminate wisely between alternatives (1:6) and to reject unwise interpretations (26:7, 9).

Certain themes and tropes recur in Proverbs, guiding interpretation of each instance. Returning to 16:16: in Proverbs, the value of "diligence" (חרוץ) is never questioned, but that of "gold" (חרוץ) is (3:14; 8:10, 19), rendering the latter meaning more fitting. Concerning 15:16: in Proverbs, "fear of the Lord" (יראת יהוה) is religious contrition, established from the outset as the "beginning of wisdom" (1:7) and foundation of ethical behavior.[87]

Constraints are also offered by the immediately surrounding discourse. Heim suggests that in a proverb cluster, each saying fleshes out the meaning of the others. Independently, he says, they are "under-determined and multi-valent," but when read together, cross-inferences can elucidate

---

86. Chevel Nachalah suggests "diligence" for Prov 10:4 but parses מן as indicating origin: "wisdom acquired by diligence." See Eliezer Ginsburg, *Mishlei: A New Translation with a Commentary Anthologized from Talmudic, Midrashic, and Rabbinic Sources*, Artscroll Tanach Series (New York: Mesorah, 1998), 309. The meaning "gold" for חרוץ is supported by evidence from cognate languages: Phoenician חרץ; Assyrian ḫurâṣu.

87. On the distinction between fear of the Lord in Proverbs and in other corpora (esp. Deuteronomy), see Joachim Becker, *Gottesfurcht im Alten Testament*, AnBib 25 (Rome: Pontifical Biblical Institute, 1965).

meaning.[88] For example, the proverbs after 16:16 further denigrate riches (16:19) and clarify why wisdom surpasses gold (15:16).[89] חרוץ "influences the meaning of vv. 15 and 17," giving them religious orientation.[90] "A little with fear of the Lord" (15:16) is implicitly equivalent to "a meal of vegetables where love is" (15:17), and the significance of the terms is fleshed out accordingly.

2.4.3.2. Contextualized by Encyclopedic Knowledge

Interpretation happens within a framework, formed by historical, sociocultural, geographical, and political dynamics.[91] This encyclopedic knowledge is important both for opening out (§2.3 above) and for constraining imagery.[92] Modern interpreters might import contemporary vegetarian ethics into the "meal of vegetables" of 15:17, but these ideas would be closed off for Israelites, who had a very different dietary world. Knowledge of institutions and practices also serves as a guide. In 16:16, "acquiring wisdom" (קנה חכמה) might plausibly refer to paid education—but only if such an institution existed in ancient Israel.[93]

2.4.3.3. Contextualized by the Situation of Use

Finally, uttering a proverb in a social context would offer decisive constraints (see §2.3.3 above). Interpretation is guided by, for example, the physical environment, the nature of the interaction, and the identity of the

---

88. Heim, *Poetic Imagination*, 106. Sometimes, however, literary context can make the sayings *more* ambiguous. See Schwab, "Sayings Clusters."

89. Heim, *Poetic Imagination*, 219–20.

90. Heim, *Poetic Imagination*, 199.

91. For the importance of cultural frameworks in Proverb interpretation, see John J. Pilch, "Proverbs in Middle East North Africa (Mena*) Cultural Context," *BTB* 45 (2015): 202–14.

92. See Rayond W. Gibbs Jr., "Multiple Constraints in Theories of Metaphor," *Discourse Processes* 48 (2011): 575–84; Hans Ijzerman and Sander L. Koole, "From Perceptual Rags to Metaphoric Riches: Bodily Constraints on Sociocognitive Metaphors: Comment on Landau, Meier, and Keefer," *Psychological Bulletin* 137 (2011): 355–61.

93. The interpretation as paid education is even more plausible in the reference to "acquiring wisdom" (לקנות חכמה) in 17:16. For the interpretive options, see Loader, "Problem of Money." See the discussion of the "schools" hypothesis in §1.2 above. The form קנה in 16:16 is an irregular infinitive construct of a ל"ה verb. See Joüon §79p.

interlocutors. Ambiguities can be resolved by prosody and visual informa-tion.[94] The interpreter searches for the relevance of the saying, and closes its ambiguities accordingly. In the next chapter, I will consider further what this process entails.

2.5. Conclusion

The meanings of proverbs, then, are not limitless. When exploring potential openness, we must be attentive to the entrenchment of certain meanings, to the verse as a whole, and to wider contexts, which might constrain interpretation. We should further acknowledge that what we perceive as ambiguity may have been unambiguous to ancient readers. What we think is clear may have been open-ended.

With due caution, however, proverbs are still characteristically open. They often display polysemy (§2.1)—that is, semantic or grammatical ambiguities. Their parallelism (§2.2) may offer interpretive questions without clear answers, or they may contain imagery (§2.3), opening up a world for the reader to explore. We will see in the next chapter how such openness helps the sayings in their didactic and proverbial functions.

---

94. For prosody, see Lyn Frazier, Katy Carlson, and Charles Clifton Jr., "Prosodic Phrasing is Central to Language Comprehension," *Trends in Cognitive Sciences* 10 (2006): 244–49; Jesse Snedeker and John Trueswell, "Using Prosody to Avoid Ambi-guity: Effects of Speaker Awareness and Referential Context," *Journal of Memory and Language* 48 (2003): 103–30. For visual information, see Falk Huettig, Joost Rommers, and Antje S. Meyer, "Using the Visual World Paradigm to Study Language Process-ing: A Review and Critical Examination," *Acta Psychologica* 137 (2011): 151–71; M. J. Spivey et al., "Eye Movements and Spoken Language Comprehension: Effects of Visual Context on Syntactic Ambiguity Resolution," *Cognitive Psychology* 45 (2002): 447–81.

3
Openness for Didactic and Proverbial Purposes

In chapter 1, I suggested that the sayings in Prov 10:1–22:16 should be seen as didactic proverbs. Accordingly, they are open to being interpreted and used either didactically, for general formation and training, or proverbially, to influence specific situations. In chapter 2, I explored how proverbs may show literary openness through polysemy, parallelism, and imagery. In this chapter, I tie these together and discuss how a proverb's openness makes it particularly useful for both didactic and proverbial functions. This will take us beyond openness in interpretation to openness in application.

3.1. Openness in a Didactic Use

Openness greatly enhances the didactic function of biblical proverbs, contributing to three key educational aims: developing a worldview, forming character, and training the intellect. In particular, openness educates by simultaneously entailing the sayings' broadness and their complexity. Let me explain.

First, the cumulative effect of the sayings is to build up a *worldview* in the student, or, more precisely, a broad framework of categories and patterns through which to view the world. Particularly important are character categories (chapter 4) and act-consequence patterns (chapter 5). The categories offered are wide and general, able to encompass a broad sweep of reality. They function as large, open boxes into which the student may fit the manifold situations of life. These boxes alone are offered as the proper rationalization system for the messiness of the world.

However, the proverbs' openness also prevents this basic framework from becoming absolute law. Openness entails complexity as well as breadth. The proverbs, like the world they represent, are ambiguous and elusive. The worldview they build must be flexible and adaptive, not rigid and dogmatic. The proverbs can be fitted together in various ways, and never reach a completed system. Their openness to different meanings allows the framework to be nuanced and shifted by the changing situations of life.

Second, the openness of the proverbs facilitates the *character development* of the student (see chapter 4). The generalized character types offer simple ideals, perhaps for the sake of the one beginning in wisdom: she must become "righteous" (צדיק) and "wise" (חכם). The proverbs tend to describe overall character, in broad terms, showing concern for total disposition. The student may fill out these open characterizations with specific actions. She can fit herself into the category and develop proper morality in the particulars of her own behavior.

Insofar as their openness also entails ambiguities, some proverbs suggest that human character is not simple. This will become evident in chapters 4–7. "Righteous" and "wicked" are not all or nothing, and there are vagaries under the surface of every proverb and every human person. Acknowledging this, Proverbs attempts to shape its reader. Openness encourages her to step inside the proverb, to be influenced and formed by it. In particular, Proverbs wants to reorient her desires toward wisdom (16:6), encouraging her to seek it not as an obligation but as a joy. It wills for her to delight in its own wise words. Indeed, the nature of its words encourages this. Their openness is often playful, alluring, and evocative. Some proverbs become intellectual games, riddles to resolve. Others invite her to explore rich and open imagery. She is tempted in, seduced into study.[1]

In doing so, she participates in Proverbs' third main didactic aim—*intellectual training.* Pondering the complexities emerging through the proverbs' openness, she cultivates particular modes of thought.[2] Proverbs do not simply teach about the faculties of wisdom, but they also train those faculties. To decipher polysemy, parallelism, or imagery, the reader must engage reason, logic, and critical discernment. She must consider

---

1. On the pedagogical power of poetry in general in Proverbs, see Stewart, *Poetic Ethics*, 43–55; Davis, *Proverbs, Ecclesiastes, and the Song*, 18–24.

2. Dave Bland, "The Formation of Character in the Book of Proverbs," *ResQ* 40 (1998): 232–33; Fox, "Rhetoric of Disjointed Proverbs," 175–76; M. Hind, "Teaching for Responsibility: Confirmation and the Book of Proverbs," *RelEd* 93 (1998): 207–24; Stewart, *Poetic Ethics.*

what is important and what is peripheral for interpretation. She must make and assess connections between phenomena and scrutinize what she sees. These skills are vital not only for textual interpretations but also for making sense of life. Proverbs' open imagery encourages the imagination, a faculty fundamental to moral reasoning.[3] To imagine entails crystalizing new insights and welcoming recategorizations. This is essential for a world where, despite the essential stability of tradition and life, newness may arise. Proverbs' openness, then, is didactically oriented, training the reader how to engage fruitfully with the changing world.

3.2. Openness in a Proverbial Use

Equally, openness is significant for the sayings' proverbial function. When a proverb is spoken, it comments on a particular situation for a particular purpose. And the proverb's meaning cannot be restricted to its textual meaning but must encompass its whole performance meaning. As defined by paremiologist Barbara Kirshenblatt-Gimblett, this consists of "participants' evaluation of the situation + participants' understanding of the proverb's base meaning + interactional strategy of the proverb user" (situation + text + purpose).[4] The openness of the text allows it to be used in many different situations for many different purposes.

3.2.1. Openness to Different Situations

3.2.1.1. How a Proverb Is Mapped

Scholars have argued that a proverb is only fully meaningful when applied to a situational context. Such situational context is lacking in a proverb collection, and many suggest that it has been functionally replaced by literary context (see §1.6 above). However, there is no reason why a student should not apply a collected proverb directly to a situation in his life; indeed, if he is serious in following the book's moral counsel, he must!—for this is how

---

3. Mark Johnson, *Moral Imagination: Implications of Cognitive Science for Ethics* (Chicago: University of Chicago Press, 1994); Stewart, *Poetic Ethics*, 170–202.

4. Barbara Kirshenblatt-Gimblett, "Towards a Theory of Proverb Meaning," in *The Wisdom of Many: Essays of the Proverb*, ed. Wolfgang Mieder and A. Dundes (New Yorks: Garland, 1981): 119; it is followed in biblical studies by, e.g., Fontaine, *Traditional Sayings*, 48–50; Camp, *Wisdom and the Feminine*, 165–67.

general principles become concrete realities. When he does so, the proverb text interacts with and maps onto the situational context.

As we have seen, a proverb is often structured as [topic—comment] (§1.5 above). The hearer maps each of these components onto some feature of the situational context (here designated as X and Y; fig. 1).[5]

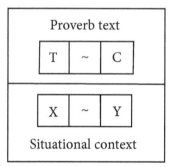

Fig. 1.

Biblical proverbs tend to have two lines; they also make a second comment on a second topic [T ~ C // T2 ~ C2]. If a proverb employs simple synonymous or antithetical parallelism, then both halves may be mapped onto a single context (fig. 2).

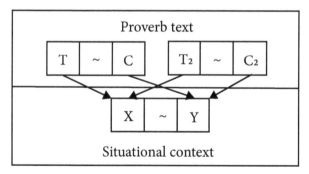

Fig. 2

The proverb provides two different, mutually affirmative views of the same situation. The repetition drums in the message and its relevance. In

---

5. Figure adapted from Peter Seitel, "Proverbs: A Social Use of Metaphor," *Genre* 2 (1969): 143–61, also followed by Fontaine, *Traditional Sayings*, 58–63. The application of metaphorical proverbs is more complex than this (see §2.3.3)

an antithetical proverb, the same principle is stated positively and negatively, bringing balance and order to what may have been an otherwise
ambiguous situation.

However, when the parallelism is imprecise or absent, it may be difficult to map both sides onto the same situation (fig. 3):[6]

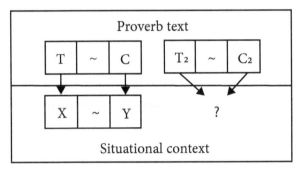

Fig. 3

A proverb like this may be more open to application because it can be
used in situations relating to either half. It begins at a certain point (the
situation of the hearer) but then develops in a direction of its own choosing. It moves beyond specific application to more general reflection. The
hearer must consider and discern why the proverb has taken this course,
learning to see his immediate situation in relation to the wider phenomena
of the world.

3.2.1.2. Openness Arising[7]

Such a mapping of a proverb onto a situational context gives rise to openness. This may be because, first, the proverb has multiple "base meanings."[8]
The base meaning is the basic interpretation of the text, without regard to
situational context. As we have seen, proverbs may be open to several such
meanings because of their polysemy, parallelism, and imagery.

---

6. Examples of this in practice are given in §5.2.2 below.

7. The ways that these different types of openness may affect interpretation are
discussed in chs. 5–7.

8. The term comes from Kirshenblatt-Gimblett, "Towards a Theory of Proverb
Meaning." For examples of how different base meanings might be used in application,
see §§4.2; 5.3.3.

It has been empirically demonstrated that users apply different base meanings to different situations. Kirshenblatt-Gimblett highlights, for example, the multiple possible base meanings of "a friend in need is a friend in deed," depending on "(1) syntactic ambiguity (is your friend in need or are you in need); (2) lexical ambiguity (indeed or in deed)."[9] Different users employ the proverb in different ways accordingly. Equally, "a rolling stone gathers no moss" yields two quite different interpretations, depending on the user's understanding of the imagery.[10] By one interpretation (prevalent in Scotland), "moss" is undesirable, and "rolling" protects against it: stagnation is prevented by keeping on the move. But by another interpretation (prevalent in England), "moss" is a sign of peace and stability, and "rolling" would destroy it: prosperity will not accumulate for the restless.

Second, a single base meaning may have multiple realizations. Even when two proverb users agree what the proverb means, they may apply it different ways. Here openness emerges not simply from the text but from the interaction between text and context. It has various manifestations:

Metaphor.[11] As discussed in §2.3.3, the world evoked by a metaphor may be blended with the situational context in an imaginative, open-ended way.

Generality.[12] The base meaning of a proverb is often a broad principle, employing general terms, which can be specified in many ways. For example, Prov 10:1b states, "A wise son makes a father glad." "Wise," like so many character terms in Proverbs, is a wide category applicable to many different people (see ch. 4). Being "glad" may manifest itself in a thousand concrete instances.

Positive or negative relation to context.[13] It is possible to apply proverbs positively or negatively, as depicting the situation of the hearer or the

---

9. Kirshenblatt-Gimblett, "Towards a Theory of Proverb Meaning," 114.

10. G. B. Milner, "Quadripartite Structures," *Proverbium* 14 (1969): 379–83; followed by Arvo Krikmann, *Some Additional Aspects of Semantic Indefiniteness of Proverbs: Remarks on Proverb Semantics 2* (Tallinn: Academy of Sciences of the Estonian SSR, 1974), 7; Kirshenblatt-Gimblett, "Towards a Theory of Proverb Meaning," 112–13; Bland, "Rhetorical Perspective," 128–29; Peter Grzybek, "Semiotic and Semantic Aspects of the Proverb," in Hrisztova-Gotthardt and Aleksa Varga, *Introduction to Paremiology*, 89.

11. Examples are given in §5.3.3.

12. See chapter 4 and §5.3.3.

13. See §5.2.2.

opposite scenario. Proverbs 10:1b could be spoken to a son who is wise (perhaps to commend him) or to one who is not wise (to admonish him). Antithetical proverbs provide both the positive and negative manifestations. Proverbs 10:1 continues, "But a foolish son is sorrow to a mother." One half is mapped by identity, and the other half by contrast. Which half is positively mapped may change the rhetorical direction of the proverb. Spoken to a wise man (i.e., if the first half is positively applied), the second half might be an afterthought. Spoken to a fool, it becomes the climax.

Opinion about the situation.[14] While most proverbs offer clear evaluative categories, some do not, and different individuals may assess them differently. One speaker might think it despicable that "the poor man is hated even by his neighbor, but the rich man has many friends" (Prov 14:20; cf. 19:4, 6, 7), and pronounce the proverb in disapproval. Another may use it simply to observe society. A third might speak it positively, sanctioning a quite proper manifestation of the social order or offering savvy advice about whom to befriend. The proverb has no clear opinion of its own, but it may be used to condemn, comment, or commend.[15]

Temporal orientation.[16] Proverbs occur with various conjugations—though *yiqtol*s and verbless clauses are most common, we also find *qatal*s and participles.[17] However, tense does not dictate temporal orientation. In proverbial use, a *qatal* (usually a past tense) might apply to a future situation, and a *yiqtol* (usually a future) to the past. All seem to express a generic, gnomic sense, a proverbial present, which can then be applied diagnostically or prognostically.[18] Though Prov 10:1b has a *yiqtol* form (ישמח), it may refer to a son who has made, is making, or will make his father glad.

---

14. See §6.3.1.

15. Cf. also proverbs about bribery, e.g., 17:8; 21:14.

16. See §§5.2.2; 6.2.1.

17. According to Cook, in the first line of the proverbs in 10:1–22:16 and 25:1–29:27, we find: 180 *yiqtol*, 202 verbless, 48 participial, 38 *qatal*, and 31 modal clauses. Johann A. Cook, "Genericity, Tense, and Verbal Patterns in the Sentence Literature of Proverbs," in Troxel, Friebel, and Magary *Seeking Out the Wisdom of the Ancients*, 124.

18. Cook, "Genericity, Tense, and Verbal Patterns." But cf. Max Roglund, *Alleged Non-past Uses of Qatal in Classical Hebrew*, Studia Semitic Neerlandica (Assen: Royal Van Gorcum, 2003), who argues that even here *qatal*s retain something of their past orientation.

Correlation of persons.[19] Finally, the correlation of persons is not evident in a proverb's base meaning. In most speech genres, speakers refer to themselves in the first-person and to their conversation partners in the second-person. Proverbs, however, are almost all in the third-person, giving them an openness to apply to *any* person. Particularly important is whether the characters in the proverb correlate with the people using the proverb. Does the speaker refer to himself (first-person correlation), the hearer (second-person), or somebody else (third-person)?

Proverbs that speak of two characters are particularly open. In application, the hearer may correlate with either, and the proverb is sometimes understood quite differently in each case. Proverbs 13:1, for example, reads בן חכם מוסר אב ולץ לא־שמע גערה ("A wise son—a father's instruction; a scoffer has not heard rebuke"). There are two main ambiguities in the base meaning here: What is the relationship between the two nominal phrases juxtaposed in the first colon? And does שמע in the second colon refer to passive hearing or active listening? The interpretation may depend on the recipient of the proverb—father or son.

If the son is the recipient, both cola will address his behavior. The second colon warns against improper behavior, with שמע as active listening. The scoffer characteristically "does not listen to/heed rebuke," but the son must. The juxtaposition in the first colon may be resolved either by gapping שמע back from the second colon or by supplying an implied verb: "A wise son listens to/follows his father's instruction."[20] So must the hearer. If the proverb instead addresses the father, the sense is quite different, for now the father's behavior is central. The first colon implies a causal relationship: a wise son is made by his father's instruction.[21] The father must instruct the son well, for wise character will follow. If the father is anything like those elsewhere in Proverbs, this will gladden his heart (Prov 10:1; 15:20; 23:15, 24; 27:11). The son's active listening is not the focus of שמע, but rather the fact that rebuke has been sounded at all. The scoffer's father

---

19. See §§6.2.1, 6.3.1. The terminology is taken from Seitel, "Social Use of Metaphor."

20. Cynthia L. Miller, though, has argued that such backward gapping is linguistically improbable; see Miller, "A Linguistic Approach to Ellipsis in Biblical Poetry," *BBR* 13 (2003): 251–70.

21. This may even be a quasi-copula: a wise son *is* the father's instruction, in that he is the product of it. See Franz Delitzsch, *Biblical Commentary on the Proverbs of Solomon*, Clark's Foreign Theological Library 4/45 (Edinburgh: Clark, 1884).

cannot have given him any rebuke, while a more attentive disciplinarian could have rectified his character. Let this be a warning.

Overall then, the usefulness of a proverb is increased by its openness, for this allows it to be applied to many different situations. A proverb may have different base meanings, and a single base meaning may be mapped in multiple ways.

3.2.2. Openness to Different Functions

3.2.2.1. Introduction

Proverbs are not only multisituational but multifunctional. A proverb is mapped onto a situation for a reason; it is, according to Fontaine, "*always purposeful.*"[22] Accordingly, the performance meaning depends not just on base meaning and situation but also on purpose (similar to Kirshenblatt-Gimblett's "interactional strategy of the proverb user").[23] This too can generate openness, for a single proverb may be put to many different ends. Paremiologist Arvo Krikmann notes that proverbs can, for example, endorse ideas, forecast, express doubts, reproach, accuse, justify, excuse, mock, comfort, jeer, repent, warn, advise, and interdict—to name but a few![24]

This relates to a wider point about language. When I speak, I do not simply exercise my vocal chords. I also do something *in* my speaking—I congratulate, command, complain, or conclude.[25] A speech is also an act. Such speech acts might be classified according to the speaker's purpose. By this measure, John R. Searle distinguished between assertives (intending to

---

22. Fontaine, *Traditional Sayings*, 64, emphasis original.

23. Kirshenblatt-Gimblett, "Towards a Theory of Proverb Meaning," 119.

24. Krikmann, *Semantic Indefiniteness*, 3; see also Outi Lauhakangas, "Proverbs in Social Interaction: Questions Aroused by the Multi-functionality of Proverbial Speech," *Proverbium* 24 (2007): 204–28; Anders Widbäck, "Summary: Proverbs in Play; Usage of Proverbs in Drama Dialogue," in *Ordspråk i bruk: Användning av ordspråk i dramadialog* (Uppsala: Uppsala Universitet, 2015), and concerning biblical proverbs, Hildebrandt, "Proverb," 7.

25. J. L. Austin, the seminal scholar for "speech act theory," distinguished the speaking and what is done *in* speaking as "locutionary" and "illocutionary" acts respectively. He also distinguished "perlocutionary" acts: what is done *by* speaking. See Austin, *How to Do Things with Words: The William James Lectures Delivered at Harvest University in 1955* (Oxford: Clarendon, 1975).

assert belief), directives (directing the hearer), commissives (committing to action), expressives (expressing feelings), and declarations (declaring that something is the case, and thereby making it so).[26]

As I will go on to show, proverbs function particularly well as assertives and directives.[27] Their purpose may be to assert some truth about the world or to direct their hearer to proper behavior. Searle distinguished assertion and direction further by the "psychological state" of their speaker and the "direction of fit between words and the world." Assertion implies *belief* that something is the case; I try to make my *words* fit the *world*. Direction implies *desire* that it be the case; I try to make the *world* fit my *words*.[28]

Used as *assertive* speech acts, biblical proverbs give not neutral facts but charged evaluations.[29] They formulate the strongly held beliefs of the sages, giving words to the way the world truly is. They create a value system through their particular categories and patterns. Categories and patterns can disambiguate and name situations, making them more manageable.[30] However disordered circumstances may seem, they fall into known types, and can be mastered. The new phenomenon is related to an existing system, the myriad experiences of life sorted into a comprehensible network. The process is iterative. A category or pattern is learned and applied to a situation. The situation then nuances how the category is understood, ready for its reapplication. This emerging com-

---

26. For example, "I hereby declare this garden party open"; "I dub thee Sir Nicholas"; "I do." Searle called this classification "illocutionary point." John R. Searle, *Speech Acts: An Essay in the Philosophy of Language* (Cambridge: Cambridge University Press, 1970), 2–3, classification on 12–20.

27. This basic distinction, or one similar, is often made by paremiologists and biblical scholars. Camp, *Wisdom and the Feminine*, 167–71; Fontaine, *Traditional Sayings*, 163–64; Robert M. Harnish, "Communicating with Proverbs," in *Cognition, Comprehension and Communication. A Decade of North American Proverb Studies (1990–2000)*, ed. Wolfgang Mieder (Baltmannsweiler: Schneider-Verlag Hohengehren, 2003), 167–68; Krikmann, *Some Additional Aspects of Semantic Indefiniteness*, 6; Lauhakangas, "Proverbs in Social Interaction," 219–20.

28. Searle, *Speech Acts*, 3–5 and 12–14.

29. I will therefore speak about using proverbs "evaluatively," rather than "assertively."

30. On disambiguation, see Lieber, "Analogic Ambiguity." On "naming" the situation, see Abrahams, "Introductory Remarks," 150; Lauhakangas, "Proverbs in Social Interaction," 220; Bland, "Rhetorical Perspective," 91–94.

plex of categories and patterns contributes to the didactic development of a worldview.

Used *directively*, these same categories and patterns become incentives for action. Do you want to fall into this category, or bring about this unfolding pattern? I direct you to behave accordingly! The speaker expresses his strong desire that you order your world according to his words. Habituating yourself in such behavior will develop your character over time (the sayings' long-term didactic goal).

3.2.2.2. Evaluative and Directive Functions

[Act—Character] Proverbs

The main categories offered in Prov 10:1–22:16 are character categories—wise and foolish, righteous and wicked (see chapter 4). These often occur within the structure [act—character]: a particular act is classified as indicating a character type. These proverbs are especially effective in an evaluative function. After a hard day in the field, I return home, and my neighbor David commends me: אגר בקיץ בן משכיל ("He who gathers in summer is a prudent son"; Prov 10:5a). Because of my behavior, David evaluates me as "prudent." This is not a neutral observation but draws in a preexisting and highly charged ethical system, structured around apparently absolute moral types.

The charged language also makes these proverbs useful in a directive function. David may quote the same proverb the following morning in order to encourage me to go into the field again—I will be prudent if I go. In Proverbs, development of wisdom and character is a great end to be desired: "How much better to get wisdom than gold!" (Prov 16:16a). Personal formation is offered as its own reward; being prudent should motivate in and of itself. This may not appeal to all students, however. Indeed, "A fool takes no pleasure in understanding" (Prov 18:2a), and the promise of prudence is unlikely to stir him. Perhaps recognizing this, proverbs also offer more material motivations.[31]

---

31. On the complexity of motivation and the "moral self" in Proverbs, see Stewart, *Poetic Ethics*, 102–29.

[Act—Consequence] Proverbs

This is where the [act—consequence] structure comes in (see further chapter 5). It gives a clear example of a pattern: a particular act leads to a particular outcome. ראש עשה כף־רמיה ויד חרוצים תעשיר: "A lazy hand brings poverty, but the hand of the diligent makes rich!" (Prov 10:4), David continues when I look unconvinced by his motivation of "prudence." Used directively, these proverbs are forceful. The book does not shy away from offering material incentives—in this case, riches. Antithetical [act—consequence] proverbs have a doubled capacity, both alluring and alarming with polarized prospects of reward and punishment.[32] Accordingly, I hurry out into the field.

The consequences offered are often extreme. This makes them motivationally powerful, but problematic if deployed to evaluative situations, for this might turn into reasoning from event to cause. If you are poor, you must be lazy; if you are suffering, you must be wicked. This is the kind of retributive logic (mis)appropriated by Job's "friends," and some scholars are keen to deny its validity in Proverbs.[33] As a genre, proverbs function through unqualified assertions, without offering counterexamples. Necessarily, they will only be true to certain situations and not to others. Only if a proverb is immediately plausible within the circumstances will its evaluative strategy succeed. Six months later, the crops have failed, and David evaluates the situation: "A lazy hand causes poverty." If I have ignored his previous advice and been idle, this proverb may find traction. It is an accurate classification of a pattern I have instigated. If, however, I have continued in my diligence, I may cast off the proverb as a misevaluation.

[Character—Consequence] Proverbs

The categories and patterns in proverbs, then, open them up to both evaluative and directive functions. The double-functionality is most evident in proverbs of a [character—consequence] structure. The character term gives a clear evaluative category, and the consequence offers powerful motivation. The following year, after an unexpected resurgence of my barley, David exclaims ברכות לראש צדיק ("Blessings are on the head of the

---

32. So Hildebrandt, "Motivation and Antithetical Parallelism."

33. See, e.g., Tomáš Frydrych, *Living under the Sun: Examination of Proverbs and Qoheleth*, VTSup 90 (Leiden: Brill, 2002), 39–40. "If the righteous accumulates wealth, is it equally true that the wealthy person is righteous? The answer to this question in Proverbs is no" (39).

righteous!"; Prov 10:6a). He has evaluated me as righteous, and directed me through the promise of future blessings. Like folk proverbs, then, the didactic proverbs of the Bible are open to many different functions, of which two are paramount: evaluation and direction.

3.3. Conclusion

My main concern in this book is with the openness of the didactic proverb. Part 1 has discussed what I mean by each of these terms and has begun to fit them together. I argued (ch. 1) that the sayings in Prov 10:1–22:16 are didactic proverbs. They invite a double strategy of interpretation and use: didactic and proverbial. This was argued on the basis of their generic relations (didactic instructions and folk proverbs), social settings (court and family), media (written and oral), self-presentation (חידות and משלים), sentential form (aphorism-like and proverb-like), and final form (whole collection and individual saying).

In chapter 2, I distinguished three main types of literary openness occurring in the proverbs and offered some constraints. Polysemy allows double meanings at the level of semantics and grammar. In parallelism, the synonymy or antithesis of the lines is sometimes unclear, and there may be an imbalance for the reader to fill out. Through imagery, the proverbs open up a world to explore and to be blended imaginatively with the target domains in the proverb text and in the reader's own life.

Chapter 3 began to discuss how the openness of the sayings contributes to their didactic and proverbial functions. Didactically, it helps to develop a broad and flexible worldview, forms the reader's character and desires, and trains his intellect. In a proverbial use, it allows application to many different situations for many different purposes. The contribution of openness, however, can only truly be seen when it is explored for oneself. To that end, part 2 turns to the text of the proverbs.

In part 2, I will explore the text of Prov 10:1–22:16 itself, interpreting the sayings as both didactic and proverbial, and giving particular attention to the way that openness contributes to these uses. I will focus on four important areas of Proverbs scholarship in order to see how reading this way might nuances our understanding. Chapter 4 considers the role of character, chapter 5, the act-consequence connection; chapter 6, the king; and chapter 7, the acquisition of wisdom. Chapter 4 looks at key terminology, and chapters 5–7 examine individual proverb texts.

Part 2
Exploring the Openness of Didactic Proverbs

4
The Openness of Character Categories
in Didactic Proverbs

תֵּן לְחָכָם וְיֶחְכַּם־עוֹד הוֹדַע לְצַדִּיק וְיוֹסֶף לֶקַח:
Give to the wise man, and he will be wiser still; teach the righteous man,
and he will increase in learning.
— Prov 9:9

4.1. Character Categories

In almost every verse of Prov 10:1–22:16, a distinctive character or pair of
characters greets us. Some of these characters occur only once—the "violent" (עָרִיצִים; 11:16), the "humble" (צְנוּעִים; 11:2), the "mighty" (עֲצוּמִים;
18:18)—but often the proverbs repeat the same key character types. Particularly in chapters 10–15, they are presented in stark contrasts, giving
the impression of a "binary anthropology": the wise against the foolish, the
righteous against the wicked.[1] This may partly stem from the generic conventions of didactic literature, with character types attested in Egyptian
didactic texts, too.[2] Proverbs, however, makes them central to its rhetoric
in a way far beyond its Near Eastern parallels.

---

1. Sun Myung Lyu, *Righteousness in the Book of Proverbs*, FAT 2/55 (Tübingen:
Mohr Siebeck, 2012), 34–37.

2. Most prominent are the "silent man" (*grw*) and the "heated man" (*šmm*), who
occur particularly often in Instruction of Amenemope. The late demotic text Papyrus Insinger uses character types more extensively, including the wise man (*rḫ*) and
the fool (*lḫ, swg, ḥn*), the man of god (*rmt nṯr*) and the wicked (*sꜣbe*). See Othmar
Keel, "Eine Diskussion um die Bedeutung polarer Begriffspaare in den Lebenslehren,"
in Hornung and Keel, *Studien zu altägyptischen Lebenslehren*, 225–34; Miriam Lichtheim, "Observations on Papyrus Insinger," in Hornung and Keel, *Studien zu altägyptischen Lebenslehren*, 283–306; Lichtheim, "Didactic Literature," 256–61; Lyu, *Righteousness*, 97–114; Shupak, *Where Can Wisdom Be Found?*, esp. 259–61; Nili Shupak,

I will argue that these character categories are open in a number of ways and that this openness contributes to how the sayings function as didactic proverbs. This is a significant claim, for many scholars see them as closed, abstract categories, without function in the real world.

4.1.1. Closed, Abstract Categories Cut Off from the World?

The apparently black-and-white depiction of character types—wise-foolish, righteous-wicked—has suggested to some scholars a loss of contact with reality. Hans Heinrich Schmid, for example, influentially argued that such binary presentation marked a hardening point in the developing wisdom tradition.[3] Older wisdom (fleetingly attested in Prov 25–27) had been concerned with navigating the contingencies of life and had accepted ambiguities of character.[4] But by the time Proverbs was fully compiled, the world had been artificially systematized into two camps: the righteous/wise on one side, the wicked/foolish on the other. This amounted to a dogmatization. Denying ambiguity, the new order was "statically fixed and established" by its closed, abstract categorizations.[5] A crisis of wisdom eventually ensued, epitomized in the cries of Job and Qoheleth, for this dogma was not played out in real life.

Other scholars have proposed similar developmental schemas, but with an additional distinction: the wise-foolish proverbs as earlier than the righteous-wicked proverbs.[6] For Claus Westermann, the former represent an early stage in the tradition, before the alleged dogmatization, and they genuinely reflect life in a folk community.[7] But the latter are late, artifi-

---

"Positive and Negative Human Types in the Egyptian Wisdom Literature," in *Homeland and Exile: Biblical and Ancient Near Eastern Studies in Honour of Bustenay Oded*, ed. Gershon Galil, Mark Geller, and Alan Millard (Leiden: Brill, 2009), 245–60.

3. Schmid, *Wesen und Geschichte*, 156–64.

4. Schmid held Prov 25–27 to be the oldest section in the book. Its sayings are the most "worldly," and it does not show the developed theologization and systematization of other sections. Schmid, *Wesen und Geschichte*, 145–46, 165–66.

5. "Statisch fixiert und fest gelegt." This fixing was also achieved, as we will see in the next chapter, by its apparently rigid act-consequence connection. See Schmid, *Wesen und Geschichte*, 159.

6. McKane, *Proverbs*; R. B. Y. Scott, "Wise and Foolish, Righteous and Wicked," in *Studies in Religion of Ancient Israel*, ed. Gary W. Anderson et al. (Leiden: Brill, 1972), 146–65; Westermann, *Roots of Wisdom*.

7. Westermann, *Roots of Wisdom*, 50–57.

cial constructions.[8] They are schematically formulated into quadripartite structures, highlighting the stark opposition between the characters and between their respective fates. Far from the changing situations of life, "anything concrete is altogether missing…; the statements are purely general and theoretical."[9] Similarly, for McKane, the humanistic wise-foolish rhetoric of "old wisdom" was dogmatized by the pious moralism of the righteous-wicked sayings. These are later theological reinterpretations and display "a kind of Yahwistic piety which is condemned to emptiness because it has disengaged itself from the realities of life."[10] However, while the two sets of characters are indeed portrayed quite differently, I will suggest that neither is in fact disengaged from reality.

4.1.2. Character Ethics in Proverbs

A more fruitful approach to the character terms might be to see them as contributions to a character-based didactic framework. The terms are not alien to lived experience but are at the very heart of how the proverbs shape lives and behavior. *Character ethics* is a burgeoning area in moral philosophy and biblical studies.[11] William P. Brown in particular has

---

8. Westermann, *Roots of Wisdom*, 75–84.

9. Westermann, *Roots of Wisdom*, 76.

10. McKane, *Proverbs*, 16.

11. Sometimes this is also called *virtue ethics*. In biblical studies, see, e.g., Bruce C. Birch, *Let Justice Roll Down: The Old Testament, Ethics, and Christian Life* (Louisville: Westminster John Knox, 1991), esp. 31–33; William, P. Brown, *Character in Crisis: A Fresh Approach to the Wisdom Literature of the Old Testament* (Grand Rapids, MI: Eerdmans, 1996); Brown, *Wisdom's Wonder: Character, Creation, and Crisis in the Bible's Wisdom Literature* (Grand Rapids, MI: Eerdmans, 2014); Waldemar Janzen, *Old Testament Ethics: A Paradigmatic Approach* (Louisville: Westminster John Knox, 1994); Jacqueline E. Lapsley, *Can These Bones Live? The Problem of the Moral Self in the Book of Ezekiel* (Berlin: de Gruyter, 2000); Cyril S. Rodd, *Glimpses of a Strange Land: Studies in Old Testament Ethics*, OTS (Edinburgh: T&T Clark, 2001), 273–82; Stewart, *Poetic Ethics*. See also collections of essays in Brown, *Character and Scripture: Moral Formation, Community, and Biblical Interpretation* (Grand Rapids, MI: Eerdmans, 2002); and M. Daniel Carroll R. and Jacqueline E. Lapsley, eds., *Character Ethics and the Old Testament: Moral Dimensions of Scripture* (London: Westminster John Knox, 2007). John Barton is skeptical of finding character ethics in the Hebrew Bible. See Barton, *Understanding Old Testament Ethics: Approaches and Explorations* (London: Westminster John Knox, 2003), 65–74; Barton, *Ethics in Ancient Israel* (Oxford: Oxford University Press, 2014), 157–84.

brought it to attention, calling it the raison d'être of the biblical wisdom literature.[12] Indeed, the book of Proverbs is increasingly being seen as rich ground for exploration.[13]

While character ethics encompasses a range of different philosophical, literary, and theological approaches, it is most strongly associated with Greek philosophers like Socrates and Aristotle. In its classical expression it is not directly transferable to Israel, but it can be a helpful heuristic framework. Character ethics is distinct from other ethical theories in its focus on character-building rather than on duties and rules (deontology) or on outcomes (consequentialism). Decisions are thought to flow from stable moral dispositions; all *doing* comes out of a prior *being*. Moral character is manifested not only in ethical dilemmas but in every decision of daily life.[14] The human person is holistic, with moral disposition inextricable from emotions, desires, intellect, habits, and so on. Disposition must be formed over time, until virtues become habitual.

Much of this is relevant to Proverbs. Despite the apparent simplicity of the character terms, the moral self that Proverbs imagines is far from simplistic.[15] Ideal characters are held up as paradigms for emulation, to be embodied through the messy contingencies of life, in the hope that readers might become wise and righteous themselves.[16]

4.1.3. Prototypes

Through its character categories, Proverbs aims to teach and form its students. To understand how, we should consider how categories are conceptualized. A category might correspond to a single word in a language (e.g., "rivers," "buildings"), but many categories are not summed up monolexically (e.g., "water features," "things to see in a town"). Equally, a word might designate more than one category (e.g., "bank"—riverside

---

12. Brown, *Character in Crisis*, 21.

13. See, e.g., Brown, *Character in Crisis*, 22–49; Dave Bland, *Proverbs and the Formation of Character* (Eugene, OR: Wipf & Stock, 2015); Lyu, *Righteousness*, esp. 60–75; Stewart, *Poetic Ethics*.

14. Daniel C. Russell, "Virtue Ethics in Modern Moral Philosophy," in *The Cambridge Companion to Virtue Ethics*, ed. Daniel C. Russell (Cambridge: Cambridge University Press, 2013), 2.

15. Stewart, *Poetic Ethics*, 6–8 and passim.

16. So Ansberry, *Be Wise, My Son*, e.g., 77; Lyu, *Righteousness*, 62–64. A "paradigmatic" approach is most fully explored by Frydrych in *Living under the Sun*, esp. 18–23.

or financial institution). In Proverbs, the central character categories are frequently labeled as חכם ("wise") and צדיק ("righteous").

Recent work on conceptual processing has suggested that categories are often understood through their *prototypes*.[17] Prototype theory views categories not as bounded and closed but as fundamentally open in a number of ways. Most important for our purposes are the following characteristics:

1. Categories cannot be defined by *necessary and sufficient conditions* for membership.
2. Instead, they are conceptualized in terms of their *central members*.
3. Radiating outward from the center are many other members, which have *graded centrality*.
4. Toward the edges of the category, it may be unclear if an item is a member or not. The category has *fuzzy borders*.

Here I will explain these features from a theoretical perspective, and in the next section I will show their relevance to didactic proverbs.

4.1.3.1. Necessary and Sufficient Conditions for Membership?

According to a classical theory of categorization, category membership is determined by necessary and sufficient criteria.[18] A word or category can be broken down into its semantic components; a "colt," for example, is [equine] [male] [young].[19] Any creature fulfilling these criteria is a member of the category, but one falling short (e.g., a female horse) is excluded.

For many words, however, this "checklist" theory breaks down.[20] Ludwig Wittgenstein famously pointed out the impossibility of finding

---

17. For a classic work on categorization employing prototype theory, see George Lakoff, *Women, Fire, and Dangerous Things: What Categories Reveal about the Mind* (Chicago: University of Chicago Press, 1987). For more recent discussions, see Croft and Cruse, *Cognitive Linguistics*, 77–92; Dirk Geeraerts, *Theories of Lexical Semantics* (Oxford: Oxford University Press, 2009), 183–203; Lewandowska-Tomaszczyk, "Polysemy, Prototypes, and Radial Categories."

18. Such as was propounded by Aristotle in his treatise *Categoriae*. For Neoclassical Theories, see Eric Margolis and Stephen M. Laurence, *Concepts: Core Readings* (Cambridge: MIT Press, 1999), 303–52.

19. See discussion in Geeraerts, *Theories of Lexical Semantics*, 70–80.

20. Thus is Fillmore's caricature; see Charles J. Fillmore, "An Alternative to Checklist Theories of Meaning," in *Proceedings of the First Annual Meeting of the Berkeley Linguistics Society* (California: University of California Press, 1975), 123–31.

necessary and sufficient conditions for the category "game." He berated his readers, "Don't say: 'There *must* be something common, or they would not be called "games"'—but *look and see* whether there is anything common to all."[21] He concluded that there was not. Rather, certain features are shared between certain games but not between others. This is somewhat analogous to a family, where some characteristics—build, temperament, facial features—may be shared by Granddad Bill and Uncle Charles but not by Great Aunt Eloise. Family resemblances characterize both kinship and semantic categories. No single member must exhibit every feature, nor must a single feature be shared by every member. The category's makeup is much more fluid and open.

4.1.3.2. Central Members

Following on from this, it was recognized that some items are cognitively central to their categories. This approach was pioneered by Eleanor H. Rosch, through her experimental work in cognitive psychology.[22] She began with the study of color terms, noticing that color categories "develop around perceptually salient 'natural prototypes.'"[23] These prototypes are the best examples we can imagine of given colors—we might think of blood red instead of maroon, grass green instead of turquoise. In other categories too, we find better and worse examples, more and less prototypical members.[24] These insights developed into a prototype theory of category structure.

According to this theory, categories gather around central, prototypical cases. Often, the central cases are representative of the category.[25] They share features in common with other items inside the category and

---

21. Wittgenstein, *Philosophical Investigations*, 31.

22. See, e.g., Eleanor H. Rosch, "Natural Categories," *Cognitive Psychology* 4 (1973): 328–50; Rosch, "Cognitive Reference Points," *Cognitive Psychology* 7 (1975): 532–47; Rosch, "Cognitive Representations of Semantic Categories," *Journal of Experimental Psychology* 104 (1975): 192–233. For an overview of Rosch's work, see Lakoff, *Women, Fire, and Dangerous Things*, 39–55.

23. Rosch, "Natural Categories," 328.

24. Rosch, for example, examined the categories of furniture, vehicles, fruit, weapons, vegetables, and clothing in "Cognitive Representations."

25. Eleanor Rosch, "Principles of Categorization," in *Cognition and Categorization*, ed. Eleanor Rosch and Barbara B. Lloyd (Hillsdae, NJ: Lawrence Erlbaum, 1978), 30.

are distinctive from items outside. Sometimes, however, central cases are stereotypes. These develop socially and (though unrealistic) become cognitively pertinent to members of that community.[26] Sometimes prototypes are ideals, presenting society's view of what *should* be the case. George Lakoff suggests that ideal members are "of great importance in culturally significant categories," shaping the way that judgments and plans are made.[27] It is in this sense that I suggest prototypes are at work in the proverbs: they present idealized examples of righteous and wise men.

4.1.3.3. Graded Centrality

The recognition of central cases has implications for category structure, which must be open to degrees. Members do not have equal status; they have *graded centrality*—some are better examples than others.[28] The precise grades envisaged might vary from speaker to speaker, but there is consistency of overall conceptualization within speech communities. Which is a better example of a "fruit," an apple or a date? Western speakers generally pick the apple.[29] From the center, radiating outward, are all the other fruits—the bananas, oranges, and melons. At the periphery fall the obscure cases—the tomatoes, avocados, and dates. Accordingly, categories are not all or nothing. Items do not have to be central to be considered members. Individuals do not have to be ideal cases to be counted as righteous or wise.

4.1.3.4. Fuzzy Borders

Finally, graded centrality raises the question of how far you have to move from the center before you are outside the category's bounds. Is an olive, for example, still a "fruit"?[30] The borderline seems somewhat fuzzy. The

---

26. Lakoff, for example, discusses the "housewife" stereotype as central to the "mother" category in *Women, Fire, and Dangerous Things*, 79–80.

27. Lakoff, *Women, Fire, and Dangerous Things*, 87.

28. This has been thoroughly demonstrated through experimental work. See Croft and Cruse, *Cognitive Linguistics*, 78–79; Rosch, "Principles of Categorization," 38–40.

29. Demonstrating the cultural specificity of this, Jordanian speakers tend to pick the date. See Croft and Cruse, *Cognitive Linguistics*, 78.

30. This example is discussed in Geeraerts, *Theories of Lexical Semantics*, 189–90.

scholarly discussion of "fuzziness" began in mathematics with Lotfi A. Zadeh's "fuzzy set" theory.[31] In classical set theory, an item's "membership function" takes a numerical value of 0 (not a member of the set) or 1 (a member). Zadeh suggested that membership functions between 0 and 1 can exist. That is, some items are not quite a member of the set, and not quite not-a-member either. The set has fuzzy borders.

Zadeh's theory was quickly applied to semantics, incorporated into prototype theory, and verified by empirical research: a category in language too may have fuzzy borders, open boundaries.[32] Without necessary and sufficient conditions for membership, there is no clear dividing line between items inside and outside. For some items, for some of the potential "righteous" or "wise," the question of category membership may remain unresolved.

4.2. The Wise and the Foolish

The character categories "wise" and "foolish" can be usefully viewed through the lens of prototype theory. The most common term to designate the "wise" is חכם.[33] But the category in Proverbs cannot simply be equated with the full semantic potential of this word. The book employs it in a distinctive way.

Some scholars suggest that in Proverbs the "wise man" (חכם) is a technical designation for a professional sage (comparable to the professional priest and prophet; cf. Jer 18:18).[34] But the strong focus on disposition and the contrast with the fool suggest something more here: wisdom as a quality of character. Elsewhere in the Hebrew Bible, being wise can be a down-to-earth skill—perhaps technical expertise (e.g., Exod 28:3) or even shrewd cunning (2 Sam 13:3)—but Proverbs elevates and aggrandizes the notion into its own idealized portrait.

---

31. Lotfi A. Zadeh, "Fuzzy Sets," *Information and Control* 8 (1965): 338–53.

32. For the application of "fuzzy logic" to natural language, see James D. McCawley, *Everything That Linguistics Have Always Wanted to Know about Logic but Were Ashamed to Ask* (Chicago: University of Chicago Press, 1981), 360–94. For verification in empirical research, see, e.g., Carolyn B. Mervis and Eleanor Rosch, "Categorization of Natural Objects," *Annual Review of Psychology* 32 (1981): 100–102.

33. There are sixty occurrences of this root in Proverbs, of which about twenty-nine designate the category type "wise man/men."

34. See, e.g., William McKane, *Prophets and Wise Men*, SBT 44 (London: SCM, 1965).

חכם seems to be something of an umbrella term, both encompassing the whole "wise man" category and occupying one space within it. Other spaces are filled by the "understanding" (איש תבונה, נבון, מבין), the "shrewd" (ערום), and the "prudent" (משכיל). There is no single umbrella term for the "fool" category, but we hear commonly of the אויל and the כסיל, along with the לץ ("scoffer"), חסר־לב ("senseless"), and פתי ("naïf").[35]

I suggest that the categories "wise man" and "fool" have open prototype structures, exhibiting the four features delineated above. What is more, each feature has implications for the functions of didactic proverbs. To preempt my conclusions, I will suggest the following:

Feature of prototype structure	Implications for didactic proverb use
Conceptualized around central cases	Motivational potential of ideals
Lack of necessary and sufficient conditions	Creation of a broad evaluative framework
Graded centrality	Character development
Fuzzy borders	Making wise the foolish

4.2.1. Central Cases and Ideals

According to prototype theory, categories are conceptualized in terms of their central members. In most instances, each proverb presents one such central case, offering an ideal example of a character. Their cumulative effect is to sketch the category's center, a portrait of the prototypical wise man or fool.

These characters are depicted with certain qualities, mainly related to their attitude toward wisdom, their use of speech, and their morality. The wise seek and attain the wisdom inaccessible to fools (14:6; 15:12; 17:24; 18:15). They treasure up or disseminate this wisdom, while fools spread folly (10:13, 14; 12:23; 13:16; 14:7, 33; 15:2, 7). Wisdom is a delight to them, but "folly is joy to the senseless" (15:21; cf. 10:23; 18:2). The wise recognize their limitations (11:2); they listen to the advice that fools spurn (10:8; 12:15; 13:1, 10; 15:5, 12), and such discipline increases their knowledge (15:31; 17:10; 19:25; 21:11). In speech, the wise benefit themselves

---

35. On the relationship between these terms, see §4.2.3 below.

and others, while fools bring harm (10:10, 18; 12:18; 13:14; 14:3; 18:6, 7). Aware of its power, the wise man knows to restrain his speech (11:12; 17:27; 18:13 [but cf. 17:28!]). In the moral sphere, the wise man pays careful attention to his way (14:8, 15; 15:21). By contrast, the fool acts wickedly (10:23; 13:19) and is imprudent, hot-tempered, and quarrelsome (12:16; 14:16, 17, 29; 19:3; 20:3).

By these characterizations, the proverbs offer students something to emulate in their own lives. Some of these behaviors are quite attainable by the novice: listening to advice takes nothing more than a humble disposition. Others are for the more advanced and aspirational: disseminating true wisdom is the prerogative of the few.

Ideal characters are here used for their motivational potential. Elsewhere, wisdom's desirability is made explicit. In chapters 1–9, wisdom is personified as a woman to adore and revere. She is "more precious than jewels, and nothing you desire can compare with her" (3:15; cf. 2:4; 8:10–11, 18–19; 16:16; 20:15; 25:12). Here the strategy is more subtle. The prototypical wise man is described again and again. This repetitive insistence drums the readers' desires into sapiential shape; wisdom comes to provide motivation in and of itself. Accordingly, these proverbs can function well directively (see §3.2.2 above). Why should I listen to advice? Because then you will be wise.

4.2.2. Scarcity of Definitional Features

According to prototype theory, categories cannot be defined by necessary and sufficient features. Similarly, in the proverbs, certain characteristics are made central, but no full definition is offered. This is part of the reason why the terms are sometimes seen as abstract and empty. However, perhaps readers are being encouraged to fill out the categories for themselves.[36] Readers are given a snapshot of the category's center and are goaded to sketch in the larger picture. They might employ various strategies to this end:

Using the prototypes themselves. The prototypical examples provide the seedbed for the full category in all its verdancy. Based on logic and experience, the readers can extrapolate from central cases: the wise man

---

36. See Hausmann, *Studien zum Menschenbild*, 95. The openness of character terms forms an important part of Hausmann's discussion.

takes advice (10:8; 12:15; 15:5), so he may also be humble, submissive, and self-aware. Readers can draw resemblances: in the proverbs, one who scorns the guilt offering is a fool (14:9); in life, one who shuns pilgrimage is probably a fool too.[37] Readers can specify the meaning of general language, pinpointing a specific "evil" from which the wise turn (14:16) and making concrete the advice to "give thought to a word" (16:20). They can imaginatively elaborate scenarios: when the wise tongue "heals" (12:18), what joys of vitality may lie in store?

Using the wider literature. Furthermore, when Proverbs is used didactically, each saying may be taken not individually but as part of the larger literary work (see §1.6 above). Accordingly, chapters 1–9 set the broad contours for understanding the "wise man" and the "fool." From wisdom's self-praise in chapter 8, for example, we learn that wisdom is noble, right, true and straight (8:6–11), entailing fear of the Lord (8:13), and demanding righteousness and justice (8:15–16, 20). A dominant binary is established in these chapters—two ways, two women, two houses.[38] Much of Prov 10–29 is structured through antithetical parallelisms, which reaffirm this division. All the positive characteristics implicitly cohabit with wisdom; all are embodied in the same individual and can flesh out what it truly means to be wise.

Using real-world experience. The categories "wise man" and "fool" can be contextualized not just by the literature but by the real world. They can be molded through proverb use. Whenever a proverb about a wise man is spoken successfully, that situation goes to nuance the hearer's understanding of wisdom. In application, the sayings are connected to real people and experiences. These individuals could draw on their personal experiences to flesh out the categories: What, in my life, has proved wise or foolish? Whom do I know to be a wise man or a fool? Such an individual could become a real life central case, his behavior observed and emulated (though the inevitable flaws in human character make this complex in

---

37. Judging by resemblance to a prototype is a type of "reference point reasoning." The reference point serves as a helpful point of comparison and as a cognitive anchor for the classification system. Rosch, "Cognitive Reference Points"; Elena Tribushinina, *Cognitive Reference Points: Semantics beyond the Prototypes in Adjectives of Space and Colour* (Utrecht: LOT, 2008).

38. Habel in particular has drawn attention to this duality in "Symbolism of Wisdom."

practice; see ch. 6).[39] Furthermore, value systems are often socially construed.[40] Social consensus may have determined what "wise" and "foolish" meant for readers, removing the need for further explanation. The proverbs could then speak the norms of their culture with an authoritative, traditional voice.

The process of fleshing out the categories—through prototypes, literature, or experience—offers intellectual training. Necessary and sufficient characteristics are not handed to the students, and the openness itself becomes a pedagogical strategy. Interpretation is the students' freedom and responsibility.[41] They must discern, imagine, and observe what is truly wise, and through the process become wise themselves.

The categories, having been fleshed out by the situations of life, are then easily reapplied to such situations. Circumstances may seem ambiguous, but the categories provide guidance on what to look for and a system for overall appraisal. They serve as a broad evaluative framework to make sense of the world and its inhabitants. When a proverb is spoken, it fits a particular instance into the framework. The highly charged valuations define what is good or bad, what is to be desired or reviled, and the proverb accordingly offers praise or condemnation. The straightforward framework requires little decipherment and can gain immediate traction with the hearer. Its familiarity suggests the stability of ancient wisdom.

4.2.3. Graded Centrality and Character Development

The third distinctive feature of prototype theory is graded centrality: some members are better examples of a category than others. Within the cate-

---

39. Such individuals can become paragons. Commenting on paragons as cognitively central to categories, Lakoff suggests that "a great many of our actions have to do with paragons. We try to emulate them … as models to base our actions on" (*Women, Fire, and Dangerous Things*, 88).

40. See James Davison Hunter, *The Death of Character: Moral Education in an Age without Good or Evil* (New York: Basic Books, 2000), 15–27; Rodd, *Glimpses of a Strange Land*, 49–51. An example of a socially construed ethical norm might be the father's revulsion at Lady Folly's sexual ethic (Prov 7). In a modern libertarian society, her acts might be seen positively, as empowering women and celebrating the fact of sexuality. Bartholomew and O'Dowd, *Old Testament Wisdom Literature*, 279.

41. Holger Delkurt, *Ethische Einsichten in der alttestamentlichen Spruchweisheit*, Biblisch-Theol. Studien 21 (Neukirchen-Vluyn: Neukirchener Verlag, 1993), 145; Hausmann, *Studien zum Menschenbild*, 349–51.

gory of the "wise," different individuals (or the same individual at different times) may display different degrees of wisdom. Conceptualizing wisdom this way makes character development conceivable. The student can position himself in the category and then move inward through the graded centrality, conforming his behavior more and more to the prototypical wise man.

Such personal development is essential to character ethics. Moral dispositions are not innate or instantly acquired but must be diligently formed throughout life, so that virtues become ingrained.[42] John Barton has argued that character development is alien to Proverbs. Conversion (wholesale shifts from one category to another) may be possible, but "everyone is either good or bad, wise or foolish, and there is little idea of moral progress."[43] According to Barton, character is "fixed and unchanging."[44] However, this view rids Proverbs of its overall didactic function (to form wise men and women), and it does not take account of graded centrality.[45]

In Proverbs, the wise man can "increase in learning" (יוֹסֶף לֶקַח; 1:5) and "become wiser still" (יֶחְכַּם־עוֹד; 9:9). Situated at the beginning and end of the prologue, these sayings are programmatic for the book. Someone can be a member of the "wise man" category yet still progress closer to its center. However, the progression is asymptotic. No one is ever completely wise, and the center remains just out of reach.[46] This keeps even the wisest of men ever striving, their faces ever set to wisdom (17:24a; cf. 15:14a; 18:15). They are not perfect but err and are rebuked (17:10). When this happens, they characteristically welcome advice (10:8; 12:15; 13:1; 15:5) and learn from it (9:9; 19:25; 21:11). This progression is inherent in how the category is conceptualized and is important in the depictions of several types of "wise man" (חכם, נבון, and מבין).[47]

In the "fool" category, we see a slightly different phenomenon. Not all the "folly" terms express a prototype of the category. Rather, different

---

42. Michael V. Fox, "The Pedagogy of Proverbs 2," *JBL* 113 (1994): 233–43.

43. Barton, *Ethics in Ancient Israel*, 159; see also Barton, *Understanding Old Testament Ethics*, 67.

44. Barton, *Ethics in Ancient Israel*, 160.

45. Barton does acknowledge this didactic function (*Ethics in Ancient Israel*, 162), but in my view does he not give it sufficient weight.

46. For a fuller discussion of the limits of man's wisdom, see §7.3 below.

47. חכם (1:5; 9:9; 10:8; 12:15; 13:1; 18:15; 21:11); נבון (1:5; 15:6; 15:14; 19:25); מבין (17:10, 24).

terms exhibit different degrees of folly. Gradation is evident in the structure of the sematic field. Space prohibits full analysis here, but the central
elements seem the hardened fool, אויל, who despises wisdom (1:7), and
the arrogant scoffer, לץ, who will never find it (14:6).[48] More intermediary
is the blundering oaf, כסיל, characterized by his complacency (1:32) and
loquacity (10:18; 12:23; 13:16; 15:2; 18:2, 6, 7). More peripheral are the
mindless ones: the brutish בער and the senseless חסר־לב. Least culpable
of all is the naïve פתי, who may be redeemable from his folly (see below).
This conceptual structure has pedagogical import. Students can progress
through the open, graded categories—toward wisdom to their good, or
toward folly to their harm.

4.2.4. Fuzzy Borders and Making Wise the Foolish

The final significant feature in prototype theory is the possibility of fuzzy
borders: sometimes it is unclear whether an individual belongs in the
category or not. This feature of conceptual structure is evident in daily
life, where not everyone is a prototypical case. Ambiguity is expected at
the borderlines.

Imagining the categories this way raises an important practical question: is it possible to cross the border? Can a fool become wise?[49] Hardened
characters, like the לץ and the אויל, seem so far sucked into the center of
folly's vortex that escape is impossible. Only in vain does the "scoffer" (לץ)
seek wisdom (14:6). Neither he nor the prime "fool" (אויל) will improve by
instruction (13:1; 15:5, 12), or even by corporeal discipline (27:22). Trying
to educate them will ultimately harm the teacher (9:7–8). However, for
those on the edges, the vortex's power wanes, and they may yet evade it.
Thus Lady Wisdom calls out to fools as well as to the "wise" (פתי, כסיל, and

---

48. The gradation presented here is based on the analysis of Fox (*Proverbs 1–9*,
28–43). Trevor Donald gives a slightly different gradation: (least culpable) פתי, בער,
נבל, לץ, כסיל, אויל (most culpable) ("The Semantic Field of 'Folly' in Proverbs, Job,
Psalms, and Ecclesiastes," *VT* 13 [1963]: 285–92). Donald takes his evidence from
Proverbs alone, while Fox uses the whole biblical corpus. Shupak proposes a similar
scale for Egyptian "folly" language (*Where Can Wisdom Be Found?*, 198).

49. Michael V. Fox discusses this as a prevalent dispute in ancient pedagogy, in
both Egypt and Israel; see Fox, "Who Can Learn? A Dispute in Ancient Pedagogy," in
*Wisdom, You Are My Sister: Studied in Honor of Roland E. Murphy, O. Carm., on the
Occasion of His Eightieth Birthday*, ed. Michael L. Barré (Washington, DC: Catholic Biblical Association of America, 1997), 62–77. See also Lichtheim, *Moral Values*, 13–18, 46.

חֲסַר־לֵב; 8:5; 9:4), and Prov 1:2–6 programmatically declares its intention "to give prudence to the naïve" (פֶּתִי; 1:4). This simpleton is the prime target for Ladies Wisdom and Folly, for he is still formable. Both women implore him to turn aside to their own abodes (9:4, 16). The implied addressee is in a state of liminality, on the threshold between youth and adulthood, folly and wisdom.[50] The hope is offered that he might step over the border. This can provide great encouragement for naïve youths seeking improvement, and for their anxious instructors. Conversely, fuzzy borders warn the wise against complacency, for remaining so is not guaranteed. All must continually press after wisdom.

4.2.5. Conclusion

Viewing the prototype structure of the categories "wise" and "foolish," then, can cast light on their usefulness in didactic proverbs. According to prototype theory, categories are conceptualized by central cases; these motivate students and provide ideals to aim for. Categories cannot be defined by necessary and sufficient criteria, which allows students to flesh them out for themselves and to construct broad evaluative frameworks for making sense of life. They have graded centrality, making character development possible, and fuzzy borders, meaning fools may become wise. The character categories are not closed and abstract, nor cut off from the world, but are open and profoundly useful for life.

4.3. The Righteous and the Wicked

But what of the categories "righteous" and "wicked"? The righteous man is the צַדִּיק. Like חָכָם, this term serves as an umbrella, encompassing a whole category of people and behaviors.[51] Like חָכָם, the category צַדִּיק in Proverbs cannot be straightforwardly equated with the whole semantic potential of the term. In the Hebrew Bible, the צדק root is often employed in a legal context. צְדָקָה ("righteousness") depicts a judicial rule of absolute equity, administered by God or the king.[52] The adjective צַדִּיק ("righteous")

---

50. Brown, "Pedagogy of Proverbs"; Leo G. Perdue, "Liminality as a Social Setting for Wisdom Instructions," *ZAW* 93 (1981): 114–26.
51. Cf. Lyu, *Righteousness*: "Righteousness is the all-encompassing quality of human or divine character in toto above and beyond specific behaviours" (14).
52. See, e.g., 2 Sam 8:15 // 1 Chr 18:14; 1 Kgs 10:9 // 2 Chr 9:8; Isa 5:16; 9:6[5];

can mean "innocent" or "vindicated" regarding a specific legal offence.[53] In Proverbs, this legal context is usually lacking, the term instead designating holistic moral character (see §4.3.2 below). Within this category, other character terms are sometimes also found: the "good" (טוב), the "blameless" (תם), the "upright" (ישר). The antithetical category is summed up by רשע ("wicked"). Again, Proverbs transfers the character type from a legal to a more generally moral context, where he is found alongside the "evil" (רע), the "sinner" (חוטא), the "godless" (חנף), and the "treacherous" (בוגד).

These categories are presented somewhat differently from their wise and foolish counterparts. Some scholars have found them to be "condemned to emptiness" by this distinctive presentation (see §1.1 above).[54] Indeed, the presentation may seem at first to cast doubt on their prototype structure and their usefulness. This is because:

1. The central cases are described in terms of unrealistic consequences that come to the characters, making them seem implausible.
2. Such presentation by consequences offer *no* characteristics, let alone ones necessary and sufficient to flesh out the categories.
3. There is little suggestion of gradation or fuzzy borders that would allow one to improve in righteousness.

I suggest, however, that despite the difference in presentation, the categories of "righteous" and "wicked" still have a prototype structure and are just as useful as their wise/foolish counterparts. The divergence stems from the different pedagogical techniques employed.

4.3.1. Problem 1: Central Cases and Unrealistic Consequences

In general, while Proverbs presents the "wise" and "foolish" in terms of what they do, the "righteous" and "wicked" are depicted through the consequences that come to them.[55] These are often extreme and exaggerated,

---

28:17; 33:5; Jer 9:23[22]; 22:3, 15; 23:5; Pss 33:5; 72:1; 99:4; 103:6. See discussion in chapter 6 on the judicial role of the king.

53. See, e.g., Exod 23:7–8; Deut 25:1; 1 Kgs 8:32; Isa 5:23.

54. McKane, *Proverbs*, 16.

55. This apparent character-consequence connection is considered in detail in chapter 5.

rarely seeming to accord with reality, and the proverbs may thus appear to be cut off from the world. The righteous receive life (e.g., 10:16, 25; 11:19), deliverance (10:2; 11:4, 6, 8, 9, 21), and blessing (10:6; 11:18, 28). All they desire will be granted (10:24; 11:23; 13:25), and they will have fullness of joy (10:28; 13:9; 21:15). The wicked, however, face death (10:25, 27; 11:19), danger (10:2, 24; 11:5, 6, 8), and hardship (10:3, 30; 11:18). This scenario—as attested Job, Qoheleth, and our own experiences—is not always reflected in life.

However, prototype theory can make some sense of this. As we have seen, the proverbs do not claim to give a full delineation of categories, nor even a representative sample of members, but rather they give ideals. They present what should be the case, not what necessarily is. In prototype theory, not only may the prototypes themselves be ideals (see §4.2.1), but categories may presuppose *idealized cognitive models* (ICMs).[56] An ICM is a simplified, idealized world. Within this imagined world, the prototype is accurate, but within the real world, it may not be.

For example, consider the category "bachelor."[57] The definition "a bachelor is an unmarried man" (Merriam-Webster) has immediate plausibility to the English speaker. Our central prototype of the category is defined in this way. But what about unmarried men who engage in long-term relationships, civil partnerships, religious celibacy, or "Tarzan" lifestyles—are they "bachelors"?[58] Only peripherally so. The prototypical definition of the category ("a bachelor is an unmarried man") seems to imagine a world where such situations do not exist—a simplified model reality without the complexities of real life. Applying the category to the real world, then, there are many unmarried men who do not fit and who are only peripherally "bachelors."

Idealized worlds such as this are presupposed in many categories—not only linguistic categories ("bachelor") but categories of moral principles

56. Lakoff, *Women, Fire, and Dangerous Things*, 68–76.

57. This term has provoked much discussion within linguistics. For a classic explanation of the term from a structural linguistic perspective, see Jerrold J. Katz and Jerry A. Fodor, "The Structure of a Semantic Theory," *Language* 39 (1963): 185–90. It was further analyzed from a cognitive linguistic perspective by Charles J. Fillmore, ("Towards a Descriptive Framework for Spatial Deixis," in *Speech, Place, and Action*, ed. R. J. Jarvella and Wolfgang Klein [London: John Wiley, 1982], 34) and employing ICMs by Lakoff (*Women, Fire, and Dangerous Things*, 69–71).

58. Lakoff, *Women, Fire, and Dangerous Things*, 70–71.

(the "righteousness-prosperity" axiom).[59] The central, prototypical principle is "the righteous prosper." But this presupposes an idealized world with an absolute moral order and intrinsic reward nexus. This does not correspond fully with the real world, and therefore lived experience may cohere to a greater or lesser degree with the prototype.

Proverbs is probably not trying to reflect reality through this idealized world. Indeed, the book is not naïve to peripheral cases and does occasionally present them.[60] But it focuses on central ideals for their pedagogic and motivational potential. The proverbs intend to incentivize their students—to immediate action (in a proverbial use) or to reflection and character development (in a didactic use). We saw above (§4.2.1) how Proverbs uses wisdom itself as a motivation—becoming wise is an end in itself. The book recognizes, however, that not all students are stirred by such noble goals. It allows for the reality of worldly self-interest and also offers material rewards. Stewart has suggested four major motivational paradigms in Proverbs, giving strong incentives for action. Righteousness leads to wealth, honor, protection, and, fundamentally, life.[61] These idealized consequences may seem to abstract the proverbs from the world. But paradoxically, they also root them in the world, for they ensure that the student will actualize their advice.

4.3.2. Problem 2: Apparent Absence of Definitional Features

The presentation by consequences raises a further problem: the proverbs offer few characteristics by which to flesh out the categories (let alone necessary and sufficient ones). How can they then function to evaluate people's behavior?

It should first be noted that some proverbs *do* present the behavior of the righteous and wicked.[62] The righteous man's speech is beneficial, while the wicked man's is harmful (10:6, 11, 20, 21, 32; 11:9, 11; 12:5, 6, 26; 13:5; 15:28). The righteous man knows his beast (12:10), walks with integrity

---

59. Johnson, *Moral Imagination*, 78–107. Applied to Proverbs by Stewart in *Poetic Ethics*, 173–81; see also Anne W. Stewart, "Wisdom's Imagination: Moral Reasoning and the Book of Proverbs," *JSOT* 40 (2016): 351–72.

60. See Stewart, *Poetic Ethics*, 179–80.

61. Stewart, *Poetic Ethics*, 107–14.

62. For a discussion of distinctive characteristics of the "righteous" in Proverbs, see Lyu, *Righteousness*, 45–59.

(20:7), and is generous (21:26). The wicked man covets evildoers (12:12), accepts bribes (17:23), and shows no mercy (21:10).

Furthermore, irrespective of their use in Proverbs, these terms have a meaning in the Hebrew language and literature: the reader already knows something of what they entail.[63] Like some psalms, Proverbs centralizes the moral aspects of righteousness.[64] Psalm 112, for example, paints a portrait of the "righteous" man (√צדק occurring in vv. 3, 4, 6, 9). Not only does he conduct his affairs with justice (v. 5), but he has a proper relationship with Yahweh, trusting and fearing him, and delighting in his commandments (vv. 1, 7; cf. Ps 18:21–25[20–24]). He is gracious and merciful (v. 4; cf. Ps 116:5) and abundant in generosity (vv. 5, 9; cf. Ps 37:21, 26). Elsewhere too צדיק co-occurs with other moral character terms, which may be included within the category in Proverbs—for example, תם ("blameless"; Gen 6:9), ישר ("upright"; Ps 33:1), טוב ("good"; 1 Kgs 2:32).

In addition, some of the strategies suggested above for fleshing out "wise" and "foolish" are equally as applicable here:

Real-world experience: Like "wisdom," "righteousness" may be defined socially. As Cyril S. Rodd put it, "Righteousness in the first place is conformity to the prevailing norms of society."[65] The student is already embedded in this society and knows its norms. She knows who is esteemed as righteous and can observe and emulate them accordingly.

Wider literary context: As used in Proverbs, "righteousness" seems to encompass the whole of moral character.[66] Any and every positive characteristic described in the book is embodied in the righteous man. We have already seen something similar in the "wise man." The relationship between these two categories has been disputed.[67] They do not have the

---

63. There have been extensive debates about the "theory of righteousness" in the Hebrew Bible (see Lyu, *Righteousness*, 15–32). The most pervasive ideas are that righteousness entails conformity to a (legal, ethical, religious) norm, or correctness in relationship (with God or other people). Within Proverbs scholarship, Hans Heinrich Schmid influentially argued that "righteousness" is "world order"; see Schmid, *Gerechtigkeit als Weltordnung: Hintergrund und Geschichte des alttestamentlichen Gerechtigkeitsbegriffes*, BHT 40 (Tübingen: Mohr Siebeck, 1968).

64. On the differences between Psalms and Proverbs, see Lyu, *Righteousness*, 115–33.

65. Rodd, *Glimpses of a Strange Land*, 49.

66. Lyu, *Righteousness*, 134.

67. Some suggest that the terms should be equated in the Proverbs. Barton suggests "a complete correspondence" between them (*Ethics in Ancient Israel*, 158);

same semantic properties and yet are clearly closely related in Proverbs. Prototype theory can help explain this. Categories are imagined first not by their semantic properties (or conditions for membership) but by their prototypical cases. The imagined, idealized prototype of the "wise man" will also be righteous. The prototypical "righteous man" will also be wise. The two are co-referential, depicting the same ideal individual.[68]

This inextricability of morality and intellect is central in character ethics and is particularly evident in Prov 1–9.[69] According to the preamble (1:2–7), the instructions will increase both the students' wisdom and their "righteousness, justice, and equity" (1:3; cf. 2:9–10). Accordingly, Lady Wisdom presents herself as the epitome of righteousness (8:6–9, 15–18, 20–21). In sentence literature, an explicit connection is made only rarely (e.g., 10:21, 31; 11:9, 30; 14:9; 19:1; 22:12). But the dominant binary rhetoric puts righteousness and wisdom together on one side, wickedness and folly on the other. If the student knows what the "wise man" looks like (see §4.2.2 above), she can use this portrait to flesh out the "righteous." Through these strategies, the student can construct a broad and meaningful evaluative framework from these apparently ill-defined terms.

4.3.3. Problem 3: Apparent Lack of Graded Centrality or Fuzzy Borders

The third problem is the apparent lack of gradation or fuzzy borders in these categories. In contrast to the proverbs about the "wise," very few sayings suggest that one can become righteous, or even improve in righteousness. It seems to be all or nothing.

Skladny calls them "synonyms" in chapters 10–15 (*Die ältesten Spruchsammlungen*, 11); according to Fox, by the time the prologue was written, wisdom was "almost identical with righteousness" (*Proverbs 10–31*, 931). The close connection also occurs in the Demotic text Papyrus Insinger; see Lichtheim, "Observations on Papyrus Insinger"; Shupak, *Where Can Wisdom Be Found?*, 258–61.

68. See also above, §1.1.6.

69. For the relationship between virtue and wisdom in ancient virtue ethics, see Rachana Kamtekar, "Ancient Virtue Ethics: An Overview with an Emphasis on Practical Wisdom," in *Cambridge Companion to Virtue Ethics*, ed. Daniel C. Russell (Cambridge: Cambridge University Press, 2013), 29–48. Fox discusses their relationship in Proverbs from a Socratic perspective (*Proverbs 10–31*, 934–45). Christopher B. Ansberry applies an Aristotelian model ("What Does Jerusalem Have to Do with Athens? The Moral Vision of the Book of Proverbs and Aristotle's *Nicomachean Ethics*," *Hebrew Studies* 51 [2010]: 157–73).

However, we should not necessarily equate this apparently binary opposition with binary thought. Graded centrality may in fact be assumed. Cognitive research suggests that this is how most categories are conceptualized, even if they at first seem absolute.[70] Indeed, in the Hebrew Bible (and in lived experience) someone may be "more righteous than" (צדיק מן) another (Gen 38:26; 1 Sam 24:18[17]; 1 Kgs 2:32; Jer 3:11; Hab 1:13). Occasional proverbs too present characters who are more peripherally righteous, like the atypical צדיק who "gives way before the wicked" (מט לפני־רשע; Prov 25:26).

Coreferential with each other, the structure of the categories "wise" and "righteous" run parallel. The evident gradation in the former implies gradation in the former. Thus when the righteous man "increases in learning" (יוסף לקח; 9:9), he moves closer to prototypical righteousness too. Good students "pursue" (√רדף; 15:9) righteousness, presumably entailing their moral improvement, and the book's programmatic intention is for students to "acquire" (√לקח; 1:3) it.[71] I suggest that this didactic goal overrides any impression of absolutism.

But if it is possible to increase in righteousness, why do the proverbs avoid mentioning it? First, it may be a pedagogical simplification, so that the novice is not confused with grey areas and marginal cases.[72] She can put people into two crude boxes as a starting point for categorizing the world. Over time she may realize the ambiguities and gradations in human character. Second, the rhetoric of these proverbs deals in absolutes and ideals. Idealized consequences are offered to those who are wholly righteous, not to any borderline cases. Motivationally, this is powerful. You should not strive after half measures or be satisfied if you are quite righteous. You must press right in to the center of the category.

---

70. For example, "dead" and "alive" at first seem to be all-or-nothing, nongraded terms. But I may easily describe someone as "more alive" than another, extending the conceptualization to include vitality, joy, and health. It is clear what constitutes an "odd number," but research shows that even this category has a graded structure. See Croft and Cruse, *Cognitive Linguistics*, 79, 88.

71. This reference to "righteousness, justice, and equity" is structurally and rhetorically central to the book's preamble, perhaps giving its highest purpose. See Brown, *Character in Crisis*, 23–30.

72. So Ansberry, *Be Wise, My Son*; Frydrych, *Living under the Sun*.

4.4. Conclusion

The categories "righteous" and "wicked" (like "wise" and "foolish") are open and didactically useful. Three objections might be made to this, but none is unanswerable. First, does the presentation by consequences cut the proverbs off from the real world? I suggest that the proverbs present conscious idealizations of righteousness and reward and expect marginality to arise. They do so to offer motivation. Second, do the consequences mean that the categories lack a definition? No; rather, several strategies are available to flesh them out and use them as an evaluative framework. Third, is righteousness all or nothing? The absolutist depiction is probably a rhetorical technique, paradoxically intended to help the student increase in righteousness.

5
Openness and the Act-Consequence Connection

צדיק מצרה נחלץ ויבא רשע תחתיו

The righteous is delivered from trouble, and the wicked comes into it
instead.
— Prov 11:8

5.1. The *Tun-Ergehen Zusammenhang*

It is not possible to read Proverbs without being struck by its repeated
insistence on a connection between acts and consequences. Everywhere
we turn, the righteous flourish, and the wicked suffer harm. Proverbs is
less explicit, however, about what brings about these consequences. Earlier scholarship had formed a general agreement on the issue: retribution
was responsible; Yahweh intervened judicially to punish sin and reward
righteousness.[1] But the consensus was rocked in 1955, when Klaus Koch
famously argued against the pervading *Vergeltungsdogma* ("retribution
dogma"), replacing it with an intrinsic *Tun-Ergehen Zusammenhang*, "act-
consequence connection."[2]

Koch argued that the judicial-theological category of "retribution"
(*Vergeltung*) is anachronistic. In the Hebrew Bible, we find no temporal

---

1. See, e.g., Walther Eichrodt, *Theology of the Old Testament*, 2 vols. (London:
SCM, 1961), 1:263–69; Johannes Fichtner, *Die altorientalische Weisheit in ihrer isra-
elitisch-jüdischen Ausprägung: Eine Studie zur Nationalisierung der Weisheit in Israel*
(Giessen: Töpelman, 1933), 105–17.

2. Reprinted in Klaus Koch, "Gibt es ein Vergeltungsdogma im Alten Testament,"
in *Um das Prinzip der Vergeltung in Religion und Recht des Alten Testaments*, ed. Karl
Koch (Darmstadt: Wissenschaftliche Buchgesellschaft, 1972), 130–80. An abridged
version published in English as Koch, "Is There a Doctrine of Retribution in the Old
Testament?," in *Theodicy in the Old Testament*, ed. James L. Crenshaw (London: SPCK,
1983), 57–87.

distinction between deed and consequence, no "previously established norm" for reward/punishment, no "levels of severity" for different cases—nothing very judicial at all.[3] Rather, he suggested, consequences (*Ergehen*) grow organically from acts (*Tun*), like plants from seeds.[4] They are internally and necessarily bound together as a synthetic whole—a *Tun-Ergehen Zusammenhang*. For Koch, such holistic thinking characterized the Hebrew mindset. He followed Scandinavian scholars like Johannes Pedersen and Karl Hj. Fahlgren, who had argued for a particular "primitive" mode of conception: a "synthetic view of life" (*synthetische Lebensauffassung*).[5] Israelites looked at the world as a totality, devoid of our modern compartmentalizing divisions that might separate deeds from their effects. For them, such separation was almost nonsensical.[6]

According to these scholars, the structure of the Hebrew language itself gives evidence of this totalizing mentality. Not only does Hebrew have no word for "punishment," but, as demonstrated by Fahlgren, a number of Hebrew roots can describe both an act (in our terms) and its consequence.[7] So אָוֶן can mean "wrong deed" (*Missetat*) and also "guilt/punishment" (*Schuld/Strafe*). רַע can mean "moral evil" (*Bosheit*) and

---

3. Koch, "Is There a Doctrine of Retribution," 59.

4. Koch, "Gibt es ein Vergeltungsdogma," 166; omitted from abridged English version.

5. Karl Hj. Fahlgren, "Die Gegensätze von sedaqa im Alten Testament," in *Um das Prinzip der Vergeltung in Religion und Recht des Alten Testaments*, ed. Karl Koch (Darmstadt: Wissenschaftliche Buchgesellschaft, 1972), 126–29. See also Johannes Pedersen, *Israel: Its Life and Culture*, 2 vols. (Copenhagen: S. L. Møller, 1926). Such ideas about "primitive" thought are nowadays seriously questioned.

6. Thus Koch describes Fahlgren's view: "In a certain time in Israel's history it could not distinguish between transgression and punishment, between righteousness and reward" ("Is There a Doctrine of Retribution," 75). John Barton caricatures the view: "The question 'Will I suffer if I sin?' becomes … a nonsense-question: if we asked an ancient Israelite he would presumably give us a blank stare" (Barton, "Natural Law and Poetic Justice in the Old Testament," *JTS* 30 [1979]: 12).

7. Fahlgren examines the roots רשע, חטא, פשע, און, עול, נבל, רע ("Die Gegensätze"). Koch explicitly draws on Fahlgren (Koch, "Is There a Doctrine of Retribution," 75–78). Such arguments are repeated and developed by, e.g., Rolf Knierim, *Die Hauptbegriffe für Sünde im Alten Testament* (Gütersloh: Gütersloher Verlagshaus, 1965), 73–77; Gerhard von Rad, *Old Testament Theology*, 2 vols. (Edinburgh: Oliver & Boyd, 1962), 1:265–66, 384–85; Gene M. Tucker, "Sin and 'Judgment' in the Prophets," in *Problems in Biblical Theology: Essays in Honor of Rolf Knierim*, ed. Henry T. C. Sun and Keith L. Eades (Grand Rapids: Eerdmans, 1997), 373–88.

"misfortune" (*Unglück*). The same word describes both; therefore "cause and effect are for the Israelite one and the same."[8]

Accordingly, Koch proposed that the ancient Israelite inhabited a *schicksalwirkende Tatsphäre*—a sphere of activity bringing about his fate. Every deed was *schicksalwirkende* ("fate-effecting"), and no foreign agent was needed (or indeed able) to intervene between the two. Yahweh was no interventionist judge, but more like a midwife, helping to deliver what had been conceived and gestated in the impersonal womb of the *Tatsphäre*.[9] Particularly significant for Koch were verbs like שׁלם, which he translated as "make complete" (*vollständig machen*), and השׁיב, which he rendered as "steer back" (*zurücklenken*).[10] In neither case does Yahweh impose external consequences, but he "does something which is intricately woven into the action itself."[11]

Koch's views acquired particular force in confluence with another emerging stream in German scholarship—*Weltordnung* ("World Order"). Hartmut Gese noted that in Egypt, the act-consequence connection was enforced by the deity *ma'at* (who embodied order, justice, and truth). He suggested something similar for Israel.[12] Schmid expanded on this: a powerful World Order was operative across the ancient Near East, encapsulated in Egyptian *ma'at*, Babylonian *Me*, and Canaanite/Israelite צדק.[13] Both cosmic and moral, it pervaded every sphere of life: law, wisdom, nature, kingship, war, and cult. In the life of the individual, it actualized itself through the *Tun-Ergehen Zusammenhang*.[14]

Together, the *Weltordnung* and *Tun-Ergehen Zusammenhang* proved a formidable torrent, flowing through and changing the landscape of wisdom studies in the second half of the twentieth century. "Order" was established as the framework for wisdom thought, and the act-consequence connection

---

8. "Ursache und Wirkung sind ... für den Israeliten ein und dasselbe" (Fahlgren, "Die Gegensätze," 90).

9. Koch, "Is There a Doctrine of Retribution," 61.

10. Koch, "Gibt es ein Vergeltungsdogma," 134, 139–40; Koch, "Is There a Doctrine of Retribution," 60, 63–64.

11. Koch, "Is There a Doctrine of Retribution," 64.

12. Hartmut Gese, *Lehre und Wirklichkeit in der alten Weisheit* (Tübingen: Mohr Siebeck, 1958). Gese, however, also argued for a *Sondergut*, distinctive to Israel: Yahweh as a free agent not bound by the order.

13. Schmid, *Gerechtigkeit als Weltordnung*. See also Schmid, *Wesen und Geschichte*.

14. See esp. Schmid, *Gerechtigkeit als Weltordnung*, 175–77.

was considered fundamental.[15] Both at the time and subsequently, however, much critical work also questioned and refined these views. Important challenges concern (1) the linguistic foundations of act-consequence connection, (2) its apparent inviolability, (3) the agent(s) behind it, and (4) whether it offers an explanation or a motivation.

5.1.1. Linguistic Foundations of the *Schicksalwirkende Tatsphäre*

Koch's *Tatsphäre* was built in part on linguistic foundations. However, many scholars have found these to be unsound, threatening the integrity of the edifice. From שלם and השיב, Koch had inferred a previous movement (internal to the act itself) that Yahweh needed only to "make complete" or "steer back." But this argument is based on the verbs' etymology (√שלם, "to be complete"; √שוב, "to go back") and falls foul of the well-known "root fallacy": word meanings reside in current (not historical) usage and must be examined in context.[16] And in context, the terms may imply active intervention.[17]

Another load-bearing datum for Koch was the lack of a Hebrew word for "punishment." But this is not conceptually relevant. Indeed, as Ka Leung Wong reminds us, "They have no word for 'schicksalwirkende Tatsphäre' either."[18] The shape of a language cannot be directly equated with the shape of thought, and this foundation of nonexistence is no foundation.[19] The same false equation of linguistic structure and thought structure is evident in Koch's other arguments too. It is not, for example, conceptually determinative that some languages have one word where others have two. English has just "to know," while French has "connaître" and "savoir," and German has "kennen" and "wissen." Is it therefore impossible for English

---

15. See, e.g., von Rad, *Old Testament Theology*, 1:265, 384–85; von Rad, *Wisdom in Israel*, 124–37. For a recent positive (though nuanced) appraisal of Koch and Schmid, see Barton, *Ethics in Ancient Israel*.

16. See James Barr, *The Semantics of Biblical Language* (Oxford: Oxford University Press, 1961), 107–60.

17. Josef Scharbert, "Šlm im Alten Testament," in *Um das Prinzip der Vergeltung in Religion und Recht des Alten Testaments*, ed. Klaus Koch (Darmstadt: Wissenschaftliche Buchgesellschaft, 1972), 300–24; P. Zerafa, "Retribution in the Old Testament," *Angelicum* 50 (1973): 477–79; Lam, *Patterns of Sin*, 114–27.

18. Ka Leung Wong, *The Idea of Retribution in the Book of Ezekiel*, VTSup 87 (Leiden: Brill, 2001), 23.

19. See Barr, *Semantics*, 33–45.

speakers to distinguish between "knowing" a person and "knowing" facts? If I know my linguistic community, I know this is not so. Similarly, Hebrew has only אָון where English has "iniquity" and "punishment," but this does not mean that the aspects were necessarily one and the same. The linguistic phenomenon does not necessitate a metaphysical connection.

That said, however, the data Koch described are real enough and deserve consideration. But instead of language structure and lexical stocks, we should examine words used in context. Indeed, in context the polysemies are striking. In the proverbs, it is sometimes unclear whether the polysemous term refers to an act or to a consequence (see §5.3 below). By this double meaning, the proverbs may poetically propose (and do not necessarily presuppose) a connection between the two. Using the same word to describe both may suggest justice, for one is appropriate for the other in degree and kind: an עין for an עין, an אָון for an אָון.[20]

5.1.2. An Inviolable World Order?

The world-order models of Schmid and Koch seemed to admit few exceptions. Acts and consequences were thought to always correspond. Apparent violations could only be temporary, and people were "hardly ever conscious" of problems.[21] According to Schmid, the world order, epitomized in the book of Proverbs, was dogmatic, and across the ancient Near East, *ma'at*, *me*, and צדק were conceived of as mechanistic. Eventually, however, the inviolable came to be seen as unviable. In Schmid's words, a *Krise der Weisheit* (crisis of wisdom) broke out across the region. Khonshopteps, Šubšis, Jobs, and Qoheleths raised their voices against the unrealistic dogma.[22] Act and consequence do not, in fact, always align.

---

20. Barton, "Natural Law"; Patrick D. Miller Jr., *Sin and Judgment in the Prophets: A Stylistic and Theological Analysis*, SBLMS 27 (Chicago: Scholars Press, 1982); Wong, *Idea of Retribution*, 196–245. It has been suggested that the "talionic principle" is the foundation of the act-consequence wordplay. Miller, *Sin and Judgment*, 105–8.

21. Koch, "Is There a Doctrine of Retribution," 78.

22. Schmid discusses these characters in *Wesen und Geschichte*. Khonshoptep (74–78) is the son of the scribe in the Egyptian New Kingdom text, the Instruction of Ani. He laments the impossibility of adhering to his father's immutable doctrine. Šubši-mašrâ-Šakkan (131–41) is the narrator of Ludlul bēl nēmeqi, a Babylonian poem that questions why the righteous suffer. Job and Qoheleth (173) epitomize the crisis in Israel.

However, there are hints of unease even *within* Proverbs, not just in later texts. Some sayings seem to violate a strict act-consequence connection.[23] We hear of the righteous in need of deliverance (Prov 10:2; 11:4, 6, 8, 9, etc.) and the wicked gaining wealth (albeit troubled; 10:2; 11:18; 15:6). A whole community might suffer unjustly (11:11; 28:15; 29:2), and readers are encouraged to have pity on the poor, as though their penury is undeserved (14:21, 31; 19:17; 22:9). The wide array of sayings reflects a diversity of experience, where ambiguity and anomaly arise. In the book as a whole, the psychological weight of these sayings may be out of proportion with their small number.[24]

Furthermore, the proverbs focus not on specific actions but on total disposition and overall character (see §4.1.2 above). As Udo Skladny suggested, the connection is more a *Haltung-Schicksal Zusammenhang* ("attitude-fate connection") than a *Tun-Ergehen*.[25] This makes it much less direct and less tangible. If we are to speak of a world order, it is more as a recognition of life's regularities than as a mechanistic principle of causality.[26] The proverbs attest to a world that is generally predictable but not inviolable.

5.1.3. The Agent(s) behind the Connection

Probably the most widespread criticism of Koch concerns the agency behind his *Tun-Ergehen Zusammenhang*. For Koch, the operative force

---

23. See, e.g., Samuel L. Adams, *Wisdom in Transition: Act and Consequence in Second Temple Instructions*, JSJSup 125 (Leiden: Brill, 2008), 53–54, 85; Hatton, *Contradiction*, 83–116; Hausmann, *Studien zum Menschenbild*, 234–37.

24. Hatton, *Contradiction*, 83. Claudia Camp suggests that, though this is a "minority report," it can still cause great anxieties; see Camp, "Proverbs and the Problems of the Moral Self," *JSOT* 40 (2015): 25–42.

25. Skladny, *Die ältesten Spruchsammlungen*, 71–75. Others speak of a "character-consequence connection," e.g., Hildebrandt, "Motivation and Antithetical Parallelism," 438. By Hildebrandt's count, in Prov 10–15 there are 152 [character—consequence] proverbs, and only 62 [act—consequence].

26. "World order" has proved a slippery term, with scholars employing it in either of these ways. Fox distinguishes them as "predictable" and "mechanistic" orders respectively. He also adds a "constructed" order, actively constituted by people's acts. Michael V. Fox, "World Order and Maʿat: A Crooked Parallel," *JANESCU* 23 (1995): 40–41. Cf. Adams, *Wisdom in Transition*, 84–85; Lennart Boström, *The God of the Sages: The Portrayal of God in the Book of Proverbs*, ConBOT 29 (Stockholm: Almqvist & Wiksell, 1990), 91, 137–38; Delkurt, *Ethische Einsichten*, 157–59.

was an impersonal nexus, with Yahweh relegated to the position of midwife. But many proverbs do speak of an active deity, who blesses (10:22; 16:20; 18:22), directs behavior (16:1, 9; 20:24), tests hearts (15:11; 17:3; 21:2), creates (16:4; 20:12; 22:2), and (despite Koch's protestations) administers rewards and punishments (12:2; 15:25; 16:5, 7; 17:5; 19:14, 17; 21:12; 22:12, 14, 22–23; 24:12). Koch does not address such verses adequately.

Some scholars explain Yahweh's presence chronologically: at first Israel understood there to an impersonal *Zusammenhang*; later a Yahwistic conception took over.[27] This impression is sometimes bolstered with an apparent parallel in Egypt: mechanistic *ma'at* was replaced by the free, arbitrary will of the deity.[28] However, there is little to signal that theological elements are late, either in Israel or in Egypt. The theological proverbs are in formal and thematic continuity with those around them, and positing an original secular understanding is a great anachronism. It is more likely that the two modes of causality coexisted from the beginning and were not held to contradict.[29] Yahweh was the omnipresent reality behind the connection and intimately involved in its operation.

In some proverbs, humankind is allowed some retributive agency of their own—they too can bless and curse (11:26). *Society* may be operative in the *Zusammenhang*.[30] The scholarly recognition of this has been prompted

27. Fahlgren, "Die Gegensätze," 126–29; Michael V. Fox, "Aspects of the Religion of the Book of Proverbs," *HUCA* 39 (1968): 55–69; Henning G. Reventlow, "Sein Blut Komme Über Sein Haupt," *VT* 10 (1960): 311–27. The classic expression of the "Yahweh redaction theory" is McKane, *Proverbs*, although he contrasts Yahweh's activity with self-confident human wisdom rather than with an impersonal world order.

28. Influentially Hellmut Brunner, "Der freie Wille Gottes in der ägyptischen Weisheit," in *Les sagesses du Proche-Orient Ancien: Colloque de Strasbourg 17–19 Mai 1962* (Paris: Presses Universitaires de France, 1963), 103–20.

29. So, e.g., Adams, *Wisdom in Transition*, 77–83; Barton, *Ethics in Ancient Israel*; Dell, *Book of Proverbs*, 105–17; Faith Huwiler, "Control of Reality in Israelite Wisdom" (PhD diss., Duke University, 1988), 12–31; Tucker, "Sin and 'Judgment.'" On Egypt, see Adams, *Wisdom in Transition*, 15–52; Fox, "World Order and Maat," 42–44; Miriam Lichtheim, *Maat in Egyptian Autobiographies and Related Studies*, OBO 120 (Göttingen: Vandenhoeck & Ruprecht, 1992). Lichtheim concludes that "over the span of two millennia, the basic understanding of Maat doing and its rewards had not changed" (97).

30. Adams, *Wisdom in Transition*, 87–88; Georg Freuling, *"Wer eine Grube gräbt...": Der Tun-Ergehen-Zusammenhang und sein Wandel in der alttestamentlichen Weisheitsliteratur*, WMANT 102 (Neukirchen-Vluyn: Neukirchener Verlag, 2004), 57–61; Bern Janowski, "Die Tat kehrt zum Täter zurück: Offene Fragen im Umkreis

partly by fresh thinking on *ma'at*. Jan Assmann has described *ma'at* not as an impersonal cosmic force but in social terms of "connective justice" and "solidarity," to be communally enacted.[31] Applying these principles to Israel, Bernd Janowski argues for "retribution as social interaction."[32] Consequences do not come naturally from acts but come through socially enforced reciprocity: whatever the doer did comes back to him through another. Some proverbs make this explicit (e.g., 11:26; 14:17; 17:13; 20:22; 24:29). Others use general language and passive formulations, which Janowski suggests should be filled out socially.[33] Perhaps, however, this inexplicit nature intentionally leaves the proverbs open to different agents, making them applicable to many situations.[34]

5.1.4. Explanation or Motivation?

Proverbs is no scientific treatise. It does not set out to describe systems of causality. Sometimes, the act-consequence sayings may be used (accurately or not) to evaluate situations (see §3.2.2 above), but their main aim seems to be to direct the behavior and shape the character of their impressionable pupils. To this end the *Tun-Ergehen Zusammenhang* may be employed: for motivation, not for explanation.[35] Indeed, the extreme consequences are obviously problematic if intended as accurate descriptions of reality (see §4.3.1 above), but they have significant force as motivational devices. The apparently inevitable connection is intended to orient the student before he acts. The proverbs express not what he *has been* until now but what he *should be* from now on, holding up prototypical ideals for his emulation. These idealized characters are central to the proverbs. Any

---

des 'Tun-Ergehen-Zusammenhangs,'" *ZTK* 91 (1994): 247–71; Carl-Albert Keller, "Zum sogenannten Vergeltungsglauben im Proverbienbuch," in *Beiträge zur alttestamentlichen Theologie: Festschrift für Walther Zimmerli zum 70. Geburtstag*, ed. Herbert Donner, Rudolf Hanhart, and Robert Smend (Göttingen: Vandenhoeck & Ruprecht, 1977), 223–38.

31. "Konnektiven Gerechtigkeit" and "Solidarität." Jan Assmann, *Ma'at: Gerechtigkeit und Unsterblichkeit im alten Ägypten* (München: Beck, 1990), passim.

32. "Vergeltung als sozial Interaktion." Janowski, "Die Tat kehrt zum Täter zurück."

33. Janowski, "Die Tat kehrt zum Täter zurück," 264–65, citing, e.g., 11:25, 27, 31; 13:13, 21; 21:13; 22:9; 24:24.

34. Boström, *God of the Sages*.

35. See, e.g., Adams, *Wisdom in Transition*, 88–93; Freuling, "*Wer eine Grube gräbt...*," 103; Wong, *Idea of Retribution*, 24.

other active parties are ignored through impersonal and passive formula-tions. The student's responsibility is stressed over any third-party agency; his devastating or joyful experience is before the readers' gaze—strong motivation for morality.

In what follows, I will examine three sets of proverbs that comment on the act-consequence connection. Each set deploys its own technique to generate openness: the first uses mainly parallelism, the second imagery, and the third polysemy (see ch. 2). Each has implications for the act-con-sequence connection and for the four debates considered above. Each will also demonstrate the didactic and proverbial power of the sayings.

5.2. Parallelism and the Predictable World Order

I suggested above (§5.1.2) that the world order in Proverbs is not invio-lable, but is predictable. The proverbs examined here imply precisely that, using a particular technique of parallelism to do so. Structurally, many proverbs are formulated as [Topic—Comment] // [Topic—Comment], with *character*, *act*, and *consequence* terms filling these slots (see §1.1.5 above). Often, the two halves of the proverb have the same arrangement, but sometimes they are unbalanced (see §2.2.3).[36] We find, for example:

a colon:	CHARACTER	ACT	[ ]
b colon:	CHARACTER	[ ]	CONSEQUENCE

In these proverbs, the character is the only repeated term, the mediat-ing figure between act and consequence, determining both. The logic of the proverb may not be immediately clear, and the reader must work to restore it, deducing the connections between the parts. She may well level the terms by supplying an *act* to the second colon and a *consequence* to the first. The proverb becomes a kind of riddle to solve, or in Fox's terms, a "folk enthymeme," a reasoning structure with suppressed premises or con-clusions.[37] Fox points out that by supplying additional terms, the reader constructs the proofs by which she is persuaded. She will be loath to con-tradict her own reasoning, and the argument thus seems incontrovertible.

---

36. This imprecision is particularly common in Prov 10–15; see, e.g., 10:6, 8, 13, 14, 16, 21, 31; 11:2, 5, 9; 12:6, 12, 20, 21, 27; 13:2, 5; 14:3, 9, 25.

37. Fox, "Disjointed Proverbs," drawing on paremiologists Green and Pepicello, "Folk Enthymeme."

5.2.1. Didactic Explorations

דבר־שקר ישנא צדיק ורשע יבאיש ויחפיר: 13:5

A lying word the righteous hates, but the wicked becomes a stench and a disgrace.

The antithetical parallelism here is clearly recognized through the proto-typical word pair "righteous-wicked," but each colon steers in a different direction. The proverb begins with the acts of the righteous, or rather (in keeping with Proverbs' concern for total disposition) their attitudes: they hate lies. This is contrasted with the consequences coming to the wicked: stinking disgrace. The proverb could be formally represented:

CHARACTER	ACT	CONSEQUENCE
The righteous	hates a lying word	
But the wicked		becomes a stench and a disgrace

Character is central, determining acts in *a* and consequences in *b*. Per-ceiving the imbalance, the reader may fill the gaps, restoring logic and relevance by leveling the terms:

The righteous	hates a lying word	[*and doesn't become a stench or disgrace*]
But the wicked	[*doesn't hate a lying word and*]	becomes a stench and a disgrace

By supplying the reversals, the reader practices a type of reasoning essen-tial for a wise life: deducing the connections between character, act, and consequence. In this world order, the *Tun-Ergehen Zusammenhang* is logi-cal, and basically predictable.

However, the leveling process also brings a certain openness: the order is not absolutely established. "Hates a lying word" is a phrase, not a single term, and either element may be reversed. Does the wicked man *love* a lying word, or hate a *truthful* word, or indeed both? יבאיש ("becomes a stench") is a metaphor evocatively expressing contemptibility.[38] In the reversal, the reader might imagine a pleasing fragrance rising from the

---

38. Gen 34:30; Exod 5:21; 1 Sam 13:4; 27:12; 2 Sam 10:6; 16:21; 1 Chr 19:6.

righteous (cf. Cant 3:6). The term may also contain a wordplay. It is pho-
nologically similar to יביש ("he brings shame"), which often occurs as
a word pair with חפר√ to express "shame and disgrace."[39] It is possible
that באש√ is a by-form of בוש√ here, and the versions seem to reflect this
understanding.[40] But a double meaning cannot be discounted for the MT:
both "shame" and "stench" for the wicked (and so too perhaps honor and
fragrance for the righteous).

Notably, these consequences are enacted by society. In community-
oriented Israel, disgrace is a terrible punishment, and a powerful incentive
against wickedness. The proverb propagates a set of social norms. By
reversing the terms, the reader deduces that the righteous deserve honor.
Through the interpretation process, then, he ascribes honor to the worthy
and is thus made to practice the very principle the proverb preaches. He
must continue to do this throughout life.

In the above interpretation, the *hiphil* verbs are understood as ingres-
sive: "becomes a stench" (cf. 1 Sam 27:12), "becomes a disgrace" (Isa 54:4).
However, the binyan presents ambiguity, and the sense may also be causal:
"causes a stench" (Exod 5:21), "causes disgrace" (Prov 19:26)—to others,
that is. The negative consequences come not to the wicked man alone but
to those around him. Ambiguity enters the act-consequence connection
here, for who is to say whether these others deserve disgrace?

חכם־לב יקח מצות ואויל שפתים ילבט: 10:8
The wise of heart receives commandments, but the foolish of lips is
ruined.[41]

חכמים יצפנו־דעת ופי־אויל מחתה קרבה: 10:14
The wise treasure up knowledge, but the mouth of a fool—destruction
is close by.

---

39. Isa 1:29; 24:23; 54:4; Jer 15:9; 50:12; Mic 3:7; Ps 71:24; Prov 19:26; Job 6:20.

40. Cf. the qere/ketiv of Isa 30:5. See, P. R. Ackroyd, "A Note on the Hebrew Roots
באש and בוש," *JTS* 43 (1942): 160–61. Pesh. (=Targ.) *ybht*; the LXX paraphrases "has
shame and disgrace" as αἰσχύνεται καὶ οὐχ ἕξει παρρησίαν, "will be disgraced and not
have boldness."

41. The precise meaning of לבט√ is disputed. Its only other occurrences are Prov
10:10 (an exact repeat of this colon) and Hos 4:14. The Arabic cognate means "to
throw down to the ground." See Fox, *Proverbs 10–31*, 516. The LXX translates it as
ὑποσκελισθήσεται ("will stumble"). Pesh. (=Targ.) has *mttḥd* ("seized"), possibly
reflecting the reading ילבד ("are captured").

These two proverbs, separated by only six verses, give very similar messages: the wise take in wisdom; foolish mouths bring destruction.[42] The first cola may be self-referential: the reader must love and treasure up the proverbs' own wisdom, contemplating their many nuances, which will educate her. A parallelism is recognized in each proverb through the antitheses of wise and foolish: these stable, recurrent prototypes determine conduct and destiny. However, the parallelism is not exact. The first cola give acts, the second consequences. The reader may *emphasize* the consequence terms, reading the proverbs as developmental. Ruin and destruction are climactic motivations. She may alternatively practice her logical skills and *level* the terms (see §2.2.3 above):

	CHARACTER	ACT	CONSEQUENCE
10:8	The wise of heart	receives commandments	[*and is not ruined*]
	But the wicked	[*does not receive commandments and*]	is ruined
10:14	The wise	treasures up knowledge	[*destruction is not close by*]
	But the mouth of a fool	[*does not treasure up knowledge and*]	destruction is close by

On the one hand, the gap-filling suggests the predictability of the world order: connections between acts and consequences can be inferred. But on the other, it allows openness, for the implied reversals are not certain. In 10:8, the terms could be simply negated or positively opposed. Does the fool "not receive" or actively spurn commandments? Will the wise "not be ruined" or positively flourish?[43] In 10:14, we find two-word phrases. Is destruction *far* from the wise, or is *restoration* or *life* close by?

---

42. Surrounding proverbs also speak of the value of good speech: 10:11, 13, 17–21. 10:10b repeats 10:8b, suggesting that one of these cola may have been displaced. Fox, *Proverbs 10–31*; Murphy, *Proverbs*; Crawford Howell Toy, *A Critical and Exegetical Commentary on the Book of Proverbs*, ICC (Edinburgh: T&T Clark, 1899).

43. Heim creatively reverses ילבט as ימלט, presumably for the pleasing soundplay. Semantically, this reversal (the wise "are delivered") is not exact. See Heim, *Poetic Imagination*, 225.

The wise "treasure up knowledge," valuing it highly. Do fools treasure up *folly* in the same way, or *devalue* knowledge, counting it as worthless? צפן suggests only sparing expenditure. While the wise are judicious in speech, perhaps the fool spews forth whatever "wisdom" he thinks he has (leaving דעת unreversed) and his extensive folly (reversing דעת) (cf. 13:16b).

Supplying the reversals ties together act, character, and consequence in the reader's mind. The details of the connection, however, are not explicit. The verb "is ruined" (יִלָּבֵט) in 10:8 is passive, and the agent of "destruction" (מחתה) in 10:14 is unspecified. The emphasis remains on the fool and his responsibility, rather than any divine, societal, or intrinsic agency (none of which are excluded). The proverbs may further suggest a complex model of causality. In the short term, the wise might receive precisely the commandments that can forestall a particular type of "ruin," imminent in their circumstances (10:8); they may treasure the knowledge to avoid this specific "destruction" (10:14). In the long term, through habitual "receiving" and "treasuring," they develop a total disposition conducive to their flourishing. Furthermore, in 10:8, a third party is suggested—the speaker of the commandments—with powerful influence over her student's fate, hinting at social agency. In 10:14, it is possible that the "destruction" does not harm the fool alone, but all those around him, deserving or not.[44] This problematizes any facile notion of an absolute act-consequence relationship.

10:16: פעלת צדיק לחיים תבואת רשע לחטאת׃
The wage of the righteous—to life; the produce of the wicked—to sin.

The form in our final example is terse, and its sense catches the reader off guard. At first, it seems to present a precise antithetical parallelism. The cola are matched by the syntax, the verbal ellipsis, the prototypical word pair רשע/צדיק, and even the vowel patterns of תְּבוּאַת/פְּעֻלַת. But after the ל in the second colon, we meet not the anticipated antithesis to "life" (i.e., "death," מות) but "sin" (חטאת). This riddle-like rupture brings a psychological disorientation appealing for resolution. The most obvious solution is to level the terms:

---

44. So Delitzsch, *Biblical Commentary*; McKane, *Proverbs*; Toy, *Critical and Exegetical Commentary*; Waltke, *Book of Proverbs 1–15*; Christine Roy Yoder, *Proverbs*, AOTC (Nashville: Abingdon, 2009).

CHARACTER	ACT	CONSEQUENCE
The wage of the righteous	[—to virtue and]	to life
The produce of the wicked	—to sin	[—and to death]

The "wage" and "produce" might have literal economic reference.[45] As elsewhere, the very suggestion that the wicked *have* produce problematizes a dogmatic understanding of the *Tun-Ergehen Zusammenhang*. The righteous use their income in life-enhancing, virtuous ways, while the wicked squander theirs on sin, ultimately leading to death. Or the proverb could speak figuratively of all that comes from and comes to the characters.[46] "Life" and "sin" are fundamental, basic ideas, general terms that could be fleshed out in various ways by the student's imagination, experience, and reason. The *b* colon may suggest that the wicked man gets ever more engrossed in sin, progressing through grades of wickedness (see §4.3.3) until it consumes his whole lifestyle and encapsulates his character. A *Haltung-Schicksal Zusammenhang* may be more appropriate here than *Tun-Ergehen*.

Through the parallelism, the reader connects this sinful behavior with death; a deduction set up to motivate righteous living. Some commentators suggest that consequences are already implicit in the term חטאת.[47] Indeed, Waltke translates it as "sin and death" (so NIV), and חטאת was one of the terms adduced by Koch and others to support the "synthetic view of life," for it apparently refers to both sin (*Sünde*) and disaster (*Unheil*).[48] However, the meaning *Unheil* is very rare if present.[49] I suggest that "death" is

---

45. So Murphy, *Proverbs*; Toy, *Critical and Exegetical Commentary*; Yoder, *Proverbs*.

46. פעלה might also be translated as "work, deeds" (cf. Ps 17:4; 2 Chr 15:7)—i.e., as referring to the acts of the righteous (cf. the LXX rendering, ἔργα). The parallelism with "produce" favors the translation as "wage," however, depicting consequences.

47. R. J. Clifford suggests that it means not "sin" but "lack" (not an act but a consequence), citing Prov 21:4 and Job 14:16; see Clifford, *Proverbs: A Commentary*, OTL (Louisville: Westminster John Knox, 1999). However, both of these instances are dubious. David Winton Thomas connects it with the Ethiopic, and suggests the meaning "penury"; see Winton Thomas, "The Meaning of חטאת in Proverbs X. 16," *JTS* 15 (1964): 295–96.

48. Waltke, *Book of Proverbs 1–15*, 464; Koch, "Is There a Doctrine of Retribution," 75; Knierim, *Die Hauptbegriffe für Sünde*, 19–112; Fahlgren, "Die Gegensätze," 93–105.

49. Koch cites this proverb and Num 12:11. BDB only gives Zech 14:19. More commonly, the noun חֵטְא may take this meaning.

not in the normal semantics of the word, nor should it feature in the translation, but this proverb closely binds the concepts together. Death clings around sin. Though far from being explicit, the proverb may suggest some form of intrinsic causality.

Of course, the reader might not supply the mental reversals. The absence of "death" is conspicuous and perhaps significant. In the balance of justice, retribution is expected but does not occur. The wicked are not, in fact, greeted with death. The disruption to the precise parallelism through the term חטאת suggests that the world order does not always click along mechanically. The student must be prepared to face ambiguity in proverbs and in the world.

5.2.2. Used as Proverbs

So far, we have explored these proverbs didactically—for the principles they teach their reader and the ways they form character and intellect. But they could also be spoken as proverbs—applied to a specific situation with a specific purpose. In chapter 3, I suggested a number of ways that a single proverb may be open to different *situations* and <u>functions</u>.[50] Here I will concentrate on our example verses and show how manipulating the variables may result in many different uses.

Most folk proverbs are a single line, but the examples here employ a distinctive parallel arrangement. They give not one topic and one comment but two paralleled topics and two very different comments. This makes their mapping onto context more complex. Adapting the diagram from chapter 3, we could represent it thus (fig. 4):

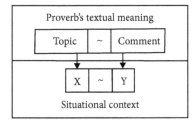

Fig. 4a. A folk proverb.

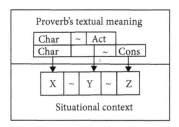

Fig. 4b. An imprecise parallelism.

---

50. In the subsequent discussions, I will italicize *situations* and underline <u>functions</u> for clarity.

Two character terms are given, one relating positively to the context (describing what is or will be the case), and one relating negatively (giving the opposite of what is or will be). The sense of bifurcation is strong: either righteous or wicked, wise or foolish. This is particularly useful <u>evaluatively</u>. We have seen how, through their prototypical character types, proverbs establish a broad framework for making sense of the world (chapter 4). Whenever such a proverb is spoken, the referent is fitted into the appropriate category. She is commended or condemned, and the categories are fleshed out accordingly, ready for reapplication in another proverb use. The constant presence of the opposing character hints at the possibility of changing sides, of crossing the fuzzy borders between categories. The fate of the wicked motivates the righteous hearer if she fears it may be her own. The actions of the wise interest the fool if she yet hopes to join them.

As well as characters, these proverbs offer an act. This is the most straightforward term to map onto context, as it gives a concrete datum, easily observable in the world. They also give a consequence. It is possible that this consequence has occurred in the context, and the proverb is spoken to explain it. More likely though, the consequence is a motivational device, facilitating the proverbs' <u>directive</u> function with the threat of punishment or hope of reward. Containing both character and consequence terms, these proverbs gain dual evaluative-directive potency.

As examples, let us take Prov 13:5 and 10:8. I will focus on the possibilities of *a positive or negative relation to context* and *a past or future orientation*. That is, does the proverb describe the current situation or an opposite situation? Is it spoken before or after the event described? As a rule of thumb, before the event it may function <u>directively</u>; afterward it may offer <u>evaluation</u>.

13:5 דבר־שקר ישנא צדיק ורשע יבאיש ויחפיר:
> A lying word the righteous hates, but the wicked becomes a stench and a disgrace.

I could speak this proverb with an entirely *future orientation*. Neither of the events described has yet happened: no one has spoken a word, no one been dishonored. The whole proverb becomes <u>directive</u>, providing motivations in both cola. "Hate lies!" I direct my interlocutor, "Then you will be righteous and will not be put to shame." The first motivation appeals to noble goals: character development as its own reward. The second is more straightforwardly self-serving, for no one wants disgrace.

Or I might speak the same words with a *past orientation*. My interlocutor has both shown himself to love lying words and been put to shame. I offer the proverb as an <u>evaluation</u>. "You love lies? You cannot be righteous," I begin, evaluating and condemning his character based on his attitudes, "and that is why you have been disgraced." The situation is an example of a recurring [act—consequence] pattern. My hearer might learn to distinguish this pattern through the ambiguities of life and evaluate future shame accordingly.

The imprecise parallelism here means that the two cola describe different events, which need not have the same temporal reference. The proverb could be spoken between the cola, as it were, with both *past and future orientations*. A friend has displayed that she hates lies. Accordingly, I <u>evaluate</u> her as righteous. She fleshes out the character type in her evaluative system and can reapply it when appropriate. I add that, should she continue in righteousness, she will not be shamed or disgraced. She is thus disinclined from wicked behavior and <u>directed</u> to further truthfulness.

In this proverbial use, the first colon has a *positive relationship to context*: it describes my interlocutor. The second colon has a negative relationship, depicting the opposite of her destiny. But it is also possible to reverse the arrangement. Another conversation partner revels in deceit. Speaking evaluatively, I condemn his character by applying the first colon negatively: he cannot be righteous. As a foreboding comment on his ensuing fate, or as a directive plea to change his ways, I add that men like him will suffer disgrace.

10:8 חכם־לב יקח מצות ואויל שפתים ילבט:
The wise of heart receives commandments, but the foolish of lips is ruined.

The same possibilities of interpretation also apply to other proverbs of this type. Proverbs 10:8 could be spoken <u>directively</u>, depicting possible *future* events: "Receive commandments! Then you will be wise and will not be ruined!" Or it may function <u>evaluatively</u>, concerning a situation in the *past*: "I am pleased that you received my commandments. I commend you as wise. This wisdom is why you have flourished." Or, reversing the *positive/negative relationship*: "You have not heeded my commands! You foolish student! Have you not suffered ruin as a result?"

Or, again, the proverb can be spoken such that the first colon lies in the *past* and the second in the *future*: "You have received my commands, so I <u>evaluate</u> you as wise. I <u>direct</u> you to more of the same, for it will dispel

potential ruin." The parallelism in these verses, then, makes them particularly useful as proverbs, able to address a number of different situations
and offer both evaluation and direction.

5.2.3. Conclusion

The openness of the parallelism in these proverbs may have implications
for how we understand the *Tun-Ergehen Zusammenhang*. These verses
do not indicate the agent behind the connection; there are various hints,
but the different possibilities—divine, social, intrinsic—remain open. The
stress is on responsibility rather than agency, both cola presenting prototypical, polar character types, determining behavior and destiny. Each
colon contains a gap, a missing act or consequence. By strongly implying
how to fill these gaps, the proverbs suggest predictable act-character-con-
sequence connections in the world. However, this parallelism also brings
ambiguity to the order. The reversals are only implied, and their precise
content is unclear; any connections must allow for flexibility.

When used as proverbs, these verses have dual evaluative-directive
potential, due to their combination of character and consequence terms.
They are able to speak with a positive or negative relationship to context, and before or after the events described. Within a didactic use too,
openness is a powerful tool, forcing serious engagement with the text and
training certain modes of thought. The readers must flesh out the open
character types through imagination and experience. They can use logical
reasoning to infer the connections between acts, characters, and consequences. This is an essential skill for negotiating an ethical path through
life. Even if connections are not obvious in events, they may be deduced
through careful observation and thought.

5.3. Imagery of the *Schicksalwirkende Tatsphäre*

In the second group of proverbs to be considered, openness is generated
primarily through imagery. Imagery in the proverbs can be rich and evocative, opening up imaginary worlds to their readers (see §2.3 above). I will
examine two such metaphorical worlds, each of which is imagined as a
schicksalwirkende Tatsphäre (a "sphere of activity effecting fate"). Within
the logic of these metaphorical worlds, act and consequence intrinsically
correspond. Deducing the connection in the metaphor trains the readers to deduce it in life and motivates them to act accordingly. The first

imaginary world draws on imagery of "the path," the second "dining on destruction."

5.3.1. The Path[51]

5.3.1.1. Introduction

"Nel mezzo del cammin di nostra vita," begins Dante's *Divine Comedy*: "In the middle of life's road." This metaphor of "del cammin di vita" is recognizable to us all, a ubiquitous trope across cultures, centuries, and religions. We need only think of Taoism (from the Chinese word for "path"), the early Christian movement of the Way (ἡ ὁδός), and the Eightfold Path of Buddhism. The imagery was employed throughout the ancient Near East and in later Zoroastrian and Greek texts.[52] Israel was no exception.

Linguists have described "life is a path" as a basic conceptual metaphor, conventional to many speech communities.[53] Conceptual metaphors are not mere embellishments but tools for structuring thought. They make complex ideas more manageable. Something difficult to understand, like life, is imagined as something simpler, like a path. Reasoning about paths can then be employed to learn about life. Properties, relations, and pat-

---

51. For a fuller exploration of this metaphor, see Suzanna R. Millar, "The Path Metaphor and the Construction of a Schicksalwirkende Tatsphäre in Proverbs 10:1–22:16," *VT* 69 (2019): 95–108.

52. Markus Philipp Zehnder surveys the metaphor in Akkadian, Ugaritic, Aramaic and Egyptian literature; see Zehnder, *Wegmetaphorik im Alten Testament: Eine semantische Untersuchung der alttestamentlichen und altorientalischen Weg-Lexeme mit besonderer Berücksichtigung ihrer metaphorischen Verwendung*, BZAW 268 (Berlin: de Gruyter, 1999), 117–292. Günter Vittmann examines it in Egypt; see Vittmann, *Altägyptische Wegmetaphorik*, Beiträge zur Ägyptologie 15 (Wein: Afro-Pub, 1999). For the metaphor in Zoroastrian and Greek texts, see Gérard-Henry Baudry, *La voie de la vie: Étude sur la catéchèse des pères de l'église*, ThH 110 (Paris: Beauchesne, 1999).

53. For a classic work on conceptual metaphor theory discussing "life is a path," see George Lakoff and Mark Turner, *More Than Cool Reason: A Field Guide to Poetic Metaphor* (Chicago: University of Chicago Press, 1989). The theory is applied to the "path" metaphor in Hebrew Bible by Alec Basson, "The Path Image Schema as Underlying Structure for the Metaphor 'Moral Life is a Journey' in Psalm 25," *OTE* 24 (2011): 19–29; Olaf Jäkel, "How Can Mortal Man Understand the Road He Travels? Prospects and Problems of the Cognitive Approach to Religious Metaphor,'" in *The Bible through Metaphor and Translation: A Cognitive Semantics Perspective*, ed. Kurt Feyaerts (Bern: Lang, 2003), 55–86.

terns of inference are transferred and blended across the domains. The
path can be explored extensively in the imagination before being applied
to interpreter's own circumstances. It brings to mind not a single image
but a whole image schema. Not only is life a path, but "conduct in life is
movement on a path," "dangers in life are hazards on a path," and "advice
about life is guidance along a path."[54]

The "path" (usually דרך) is employed throughout the Hebrew Bible,
especially in Deuteronomy, Psalms, and the prophets.[55] In Proverbs, it has
some distinctive features. In particular, it is removed from its nomistic
and salvation-historical frameworks. It is not linked with the Torah, with
"straying" implying idolatry, nor is it a reminder of the God-led Exodus.[56]
Furthermore, in 10:1–22:16 (in contrast to chapters 1–9), God seems
all but entirely absent along the path.[57] Once we hear of the "way of the
Lord" (דרך יהוה; 10:29), and twice he controls a man's "steps" (צעדו; 16:19;
מצעדי־גבר; 20:24), but elsewhere he is silent. As in many act-consequence
proverbs, divine agency is elusive.

The image may bring various associations. We should not look for
absolute consistency between proverbs but allow the path new undula-
tions each time it is evoked.[58] Its metaphorical world allows for openness
and imagination. Sometimes, the path depicts overall lifestyle, the total
moral course of life. Along the straight path, every step heads straight;

---

54. For fuller elaboration of the schema, see Jäkel, "How Can Mortal Man
Understand."

55. The most comprehensive study is Zehnder, *Wegmetaphorik*. See also Basson,
"Path Image Schema"; Baudry, *Voie de la vie*; Brown, *Seeing the Psalms*, 31–54; André
Gros, *Je suis la Route*, Thèmes Bibliques (Paris: Desclée de Brouwer, 1961); Jäkel,
"How Can Mortal Man Understand"; Øystein Lund, *Way Metaphors and Way Topics
in Isaiah 40–55*, FAT 2.28 (Tübingen: Mohr Siebeck, 2007); Friedrich Nötscher, *Got-
teswege und Menschenwege in der Bibel und in Qumran*, BBB 15 (Bonn: Hanstein,
1958). On roads in ancient Israel, see David A. Dorsey, *The Roads and Highways of
Ancient Israel*, ASOR Library of Biblical and Near Eastern Archaeology (Baltimore:
Johns Hopkins University Press, 1991).

56. This is the case particularly in Isa 40–55. See Gros, *Je suis la Route*; Lund, *Way
Metaphors*. On this in Psalms, see Brown, *Seeing the Psalms*, 31–54. Weeks suggests,
however, that the postexilic readers of Proverbs 1–9 may have found such covenantal
connotations (*Instruction and Imagery*, 148–54).

57. The path in Prov 1–9 is more explicitly theological (e.g., 2:7–8; 3:7, 26; 5:21).
See Habel, "Symbolism of Wisdom"; Weeks, *Instruction and Imagery*, esp. 73–79,
148–54.

58. Lam, *Patterns of Sin*, 163–65.

from the upright man, every deed is upright. In this book of character-based ethics, total disposition determines individual actions. Or, shifting the metaphor, it may imply moral progress, for where is the path heading? Character development is a journey, not an achieved destination.

Many scholars have commented on the image of two paths in Proverbs, separate and unbridgeable.[59] Reveling in absolutes, Proverbs presents the prototypical righteous walking one course, the prototypical wicked another. However, this simplistic polarity is sometimes ambiguated, with the imagery more of "many paths" than of two.[60] Sometimes the wicked and the righteous walk the same path, the former laying snares for the latter (e.g., Prov 1:10–19; 12:6; 22:5).

In general, when the paths are separate, the righteous course is both morally upright and pleasant, the wicked way both corrupt and hazardous.[61] Thus the image combines both act and consequence. In so doing, it creates a metaphorical *schicksalwirkende Tatsphäre*. Many correspondences between deed and outcome are evident in this metaphorical world (explored below). The proverbs suggest that these can be transferred to the target domain of the real world and are true there too. The vagaries of life are clarified by this didactic, simplifying metaphor. It offers a clever rhetorical strategy, encouraging the reader of the truth and obviousness of the connection and motivating him to a proper ethical course.

5.3.1.2. Didactic Explorations

16:17: מסלת ישרים סור מרע שמר נפשו נצר דרכו׃

The highway of the upright is a turning-aside from evil/disaster; he who watches over his path preserves his life.

The first colon of this proverb transports us to a highway traversed by upright men. Its course depicts their conduct, "turning aside from evil" (סור מרע).[62] The infinitive construct allows ambiguity in the subject here.

---

59. See, e.g., Baudry, *Voie de la vie*; Daniel, P. Bricker, "The Doctrine of the 'Two Ways' in Proverbs," *JETS* 38 (1995): 501–17; Habel, "Symbolism of Wisdom."

60. Fox, *Proverbs 1–9*, 129–31.

61. Brown, *Seeing the Psalms*, 36–39; Freuling, *"Wer eine Grube gräbt…,"* 37–39; Klaus Koch, "דרך," *TDOT* 3:270–93, 271–73; Koch, "Is There a Doctrine of Retribution," 135, 164; Nötscher, *Gotteswege und Menschenwege*, 60–64; Zehnder, *Wegmetaphorik*, passim.

62. Cf. Isa 59:15; Pss 34:15[14]; 37:27.

Perhaps the whole highway "turns." The entire course of life is in focus, one's total disposition. Or it may be the individual traveler, in the specific steps he takes. Even upright men might feel temptations to wickedness and must actively "turn" at these moments, training their desires in morality.

In so doing, they also end their trajectory to tragedy, for סור מרע may take a double meaning.[63] רע is polysemous: both "moral evil" and "disaster." Accordingly, misconduct and misfortune are both averted; "turning" becomes a fate-effecting deed. The reader learns to link act and consequence in this metaphorical world, and in his own life. Elsewhere in Proverbs, travelers "turn" (סור) from Sheol (15:24) and from the "snares of death" (13:14; 14:27). Here, the nature of the hardship is open to the imagination. An undisclosed calamity lurks ominously, motivating wayfarers to change their course.

It may be significant that this is not a generic דרך ("path") but a מסלה ("highway"), probably a carefully constructed road (Isa 40:3; 49:11; 62:10).[64] N. L. Tidwell suggests that a מסלה is broad and easily passable, with a gentle gradient. It is well kept and possibly surfaced, so the traveler stumbles over no rocks nor slips in any mud. It is direct and purposeful, well delimited, so he cannot wander off course.[65] It is precisely the type of road that "avoids harm"—סור מרע. Captured by the appealing prospect of safe passage, the reader is motivated to uprightness.

The second colon pleases the ear with its tight internal parallelism: שֹׁמֵר נַפְשׁוֹ ("preserves his life") closely mirrored by נֹצֵר דְּרְכּוֹ ("watches over his path").[66] As I have translated them, the former refers to a consequence and the latter to an act. Through phonological and morphological correspondence (both phrases consisting of a *qal* masculine singular participle and a segolate noun with third-person masculine singular suffix), the deed and effect are linked together, fitting for one another. The

---

63. The double meaning is recognized by Delitzsch, *Biblical Commentary*; Fox, *Proverbs 10–31*; Heim, *Poetic Imagination*; Waltke, *Book of Proverbs 1–15*.

64. There is some dispute about the referent of this term. Dorsey believes it is a major public route: a major regional road, national highway, or international thoroughfare (*Roads and Highways*, 228–33). This remains the standard explanation. N. L. Tidwell disputes this for the biblical period, suggesting that it is an approach road to a city, turning off the regional roads and ascending to the city gate ("No Highway! The Outline of a Semantic Description of *Mesillâ*," *VT* 45 [1995]: 251–69). These differences in opinion do not greatly change the interpretation of this proverb.

65. Tidwell, "No Highway!," 266, 269.

66. Cf. Prov 13:3a: נצר פיו שמר נפשו.

arrangement could be subject-predicate or predicate-subject, suggesting
the mutual entailment of act and consequence. Furthermore, each phrase
may intertwine the halves within itself. Elsewhere in Proverbs, שמר נפשו
refers to preserving one's own life (13:3; 19:16; 22:5), giving individuals responsibility over their own destiny. The phrase, however, may be
polysemous and elsewhere can mean "watch yourself," take care of your
ethical behavior (Deut 4:9; cf. Deut 4:15; Josh 23:11), thus implying an act
as well as a consequence.[67]

Similarly, נצר דרכו may have a double significance. "Watching over
your way" may suggest moral conduct. Elsewhere in Proverbs נצר refers
to "keeping" moral precepts or "paying attention" to behavior.[68] Here, you
must carefully attend to your moral course, without blithe assumptions of
correctness, prepared to turn from any temptation to evil. In so doing, you
will "protect your way," keeping it safe (cf. 2:8, 11; 4:6; 13:6; 20:28). "Guard
the ramparts, watch the road!" (נצור מצורה צפה־דרך) this proverb might
say with Nah 2:2[1], for you are responsible for your own safety. Attending
to the path becomes a *schicksalwirkende Tat*, impacting both course and
condition, conduct and consequence. Ruminating on the interwoven acts
and consequences, the reader learns to connect them in his own life.

This interpretation has taken the participles to refer to the traveler.
However, if both phrases depict consequences, this may not be necessary.
Perhaps "the one who guards the traveler's path [i.e., God] preserves his
life." Yahweh has set the highway to avoid harm (cf. 10:29). He will watch
over the upright man's life (24:12) and protect his way (2:8).[69] Yahweh may
stand in the shadows of this constructed world. Through the interpretation process, the reader is trained to peer into the corners of life, and there
he might find the divine.

---

67. Noting the similarity with the phrase שמר פיו (Prov 21:23), some scholars
suggest this phrase can refer to "watching what you say" (see, e.g., Heim, *Poetic Imagination* on 13:3; Clifford, *Proverbs* on 22:5). This may be supported by the LXX, which
includes the phrase φείσεται στόματος αὐτοῦ ("restrains his mouth"). However, the
LXX is very expansive here, and while נפש can mean "throat," it is nowhere an organ
of speech, so this interpretation seems unlikely.

68. Prov 3:1, 21; 4:13, 23; 5:2; 6:20; 13:3; 28:7; cf. נצר + דרך in an ethical sense in
Ps 119:33.

69. Cf. Pss 25:20; 86:2; 97:10; 121:7. Sometimes personified virtues take this role
in Proverbs: 2:11; 4:6; 13:6; 20:28.

14:22: הלוא־יתעו חרשי רע וחסד ואמת חרשי טוב

Do they not go astray, those who devise evil? But kindness and loyalty—
those who devise good.

This proverb contrasts two polar character types: the "devisers of evil"
(חרשי רע) and the "devisers of good" (חרשי טוב).[70] The terms imply internal dispositions and thought-worlds before any specific actions, and the
general designators "evil" and "good" allow an abundance of content. The
former characters "go astray" (יתעו).[71] This may refer to moral deviation,
like that of the Israelites whom Manasseh "led astray [*hiphil*] to do evil"
(ויתעם ... לעשות את־הרע; 2 Kgs 21:9 // 2 Chr 33:9). The image presupposes
an ethical norm, a set path. Usually in the Hebrew Bible, this is the divinely
given law, but in the noncovenantal discourse of Proverbs, it may suggest
wise instructions, societal values, or an inbuilt moral plumb line. √תעה can
also suggest "to stagger about," as though inebriated (Isa 28:7; Job 12:25);
these apparent "artisans" (חרשים) of evil have the true intellectual clarity of
drunks.[72] Through its rhetorical question, the colon directly addresses its
reader, forces her to think, and compels her assent. She is goaded to view
the world through the categories of the sages.

Further, within the proverb's metaphorical framework, straying implies
harmful consequences.[73] It is a fate-effecting deed. As she imagines straying
from the path, the reader wanders aimlessly, without direction or purpose,
like a desolate nomad (Gen 21:14) or a forlorn beast (Exod 23:4; Isa 53:6; Ps
119:176). The scorching heat of trackless wastes (Ps 107:4; Job 12:24) is the
inevitable fate of deviants—strong motivation against moral error.

In the second colon, "kindness and loyalty" (חסד ואמת) are linked
with the "devisers of good," but the nature of the link is not clear.[74] The

---

70. The LXX preserves two versions of this proverb (14:22a–b and 14:22c–d, followed by Pesh.). In the first, the LXX seems to read חרשו for חרשי, translating it as an
active verb τεκταίνουσι ("they devise").

71. Prov 14:22c in the LXX seems to read ידעו here, translating οὐκ ἐπίστανται
("do not understand").

72. Sometimes, the term חרשים can refer to skillful craftsmanship (Gen 4:22; 1
Kgs 7:14). This impression is even stronger in the cognate noun חָרָשׁ (e.g., Exod 35:35;
2 Sam 5:11; 2 Kgs 24:16; Jer 10:9).

73. Toy paraphrases "go astray" as "go to destruction" (*Critical and Exegetical
Commentary*, 95). So Delitzsch, *Biblical Commentary*, 237.

74. The ambiguity is retained in the LXX (14:22d): kindness and loyalty "are with"
(παρὰ) the devisers of good (followed by Pesh., which has ʿm ["with"]).

reader must infer the connection between the juxtaposed phrases, forging associations between previously unconnected phenomena. It may be predicate-subject: such men are benevolence itself![75] The hyperbolic identification has rhetorical force, and it fleshes out "goodness" with social solidarity. The reader must embody beneficence in her own community, so that it characterizes her whole being.

Alternatively, "kindness and loyalty" may suggest not acts but consequences. The reader may deduce a double meaning and transfer it to her own life. Perhaps "kindness and loyalty *meet* the devisers of good."[76] In *The Pilgrim's Progress*, Christian meets many on the road—Piety, Charity, Watchful, Mr. Feeble-Mind. Similarly, our travelers here are greeted by Kindness and Loyalty. Just as Righteousness "protects" (13:6) and Evil "pursues" (13:21), these personifications treat the wayfarer according to their natures. They are trustworthy guides, preventing the travelers from straying, watching over them as diligently as they watch over the king (20:28). Elsewhere they are God's heralds on the road (Ps 89:15[14]). A divine sender is not mentioned here but may be hidden in the vagaries of proverbs and life.

10:17: ארח לחיים שומר מוסר ועוזב תוכחת מתעה:
A path to life—one who heeds discipline, but one who rejects reproof leads astray.

This proverb draws the reader in with a grand offer of "a path to life" (ארח לחיים). Life, as the epitome of all that is good, is an enticing allure. The path is connected with a character, but the blunt juxtaposition of the nominal phrases means that the relationship between the two is not entirely clear.[77] The reader must discern such links for himself. Perhaps this man walks this path. He is not described as an absolute moral type (like the "righteous") but as "one who heeds discipline" (שומר מוסר). Accordingly,

---

75. Cf. NIV margin, ESV margin: "show love and faithfulness." REB: "are loyal and faithful."

76. Many translations and commentators: ESV, HCSB, KJV, NASB, NIV, RSV; Clifford, *Proverbs*; Delitzsch, *Biblical Commentary*; Murphy, *Proverbs*; Toy, *Critical and Exegetical Commentary*; Waltke, *Book of Proverbs 1–15*.

77. Most LXX manuscripts take the syntax differently—a testament to the openness of the proverb. They construe מוסר as the subject of the verb שומר: ὁδοὺς δικαίας ζωῆς φυλάσσει παιδεία ("education guards the ways of righteous life"). "Righteous" is a moralizing interpolation.

the moral walk is a communal enterprise, requiring wise guides and dis-
cipliners, for no traveler has perfect command of the route. And it is a
journey "to life," not an achieved destination.[78] Development of character
and conduct are possible, and by heeding advice (even this proverb's own
advice), the reader may approach this salutary goal. Conversely, "The one
who rejects reproof leads astray." The *hiphil* מתעה here may be internal:
he "leads *himself* astray."[79] As in 14:22, √תעה may take the double sense
of straying ethically and into disaster. Forsaking instruction, the student
forges his own ethically dubious paths and blindly takes himself into deso-
lation.

But another interpretation is also possible: the proverb focuses not
on the heeder and the rejecter alone but on their actions toward others.
The first colon may be equational: the disciple *is himself* a path to life—
for others. This counterintuitive metaphor flexes our interpretive muscles.
Others have instructed him; now he himself shows the way. Equally,
the untrained man in the second colon leads *others* astray (causative
hiphil).[80] The overall interpretation is complex, a mental challenge to
train the reader. It involves three characters in each colon: implicitly, A
"disciplines"/"reproves" B; B "heeds"/"rejects" this, and then instructs C; C
is consequently led either "to life" or "astray." The proverb thus describes
the acts of B, and the consequences not for himself but for C. A note of
trepidation may enter here, for C, the one "led astray," may be no moral
reprobate but simply a naïve follower, now lost in arid wastelands. Undeserving of his fate, he hints at problems in an overdogmatic *Tun-Ergehen
Zusammenhang.*

However, character B is not let off freely. In this communal world,
guides walk with their travelers, experiencing the same safe paths or trackless deserts. Where he leads others, there he leads himself. The reader
takes this connection, evident in the metaphorical world, and applies it to
his own world. In Prov 10, your attitude to speech and instruction affects
your own destiny (10:8b=10b), the destiny of others (10:11a, 13, 21a), and

---

78. But cf. Prov 2:19; 5:6; 15:24.

79. Internal *hiphils* are not uncommon for verbs of motion. For example, הקריב
("to [cause oneself to] come close"; e.g., Exod 14:10) and הרחיק ("to [cause oneself to]
go far away"; e.g., Gen 44:4). Though the passage is difficult, an internal *hiphil* of התעה
("to [cause oneself to] go astray") may also occur in Jer 42:20. See *IBHS*, 27.2g. This
understanding is reflected in Pesh. and Targ., which use the G rather than C stem.

80. The object is elided, as in Isa 3:12; Hos 4:12.

sometimes both (10:6b=11b, 14b).[81] The layers of double meaning imply both here.[82]

צדקת תמים תישר דרכו וברשעתו יפל רשע: 11:5
The righteousness of blameless men straightens/levels his way, but in his wickedness the wicked man falls.

If those in 14:22a and 10:17b are going astray, those in 11:5a are doing their utmost to avoid this. They intentionally "straighten" (תישר) their way against tempting deviations (cf. Prov 4:25; 9:15; 15:21), walking the ethical line set by God, society, or inbuilt morality. This action stems from their "righteousness" (צדקה), character determining conduct. In תישר, they also "level" their way: removing obstacles, smoothing the surface (e.g., Isa 40:3–4; 45:2).[83] Undoubtedly a laborious process, this metaphor suggests the careful, wearisome work required for ethical development. The result, however, is worth the effort. The straight/level path is smooth and easily traversable, giving no cause for stumbling (Jer 31:9). It is direct, destination in sight (Ps 107:7), promising a safe passage (Ezra 8:21). In this metaphorical world, straightening/leveling one's path is a *schicksal-wirkende Tat*, leading to a prosperous journey. The reader deduces this connection, blends it with the situations of her own world, and is motivated to righteousness.

The wicked man, however, walks a very different path, which the reader infers (through the imprecise parallelism) cannot be smooth or straight. Indeed, along its course, he "falls." The fall, however, cannot be

---

81. This assumes that 10:13b provides a second subject for תמצא in 13a: "On the lips of the discerning is found … a rod for the back of the senseless." The wise punish fools through their words. In 14b, the fool's mouth brings ruin to himself and others (see above, §5.2.1). 10:6b=11b reads ופי רשעים יכסה חמס. There is a subject-object ambiguity here, so the colon could mean "The mouth of the wicked covers violence" or "Violence covers the mouth of the wicked." The first arrangement might suggest that the wicked do violence and seek to hide it through words (act); see, e.g., Fox, *Proverbs 10–31*. This would provide an antithetical parallelism to 11a, which speaks of words' effect on others. In the second arrangement, perhaps violence comes upon the wicked man (consequence), just as blessings come upon the righteous in 6a; see, e.g., Clifford, *Proverbs*.

82. This double meaning is recognized by Clifford, *Proverbs*; Murphy, *Proverbs*; Waltke, *Book of Proverbs 1–15*.

83. Luis Alonso Schökel, "ישר," *TDOT* 6:463–72; Dorsey, *Roads and Highways*, 3.

blamed on extraneous circumstances, but only on his own character: it is "because of his wickedness" (ברשעתו, parsing the ב causally).[84] Or, he falls *into* his wickedness (the ב interpreted locatively). Perhaps wickedness encloses his character, ingraining him in patterns of sin from which he cannot escape. Furthermore, it suggests his consequent downfall. Far from straight level paths, pits and snares may hide round a corner or beneath the uneven surface (cf. Prov 13:14; 14:27; 22:5; 26:27; 28:10).[85] In the reader's imagining, "his wickedness" (רשעתו) might become "his net" (רשתו), to entangle and entrap. Perceiving the soundplay, the reader connects act and consequence. This is "his" wickedness/net—completely in line with his character, entirely his responsibility. Elsewhere, a psalmist pleads, "Let the wicked fall into their own nets" (יפלו במכמריו רשעים; Ps 141:10); here, he has his wish. The wicked man characteristically lays traps for others, but he becomes his own prey (cf. Prov 26:27; 28:10).[86] Just recompense provides a heavy disincentive from wickedness.

5.3.1.3. Conclusion

Weaving through their metaphorical worlds, the proverbs' open paths can be explored extensively. In these worlds, act and consequence often correspond. Disciples offer "a path to life" to others, and they walk one themselves (10:17). Do-gooders act in and experience "kindness and loyalty" (14:22). Some deeds prove fate-effecting, with a single phrase encompassing both act and consequence. "Watching over" and "straightening" your way ensure good conduct and consequences simultaneously. "Straying" and setting traps are ethical misdemeanors and harbingers of destruction. Within the logic of this metaphorical world, such connections are obvious. The readers discern the patterns and can blend them imaginatively with the situations of their own lives.

---

84. Williams, *William's Hebrew Syntax*, §247.

85. The "hazard" metaphor is continued into the following proverb, which seems paired thematically, lexically, and syntactically with this one. 11:6b reads ובהות בגדים ילכדו ("In the desire/disaster of the treacherous, they are captured"). The meaning of הות is disputed. It may be a by-form of אוה ("desire"; cf. Prov 10:3; Mic 7:3; Ps 52:9[7]), or an unusual singular form of הוות ("disaster; cf. Job 6:2; 30:13). It is possible that a wordplay is intended, connecting act with consequence. Either way, the hazard metaphor entraps wrongdoers here too.

86. Cf. also Pss 9:16–17[15–16]; 57:7[6].

This may provide strong incentive to good behavior. Why stray morally if it means wandering in the wilderness? Why lay a net if you will get tangled in it yourself? Your choice of path, your total disposition, determines each fate-effecting deed, making character development paramount. Life is a journey, and with careful and constant attention, progress is possible.

No interventionist agents are named. If I find myself forlornly wandering the wilderness, I have my own ethical wanderings to blame. No external agent is needed for "straying" to entail "straying." Sometimes, though, a divine mapmaker may be implicit. Sometimes social agency is stressed: we are each other's guides. Through this, a hint of unease enters the act-consequence connection, for it is possible to lead undeserving victims astray (14:22; 10:17) or to set a net for their feet (11:5).

5.3.2. Dining on Destruction

5.3.2.1. Introduction

Our second metaphorical schema welcomes the reader into the banquet hall. From Lady Wisdom's feast (9:1–6) to the "delicious morsels" of the whisperer (18:8; 26:22), food metaphors abound in Proverbs, whetting the reader's tastebuds or setting him retching in disgust.[87] The metaphor is accessible to all and provides training for the sensory imagination. In the proverbs examined here, individuals eat, ingest, and are filled with evil itself. It may empower their activity, energizing their wicked deeds, but it may also prove a poison.

In the Hebrew Bible, wicked qualities sometimes become a foodstuff, greedily consumed by wrongdoers, and characterizing their subsequent action. Men drink "injustice" (עולה) and "scoffing" (לעג) like water (Job 15:16; 34:7). They salivate over the sweet savor of sin, hiding "trouble" (עמל), "iniquity" (און), and "evil" (רעה) under their tongues (Ps 10:7; Job 20:12). They feast on the "bread of wickedness" (לחם רשע) and "wine of violence" (יין חמסים; Prov 4:17). Fools feed on "folly" (אולת; Prov 15:14).[88] Such food energizes them and creates their character, for in this metaphorical

---

87. See Brown, "Didactic Power."

88. Cf. also imagery of being "filled with" (מלא) negative behavior, e.g., "violence" (חמס) in Ezek 28:16; Mic 6:12; "indignation" (זעם) in Jer 15:17; "wrath" (חמה) in Jer 6:11.

world, "You are what you eat."[89] But as much as food empowers, it can also poison.[90] The Lord pours the foaming cup of his wrath and fills the belly with "his fury" (חֲרוֹן אַפּוֹ; Job 20:23).[91] Lamenting psalmists drink deeply of anguished tears (Pss 42:3; 80:6[5]; 102:9). Men are filled with "sorrow" (יָגוֹן; Ezek 23:33) and sated with "shame" (קָלוֹן; Hab 2:16), and they drink the "violence" they suffer (חָמָס; Prov 26:6).

Thus eating may be a *schicksalwirkende Tat*—at once empowering activity and effecting consequences. In the proverbs examined here, an individual consumes evil. Act and consequence are infused together in a single draft: an elixir that energizes evil activity but simultaneously poisons its drinker. Adding this to the mix of her own life, the reader is powerfully disincentivized from evil.

5.3.2.2 Didactic Explorations

עֵד בְּלִיַּעַל יָלִיץ מִשְׁפָּט וּפִי רְשָׁעִים יְבַלַּע־אָוֶן׃ 19:28:
A worthless witness scoffs at justice, and the mouth of the wicked scoffs down iniquity/trouble.

This proverb begins in the law court, with a man of such perverted values that he mocks justice. The second colon explains his behavior: the "worthless man" (בְּלִיַּעַל) scoffs because he is full of the iniquity he has "scoffed down" (יְבַלַּע).[92] Repetition of ע-ל-ב and double *patakh* patterns forge a phonic and conceptual unity here.[93] "Iniquity" (אָוֶן) comes into the man; scoffing comes out. Iniquity is almost an independent force,

---

89. Greg Schmidt Goering, "Honey and Wormwood: Taste and the Embodiment of Wisdom in the Book of Proverbs," *HBAI* 5 (2016): 23–41.

90. On the "bad taste" metaphor for distress, see Phil D. King, *Surrounded by Bitterness: Image Schemas and Metaphor for Conceptualizing Distress in Classical Hebrew* (Eugene, OR: Pickwick, 2012), 322–54.

91. Cup of wrath: Isa 51:17, 22; Jer 25:15; Ezek 23:33; Zech 12:2; Hab 2:16; Pss 11:6; 75:9[8]; Job 21:20.

92. The translation (with "scoffs" framing the center of the verse) intends to capture the aesthetic effect of the wordplay.

93. This striking assonance is probably why *piel* was chosen here rather than *qal*. In *qal*, √בלע means "to swallow down," but in *piel*, it usually means "to destroy." An "eating" sense here is accepted by most commentators and is suggested by (1) the reference to the "mouth" (פִי); (2) the antithesis with the *a* colon (giving out—taking in); (3) the semantic difficulty of the usual *piel* sense ("destroys iniquity"?); (4) the possible meaning "devour" for *piel* √בלע in Prov 21:21; (5) the LXX's translation as καταπίεται,

poisoning his actions, ingraining him in sin.[94] We act out of what we have internalized to our characters, and here character has become extreme, prototypically wicked.

In Proverbs' urgency to shape the holistic moral self with its desires, this metaphor suggests the wicked man's appetite for wrongdoing. He devours it, greedily gobbling it up, for evil tastes sweet to the wicked (Job 20:12; cf. Prov 9:17; 18:8=26:22). The reader deduces that this is an abominable desire and shapes his own desires in opposition. The language suggests the man's thoughtlessness: he acts impulsively from his unrestrained appetite, without consideration of consequences.

But consequences will come. The promised feast turns to poison, and the meaning of אָוֶן turns from "iniquity" to "trouble." With caricatured idiocy, the wicked man gobbles up his own punishment, and the reader is goaded to judge his sensibleness. No external agency is indicated; the disaster is entirely self-inflicted. The content of this disaster, gut-wrenching and inescapable, is left to the reader's imagination, repulsing him from wickedness. The reader deduces the inevitable connection between act and consequence in this proverb.[95] Using the same word, אָוֶן, to depict both suggests that they are appropriate to one another in degree and kind. Devouring iniquity is fate-effecting, and the ensuing disaster is of bowel-trembling intensity.

12:21: לֹא־יְאֻנֶּה לַצַּדִּיק כָּל־אָוֶן וּרְשָׁעִים מָלְאוּ רָע׃
No harm befalls the righteous, but the wicked are full of evil/disaster.

---

which frequently translates qal √בלע ("to swallow") elsewhere; and (6) the proverb's resultant fit within the metaphorical schema delineated here.

94. This act interpretation is accepted by, e.g., Barucq, "Proverbes (Livre Des)"; Clifford, *Proverbs*; Delitzsch, *Biblical Commentary*; Fox, *Proverbs 10–31*; Victor Avigdor Hurovitz, "Unsavoury Personalities in the Book of Proverbs in Light of Mesopotamian Writings," *HS* 54 (2013): 93–106. Some reject it because iniquitous acts should be given out, not taken in (cf. Targ. מפיק ["gives out"]) and propose emending to יביע ("he utters"): *BHS* (though not *BHQ*); Toy, *Critical and Exegetical Commentary*; Gemser, *Sprüche Salomos*; Helmer Ringgren, Urtur Weiser, and Walther Zimmerli, *Sprüche/Prediger*, ATD 16 (Göttingen: Vandenhoeck & Ruprecht, 1962). However, this disrupts the soundplay and is unnecessary. Others suggest a connection with the Arabic root balaġa ("to be eloquent"). *HALOT*; McKane, *Proverbs*. But this is a speculative stretch for a common Hebrew verb.

95. The double meaning is recognized by Waltke (*Book of Proverbs 1–15*) and hinted at by Luis Alonso Schökel (*Proverbios*, Nueva Biblia Española, Sapienciales 1 [Madrid: Cristiandad, 1984]) and Roland E. Murphy (*Proverbs*).

רע fills the wicked. While the opposite prototype, the righteous man, avoids even external harm (21a), the wicked are saturated with disaster, total and all-consuming.[96] Elsewhere, the Lord "fills" the hungry with "good" (מלא טוב; Ps 107:9; cf. 104:28), but here, the stative verb (מלא, *qal*) means there is no hint of external agency. Our fixed and sickened gaze is on the wicked man's self-inflicted and irremediable state, capturing the imagination and powerfully motivating us to avoid wickedness.

However, רע is polysemous and may refer not just to disastrous conse-quences but to the man's evil *acts*.[97] Some scholars reject this interpretation, arguing that because consequences are depicted in the *a* colon, parallel consequences are needed in *b*.[98] However, as we have seen (§5.2), Proverbs revels in such imprecision for the gap-filling potential it provides. Perhaps "the wicked are filled with evil acts [*and harm befalls them*]" (supplying a reversal from *a*). The reader thus works out the connection between act and consequence. The very preceding verse has the same imbalance. In 12:20, the good receive joy (a consequence; 20b), but the evil have deceit in their hearts (an act; 20a). The heart in 12:20 houses deceit, presumably determining character and activity (cf. 12:23). The whole being in 12:21 is pervaded with evil; how much more will this infiltrate their deeds? Just as Jeremiah cannot hold in the wrath that "fills" him (מלא; Jer 6:11), our wicked man brims with an evil that will inevitably overflow into action. The proverb is stark in its absolute statement: wicked men are full of evil, and that alone.

The proverb, then, is open to implications of both act and consequence, and presents them together under the figure מלאו רע.[99] In this metaphori-cal world, allowing evil to fill you becomes a *schicksalwirkende Tat*. The wicked man may think he has mastery over it, but he gets ingrained in patterns of ill, whose potency rebounds and infects his being with disaster. The metaphor is didactic, making accessible this somewhat complex view

---

96. Thus, in the MT, the *a* colon depicts consequences. In the versions, it depicts acts/attitudes. The LXX and Pesh. (=Targ.) seem to reflect the reading יגאה instead of יאנה (metathesis)—no injustice "will please" (ἀρέσει; Pesh. has *špyr* ["is beautiful to"]) the righteous. See McKane, *Proverbs*; Murphy, *Proverbs*; Waltke, *Book of Proverbs 1–15*.

97. Yoder, *Proverbs*.

98. Waltke, *Book of Proverbs 1–15*.

99. Double meaning is recognized by Clifford (*Proverbs*) and Fox (*Proverbs 10–31*).

of morality. It further suggests that the connection is inevitable and obvious: of course you will suffer if you fill yourself with such poison.

מפרי פי־איש יאכל טוב ונפש בגדים חמס: 13:2

From the fruit of a man's mouth, one/he will eat good;
>> but the throat of the treacherous (will eat) violence.
>> but the desire of the treacherous is for violence.

Three threads of double meaning intertwine in 13:2a. First, it offers us "the fruit of a man's mouth" (cf. 12:14; 18:21). On the one hand, this metaphor may depict speech, the fruit that the mouth produces (an act). The fruit here proves "good" (טוב), so the reader deduces that the speaker (simply designated a "man" [איש]) is good, too.[100] The lack of the expected character ascription leaves us wondering and encourages us to apply an important principle: character is known through speech and action. But on the other hand, the metaphor also suggests consequences—the fruit the mouth enjoys. Here, the identity of the eater is unclear, providing the second thread of double meaning. יאכל has no explicit subject: a second individual or the speaker himself may "eat" (translating "one" and "he" respectively).[101] That is to say, the speaker gives good fruit to others (an act) and enjoys it himself (a consequence). Third, the good that is consumed may both empower the eater's actions and characterize the benefits he receives.

Conversely "the throat of the treacherous eats violence." This interprets נפש in its physiological sense, "throat," and assumes יאכל to be gapped into the second colon.[102] Earlier in Proverbs, the wicked "drink the wine of violence" (4:17). Here the treacherous eat it, taking it in as the directing and energizing fuel for their acts. The verb here (אכל) is less forceful than "devour" (בלע) in 19:28. Violence has become commonplace, as natural

---

100. The lack of explicit character qualification may have been problematic for the Greek translator, who takes טוב as the subject (ἀγαθός), and changes איש ("man") to δικαιοσύνης ("righteousness")—"The good man will eat from the fruits of righteousness."

101. Or, following the LXX, the subject may be טוב—"The good man eats from the fruit of a man's mouth."

102. So, e.g., KJV; Fox, *Proverbs 10–31*. Some object to this interpretation because the נפש is nowhere else said to "eat." See, e.g., Toy, *Critical and Exegetical Commentary*. But elsewhere it is hungry, thirsty, satisfied, and filled, so this seems a natural extension.

as eating and drinking. Mealtime routine structures the day, and violence structures the lives of the wicked. Developing the habits, and hence the character, of the "good" must fuel the reader instead.

Alternatively, "eating violence" may depict a consequence (cf. Prov 26:6). Its poison burns the insides and cannot be escaped, as surely as you cannot escape from yourself. The treacherous men in this proverb, then, are immensely foolish. They intend violence to be their elixir, but it inevitably turns toxic. It is fate-effecting to dine on such destruction, and no external agent can be blamed. The metaphor teaches the reader to conceptualize good and violence in this new and didactically useful way. Through the imaginative leap, she learns that act and consequence are baked together in a single dish.

Proverbs 13:2–4 focalizes the נפש, with even an acrostic in the central proverb (the first letters of the words in 13:3 are נפשנפש). The term occurs in each of these verses, and its various meanings are played with, prohibiting a simple, unified translation—NABRE gives "throat," "self," "appetite"; ESV gives "desire," "life," "soul" for the verses respectively. Possibly, it expresses the "living self/person" of the treacherous here, in a blunt juxtaposition: "the treacherous person—violence!" By this interpretation, he may act in violence or suffer from it.[103]

The throat, as the locus of the appetite, can also provide a semantic extension to "desire." This may be the case in 13:2, requiring the syntax of *b* to be reparsed as an equational clause: "the desire of the treacherous is (for) violence."[104] This creates an unbalanced parallelism in the proverb, from which the reader infers that the man in *a* does *not* desire violence and that the treacherous will *not* eat good.[105] Improper desire may be faintly hinted in 13:3, and it is outright condemned in 13:4: "The נפש of the slug-

---

103. נפש is frequently used to represent the acting person in Priestly legislation (e.g., Lev 2:1; 4:2, 27). Cf. also Prov 11:25 נפש ברכה ("the person who blesses"). In a number of instances, נפש is in construct with a person/type ("life of X"), in contexts expressing potential harm to that person's life (e.g., Num 35:31; 1 Sam 25:29; 2 Sam 19:6; 1 Kgs 1:12; 3:11; Jer 20:13; Ps 74:19). The LXX may be unpacking the logic of this in its paraphrase: "The souls of lawbreakers will untimely perish" (ψυχαὶ δὲ παρανόμων ὀλοῦνται ἄωροι). Cf. also Pesh.—*wnpšthwn d'wl' n'bdn* ("The *npš* of the wicked will perish").

104. So Delitzsch, *Biblical Commentary*; Toy, *Critical and Exegetical Commentary*; Waltke, *Book of Proverbs 1–15*. נפש rarely refers to righteous desires, but it designates those of evil men in, e.g., Exod 15:9; Ezek 16:27; Ps 27:13[12].

105. The lack of precise parallelism has proved difficult for some interpreters (see

gard craves and gets nothing."[106] The triad of proverbs aims to shape the reader's desires as well as her actions. Woe betide her if she fosters violent longings; she must look only to good fruit (13:2a).

The two parsings of *b* may work together, one providing the logical precursor to the other. "The desire of the treacherous is for violence." So, imprudently, they make it their meal, and "the throat of the treacherous eats violence." They will suffer accordingly. Working out, imagining, and elaborating such a narrative trains the reader to internalize Proverbs' logic for her own life.

ערב לאיש לחם שקר ואחר ימלא־פיהו חצץ: 20:17
Sweet to a man is the bread of lies, but afterward his mouth will be filled with gravel.

The foodstuff here is more concrete than in previous examples: "bread of lies" (לחם שקר). Perhaps this is physical food, earned through deceitful enterprise (genitive of means), a practice elsewhere condemned in Proverbs (11:18; 13:11).[107] Or perhaps the bread is figurative, the "lies" describing not its source but its constitution (attributive genitive). The man delights in falsehoods and indulges in them as his meal. Deceit thereby enters his very being. It becomes his daily bread, habituated into his character. As in Prov 13:2, he is simply a "man" (איש), without ethical qualification; the reader must evaluate his morality for himself.

The "sweetness" (√ערב) of this bread is an acute psychological insight: the sensual pleasures and immediate gratification of wrongdoing can be seductive. The wicked refuse to spit out the evil that they suck (Job 20:12–13), while Lady Folly's lips drip honey (Prov 5:3). The reader is teased with a promise that may tempt every "man" (איש). However, sweetness turns to venom (Job 20:14) and honey to wormwood (Prov 5:4). Here, in what is possibly a subtle soundplay, "desire" (חפץ) dissipates as bread turns to "gravel" (חצץ).[108] This has the last word, and

---

discussion in J. A. Emerton, "The Meaning of Proverbs XIII.2," *JTS* 35 [1984]: 91–95), and some suspect textual corruption (e.g., Toy, *Critical and Exegetical Commentary*).

106. The one who "opens wide his lips" (פשק שפתיו) in 13:3 is probably a rash talker, but in the context of 13:2 and 13:4 could hint at the greedy man too.

107. Williams, *William's Hebrew Syntax*, §45b; Delitzsch, *Biblical Commentary*; McKane, *Proverbs*. See pp. above §2.1.2 on polysemies in these verses.

108. So Stewart, *Poetic Ethics*, 149.

the sensory experience is reoriented. A jolt of the jaw as it grinds on gravel (cf. Lam 3:16), disgust replaces the pleasantries, and the senses are stirred against deceit. The psychological jolt occasioned by the unexpected trains the reader for encountering unforeseen events in life, even if they are as absurd and vile as a faceful of stones.

This leads to a second interpretation of שׁקֶר—not as lies the man engages in, but as a quality of the bread itself, for it deceives its eater.[109] Elsewhere, rulers offer "deceptive food" (לֶחֶם כְּזָבִים; Prov 23:3) that provides no sustenance. Here, no third party is involved; interest is solely on the eater and his responsibility. As Waltke remarks, "In poetic justice, the deceptive fare the liar and cheat dished out to others now turns around and deceives him."[110] This is a true correspondence of act and consequence: a lie for a lie. While the previous proverbs stressed the sheer obviousness of the connection, a nuance is added here. For those not trained in wisdom, wicked acts are deceptive. They may look beneficial, but they will harm you in the end (cf. Prov 14:12=16:25). The proverbs thus counsel scrutiny: "Observe carefully what is before you" (Prov 23:1).

5.3.2.3. Conclusion

These four proverbs offer a rich metaphorical world, open to exploration. The controlling image is "dining on destruction": the individual consumes something evil, and his acts and their consequences are characterized accordingly. The readers are encouraged to explore this world—with its implications, patterns of reasoning, and nuances—and to blend it into the situations of their own worlds. Openness occurs through the generality of the key terms—אָוֶן, רַע, חָמָס, שֶׁקֶר—which may refer to acts or to consequences. Designated by the same word, the latter befits the former. In this metaphorical world, consumption is *schicksalwirkend*, fate-effecting. If you internalize evil, it will inevitably harm you. Applied to the reader's own world, such patterns of reasoning provide strong moral motivation.

Unlike elsewhere in the Hebrew Bible, where harmful food is given by another, no external agents are named here.[111] Rather, the eater himself is

---

109. Fox, *Proverbs 10–31*; Raymond C. van Leeuwen, "Proverbs," in *A Complete Literary Guide to the Bible*, ed. Leland Ryken and Tremper Longmann III (Grand Rapids: Zondervan, 1993), 256–67.

110. Waltke, *Book of Proverbs 1–15*, 146.

111. See, e.g., King, *Surrounded by Bitterness*, 348.

responsible. His character is paramount, controlling both what he does and what he experiences. As food enters the digestive system and energizes the body, wickedness enters the wrongdoer and empowers his activity. It takes hold of him, ingraining him in patterns of wrong. Hence the importance of character development, habitually nourishing yourself through proper practice. The proverbs show the appetites of the wicked and even make them look "sweet" (20:17). But they teach condemnation of such cravings, shaping the reader's own desires.

Thus the proverbs offer their own categories and patterns as a lens for viewing the world. Their metaphorical framework simplifies a complex view of morality, and the readers are powerfully disincentivized through their promise of poison. Consider your food before you eat, lest it turn toxic. Consider your deed before you do it, lest it prove a *schicksalwirkende Tat*.

5.3.3. Used as Proverbs

In addition to its didactic benefits, the openness of these "path" and "dining" sayings helps them to function as proverbs. They become multi-situational and multifunctional. In part, this is due to their generality and metaphor, and their multiple base meanings. I will use 16:17 and 19:28 as examples here, though the principles apply more widely.

16:17: מסלת ישרים סור מרע שמר נפשו נצר דרכו:
The highway of the upright is a turning-aside from evil/disaster; he who watches over his path preserves his life.

19:28: עד בליעל יליץ משפט ופי רשעים יבלע-און:
A worthless witness scoffs at justice, and the mouth of the wicked scoffs down iniquity/trouble.

In the imprecise parallelisms of the previous section, the proverbs each contained a concrete act, easily mapped onto the context. Someone "hates a lying word" (13:5); another "receives commandments" (10:8). No such straightforward description occurs in the proverbs here. Rather, they are expressed through metaphor: someone "walks a path"; another "consumes a meal." Applying a metaphor to a situational context is a complex, imaginative process (see §2.3.3 above). Saying "my pathway turns" (16:17), I might blend my encyclopedic knowledge of this image with many different situations. If I discover minor ills that need careful negotiation, my imagined path might undulate gently. If I foresee a major disaster, it makes a hairpin. The "highway" might run through my economic enterprises (I perhaps recall its careful construction), social relationships (imagining fellow travelers), or religious affairs (picturing a pilgrimage procession).

The presence of the "worthless witness" means that 19:28 is most obviously applied in the judicial sphere. But the witness may also be figurative of unjust individuals more broadly. Then the connotations of "scoffing down" might change too. In economics, it may imply money-grubbing; in society, selfishness; and in religion, thoughtless irreverence.

Furthermore, the generality in these proverbs makes them multiapplicable. What is the "evil" from which my pathway turns? What is the "iniquity" in which the wicked indulge? Scamming a customer (e.g., 11:1)? Quarreling with a spouse (21:9)? Scorning an offering (14:9)? These general terms also increase the proverbs' evaluative potential. If I say "The highway of the upright turns from evil" (16:17), I have evaluated not only my interlocutor as upright but the action avoided as evil. If "wicked men gobble up iniquity" (19:28), my referent is "wicked," and furthermore his acts are "iniquitous." By speaking the proverb, I have claimed the situation for my evaluative system, applying and nuancing the categories inherited from the sages. I call on my hearer to do the same.

The proverbs are not, however, so vague that they cannot find traction in the circumstances. Most do contain some indication of a concrete action, some hook to attach onto the context.[112] 19:28a entails that the wicked man has made a mockery of justice. In 16:17a, not only has my hearer not done evil, but he has actively turned from it, implying some previous temptation to take a wicked course.

Finally, as shown throughout this chapter, the "path" and "dining" proverbs are open to different base meanings. In particular, they might describe the act done or the consequences received. "Turning from רע" means avoiding not only ethical "evil" but consequential "disaster." "Gobbling up און" is not only acting in "iniquity" but suffering the resultant "trouble." Applied to a context, one or other of these nuances may come to the fore. Accordingly, the proverbs may not only evaluate but motivate

---

112. These proverbs could be spoken when someone has, for example, devised good/evil (14:22), shown kindness/loyalty (14:22), received/not received discipline (10:17), "straightened" their way (11:5), "fallen" (11:5), scoffed (19:28), engaged in/desired violence (13:2), or indulged in bread/benefits/lies (20:17). Only 12:21 seems to have no concrete hook.

and <u>direct</u>. "Be upright!" I imply, "so that your path turns from disaster" (16:17). "Don't be wicked! Or you'll be gobbling up trouble" (19:28). Powerful incentives lie in these dramatic consequences, expressed inexplicitly to entice the mind. Hearers are left to imagine and thereby to disincentivize themselves. The double meanings, if perceived, allow the proverbs simultaneously to evaluate and direct.

5.4. Problematizing Polysemies

We have considered proverbs opened by parallelism and imagery. The final examples in this chapter mainly use polysemy. Through their openness, they may undermine a dogmatic understanding of the act-consequence connection. The proverbs in §5.2 above stressed the predictability of the world order but gave hints of ambiguity. Here the ambiguity is more prevalent. I suggest that these proverbs each have a double interpretation. One interpretation affirms the world order and its act-consequence nexus; the other subverts it. Contradictions may therefore emerge not only *between* proverbs but even *within* them, between different interpretations of the polysemy.[113] Readers may be torn between the meanings or may apply each to a different situation.

5.4.1. Didactic Explorations

11:24: יש מפזר ונוסף עוד וחושך מישר אך־למחסור:
There is one who scatters, and he is increased more, and one who holds back from uprightness—only to scarcity.

Proverbs 11:24 provokes the reader with its bald assertion of paradox: giving out gives back; holding back backfires.[114] Aphorism-like, its enigma draws the reader in so as to train his mind. Furthermore, there is an additional complexity: the evaluation of the characters' morality, and hence whether they deserve their destiny, is open to interpretation. By one reading, the proverb affirms the act-consequence connection, but problematizing polysemies may undermine it.

---

113. On contradictions between proverbs, see, e.g., Hatton, *Contradiction*.

114. Proverbs beginning with יש often present paradoxes (e.g., 13:7, 23; 14:12 = 16:25; cf. Qoh 2:21; 7:15; 8:14; Sir 4:21; 6:9, 10; 10:31; 11:11, 12).

Rather than describe a prototypical character type, the first colon introduces the מפזר—the "scatterer." The verb suggests wide and haphazard dispersal. This may depict charitable giving. Like the righteous one who "has scattered [פזר], has given to the poor" (Ps 112:9), the man here may be a model of magnanimity, liberally bestowing his own bounty on all (cf. Prov 14:21, 31; 19:17; 21:26; 22:9). For the student, he becomes a paradigm for emulation. But the verb itself is vague, reticent about its object and motive.[115] The mere activity of scattering does not reveal the character beneath (in contrast with the obvious manifestations of character in acts elsewhere). Economically, it may suggest broad investment of personal finances, for who knows "which will prosper, this or that" (Qoh 11:1–6). The proverb would then offer morally neutral business acumen.[116] Or the "scatterer" may be a reckless spender.[117] Elsewhere, Proverbs commends financial prudence (e.g., 11:15; 17:18; 20:16) and warns that the "lover of wine and oil will not be rich" (21:17). Here, the character may have no such quibbles but indulges his fancies with unrestrained relish.

In contrast is set the חושך מישר, "the one who holds back from uprightness." If the scatterer is generous, he is the opposite: an antisocial, tight-fisted miser.[118] ישֶׁר is here taken metonymically, "what is right" (cf. Job 33:23). The מן may be ablative—"holds back (from doing) what is right"—or comparative—"holds back (more than) what is right."[119] Either way, he is an antitype to avoid. Niggardliness in Proverbs may bespeak deeper ills, for "the righteous gives and does not hold back [לא יחשך]" (Prov 21:26). But "holding back" is not always negative. In fact, perhaps the man holds back—that is, saves money—"because of his uprightness" (מישר, parsing the מן causally and taking ישר in its usual sense as a character quality).[120] The proverb then speaks of prudence, financial decisions rooted in an upright character.

---

115. Elsewhere, the objects are diverse: sheep (Jer 50:17), bones (Pss 53:6[5]; 141:7), enemies (Ps 89:11[10]), frost (Ps 147:16), nations (Joel 4:2[3:2]; Esth 3:8).

116. Murphy, *Proverbs*; possibility raised by McKane, *Proverbs*; Yoder, *Proverbs*.

117. Fox, *Proverbs 10–31*.

118. Negative character types are evident in the moralizing paraphrases of Pesh. (ʿyt ddʾ dylh mknš ["one who gathers what is not his"]) and Vulg. (*alii rapiunt non sua* ["others seize what is not theirs"]).

119. For the former of these interpretations, cf., e.g., 1 Sam 25:39: חשך מרעה ("he held back from [doing] evil"); cf. also Ps 19:14[13].

120. Fox, *Proverbs 10–31*. On causal *min*, see Williams, *William's Hebrew Syntax*, §319. Cf. 2 Sam 3:11; Ish-bosheth could not answer "because of his fear" (מיראתו).

Overall, then, the proverb may contrast the generous with the miserly, or the reckless with the cautious. They all get the opposite of what their behavior would suggest. The scatterer "is increased again" (נוֹסָף עוֹד), and the refrainer comes "to poverty" (אַךְ לְמַחְסוֹר; cf. 14:23; 21:5; 22:16). No agent is specified behind these fates; indeed, the first colon gives a passive conjugation and the second gives a blunt juxtaposition. The connection remains unexplained, impelling the reader to wonder.

If the generous and miserly are in view, then the proverb upholds the act-consequence connection. Unambiguously in 28:27, and implicitly here too, "whoever gives to the poor will have no scarcity [אֵין מַחְסוֹר]" (cf. also 22:16). Acts will be recompensed in kind—by Yahweh, by society, by some intrinsic causality, the options are open. The proverb motivates the reader to embody beneficence and shun parsimony. This interpretation is supported by literary context. The proverb compilers have followed this verse with two similar sayings, each emphatically affirming the *Zusammenhang*: "The person who blesses will be enriched, and one who waters, he too will be watered. The one who holds back grain, the people curse, but blessing is on the head of the one who sells it."

However, each proverb must also be allowed to speak in its own right. As the reader ponders 11:24, he may contemplate the possibility of the reckless man's riches and the prudent man's penury, contradicting act-consequence logic. Such cynical paradoxes are known from late Egyptian texts. So P.Ins. 7.15–16: "It is not the wise man who saves who finds a surplus. Nor is it the one who spends who becomes poor."[121] In Prov 11:24, the possible double meaning may serve to train the reader's mind. He must acknowledge ambiguities in proverbs and the world, judging the interpretations through wisdom and experience.

11:16: אֵשֶׁת־חֵן תִּתְמֹךְ כָּבוֹד וְעָרִיצִים יִתְמְכוּ־עֹשֶׁר:
The gracious woman takes hold of honor; ruthless men take hold of riches.

The beginning of 11:16 seems to present clear *Tun-Ergehen* logic. Like the widely praised "woman of valor" (אֵשֶׁת־חַיִל; Prov 31:28, 31), the "woman of grace" (אֵשֶׁת־חֵן) attains society's greatest reward: honor. The *b* colon provides parallel syntax and verbal repetition, suggesting that its message will be complementary. But instead, the *Zusammenhang* seems violated, for it

---

121. See the whole of P.Ins. 7.13–19, *AEL* 3:191; also Instruction of Ankhsheshonq 26.7, *AEL* 3:179. Fox, *Proverbs 10–31*, 542.

is "violent men" (עריצים) who attain wealth. The psychological jolt forces deep reflection. (How) can the saying be true? How can the unexpected be managed, in proverbs and life?

Assured in the conviction that good people get good things, the reader might search for a positive meaning in the second colon. Some suggest emending עריצים to חרוצים ("diligent men").[122] The versions possibly offer some support for this, but it is more likely that they were smoothing over difficult Hebrew than that they were working from a different *Vorlage*.[123] Others propose that עריץ has a positive connotation here. Thus "strong men" (as per Roland E. Murphy) are rewarded with riches.[124] The proverb would commend graciousness to women and energetic vitality to men, as gender-appropriate routes to success.[125] G. R. Driver draws attention to an Arabic cognate *ʿariṣim*, referring to vigorous activity without value judgment.[126] Arguments from cognates, however, are notoriously difficult, and this meaning is unsupported in Hebrew.[127] Indeed, elsewhere עריץ is clearly negative, associated with the "wicked" (רשעים; Isa 13:11; Ps 37:35; Job 15:20; 27:13), the "evil" (רעים; Jer 15:21), and the "arrogant" (זדים; Isa 13:11; Ps 86:14). Elsewhere, Proverbs condemns the violent.[128] Here, the reader is goaded to evaluate them for himself: does their connection with wealth give them worth?

---

122. *BHS*, possibility noted in BHQ; Alonso Schökel, *Proverbios*; Fox, *Proverbs 10–31*; Gemser, *Sprüche Salomos*; Oesterley, *The Book of Proverbs*; Ringgren and Zimmerli, *Sprüche/Prediger*.

123. The LXX has ἀνδρεῖοι (manly, vigorous), which translates חרוץ in Prov 10:4; 13:4, and Pesh. (+ Targ.) has 'šyn' (strong), which translates חרוץ in Prov 12:24; 13:4. The change in the MT may have been provoked by mishearing ח for ע. However, the LXX and Pesh. both have an extra couplet inserted in between the cola and seem to be creative reworkings. On the Greek translation, see Hatton, *Contradiction*, 108–9.

124. Murphy, *Proverbs*; cf. Barucq, "Proverbes (Livre des)," "les hommes énergetiques." Early vernacular translations seem to have preferred this option: KJV (1611) "strong men"; Coverdale (1535) "the mightie"; *Giovanni Diodati Bibbia* (1649) "i possenti"; *Reina Valera Antigua* (1602) "los fuertes."

125. McKane, *Proverbs*.

126. G. R. Driver, "Problems in the Hebrew Text of Proverbs," *Bib* 32 (1951): 180.

127. See James Barr, *Comparative Philology and the Text of the Old Testament* (Oxford: Oxford University Press, 1968). Driver supports the Hebrew usage with reference to Ps 37:35, but here it is clearly a bad characteristic, connected with the רשע ("wicked").

128. See Karen Engelken, "Erziehungsziel Gewaltlosigkeit? Überlegungen zum Thema 'physische Gewalt' im Buch Proverbien," *BN* 45 (1988): 12–18.

Responding in the negative, but still affirming an act-consequence connection, the reader might devalue wealth. *Bad people do not get truly good things.* Gracious women have real riches—that is, honor. But ruthless men have only material goods.[129] The cola are now antithetical, pitting relative values against each other. While honor is universally positive in Proverbs, wealth is more ambiguous. Indeed, "favor [חֵן] is better than silver or gold" (Prov 22:1b). Many such "better than" sayings affirm that wealth is only of relative worth.[130] Thus interpreted, the proverb is didactically powerful, encouraging the reader to deduce the value system and make it her own, assimilating her desires and lifestyle accordingly.

She may remember, and is reminded just two verses later, that "the wicked earns deceptive wages" (Prov 11:18a; cf. 10:2; 11:4; 21:6). The apparent breach of the act-consequence connection may be restored in time.[131] The עָרִיץ may "heap up silver like dust" (Job 27:16) but will not enjoy it (27:17), may "spread himself like a green tree" (Ps 37:35) but will ultimately disappear (37:36). None of this, however, is explicit in the proverb. Indeed, commentary is conspicuously absent. Furthermore, כָּבוֹד ("honor") and עֹשֶׁר ("riches") are nowhere else opposed in Proverbs but are equivalent goods, offered together by Lady Wisdom herself (Prov 3:16; 8:18).[132]

Perhaps, then, the proverb simply and cynically asserts that bad people get good things.[133] The ruthless men rip *Tun* and *Ergehen* apart. And as for the woman, with graceful allure she seduces the consequence away from its rightfully wedded act—to her own bed. Indeed, the אֵשֶׁת־חֵן may not be as noble as the אֵשֶׁת־חַיִל whom she mimics. Sirach warns against her: "Hide your eye from a gracious woman [אֵשֶׁת־חֵן]; ... she has burned up her lovers in fire" (Sir 9:8; cf. Nah 3:4). Grace is indeed deceitful (Prov 31:30), an ambiguous quality that can be used for good or ill within the complex-

---

129. HCSB, NIV, and REB supply "only" in the second colon. Cf. Delitzsch, *Biblical Commentary*; Toy, *Critical and Exegetical Commentary*; Waltke, *Book of Proverbs 1–15*.

130. Prov 3:14; 8:11, 19; 15:16–17; 16:8, 16, 19; 17:1; 19:1, 22; 22:1; 28:6. On the value system, see esp. Theodore A. Perry, *Wisdom Literature and the Structure of Proverbs* (University Park: Pennsylvania State University Press, 1993); Sandoval, *Discourse of Wealth and Poverty*.

131. Clifford, *Proverbs*; Waltke, *Book of Proverbs 1–15*.

132. Cf. 1 Kgs 3:13; Prov 3:16; 8:18; 22:4; Qoh 6:2; Esth 1:4; 5:11; 1 Chr 29:12, 28; 2 Chr 1:11, 12; 17:5; 18:1; 32:27.

133. Clifford, *Proverbs*; Hatton, *Contradiction*, 103–9.

ity of human character. Here the woman is ascribed "honor" (כבוד) for her grace. When society is the agent of the *Tun-Ergehen Zusammenhang*, there is no guarantee of its justice.[134] Glory can be conferred on the undeserving, like binding a stone in a sling (Prov 26:8).

The proverb, then, creates subtle polysemies with huge repercussions: the act-consequence connection is upheld or torn down. Often the exploratory process taken to get to the final interpretation is as significant as the interpretation itself. The connotations and ambiguities encourage deep reflection on the reality of the world, its justice, and its host of characters from whom to learn.

5.4.2. Used as Proverbs

As well as being stimuli for didactic reflection, these verses could be applied as proverbs to specific situations with specific functions. The most striking differences in use will of course stem from which base meaning is intended, the speaker's context and manner probably making this clear. The subversive interpretations open the proverbs to various <u>different functions</u>, beyond simple direction and evaluation.

I say to a potential almsgiver in my community, "There is one who gives freely, and he is increased more, and one who holds back more than what is right, only to scarcity" (יש מפזר ונוסף עוד וחושך מישר אך־למחסור; 11:24). The relevance of the proverb for the situation is immediately grasped. It functions just as any [act—consequence] proverb might: <u>directing</u> and motivating correct behavior through the hope of reward. My hearer should increase his charity, for it will be duly recompensed. He is warned against miserliness, lest poverty ensue.

But I may also speak the proverb quite differently, with reference to a financial squanderer. "There is one who spends recklessly, and he is increased more; and one who holds back because of his uprightness, only to scarcity!" By saying this, I do not mean to direct my hearer to recklessness. Rather, my utterance might be an <u>outraged cry</u> at the injustice around me, a <u>cynical comment</u> on the way the world is, or a <u>humble recognition</u> of reality's disorder, in hope of some small mastery over it.

The same sorts of multiple usage are evident in Prov 11:16. The different base meanings allow it to be spoken about a seductress or a truly

---

134. Janowski, "Die Tat kehrt zum Täter zurück," 271.

gracious woman, about a violent man or (possibly) an energetic zealot. "A gracious woman attains honor!" I say, <u>directing</u> my hearer to graciousness through the promise of social standing. Or, to a woman already honored, these words may <u>evaluate</u> her congenial character. If she is poor, the proverb may provide <u>comfort</u>, for though others attain fleeting material wealth (*b* colon), a far greater reward is hers. Or, by the same Hebrew, I might <u>rage</u> against, <u>complain</u> of, or <u>resign</u> myself to apparent injustices. "The seductress gets honor. The violent get rich."

5.4.3. Conclusion

The polysemy in these proverbs opens each of them up to two quite different interpretations, one affirming the *Tun-Ergehen Zusammenhang*, the other undermining it. Accordingly perhaps, the world order is sometimes upheld, sometimes violated, and the proverbs may be spoken into either situation. Furthermore, character is much more complex than simply "righteous" or "wicked." "Scatterers" are sometimes generous men, sometimes reckless spenders; the "gracious woman" may be noble or seductive. The proverbs do not make explicit the agent(s) behind the consequences. If Yahweh is active, perhaps he may be trusted to enforce just retribution, but the same guarantee cannot be made for social agency. Readers are not forced into a particular interpretation but are encouraged to explore and consider, weighing and evaluating possibilities. Contradictory interpretations and contradictory experiences are encountered throughout life: interpreting these proverbs becomes training for living.

5.5. Conclusion

This chapter has focused on proverbs that comment on the act-consequence connection. They are open to extensive exploration, mainly due to their parallelism, imagery, and polysemy. At the start of the chapter, I highlighted four key scholarly discussions. Our explorations have had implications for each:

(1) *The* schicksalwirkende Tatsphäre *and its linguistic foundations.* I have suggested that the act-consequence polysemy of terms like רע ("evil"/"disaster") does not itself imply an ontological connection between the two. However, the proverbs exploit such polysemies to their own ends. Some proverbs construct metaphorical worlds in which there *is* an obvious connection between *Tun* and *Ergehen*. If you swallow "evil" (רע) into

your character, of course it will poison you (§5.3.2). If you "stray" [√תעה] from the path, of course your journey will be punishing (§5.3.1). The reader takes these connections from the source world and applies them to the target world, where they may not have been obvious before. The *schicksalwirkende Tatsphäre* is not so much a presupposition as a metaphorical construction for didactic ends.

(2) *An inviolable world order?* For Koch and Schmid, the act-consequence connection in Proverbs was basically inviolable. My discussion has suggested that while the world's order may be predictable, it admits of exceptions. The parallelisms in §5.2 offer a straightforward way for readers to infer acts and consequences. But they do not absolutely determine the process. Furthermore, the polysemous proverbs in §5.4 admit subversive interpretations, violating the *Tun-Ergehen Zusammenhang*. These problematic elements are on the fringes in Proverbs, but their persistent presence suggests that the sages had no naïve, dogmatic worldview.

(3) *The agent(s) behind the connection.* In general, the proverbs examined here (like many in the book) do not specify an agent. Occasionally they hint at one—intrinsic causality, Yahweh, or society—but little is explicit. The openness suggests that any of these could be active. The focus is on the character in the proverb: his responsibility is more important than any technical agency.

(4) *Explanation or motivation?* The focus on responsibility ties in with Proverbs' didactic purposes: the sayings motivate *character development* in the responsible individual, rather than explaining mechanisms of causality. The proverbs are concerned with total disposition—the overall path a person walks—more than with individual acts; more *Haltung* than *Tun*. And disposition includes emotions and desires, evocatively captured through, for example, dining imagery. The proverbs recognize the complexity of human character and that life is a journey of development.

Furthermore, the process of exploring the openness proves to be intellectual training for the reader. The parallelisms encourage their readers to use logic and deduce the connections between act and consequence, in proverbs as they must in life. The imagery prompts imaginative explorations, fresh modes of thought, and the blending of inference patterns across domains. The polysemies teach their readers to hold apparent contradictions in tension and to confront ambiguities. Apparently incompatible ideas may in fact each be appropriate when applied thoughtfully to different situations.

This is particularly apparent when the verses are used as proverbs. Each time a proverb is spoken, it interprets a new situation and is given a fresh function. The proverbs are open to positive or negative application to context, and to past or future orientations. Their general and metaphorical terms make them applicable to many different circumstances. They are especially suited to evaluate (through their character terms) and to direct (through their act-consequence motivations). When the straightforward connections are problematized, many other possible functions open up.

Such problematic elements will come to the fore more in the next chapter. We will hone in on one particular character—the king—with his acts and the consequences that come through him. We will see that these proverbs offer no straightforward evaluation or direction, no clear-cut character types to emulate or righteous acts to copy. It is uncertain how to bring about the consequences they offer.

6

The Openness of Didactic Proverbs about the King

משלי שלמה בן־דוד מלך ישראל:

The proverbs of Solomon, son of David, king of Israel
— Prov 1:1

6.1. The King in Proverbs

From the Solomonic heading to the cluster of monarchical maxims in chapter 16 to the maternal address to King Lemuel in chapter 31, the king has an important role in Proverbs. This chapter will explore the kingly proverbs in 10:1–22:16, examining their openness and its implications. I will begin by discussing some issues in current scholarship: the depiction (§6.1.1), social context (§6.1.2), and pedagogical function (§6.1.3) of the kingship sayings. I will then explore some specific proverbs: those about the king's judgment (§6.2) and about his favor and wrath (§6.3).

6.1.1. The Depiction of the King in the Royal Proverbs

The king is one of the few cameo parts allotted to a social figure in Proverbs, sketched in many sayings.[1] Here I will focus on two key questions: How favorable is the proverb's depiction of the king? What is the relationship between Yahweh and the king?

A cursory glance at the kingship sayings in Prov 10:1–22:16 (esp. 16:1–22:16) reveals a powerful figure.[2] He is a sovereign authority, allotting life and death (16:14, 15; 20:2). He is the supreme and righteous judge

---

1. Other roughly comparable roles include the father, wife, and neighbor.

2. The king is only mentioned twice in chapters 10–15: 14:28 and 14:35. Cf. also 11:14. On the significance of these verses in their literary context, see Ansberry, *Be Wise, My Son*, 80–84.

(16:10; 20:8, 26), delighting in rectitude (14:35; 16:13; 22:11) and despising wickedness (16:12; 20:26); his throne is established on righteousness and love (16:12; 20:28).

Furthermore, he seems to have a close relationship with Yahweh (though it is rarely made explicit). Editorially, a cluster of kingship sayings in 16:10–15 is linked to a section on Yahweh immediately preceding it, 16:1–9.[3] Verbal repetitions connect the passages (כפר, תועבה, רשע, בון, רצון/רצה), and there are interlocking verses. Verse 8 comes one verse before the end of 16:1–9 and, alone in this cluster, does not mention יהוה. It links forward by introducing "justice" (משפט; vv. 10–11) and "righteousness" (צדקה; vv. 12–13). Verse 11 comes one verse after the beginning of 16:10–15 and is the only verse not to speak of the king. It links back with its reference to יהוה.

The effect is to set the kingship proverbs within a theological context. Yahweh's dominant and sovereign role (vv. 1–9) is passed to the king (vv. 10–15). He is God's human representative, with divine prerogative to impose his rule on earth. The king's qualities here are Yahweh's elsewhere: his concern for justice (16:10), his righteousness and uprightness (16:12–13), and his power over life and death (16:14–15).[4]

In Egypt, the king was the divine son of Re, and as such, became the earthly guardian of Maʿat.[5] When scholars transferred Maʿat to Israel in the form of "world order" (see §5.1 above), she brought this guardian with her. Thus in Israel too the king became the *Garant des Schicksal-Haltung-Zusammenhangs* ("Guarantor of the attitude-fate connection"), and Schmid's five spheres of *Weltordnung* (law, wisdom, fertility, war, cult) apparently coalesced under his just administration.[6] However, we have seen that *Zusammenhang* and *Ordnung* are problematic notions

---

3. Ansberry, *Be Wise, My Son*, 104–7; Hee Suk Kim, "Yhwh Sayings and King Sayings in Proverbs: 10:1–22:16," *Korean Journal of Christan Studies* 75 (2011): 83–104; Whybray, "Yahweh-Sayings." The kingship cluster is internally bound by the term מלך (in all but 16:11): Prov 16:12–13 coheres in syntax, the plural מלכים, and the root צדק; 16:14–15 employs the antonyms of life and death and a wordplay on מלך—מלאך—מלקש. Interconnected Yahweh and kingship sayings also occur in 20:22–21:3.

4. See Skladny, *Die ältesten Spruchsammlungen*, 28. For examples of justice, see 16:11; 21:3; 28:5; 29:26; for righteousness, see 3:33; 10:3; 15:9, 29; 17:15; 18:10; 21:3; for uprightness, see 3:32; 15:8; for life and death, see 14:27; 19:23; 22:4.

5. Assmann, *Maʿat*, 200–212.

6. Skladny, *Die ältesten Spruchsammlungen*, 38; Schmid, *Gerechtigkeit als Weltordnung*, 23, 83–89.

when applied to Israel, and furthermore, the king is nowhere shown to control them as Yahweh does. Indeed, he is not divine but is fundamentally subordinate to the Lord, only gaining authority through Yahweh's gracious bestowal, ever subject to his will (21:1). Proverbs 16:1–9 (which juxtaposes the kingship sayings in 16:10–15) emphatically declares God's control over human destiny (esp. 16:1, 3, 9; see §7.3). This presumably includes the king's own destiny. The relationship thus involves both authorization and subordination.[7]

The collections of sayings after 22:16 comment on the king in distinctive ways. In 22:17–24:34, occasional sayings seemingly presuppose a courtly addressee, who can "stand before kings" (22:29) or "eat with a ruler" (23:1). Yahweh and the king are paired in one proverb: both are to be feared (24:21). At the start of chapter 25, a kingship cluster occurs. God conceals, and the king "searches" (חקר√; 25:2). His own heart, however, "is unsearchable" (אין חקר; 25:3). You should remove the wicked from "before the king" (לפני מלך) like dross from silver (25:4–5). You should remove yourself from "before the king" (לפני מלך), lest he debase you (25:6–7).

Chapters 28–29 are the most striking, containing several distinctly unflattering portraits, removing any notion of a divine monarch. They speak of a "wicked ruler," with the wildness of a rampaging beast (28:15), and of a noble oppressing subordinates (28:16). They describe the abuse of power, court machinations, and economic injustice (29:4, 12, 26). Not every proverb writer was an ardent royalist. Hatton suggests that the book is "no tame supporter of the *status quo*," undermining the monarch even as it seems to glorify him.[8] Noting the political sensitivity of the theme, he suggests that the proverbs are stated subtly, "in such a way that any subversive intention could be denied."[9] I will suggest that even in 10:1–22:16, where the king seems at his most glorified, there are hints of unease beneath the surface.

---

7. Katharine J. Dell argues for divine authorization: the king is "part of the manifestation of God to humanity, standing at the crossroads of the human and the divine." See Dell, "The King in the Wisdom Literature," in *King and Messiah in Israel and the Ancient Near East: Proceedings of the Oxford Old Testament Seminar*, ed. John Day (London: Bloomsbury T&T Clark, 2013), 163–86, quote at 185. W. Lee Humphreys stresses subordination: the proverb writers wanted to avoid any implications that the king might be divine; see Humphreys, "The Motif of the Wise Courtier in the Book of Proverbs," in *Israelite Wisdom: Theological and Literary Essays in Honor of Samul Terrien*, ed. John G. Gammie et al. (Missoula, MT: Scholars Press, 1978), 177–90.

8. Hatton, *Contradiction*, 135.

9. Hatton, *Contradiction*, 118.

6.1.2. The Context and Addressees of the Royal Proverbs

A second area of debate concerns context and addressees. The wider discussions surrounding the book's social setting have already been considered (§1.2. above). Here, I will limit my focus to kingship sayings. Must they relate to an actual court setting?

Of all the proverbs, they are the strongest contenders for this setting. Perhaps the sections where kingship sayings are prominent came from the court, even if the whole book did not. In this vein, Bruce V. Malchow describes Prov 28–29 as a "manual for future monarchs," and Glendon E. Bryce distinguishes Prov 25:2–27 as an independent wisdom book, used to train aspiring courtiers in "the proper kind of behaviour for success and promotion."[10] Most extensive and influential was Skladny, whose delineation and characterization of four collections within chapters 10–29 were largely derived from their kingship sayings.[11]

However, such dissection attempts seem speculative, and scholars have questioned whether royal content really necessitates a royal context.[12] Indeed, the proverbs were retained and therefore presumably still considered relevant, even into postmonarchic times. Friedemann Golka has proposed African parallels as empirical evidence that royal sayings can be coined in the *Volksmund*.[13] As in Africa, he says, so in Israel. However, Golka's method should be viewed with caution. Direct comparison is difficult between societies so divergent, and between proverbs with such formal and stylistic distinctions.[14] Many of his specific parallels are

---

10. Bruce V. Malchow, "A Manual for Future Monarchs," *CBQ* 47 (1985): 238–45; Glendon E. Bryce, *A Legacy of Wisdom: The Egyptian Contribution to the Wisdom of Israel* (Lewisburg: Bucknell University Press, 1979), 147. Similarly, Humphreys argues that 16:1–22:16 and 25:2–27 may have been for the education of "wise courtiers" ("Motif of the Wise Courtier").

11. Skladny, *Die ältesten Spruchsammlungen*, 7–67.

12. See, e.g., Dell, "King in the Wisdom Literature"; Weeks, *Early Israelite Wisdom*, 41–56; Westermann, *Roots of Wisdom*, 31–35; R. N. Whybray and Robert Morgan, eds., *The Book of Proverbs: A Survey of Modern Study*, History of Biblical Interpretation Series 1 (Leiden: Brill, 1995), 45–59.

13. Golka, *Leopard's Spots*, 16–35.

14. In particular, many of Golka's examples come from societies where there is no king as such. Golka's African examples are folk proverbs without the literary characteristics of Prov 10:1–22:16 (e.g., parallelism).

strained.[15] He does show, however, that kingly figures can be common in the proverbs of ordinary people.

Golka finds further support for his thesis in the "commoner's perspective" he can apparently distinguish.[16] There is an uneasy tendency noticeable in scholarship here: whatever the proverbs say about the king, scholars can fit it to their thesis. The critical voice of chapters 28–29 might be the enraged cry of the common people or an educational tool for the king himself.[17] The apparent glorification of 16:1–22:16 might come from the king's sycophantic inner circle or from the naïve minds of the common folk.[18]

Scholars cannot agree on the context, addressee, or perspective of the sayings, and this, I suggest, is because they are open to a number of contexts, addressees, and perspectives. They could be spoken in the royal court—to the monarch or his courtiers—but they need not be. While the historical king did have a certain special status not applicable to others, he might also function figuratively, so as to encapsulate wider principles.[19] The proverb genre is particularly open to metaphorical applications. It delights in hyperbole and exaggerations—hence its use of this most majestic figure. He is an easily interpreted symbol for authority, and the king-courtier dynamic may serve as the epitome and paradigm for many relationships within a stratified society.

6.1.3. The Pedagogical Function of the Royal Proverbs

The possibility of a figurative reading allows us to consider these proverbs as widely applicable pedagogical tools, in which the reader might critically observe the characters or imaginatively align himself with them. So how does the figure of the king function pedagogically?

---

15. For example, he compares Prov 16:13—"Righteous lips are the delight of a king / and he loves him who speaks what is right"—with the African proverb "You cannot dig up the hole of the anteater / but you may peep into it," on the grounds that both may implicitly advise not causing offense to a superior (Golka, *Leopard's Spots*, 29).

16. Golka, *Leopard's Spots*, 34.

17. For the former, see Golka, *Leopard's Spots*, 32–34; Westermann, *Roots of Wisdom*, 33–34; Whybray, *Wealth and Poverty*, 53–54. For the latter, see Skladny, *Die ältesten Spruchsammlungen*, 57–58; Malchow, "Manual for Future Monarchs."

18. For the former, see Skladny, *Die ältesten Spruchsammlungen*, 25–46. For the latter, see Whybray, *Wealth and Poverty*, 48–52.

19. Dell, "King in Wisdom Literature."

If the king is interpreted positively, he may serve as a paradigm for emulation, similar to the "righteous" and "wise" (see chapter 4). In the reader's own positions of authority, he should aspire to this ideal and assimilate his behavior. Aligning himself instead with the courtier in the proverb, the reader may learn of the appropriate response to authority. In this positive depiction, the proverbs may also become standards for comparison, by which the reader can assess his own rulers. Here, however, the idealization in the text may provoke criticism of society. For the real king may fall short of the ideal.[20]

Furthermore, some proverbs do not in fact present an ideal but show the king behaving reprehensibly (esp. Prov 28–29). The locus of normative morality shifts: the proverbs no longer provide standards for judging the world; the world must provide standards for judging the proverbs. Across the book as a whole, the king is not a type like the "righteous" or "wise," with utterly consistent ethical behavior, but an example of the complexity of human character, containing both good and bad. In his hyperbolic depiction, both are taken to extremes. The reader is called upon to observe him, in proverbs and life, analyzing his ethics.

Brown also has argued for a model of merging and diverging student-king identities, but for him there is a pedagogical progression in the book.[21] The first chapters (1–9) speak to the reader as a naïve son; the final chapter addresses him as the king (31:1–9). He is called upon to grow from one identity to the other. The intervening chapters show a politicization and widening social sphere to enable the shift. Alongside the child's development toward kingship comes, counterintuitively, increasing criticism of kingship. The erstwhile "earthly embodiment of divine *mysterium tremendum*" is later displayed in distinctly unflattering terms (chapters 28–29).[22] According to Brown, this too is pedagogical. "As the king becomes an object of critique, so the reader must cultivate self-criticism."[23] The closing pronouncement (31:1–9) sees the king under the sway of his mother, subject to unswerving rebuke. Though the reader has progressed from child to king, he is ever more a student.

---

20. Hausmann, *Studien zum Menschenbild*, 136.
21. Brown, "Pedagogy of Proverbs," followed by, e.g., Ansberry, *Be Wise, My Son*; Yoder, "Forming 'Fearers of Yahweh.'"
22. Brown, "Pedagogy of Proverbs," 180.
23. Brown, "Pedagogy of Proverbs," 181.

Brown's account is compelling, though I would challenge the alleged simplicity of the earlier collections. I will argue that the depictions of the king in 10:1–22:16 are complex and ambiguous. The reader must ponder and test them and, in so doing, train his mind. Does the king really provide a standard for evaluation, or must I evaluate him by external standards? Does he offer a paradigm or an antitype? Bold and even subversive readings are permitted, calling for courage in interpreting life and proverbs.

In the discussions that follow, we will see the contribution of the proverbs' openness to these debates. Openness allows them to give positive and negative depictions of the king. It makes them applicable to different contexts and addressees when spoken proverbially. It also turns them into complex didactic tools, useful for forming a worldview, developing character, and training the intellect.

6.2. The King's Judgment

Against this background, let us turn to the proverbs themselves. We will first confront the king's judgment (here), and then his favor and wrath (§6.3). We will focus on the proverbs' implications for the scholarly questions considered above, and how their openness contributes to their proverbial and didactic uses.

Israelite royal ideology makes the king the supreme judicial authority.[24] As the Hebrew Bible portrays it, the premonarchic era was a time of lawlessness because "there was no king in Israel" (Judg 17:6; 21:25); the judges were apparently inadequate. The elders therefore demanded a new model of leadership: "a king to judge us" (1 Sam 8:4–6). With the establishment of a monarchy came a centralized judiciary and a supreme adjudicator (the king), to whom legal cases could apparently be brought directly (2 Sam 12:1–6; 14:1–20; 1 Kgs 3:16–28; 2 Kgs 6:26–31; 8:1–6).[25] In this role, David "administered justice and equity to all his people" (2 Sam 8:15), and Solomon executed "justice and righteousness" (1 Kgs 10:9). If

---

24. Hans Jochen Boecker, *Law and the Administration of Justice in the Old Testament and Ancient East* (London: SPCK, 1980); Keith W. Whitelam, *The Just King: Monarchical Judicial Authority in Ancient Israel*, JSOTSup 12 (Sheffield: JSOT Press, 1979); Robert R. Wilson, "Israel's Judicial System in the Preexilic Period," *JQR* 74 (1983): 229–48.

25. David C. Flatto, "The King and I: The Separation of Powers in Early Hebraic Political Theory," *Yale Journal of Law and the Humanities* 20 (2008): 74–75.

he failed in these duties, the king could find his position threatened (2 Sam 15:1–6; Jer 22:15–17).

The historical accuracy of this picture is questionable, but its ideological roots are deep. Indeed, across the ancient Near East, the king was the divinely endowed administrator of justice.[26] The Mesopotamian monarch Hammurabi describes himself as the *šar mēšarim*, the "just king," and boasts that he is appointed "to cause justice to prevail in the land, to destroy the wicked and evil."[27] Equally, in Israel, justice is the foundation of the king's throne (Prov 16:12; 20:28; 25:5; Pss 89:15[14]; 97:2) and becomes a key component of messianic expectations (e.g., Isa 16:5; 32:1; Jer 23:5–6). The proverbs considered here may reflect this judicial ideal.

6.2.1. Used as Proverbs

In chapter 5 I began with didactic explorations of the verses and then proceeded to their use as proverbs. Here I take the reverse arrangement, for in life there is no linear progression between uses, and either order might occur. There are three verses to consider:

16:10: קסם על־שפתי־מלך במשפט לא ימעל־פיו:

An oracle is on the lips of a king; in judgment/with justice his mouth does not break faith.

20:8: מלך יושב על־כסא־דין מזרה בעיניו כל־רע:

The king sits on the throne of judgment, scattering/winnowing all evil with his eyes.

20:26: מזרה רשעים מלך חכם וישב עליהם אופן:

A wise king scatters/winnows the wicked and brings the wheel back over them.

Each of these proverbs suggests the judgment of the king, perhaps presuming him to preside over a legal case, maybe even spoken before the judicial throne itself (20:8; cf. 1 Kgs 7:7; Isa 16:5; Ps 112:5).[28] Or they might

---

26. Whitelam, *Just King*, 17–29.

27. *ANET*, 164.

28. Some scholars have argued for a common origin for proverbs and law. See, e.g., J. P. Audet, "Origines comparées de la double tradition de la loi et de la Sagesse dans le Proche-Orient ancien," in *Twenty-Fifth International Congress of Oriental-*

be applied more broadly to any situation requiring justice, the "king" acting as a cipher for an authority figure. Proverbs 16:10 affirms that the judgment is perfect, 20:8 affirms that it ousts evil, and 20:26 affirms that it retributes the wicked.

The proverbs imply an interaction between judge-king and defendant. The correlations of person between these textual characters and the people using the proverb may be various. I might speak the proverbs to either party (construed literally or metaphorically), or to another, like the plaintiff. Furthermore, I could speak with different temporal orientations: before the crime, between the crime and the verdict, or after the verdict. In each of these permutations, the proverb's <u>function</u> will change.

6.2.1.1. Spoken to the Defendant

These proverbs might be spoken to the potential criminal. They may, in fact, forestall the criminality, uttered *before the crime* has been committed. In this case, they can function <u>directively</u>, offering behavior and motivation. "Don't be evil," counsels 20:8; "don't be wicked," advises 20:26; in fact, "don't do anything worthy of condemnation!" (16:10), lest the "king" find out and punish you. The proverbs employ generality, leaving the contents of the crime open to many possible manifestations. Equally, the punishment is inexplicit (16:10) or metaphorical (20:8, 26), to be filled out by the hearer's imagination, blended with the situation of his own life. He thus constructs his own disincentive.

The proverbs may also address the defendant *between the crime and the verdict*. 16:10 pronounces that the judgment will be just, <u>providing encouragement</u> for the innocent, <u>striking fear</u> into the guilty. By the other two proverbs, I might <u>predict</u> the outcome: guilty. The trial occurs, and the condemnation is pronounced. *After the verdict*, I proclaim the proverbs

---

ists (Moscow: 1960), 352–57; Joseph Blenkinsopp, *Wisdom and the Law in the Old Testament: The Ordering of Life in Israel and Early Judaism* (Oxford: Oxford University Press, 1983); E. Gerstenberger, *Wesen und Herkunft des "apodiktischen Rechts,"* WMANT 20 (Neukirchen-Vluyn: Neukirchener Verlag, 1965). Some envisage the use of proverbs at court, to give the verdict or summarize a case. See, e.g., Berend Gemser, "The Importance of the Motive Clause in Old Testament Law," in *Congress Volume Copenhagen 1953* (Leiden: Brill, 1953), 64–66; Hillary Nyika, "The Traditional Israelite Legal Settings: Social Contexts in Proverbs," in *Wisdom, Science, and the Scriptures: Essays in Honor of Ernest Lucas*, ed. Stephen Finamore and John Weaker (Eugene, OR: Wipf & Stock, 2015), 34–55.

evaluatively. Adding my insult to the injury of ensuing punishment, I supplement the king's judgment with my own. The proverbs serve as a final
summary, a "case closed." "You are evil (20:8)," I imply, "wicked (20:26),
and worthy of condemnation (16:10)." These are not only legal but moral
indictments, ascribing particularly heinous character types.

6.2.1.2. Spoken to the Plaintiff

Alternatively, I may speak to the plaintiff, the one wronged by the evil/
wicked men. *Before the verdict*, the proverbs may provide <u>encouragement</u>
and <u>consolation</u>. Do not fear; justice will be done. The ruler will distinguish wickedness infallibly, and deal with it appropriately. *After the verdict*,
they may <u>celebrate</u> with the plaintiff, pronouncing the triumphant ruling.
Justice has reigned; the plaintiff has been vindicated.

6.2.1.3. Spoken to the Judge-King

Finally, the proverbs could be spoken to the king himself, or to anyone
presiding over justice. *Before the verdict*, they may function <u>directively</u>,
presenting an ideal to emulate. Stated as indicative observations and not
as imperatives, they avoid the potential affront of presuming to command
the king. The monarch does not (i.e., must not) speak unjustly (16:10). He
has (i.e., should have) hatred for wickedness and evil, dealing with them
accordingly (20:8, 26). *After the verdict*, the proverbs might <u>evaluate</u> and
<u>glorify</u> him. The king has infallibly removed all evil (20:8) and wickedness
(20:26)! O wise one (20:26), with oracular power and perception (16:10)!
Glory be to the king!

6.2.2. Didactic Explorations

 As proverbs, then, these sentences are open to application in many different situations and functions. Their openness also contributes to their
didactic usefulness, shaping a worldview, facilitating character development, and training the intellect.

20:8 מלך יושב על־כסא־דין מזרה בעיניו כל־רע:

The king sits on the throne of judgment, scattering/winnowing all evil
with his eyes.

20:26 מזרה רשעים מלך חכם וישב עליהם אופן:

A wise king scatters/winnows the wicked and brings the wheel back over them.

Grand, stately, and unmoving, the king sits upon the judicial throne (20:8a). Elsewhere Yahweh's seat (Ps 9:4, 7–8), this is now the locus of his own righteous justice (cf. Prov 16:12; 25:5), from which (in an unexpected shift of imagery) he "winnows/scatters" (מזרה). This imagery is polyvalent, open to connotations of punishment or separation. To begin with punishment, √זרה (*piel*) often means "to scatter." Just as Yahweh scatters nations for their unrighteousness, implying their devastation and destruction, so the king executes quasi-divine justice on his subjects.[29] In 20:8, he needs no secondary agents or instruments; his "eyes" alone will do it. For any king or leader reading this proverb, strict retributive justice becomes a behavioral ideal. For any subordinate, it strongly motivates one not to be "evil" (20:8) or "wicked" (20:26).

√זרה can also denote "to winnow": grain and chaff are tossed into the air and the latter is scattered to the wind.[30] Agriculture is an unexpected complement to kingship, but it lures in the everyday reader, training his imagination through mental exploration of a familiar world. As a trope for judgment (usually divine, here monarchic), winnowing imagines the wicked as chaff.[31] Despite any appearances, they are worthless and insubstantial, blown away to destruction. Wickedness is, accordingly, futile.

The subsequent imagery in 20:26 has perplexed interpreters: the king "brings the wheel back" (וישב ... אופן) over the wicked. Some scholars suggest that this is a "torture wheel," others the "wheel of fortune," but these explanations have little to support them.[32] Some interpreters resort

---

29. Most commonly Israel and Judah, but also other nations (Jer 49:32, 36; 51:2; Ezek 29:12; 30:23, 26).

30. This meaning is more common in the *qal* (Isa 30:24; 41:16; Jer 15:7; Ruth 3:2), but *piel* occurs in Ps 139:3 (figurative). For a description of winnowing in ancient Israel, see Oded Borowski, *Agriculture in Iron Age Israel* (Winona Lake, IN: Eisenbrauns, 1987), 65–70.

31. Cf. Isa 17:13: 29:5; Hos 13:3; Pss 1:4; 35:5; Job 21:18. For winnowing (זרה) as a trope for divine judgment, see, e.g., Isa 41:16; Jer 15:7.

32. A few scholars speculate that this was a punitive instrument in Israel (so Toy, *Critical and Exegetical Commentary*; Gemser, *Sprüche Salomos*; BDB). Daniel C. Snell likens it to torture instruments in ancient Greece and seventeenth-/eighteenth-century Europe. Snell adduces Hittite parallels, apparently showing a "wheel" in judicial con-

to textual emendation.[33] Most plausibly, the image continues the agricultural metaphor and refers to a threshing wheel.[34] During the ingathering
process, threshing occurred before winnowing. The order is reversed here,
disorienting readers and spurring their imaginations. Minds set in reverse,
they may search for previous stages, the acts that could have led to such
outcomes. In ancient Israel, the precious grain was probably threshed from
its husks and stalks with sticks/flails, animals, sledges, and carts.[35] The

texts. See Snell, "The Wheel in Proverbs XX 26," *VT* 39 (1989): 507 n. 12. However,
the meaning, significance, and even presence of the Hittite *ḫurki* "wheel" are disputed
in these texts. Driver bases the "wheel of fortune" reading on a Sophocles fragment
reading "Fortune revolves on the frequent wheel of a god" ("Problems in the Hebrew
Text," 184, followed by REB). There is no supporting evidence from Hebrew usage.

33. Arnold B. Ehrlich, *Randglossen zur hebräischen Bibel: Textkritisches, sprachliches und sachliches* (Leipzig: Hinrichs, 1908), vol. 6; *BHS* (though not *BHQ*). Changing
אֹופַן ("wheel") to אוֹנָם ("their iniquity") would give the retributive sense "he returns
their iniquity to them" (cf. Ps 94:23). But there is no textual or versional support, and
the imagery can be interpreted as it stands.

34. Followed by many commentators, and a number of translations who give
"threshing wheel" (HCSB, NASB, NIV, NKJV). See D. Winton Thomas, "Proverbs XX
26," *JJS* 15 (1964): 155–56; Majella Franzmann, "The Wheel in Proverbs XX 26 and
Ode of Solomon XXIII 11–16," *VT* 41 (1991): 121–23. The imagery is possibly reso-
nant because legal trials sometimes took place at the threshing floor. In the Ugaritic
tale of Aqhat, king Dan'ilu twice judges at the threshing floor (*KTU* 1.17.5.6–8 and
1.19.1.19–25). In 1 Kgs 22:10 (// 2 Chr 18:9) the threshing floor is at the city gate, a
usual location for legal judgments (e.g., Deut 21:19; 22:15; Ruth 4:1–11; 2 Sam 15:1–
6), and the ensuing dialogue takes the form of a legal trial. Andrew Tobolowsky argues
that threshing floors functioned as "sites of divine communication and of momentous
decision-making" ("Where Doom Is Spoken: Threshing Floors as Places of Decision
and Communication in Biblical Literature," *JANER* 16 [2016]: 97). For the threshing
floor at the city gate, see M. Anbar, " 'L'aire à l'entrée de la porte de Samarie' (1 R. XXII
10)," *VT* 50 (2000): 121–23; Sidney Smith, "The Threshing Floor at the City Gate," *PEJ*
78 (1946): 5–14. Another suggestion that continues the agricultural imagery is that the
אוֹפַן here is not a wheel but a tuyere—a nozzle through which air is blown on the grain
to remove the chaff. This would be the only attestation of this meaning in Hebrew,
and it would have been misinterpreted by the versions, which have "wheel" here (LXX
τροχόν; Pesh. [=Targ.] *glgl'*). See Nissim G. Amzallag, and Shamir Yona, "The Meaning
of 'Ôpan in Proverbs 20.16," *BT* 67 (2016): 292–302.

35. Flails appear in Isa 28:27; animals appear in Deut 25:4; Hos 10:11; Mic 4:13.
The instruments are explained by Borowski, *Agriculture in Iron Age Israel*, 62–65;
L. Cheetham, "Thresh and Winnowing: An Ethnographic Study," *Antiquity* 56.217
(1982): 127–30; Jaime L. Waters, *Threshing Floors in Ancient Israel: Their Ritual and
Symbolic Significance* (Minneapolis: Fortress, 2015), 2–4.

threshing sledge may have been fitted with iron or stone teeth (cf. Amos 1:3; Isa 41:15) and the cart with sets of heavy wheels, like this one. This was a violent procedure, unsuitable for delicate crops (Isa 28:27), and it occurs as a common figure for divine retribution.[36] Imaginatively blending the image with her own envisaged punishment from a quasi-divine monarch, the reader might react viscerally. The weight of the device crushes her bones, and she is powerfully disincentivized from wrongdoing.

As well as punishment, these proverbs may suggest separation, and by extension discernment of types. Both threshing and winnowing entail separation. The laborer separates the grain from the husks and stalks, then from the chaff, just as the king separates the righteous from the wicked. On the one hand, moral types, like agricultural products, have crucial and obvious differences. On the other, they are muddled together in life's threshing floor, and separating them requires skill. Indeed, the literary context may suggest that moral confusion is rife (see discussion of 20:11 in §7.2.1.2). For his winnowing fork, the king uses his "eyes" (20:8b), a tool created by the Lord (20:12) and bestowed on all. The reader can imaginatively align herself with this infallible scrutineer, learning to decipher good and evil herself. She must search not only for "evil men" (taking רע metonymically, as above) but for all "evil" (taking רע in an abstract sense): evil actions and situations, even evil within her own character.

Gazing a little deeper, however, she might see something disconcerting "in his eyes." בעיניו might modify not מזרה (he "winnows with his eyes") but כל־רע ("all that is evil in his eyes").[37] The Masoretic accents certainly point in this direction.[38] And this king, unlike his counterpart in 20:26, is not said to be "wise."[39] Indeed, only the fool's way (or the way of the kingless vagabond) is right "in his own eyes" (12:15; 16:2; 21:2).[40] The phrase is frequent in Proverbs, each time suggesting an alarming distortion of the

---

36. Isa 21:10; 41:15–16; Jer 51:33; Amos 1:3; Mic 4:12–13; Hab 3:12.

37. The inverted word order, modifier before noun, would be unusual, but it may be an emphatic fronting. Even if "ungrammatical," it may have been recognizable to the reader because the expression "in his eyes" has an expected meaning in Proverbs.

38. There is a disjunctive *tipḥaʾ* accent on מזרה, separating it from what follows, and a conjunctive *munnaḥ* on בעיניו, implying that it should be construed together with כל־רע.

39. Against the ambiguous character in the Hebrew, a moralizing clarification is given in the LXX, which designates him as a βασιλεὺς δίκαιος, "righteous king."

40. Judg 17:6; 21:25: "In those days there was no king in Israel. Everyone did what was right in his own eyes."

value system.[41] Ethical norms are personally construed; the king chooses good and evil for himself.

This gives the proverb a possible subversive undertone: the king judges unjustly, with none to hold him accountable, problematizing his apparent idealization and paradigmatic status. If spoken in a suitable context, with appropriate intonation, these connotations could ring out. The reader must not be naïve but should judge even the king's judgment. She herself should discern "evil" (according to Proverbs' own standards) and flesh out the category, developing her character accordingly. There are complexities to examine—complexities in characters and language—and nondominant interpretations to hear—of situations, people, and proverbs.

16:10: קסם על־שפתי־מלך במשפט לא ימעל־פיו׃
An oracle is on the lips of a king; in judgment/with justice his mouth does not break faith.

Most obviously, this proverb may express the supreme, infallible judgment of the king. He is a paradigm of piety and justice, a standard for all authority figures. In legal practice, he does not "break faith" (ימעל). This verb suggests a breach of relationship and almost always refers to religious devotion, perhaps suggesting God beneath the surface here.[42] Continuing the piety of the immediately preceding Yahweh cluster (16:1–9), the king does not break faith (implicitly) with the Lord. This interpretation takes משפט as "judgment" (as in Prov 16:33; 24:23) and ב as "in, with regard to," combining to give a circumstantial phrase approximating "whenever the king judges."[43] Alternatively, משפט could be "justice" (its more common sense in Proverbs), with ב taking its usual role with √מעל, introducing the injured party.[44] The king does not "break faith with justice."[45] Unlike the worthless witness who "scoffs at justice" (יליץ משפט; 19:28; see §5.3.2.2), the king adheres to it with an almost religious devotion, and so, too,

---

41. Prov 3:7; 12:15; 16:2; 21:2; 26:5, 12, 16; 28:11; 30:12.

42. The exception is Num 5:12, 27.

43. This is not common in the colocation ב מעל, but it does occur; see the phrase "break faith with regard to the devoted things" (Josh 7:1; 22:20; 1 Chr 2:7).

44. This meaning of משפט includes two verses in the immediate literary context here (16:8, 11; cf. Prov 1:3; 2:8, 9; 8:20; 12:5; 13:23; 17:23; 18:5; 19:28; 21:3, 7, 15; 28:5; 29:4, 26).

45. So BDB: "act treacherously against justice"; NIV: "betray justice."

must the reader. Emphatically fronted at the start of the colon, justice has become a personified virtue to revere.[46]

The first colon is more problematic for the royalist. קֶסֶם refers to an "oracle" or "divination" and is almost always condemned in the Hebrew Bible. Here alone does BDB give provide the meaning "in good sense." It possibly refers uniquely here to a legitimate legal-religious practice for decision making.[47] Most scholars interpret it as figurative for divinely given accuracy. Like the wise woman who esteemed David's judgments "as the wisdom of the angel of God" (2 Sam 14:17, 20), so wise proverb readers must regard their king's words as supernaturally bestowed.

It may also be possible, however, that קֶסֶם retains its negative connotations. The first colon is then a cynical comment on the king. Divination—that abominable practice co-occurring with child sacrifice (Deut 18:10; 2 Kgs 17:17) and rebellion (1 Sam 15:23), the method that delivers only lies (Jer 14:14; Ezek 13:6; cf. Ezek 21:28[23], 34[29]; 22:28)—that is the king's judgment for you. When an Israelite king does use קֶסֶם (1 Sam 28:8), it is certainly not legitimate. The reader's mind is trained by assessing this possibility.

He might reject the possibility when faced with the apparently unswerving positivity of the second colon. Or he might uncover hidden condemnation there too. The second colon may simply be ironic: the king's grandiose proclamation on his own infallible judgment, his inerrancy "in his own eyes."[48] Perceptions and values have been distorted. The speaker's tone of voice could easily convey this sense. Alternatively, we could follow Fox's interpretation: "In judgement no one can defy what he says."[49] You cannot resist the king's word, even if illegitimate; such is its power. The

---

46. Cf. the personification of "wisdom" (throughout Prov 1–9), "discretion" and "understanding" (2:11), "righteousness" (13:6), "kindness and loyalty" (14:22, see §5.3.1.2; 20:28), and, conversely, "wickedness"/"sin" (13:6) and "evil" (13:21).

47. McKane suggests that it refers to the Urim and Thummim, which the king (legitimately) consults in 1 Sam 14:41 (*Proverbs*). However, there is no evidence that קֶסֶם could designate this. Eryl W. Davies suggests that קֶסֶם in Ezek 21:26–28(21–23) refers to the shaking of arrows, and accordingly in Prov 16:10 it designates decision by lot. However, the reference in Ezekiel is not certain, and there is no other evidence for this specialist sense of קֶסֶם. Furthermore, in Ezekiel it is hardly a legitimate practice, paralleled with consulting teraphim and observing the liver. See Davies, "The Meaning of Qesem in Prv 16,10," *Bib* 61 (1980): 554–56, followed by Heim, *Poetic Imagination*.

48. So Rabbi Alshich, cited in Ginsburg, *Mishlei*.

49. Fox, *Proverbs 10–31*.

subject of יַעֲלֶה is now an impersonal "one." Its object is פִּיו, which is no longer a physical "mouth," but a metonymy for speech, "what he says." It would be unique for √מעל to take a direct object like this, but it may be possible. On the surface, then, this proverb proclaims the infallible judgment of the king, but it may contain hints of subversion. The reader must think carefully before glorifying the monarch or using him as a paradigm and standard.

6.2.3. Conclusion

The didactic explorations of these three proverbs have revealed their alluring openness, generated mainly through their polysemy and imagery. Their openness is increased when spoken proverbially, in the royal court or among commoners, during a legal trial or a nonjudicial case. They may be spoken to the defendant, the plaintiff, or the king (or the one imaginatively aligned with these characters), and at various stages in the trial process. In each case, their function might be different.

When used didactically, these proverbs facilitate the readers' character development. In 20:8 and 20:26, the reader is presented with the antitypes "evil" and "wicked," whose behavior they must avoid. The king himself may be a paradigm of justice for emulation. But the readers must think carefully before assimilating their behavior: there are undertones and complexities to be acknowledged. In the king, as in the world, good and evil can be distinguished, but only through a careful winnowing.

The readers' main impression regarding worldview may be the idealization of the king. He is closely aligned with Yahweh, scattering, winnowing, and threshing wrongdoers as he sits enthroned (20:8, 26). His judgment is as infallible as a God-given "oracle" (16:10). However, there are subtle subversive elements: perhaps the king only punishes what is evil "in his own eyes" (20:8); perhaps his judgment is as void as false religion (16:10).

These impressions are not paramount, but they may arise when the readers ponder and exercise their minds. Skills vital for success in life are practiced here. The readers must use reason and discernment, engage the imagination, and work out the implications of events. They must learn to question what they see, judging for themselves. They must not simply follow dominant voices, however authoritative they may seem.

6.3. The King's Favor and Wrath

6.3.1. Used as Proverbs

For the monarchist, the most worrying depiction of the king occurs in those proverbs describing his favor and wrath. His favor presents few problems. It suggests a social harmony and generosity to which all can aspire. His wrath, however, is more troubling, for wrath is unequivocally condemned elsewhere in Proverbs (e.g., 14:29; 15:18; 22:24; 29:22). When ascribed to the king, however, no moral commentary is given. Perhaps in certain persons and circumstances, anger is justified. Indeed, the Lord himself may be angry (22:14, and commonly in the Hebrew Bible), and he sometimes uses the king as a conduit for his wrath (1 Sam 28:18). Pro-monarchic ancient Near Eastern material sometimes revels in the king's magnificent rage.[50] Here, the monarch may have special status. Or, possibly, the principles might be extrapolated. In state and household alike, effective leadership is authoritative leadership, which sometimes requires severity (e.g., 13:24). Much will depend on the circumstances in which the proverbs are used.

We will focus on five verses:

16:14: חמת־מלך מלאכי־מות ואיש חכם יכפרנה׃
The anger of the king—messengers of death; a wise man will appease it.

20:2: נהם ככפיר אימת מלך מתעברו חוטא נפשו׃
Growling like a lion—dread fear of the king; the one who enrages him forfeits his life / sins against himself.

19:12: נהם ככפיר זעף מלך וכטל על־עשב רצונו׃
Growling like a lion—the anger of the king, but like dew on the grass is his favor.

16:15: באור־פני־מלך חיים ורצונו כעב מלקוש׃
In the light of the king's face is life, and his favor is like a cloud of spring rain.

---

50. Brent A. Strawn discusses this particularly in relation to lion imagery; see Strawn, *What Is Stronger Than a Lion? Leonine Imagery and Metaphor in the Hebrew Bible and the Ancient Near East*, OBO (Fribourg: Academic Press; Göttingen: Vanden-hoeck & Ruprecht, 2005), 174–81.

21:1 פְלֵגי־מַיִם לֶב־מֶלֶךְ בְּיַד־יְהוָה עַל־כָּל־אֲשֶׁר יַחְפֹּץ יַטֶּנּוּ:

Channels of water—the king's heart in Yahweh's hand; he turns it to all that he desires.[51]

Two images are used to depict the king's wrath: "messengers of death" (16:14) and "growling like a lion" (19:12; 20:2). Three envision his favor: "dew on the grass" (19:12), "a cloud of spring rain" (16:15), and "streams of water" (21:1). Like all proverbs, these verses are open to multiple situations and functions. I will focus on the *correlation of persons*—is it addressed to the king (the superior) or to his subject (the subordinate)?—and the *opinion about the situation*—is the favor/wrath a good thing?

6.3.1.1. Addressing the Subordinate

Though they do not all mention him explicitly, these proverbs imply the presence of a subordinate, who experiences the king's wrath or favor. After this experience, the proverbs might <u>evaluate</u> it. The sudden sorrow or success is not of the subordinate's own making. Prosperity has its primary basis not in good fortune or hard work but in the benefactor. Or, before the experience, the proverbs might be spoken <u>directively</u>. Graphic imagery provides strong motivation: the king's wrath destroys like a lion (avoid it!); his favor vivifies like water (seek it!).

How to do so, however, is less clear. Proverbs 16:14 encourages wisdom through [character—consequence] logic: the "wise man" will not fall foul of the king's rage. But the other proverbs offer no behavioral types. The speaker may assume that the hearer already knows what would rouse the king, or he may call on her to work it out. Perhaps she has learned from elsewhere that the king bestows his favor on the wise (14:35), righteous (16:13), and pure (22:11), and she may be prompted to act accordingly. But the proverbs themselves here make no such claims. They might in fact be spoken to one whose king rejoices in evil (cf. Hos 7:3); what direction do they then offer?

6.3.1.2. Addressing the Superior

These proverbs express no independent opinion of the king, allowing the speaker to superimpose his own. He might speak *affirmatively*. The

---

51. As this proverb does not explicitly mention favor or wrath, it may not be obvious why it is included here. But its connection with favor will become apparent below.

king's favor is as generous and life-giving as abundant waters. His wrath is powerful, magnificent, and terrible. Thus understood, the speaker might <u>evaluate</u> and <u>exalt</u> the ruler. Or he might <u>direct</u> the ruler to proper leadership behavior, presenting it as though it were already the case to avoid offending this powerful interlocutor.

But the speaker might also pronounce the proverbs *negatively*. Deathly messengers and roaring lions are no friendly playmates. Even when depicting the king's favor, the speaker might bring out disturbing nuances (see the didactic explorations below). He thus <u>condemns</u> the king's character— a brave (and foolhardy?) move if in his presence. Or he might <u>lament</u> the injustice of society, speaking safely out of earshot (though cf. Qoh 10:20).

6.3.2. Didactic Explorations

6.3.2.1. The King's Favor

16:15: באור־פני־מלך חיים ורצונו כעב מלקוש:
In the light of the king's face is life, and his favor is like a cloud of spring rain.

This proverb employs two images, both open to exploration, to portray the life-giving favor of the king. The first is "light" (אור), emanating from the face, possibly a metaphor for a physical smile.[52] This trope occurs across the ancient Near East, especially of the deity's face shining with favor.[53] Biblical psalmists frequently implore the Lord to show the "light of his face," akin to bestowing peace, prosperity, and victory.[54] The Ketef Hinnom inscriptions further attest to the trope's currency in Israel.[55] Thus

---

52. Toy, *Critical and Exegetical Commentary*; cf. Clifford, *Proverbs*; Delitzsch, *Biblical Commentary*; Fox, *Proverbs 10–31*. In Job 29:24, אור פני ("the light of my face") is parallel to אשחק ("I will laugh"). Vulgate gives "cheerfulness" (*hilaritate*) instead of "light." The LXX seems to read בני here—υἱὸς βασιλέως ("son of the king").

53. This occurs in Babylonian, El Amarna, and Ugaritic texts; see Bruce K. Waltke, *The Book of Proverbs: Chapters 16–31*, NICOT (Grand Rapids, MI: Eerdmans, 2005), 21.

54. "Light of the face" occurs in Pss 4:7[6]; 44:4[3]; 89:16[15]; "Make the face shine" occurs in Pss 31:17[16]; 67:1; 80:4[3], 8[7], 20[19]; 119:135.

55. Ketef Hinnom 1.16–18: "[יו]ר יהוה פנ[יו]"; 2.8–10 "אל[יך]"; "יאר יה[ו]ה פניו [אל]יך"; this closely resembles Num 6:24–26. See Gabriel Barkay et al., "The Amulets From Ketef Hinom: A New Edition and Evaluation," *BASOR* 334 (2004): 41–71.

the king here is intimately related to God.[56] This favor-filled light brings its corollary, "life" (חיים), in stark contrast with the "death" of the previous verse (see discussion of 16:14 below).[57] "Life" designates not so much physical existence as life in its fullness: secure, prosperous, abounding in joy.[58] The reader may be allured by this promise, imagining what it could mean blended with his own circumstances, and thus may be motivated to pleasing behavior.

Juxtaposed with this brightness, the darkening "cloud of spring rain" (עב מלקוש) creates a powerful sensory experience (cf. Ezek 1:28). The reader's explorations are informed here by encyclopedic knowledge. There are two major seasons in Canaan: the hot, dry "summer" (קיץ) and the cool, wet "winter" (חרף). The wet season opens with "autumn rains" (יורה) in October and concludes with "spring rains" (מלקוש) in April and May. Vital for agricultural life, these spring rains bring the year's final precious moisture, preparing the ground for the summer crops and ripening those that have germinated over the winter.

In the Hebrew Bible, meteorological activity is a divine prerogative, and rain is a gift of God, emblematic of his generosity and care, while withholding it is his curse.[59] Furthermore, the Lord himself "will come to us as the showers, as the spring rains [מלקוש] that water the earth" (Hos 6:3). Once more, conventional Yahweh imagery connects divine and human monarchs (cf. 2 Sam 23:4; Ps 72:6). The king is celestially abundant in generosity, an ideal of magnanimity to which all may aspire. The proper response to such favor is given by Job: "They waited for me as for the rain, and they opened their mouths as for the spring rain...; the light of my face they did not cast down" (Job 29:23–24). The courtier must eagerly seek the king's favor, openmouthed at the blessings he could bestow.[60] As the proverb does not elucidate, he must work out for himself how best to elicit it.

---

56. Perhaps like Moses, whose face shone after his divine communication (Exod 34:29–30).

57. For the corollary "life," see Prov 13:9; 20:20; Job 3:16; 33:28, 30; Pss 56:14[13]; 58:9[8]; Qoh 6:4.

58. Stewart, *Poetic Ethics*, 112–14.

59. Philippe Reymond, *L'eau, sa vie, et sa signification dans l'Ancien Testament*, VTSup 6 (Leiden: Brill, 1958), 41–53. The Lord gives מלקוש in Deut 11:14; Jer 5:24; Joel 2:23; Zech 10:1. Cf. also Lev 26:4; 1 Kgs 17:14; Ezek 34:26; Ps 68:10[9]. God withholds מלקוש in Jer 3:3; cf. Deut 11:17; 1 Kgs 8:35(// 2 Chr 6:26); Isa 5:6; Zech 14:17; 2 Chr 7:13.

60. Attesting to the openness of the text, the LXX interprets רצונו not abstractly as "favor" but metonymically as "those who are favorable to him" (οἱ δὲ προσδεκτοὶ αὐτῷ).

While the overall impression of this proverb is glowing, however, dark clouds may linger. Yes, rain usually brings life, but not always (Prov 28:3). A deluge might cause destruction.[61] Spring rains suggest the ominous necessity of a long, hard summer to come. They are unpredictable, and irregular—is the king's favor the same?[62] A stormy, erratic character can provide no straightforward paradigm of morality. Like the forces of heaven, he is impossible to control; who knows how to secure his capricious favor? Pondering this proverb, the reader evaluates situations and explores possibilities. He casts rains, monarchs, and his own circumstances into an imaginative, life-shaping blend.

21:1 פלגי־מים לב־מלך ביד־יהוה על־כל־אשר יחפץ יטנו:
Channels of water—the king's heart in Yahweh's hand; he turns it to all that he desires.

The rains of 16:15 here become "channels of water" (פלגי מים), which are presented as an image for "the king's heart" (לב מלך). The equation is not obvious, and the reader looks for an explanation in the second colon. But, riddle-like, its relevance is at first unclear: "he turns it to all that he desires." The subject of the verbs here (though ambiguous) is likely to be the Lord, as suggested by the mention of his "hand" (an instrument of turning). The object "turned" has double reference: the water and the heart. In the Hebrew Bible, the heart can be turned toward other gods (1 Kgs 11:2–4) or Yahweh (Josh 24:23), toward wickedness (Ps 141:4) or wisdom (Prov 2:2). It suggests full-blooded devotion. Concerned with internal disposition, Yahweh inclines the king's desire according to his own, to "all" (כל) he sees fit. כל is expansive and underdetermined; the reader could fill it out in many ways.

The "channels of water" seem incongruous with the bodily imagery of hand and heart. Proverbs employs its favorite technique of juxtaposing the unlike, the psychological disorientation challenging conventional categories and associations.[63] Human character is an elusive, flowing stream. Grasping it may seem impossible (cf. Prov 27:16), but it is as nothing

---

61. See, e.g., Gen 6–9; Ezek 13:11–13.

62. Cf. Amos 4:7; R. B. Y. Scott, "Meteorological Phenomena and Terminology in the Old Testament," *ZAW* 64 (1952): 19.

63. Some examples of unlike parings: a crown with rottenness in 12:4, a fountain with snares in 13:14//14:27, and a lion with dew in 19:12 (see below).

to the Lord (cf. Isa 40:12). He has full control of this פלג, an artificially constructed canal under his management.[64] In Egypt and Mesopotamia, farming seems to have depended on such artificial irrigation, but it was probably not common in Palestine.[65] It may, however, have occurred in urban environments (Ps 46:5[4]), or the luxuriant gardens of the upper echelons.[66] In his kingly role-play, Qoheleth declares, "I made myself gardens and parks … pools from which to water the forest of growing trees" (Qoh 2:5–6; cf. Ps 1:3; Cant 4:12–15; Neh 3:15). In order to water, artificial pools need artificial waterways.

Accordingly, the reader might be transported to a beautiful and abundant landscape, the king's garden with its sights, smells, and sounds. כל might be translated not as "everything" but as "everyone." The king's favored ones abound with all manner of luxuries. The king is liberal and generous, superabundant with gracious gifts, a paradigm and standard of generosity. Furthermore, a פלג is dependable: "Whereas a river (nāhār) might run wild, and a wadi (nāḥāl) [sic] run dry, the artificial stream of water provides a steady, directed, full supply of refreshing, living giving water."[67]

This is a rare proverb explicitly connecting the king and Yahweh (cf. elsewhere only in 24:21 and 25:2), and it stands at the heart of a king-God cluster (20:22–21:3).[68] But the significance of the connection is not read-

---

64. This seems to be the primary reference of this term. See BDB; Reymond, *Eau*, 129, cf. Fox, *Proverbs 10–31*, 679. Compare also the commonly attested Assyrian *palgu*, meaning "canal, irrigation ditch"; see Martha T. Roth, *The Assyrian Dictionary* (Chicago: Oriental Institute of the University of Chicago, 2005), 12:62.

65. Climate and terrain probably rendered it unnecessary, in distinction to the Mesopotamian/Egyptian model of canals from major rivers (the Euphrates and the Nile), cf. Deut 11:10–11. O. Borowski, "Irrigation," in vol. 3 of *The Oxford Encyclopedia of Archaeology in the Near East*, ed. E. M. Meyers (Oxford: Oxford University Press, 1997), 181–84; Hendrik J. Bruins, "Runoff Terraces in the Negev Highlands During the Iron Age: Nomads Settling Down or Farmers Living in the Desert?," in *On the Fringe of Society: Archaeological and Ethnoarchaeological Perspectives on Pastoral and Agricultural Societies*, ed. Benjamin A. Saidel and Eveline J. van der Steen (Oxford: Archaeopress, 2007), 37–43; Reymond, *Eau*, 126–31.

66. Borowski, "Irrigation," 183; Kivatsi Jonathan Kavusa, "The Life-Giving and Life-Threatening Potential of Water and Water-Related Phenomena in the Old Testament Wisdom Literature: An Eco-Theological Exploration" (PhD, University of South Africa Press, 2015), 182–91; Reymond, *Eau*, 128.

67. Waltke, *Book of Book of Proverbs 16–31*, 168.

68. Yahweh appears in 20:22, 23, 24, 27; 21:1, 2, 3; the king appears in 20:26, 28; 21:1.

ily apparent. It exalts the king as the ultimate earthly fulfiller of Yahweh's will. But it also limits him: as free and unsearchable as he may think his heart is (Prov 25:3), it is simply a tool for the deity. And (how) can the principles be applied beyond the courtly circle? *Only the king* enjoys this special relationship, not the mere commoner? Or *even the king* is under Yahweh's control, how much more the common folk?

19:12: נהם ככפיר זעף מלך וכטל על־עשב רצונו׃

Growling like a lion—the anger of the king, but like dew on the grass is his favor.

Our final favor proverb contains two images for the king—lion and dew. Here we will concentrate on the latter, completing our triad of water metaphors. The king's favor is "like dew on the grass," shimmering in the dawn air of the reader's imagination. The Hebrew Bible explains the mysterious morning presence of dew as a dropping from heaven (Deut 33:28; Prov 3:20) and implies that it has fertilizing effects. Indeed, it parallels "rain" in life-giving potential (Deut 32:2; 2 Sam 1:21; 1 Kgs 17:1) and can bring healing (Sir 43:22) or even resurrection (Isa 26:19).[69] Blended with the target domain of the king's favor, the latter becomes similarly salubrious. The king, and every benefactor, is encouraged to abundant generosity. The courtier, and every beneficiary, is inspired to please him.

Like the spring rain, dew comes from Yahweh as a sign of his favor.[70] Withholding it is a curse.[71] Yahweh himself is even likened to dew, causing Israel to "blossom like the lily" and "take root like [the trees of] Lebanon" (Hos 14:6[5]). The earthly king now adopts this role for his people. Dew is no deluge but is quiet and gentle (Deut 32:2; Isa 18:4). Likewise, the king's favor may be not monumental but subtle. Dew is widespread and far-reaching—is royal benevolence so too? It can still accumulate over the rainless summer and provide some moisture for the hardened earth.[72] There is hope for the reader suffering drought in her life.

---

69. Dew and resurrection are increasingly associated in later Jewish and Christian tradition. See, e.g., Brigitte Kern-Ulmer, "Consistency and Change in Rabbinic Literature as Reflected in the Terms Rain and Dew," *JSJ* 26 (1995): 71–74.

70. Gen 27:28; Deut 33:28; Zech 8:12.

71. Gen 27:39; 2 Sam 1:21; 1 Kgs 17:1; Hag 1:10.

72. So Fox, *Proverbs 10–31*, 654.

The imaginative elaboration process, however, may lead to some darker undertones, particularly if the reader's own "king" is not so beneficent. Is dew really conducive to flourishing, or is it simply a necessity? Is it even that? Dew comes silently and unpredictably; it will not "wait for the children of man" (Mic 5:6[7]; cf. 2 Sam 17:12), and its levels can vary greatly.[73] The king's subject cannot affect where his favor falls, making futile any attempts to garner it through good behavior. Dew is ephemeral and fleeting, "going early away" (משכים הלך; Hos 6:4; 13:3). The king's favor may dissipate as quickly as it formed. Like the natural world, the king's character (and all human character) contains good and bad. Though here he may sit atop the natural and social orders, his position atop the moral order is not so secure. He is a problematic paradigm. The reader is trained to explore such connotations, subversive and courageous. She must not be afraid of possibilities but must give full examination to the ambiguous phenomena of life.

The water imagery in these proverbs—spring rains, streams, and dew—opens them up to imaginative exploration, multiplying their didactic potential. Addressed to the courtier-beneficiary, they motivate him to develop a *character* that the king would find pleasing. Addressed to the king-benefactor, they advocate generosity. But there are ambiguities. The king's character is complex and may not prove a perfect paradigm. The readers align their *worldviews* accordingly. The king may be magnanimous, the quasi-divine bestower of the waters of life. But rain can be sporadic (16:15), and dew fleeting (19:12). Neither is predictable or controllable. So too the king's favor? These connotations are deep below the stream's surface and perhaps as fleeting as the dew itself, but they should not be dismissed immediately. Discerning them serves as *mental training*, giving rein to the readers' imagination and reason. The proverbs invite readers to evaluate interpretations, even if quiet or subversive.

6.3.2.2. The King's Wrath

19:12: נהם ככפיר זעף מלך וכטל על־עשב רצונו

Growling like a lion—the anger of the king, but like dew on the grass is his favor.

---

73. See M. Gilead and N. Rosenan, "Ten Years of Dew Observation in Israel," *IEJ* 4 (1958): 120–23.

In multisensory juxtaposition, Prov 19:12 combines the delicate moisture of dew on the feet with a fearsome growling in the ears.[74] The lion was probably familiar in ancient Israel/Judah, if not through personal experience, then through popular conception. Lions could apparently roam near human habitation (e.g., Judg 14; 1 Sam 17:34–37), offering the sluggard an excuse to stay indoors (Prov 22:13; 26:13). Across the ancient Near East, lions are "the mightiest among beasts" (Prov 30:30), commonly associated with kings for their power and majesty. The king here is not comfortable and affectionate but fear-inspiring. Egyptian, Mesopotamian, and Hittite royal inscriptions employ the motif, and leonine iconography occurs on royal ships, chariots, and thrones.[75] Kings boast of their power over lions, and even describe themselves in such terms: "I am king, I am lord, I am powerful, … I am a virile lion, … I am raging" (Adadnarari II).[76]

The Hebrew Bible, however, is much more reticent about the king-lion connection, and Israelite monarchs are almost never described as such.[77] Rather, the language is reserved for God himself. He is likened to a lion more than to any other creature, the one who "roars from Zion."[78] In this guise, he destroys wicked peoples, suggesting his great and untameable power, put to a righteous end. Strikingly, the king here assumes this role as an unstoppable, divinely authorized instrument of justice, one to be exalted and feared. The proverb perhaps inspires leaders to cultivate such a persona.

However, such connotations may not be found by every reader, particularly if her own king shows no godlike justice. Indeed, later in Proverbs, "a roaring lion [אֲרִי־נֹהֵם] or a charging bear is a wicked ruler over a poor people" (28:15). Perhaps the king has usurped Yahweh's role without authorization. Lions are a common biblical metaphor for destructive ene-

---

74. Instead of a growl, the LXX has a "bite" here (βρυγμῷ).

75. Strawn, *Stronger Than a Lion?*, 174–84.

76. Strawn, *Stronger Than a Lion?*, 179.

77. The only examples are: Saul and Jonathan were "stronger than lions" (2 Sam 1:23), Solomon's throne was flanked by lions (1 Kgs 10:19–20), and two foreign kings are depicted as lions (Ezek 32:2–3; Jer 50:17). Strawn suggests that this is a "glaring omission when seen in the light of the ancient Near Eastern data" (*Stronger Than a Lion?*, 236). He suggests that this is because the writers did not want to import any of the divine connotations of the lion image onto a human figure.

78. Joel 4:16[3:16]; cf. Isa 31:4; Jer 25:30, 38; 49:19; 50:44; Hos 5:14; 13:7–8; Amos 3:8. See Strawn, *Stronger Than a Lion?*, 58.

mies.[79] In ancient Near Eastern iconography, they are terrifying beasts and sometimes depict demons.[80] These may provoke terror in the reader. The proverb invites her into the start of a story: the growl before the attack. She can elaborate the grim continuation for herself. "The lion has roared; who will not fear?" (Amos 3:8a).

The lion-king of 19:12 may be violent and merciless. His methods are brutal and indiscriminate, his rage unrestrained. He roars against the "good sense" of the previous verse, which makes one "slow to anger" (19:11a). The proverb can condemn as ferociously as it glorifies. Employed to different ends, leonine traits may be desirable or abhorrent, for, as Brent A. Strawn put it, "the lion is a *polyvalent symbol.*"[81] The reader must adjudicate between interpretations and deploy them discriminately.

Furthermore, this image must be held together with the other in the proverb—"dew on the grass"—for both apply to the same king. This provides an intellectual puzzle, a challenge to reconcile seemingly irreconcilable realities.[82] Incongruous characteristics are simultaneously embodied by the same individual. Despite the all-or-nothing impression of some proverbs, character is endlessly complex. Placed side by side, the images play off each other. As the reader ponders them, categories and images shift and are reinterpreted. Taking the parallelism as synonymous ("and"), their similarities come to the fore. In both images, the king has supreme, uncontrollable power over the human and natural world. Taken as antithetical ("but"), differences are highlighted. The most pertinent is the polarization of destroying and giving life, but others too may emerge.

---

79. כפיר in Jer 2:15; 51:38; Pss 35:17; 58:7[6]; cf. also Isa 5:29; Jer 4:7; 50:17; Joel 1:6; Amos 3:12; Zech 11:3; Pss 7:3[2]; 10:9; 17:12; 22:14[13].

80. Strawn, *Stronger Than a Lion?*, 134–51; Othmar Keel, *The Symbolism of the Biblical World: Ancient Near Eastern Iconography and the Book of Psalms* (New York: Seabury, 1978), 86.

81. Strawn, *Stronger Than a Lion?*, 26 (italics original); cf. I. Cornelius, "The Lion in the Art of the Ancient Near East: A Study of Selected Motifs," *JNSL* 15 (1989): 65.

82. Some think they are too different to be compatible and have sought emendation by deleting נהם and changing ככפיר to ככפר ("like the hoarfrost"). This would provide a tighter parallelism with טל ("dew"), with which hoarfrost is paired in Exod 16:14. Gemser, *Sprüche Salomos*; Ehrlich, *Randglossen*; Isac Leo Seeligmann, "Voraussetzungen der Midraschexegese," in Anderson, *Congress Volume Copenhagen 1953*, 150–81. However, this emendation has no textual support and is unnecessary. Proverbs allows interesting juxtapositions of images, and the combination of a lion and dew is known in Mic 5:6–7[7–8].

The lion ravages individual victims, whereas dew covers everything. Lions are rare, but dew is common. Does the king bestow his wrath on the unfortunate few but his favor on the masses? The lion creates a strong response of terror, but the dew is understated. Is the king's wrath to be feared more than his favor is to be desired? The proverb opens up questions and lets the reader explore so as to train her mind.

20:2 נהם ככפיר אימת מלך מתעברו חוטא נפשו:

Growling like a lion—dread fear of the king; the one who enrages him forfeits his life/sins against himself.

This proverb uses the same motif as 19:12—a growling lion—with all its ambiguities of characterization. However, the Hebrew is particularly difficult, and each of the other phrases—אימת מלך, מתעברו, and חוטא נפשו—is disputed in scholarship. אימת מלך describes the "dread fear of the king," depicting the terrified courtier. But how can this be a source of "growling"? Growling would more logically come from the angry king himself (as in 19:12).[83] The two parts of the colon press together; their relationship is oblique, left for the reader to decipher. Possibly, the relationship is cause and effect: (I hear a) growling like a lion; (I feel) dread fear of the king.

The next problematic element is מתעברו. √עבר occurs in the *hithpael* five times outside Proverbs, in the reflexive meaning "to enrage oneself."[84] But this does not explain the third-person masculine singular suffix here (*"he enrages himself him"?), and the sense seems to require that the king is angered, not "oneself."[85] Most plausibly, the *hithpael* may be understood as an indirect reflexive—"to enrage *against* oneself"—with the suffix as a direct object ("him" = the king).[86] The advice not to provoke the king

---

83. Some find this too problematic and accordingly suggest emending to חמת ("anger"). André Barucq, *Le livre des Proverbes*, SB (Paris: [s.n.], 1964); Clifford, *Proverbs*. Perhaps struggling with this problem, the LXX has the king's "threat" (ἀπειλή) here.

84. Deut 3:26; Pss 78:21, 59, 62; 89:39[38]. The other occurrences in Proverbs (14:16 and 26:17) are also difficult.

85. Hatton retains the reflexive sense "enrages himself" and suggests that the suffix simply emphasizes "himself," but this seems elsewhere unattested in Biblical Hebrew (*Contradiction*, 134).

86. So many commentators (implicitly or explicitly); see, e.g., Barucq, *Le livre des Proverbes*; Delitzsch, *Biblical Commentary*; Fox, *Proverbs 10–31*; Gemser, *Sprüche*

would accord with the next verse's commendation of "keeping away from strife" (שבת מריב; 20:3a).

Also difficult is the subsequent phrase חוטא נפשו (cf. Hab 2:10). Both terms are polysemous, and their grammatical relationship is unclear. Possibly there is a double meaning.[87] חטא may be close to its etymological sense "to miss," extended here to "to forfeit," and נפש may mean "life": he who angers him "forfeits his life" (cf. the common converse "preserves his life" [שמר נפשו]; Prov 13:3; 16:17; 19:16; 21:23).[88] The act-consequence logic provides strong motivation to discern pleasing behavior.

Alternatively, √חטא may be taken in its usual sense as "to sin," with נפשו as a reflexive pronoun. √חטא usually takes a separate preposition "against" (ל/ב), but it might admit a direct object too (cf. Prov 8:36). Thus here, he "sins against himself."[89] This sophisticated interiority and self-alienation—

Salomos; Yoder, *Proverbs*. This seems to be the understanding of the versions. The LXX has "the one who provokes him" (ὁ δὲ παροξύνων αὐτὸν), and Pesh. (=Targ.) has "the one who angers him" (*dmḥmt*). See *IBHS*, §26.2d; GKC, §54f. Indirect reflexives may take direct objects—e.g., Exod 32:3 ויתפרקו ... את־נזמי הזהב ("they tore off [*from themselves*] ... the gold rings"); Mic 6:16 וישתמר חקות עמרי ("he kept [*for himself*] the statutes of Omri" [cf. also Exod 33:6; Josh 9:12; 1 Sam 18:4; Isa 52:2]). Though the text is difficult, Mic 6:16 may form a particularly apt parallel. השתמר is elsewhere a regular reflexive "to keep oneself" (Ps 18:24 // 2 Sam 22:24), but this does not exclude an indirect reflexive in Micah. Similarly, התעבר usually means "to enrage oneself," but "to enrage against oneself" may be possible here. Fox suggests this sense for Sir 16:8 too (המתעברים) (*Eclectic Edition*). Other interpretations have also been suggested. Heim takes it as from √עבר I ("to transgress against"), though the *hithpael* of this root would be an unexplained *hapax legomenon* (*Poetic Imagination*, 456). This seems to be the understanding of MSS α΄σ΄θ΄, who have ὑπερβαίνων "transgress" here. G. R. Driver relates מתעבר to the ithpael of Syr '*br* and Arab *ǧabara*, translating accordingly as "he that is negligent"; see Driver, "Hebrew Notes on Prophets and Proverbs," *JTS* 41 (1940): 174. There is, however, no other evidence for this meaning in Hebrew. Some scholars have related the sense to √ערב ("to mix up") (though unattested in verbal form in Biblical Hebrew): "he who meddles with him" (discussed by McKane, *Proverbs*; Fox, *Proverbs 10–31*). They suggest either textual corruption through metathesis of ר and ב, or a semantic conflation of these roots. Some LXX manuscripts may support this reading, as they add καὶ ἐπιμιγύμενος ("and he mixes") to the *b* colon.

87. Waltke, *Book of Book of Proverbs 16–31*; Yoder, *Proverbs*; Heim, *Poetic Imagination*.

88. Gemser, *Sprüche Salomos*; Ringgren and Zimmerli, *Sprüche/Prediger*; McKane, *Proverbs*. The possibility of this semantic extension of √חטא, however, is unclear. BDB gives this meaning for חטא for this verse; see also Hab 2:10; Prov 8:36; 19:2; Job 5:24.

89. So LXX (ἁμαρτάνει εἰς τὴν ἑαυτοῦ ψυχήν), Vulg., Barucq, *Le livre des Proverbes*.

separating the "I" who sins from the "I" who is offended—may seem foreign to Proverbs. But there are parallels: elsewhere one "despises" (מוֹאֵס;
15:32), "hates" (שׂוֹנֵא; 29:24), and "does violence to" (חֹמֵס; 8:36) "himself"
(נַפְשׁוֹ). There is complexity in character far beyond the wicked (who sins)
and the righteous (who feels offense). Furthermore, it is the courtier here
who sins, not the king, whose behavior (even if filled with leonine wrath)
remains uncondemned.[90] This ambiguates the ethical system: sin seems to
be mapped in relation to the social hierarchy (cf. Qoh 10:4). Perhaps sin-
less behavior would amount to political savvy or sycophancy.

The reader can explore these complexities of characterization of courtier and king in order to discern whether either is worthy of emulation. If
the double meaning of חטא נפשׁו is discerned, then the phrase reflects both
an act (sinning) and a consequence (forfeiting your life). The reader is
taught to connect the two halves in language and in life (see chapter 5).

16:14: חֲמַת־מֶלֶךְ מַלְאֲכֵי־מָוֶת וְאִישׁ חָכָם יְכַפְּרֶנָּה׃
The anger of the king—messengers of death, a wise man will appease it.

Our final proverb connects the king's wrath with מַלְאֲכֵי־מָוֶת ("messengers of death"). The genitive may be attributive ("messengers consisting of
death") or resultative ("messengers leading to death"). Similarly, the juxtaposition of phrases may indicate a metaphorical equation (the anger *is* the
messengers) or an outcome (the anger *results in* the messengers). Furthermore, the identity of the messengers has been subject to much scholarly
dispute. מַלְאָךְ is polysemous and allows both literal and metaphorical
interpretations.

Some suggest that the proverb draws on Ugaritic mythology, with מָוֶת
alluding to a god and the genitive giving the origin: "messengers from
Mot."[91] But this is an unnecessary speculation, and there are more plau-

---

Alternatively, perhaps, an apposition of instrument: "He sins [with/in] his soul" (cf.
Mic 6:7).

90. For an alternative interpretation, see Hatton, *Contradiction*, 134.

91. H. L. Ginsberg argued that in Ugarit, Baal sent his messengers in pairs ("Baal's
Two Messengers," *BASOR* 95 [1944]: 25–30). When Baal's attendants *Gpn* and *'Ugr*
are referred to, the form is probably dual. Dahood relates this to the present verse
of Proverbs, translating "Death's two messengers" (*Northwest Semitic Philology*, 36).
Waltke suggests that here the metaphor "is an allusion to an Ugaritic myth … because
the form is probably dual" (*Book of Proverbs 16–31*, 21). But the logic must run the
other way. Nothing suggests a dual form (morphologically identical to a plural in the

sible options. First, מלאכי could refer to literal human messengers (cf. 13:17), presumably ready at the king's disposal. Solomon sends Benaiah to kill his opponents (1 Kgs 2), and Saul has Doeg slaughter the priests of Nob (1 Sam 22); the king's henchmen here too inflict death (cf. also Jer 26:22–23; 2 Kgs 6:32–33). This culturally plausible scenario provides concrete motivation against inciting wrath. Second, מלאכי could be taken as divine messengers, angels. Elsewhere, the Lord sends an "angel" (מלאך) to inflict his deathly punishment; perhaps the earthly king too has access to such heavenly sources.[92] His grandeur and power rise to quasi-divine status, increasing the subject's fear of him: who can stop such supernatural wrath? Third, מלאכי could be an open metaphor for any number of punishments. The reader may imagine their specific form in particular circumstances and elaborate on the emergent story. מות in Proverbs is not just physical death, but it is a cipher for any calamity. Undisclosed disaster arrives at the offender's door, ready to deliver his poisonous package.

However interpreted, the first colon suggests the king's absolute power. The subsequent verse makes him lord over "life" (16:15a, see above, §6.3.2.1); here his dominion is "death." The proverb pair gives the same polar depiction as we saw condensed into 19:12. The proverb does not disclose its own evaluation, merely stating the fact and allowing the reader to make up her own mind as she confronts the realities of character and society. She might stand in awe, finding a paradigm for her own domestic dominion. Or she may be outraged, standing above the king in the moral hierarchy and condemning his murderous wrath (cf. 16:32).

In self-protection, she might align herself with the "wise man," who "will appease" the king's anger.[93] This second colon can function in two quite different ways. First, it may extol the value of wisdom. The prototypical wise man overflows with qualities guaranteed to quash the flames (cf. 29:8). Filling out the characterization, the reader might consider gracious speech, which can "turn away wrath" (15:1) and persuade a ruler

---

construct state) apart from the possible Ugaritic allusion. Very little suggests that allusion. Indeed, apart from one contested passage (Baal I ii.16–17; cited in Ginsberg, "Baal's Two Messengers," 29 n. 20), the two Ugaritic messengers belong not to "Death" (Mot) but to Baal.

92. See 2 Sam 24 // 1 Chr 21; 2 Kgs 19:35 // Isa 37:36 // 2 Chr 32:21; Ps 35:5.

93. Etymologically related to "covering," √כפר (piel) usually means "to atone for (sin)" (e.g., 16:6), but this sense does not fit here. Rather, it seems to mean "to cover over, pacify" (BDB 1), as in Gen 32:21[20].

(25:15). Indeed, the previous verse affirms that the king loves righteous lips (16:13). The colon then has a [character—consequence] structure and can function evaluatively or directively. To pacify the king, I *direct* you to become wise. Once pacified, I commend you for it and *evaluate* you as wise.

Alternatively, the pacifying may be a deliberate *act* (rather than a consequence).[94] It would be wise, advises this savvy political note, to assuage the king's anger when it arises. Attempting to bear it only heralds death. The astute reader, holding the king's anger contemptibly, and aware of the possibility of persuasion, can discern how to achieve this. Wisdom here, like sin in 20:2, is defined in terms of society and of personal/political ends, challenging the neat moral classifications offered elsewhere.

These final three proverbs graphically depict the king's wrath through imagery open for exploration. The readers can evaluate the character of both king and courtier. Is the king's wrath a paradigm for the leader? Is a courtier's morality best judged by his political acumen? Simple character classifications are found wanting in the complexity of real life, and the machinations of the court. The worldview espoused is somewhat ambiguous. The king may be a majestic, quasi-divine lion, deserving the highest respect. Or his anger may be an abominable character flaw. Confronted with these conflicts, readers are forced to exercise their minds. They must adjudicate between interpretations without fearing subversive or challenging ideas.

6.4. Conclusion

This chapter has explored a selection of proverbs about the king in order to show their openness and its contribution to their double use as didactic proverbs. Three scholarly questions were raised at the start of the chapter: what is the depiction of the king (how favorable; how closely associated with Yahweh)? Do the proverbs need a courtly setting? How do they function pedagogically? Regarding *setting*, I have suggested that a literal court is not necessary (though it is possible). As proverbs, the verses could be spoken to many different people, in many different situations, for many different reasons. The king and courtier might be idealized figures, *pedagogically* designed as standards for evaluation or paradigms for emulation.

---

94. So, e.g., Toy, *Critical and Exegetical Commentary*.

However, there are subversive elements; this is no straightforwardly favorable *depiction*.

If the courtier is a paradigm in these proverbs, the reader is called upon to develop a *character* pleasing to the king. Motivation is strong in light of the king's righteous judgment, magnificent favor, and terrible wrath. If the king is truly just, then righteousness is the aim. However, this may not be so, and morality might be reoriented by political savvy and personal ends. If the reader instead aligns himself with the king, he is encouraged to embody justice, beneficent favor, and (perhaps) righteous anger. But the king's character is not unthinkingly glorified. Like all human character, it is complex, and even in the positive portrayals, there are disturbing ambiguities. The picture is darkest when displaying his wrath.

Imagery elsewhere used of Yahweh is passed to the monarch in these proverbs, perhaps suggesting that he is the divine viceroy, instigating God's rule on earth. Or perhaps the king has usurped the role illegitimately; Yahweh is nowhere to be found when the lion-king roars unjustly. When the relationship is explicit, the monarch seems to be subordinate, with no true authority of his own (21:1).

These ambiguities strongly encourage the reader's *intellectual engagement*. Her assumed identity shifts—courtier, king, critic—necessitating dynamic interpretation. The moral norm is sometimes dislocated from the proverbs themselves, provoking her to seek it elsewhere. She must use imagination, logic, and experience to evaluate king and proverb, to weigh possible interpretations. Such explorations require courage and sensitivity, giving ear to nondominant views. Even if the resultant interpretations are ultimately rejected, the process of interpreting is formative.

These elements of character development, worldview, and intellectual training give the proverbs strong didactic potential. They help their addressee to acquire wisdom about the world. She listens to the general principles about the king and weighs them in light of specific situations. She engages her mind to scrutinize both proverb and king, and embodies their wisdom into her own character. The next chapter will focus more intentionally on the process by which such wisdom is gained.

7
Acquiring Wisdom through the
Openness of Didactic Proverbs

ראשית חכמה קנה חכמה ובכל־קנינך קנה בינה:
The beginning of wisdom: get wisdom! And whatever you get, get insight.
— Prov 4:7

7.1. Wisdom Mediated by the Didactic Proverb Genre

Proverbs calls upon its students to get wisdom. This is not just a commendation of propositional knowledge but a call to exist in the world in a new way, a way shaped by Proverbs itself. This chapter will consider what that process entails.

Scholars have distinguished several tensions in the way Proverbs expresses its wisdom. Is wisdom more concerned with the textual or the extratextual world? The general or the specific? The moral or the intellectual? The religious or the secular? Scholars may situate themselves on one side or the other, or attempt to mediate between them. I suggest that each of these tensions can be explained and clarified by considering the double didactic-proverb genre. What is more, the text's openness allows wisdom to be carried through the tensions. The first three of these tensions will be considered in this section, and the fourth later (§7.3), in order to begin to answer the pressing question of the sage: "Where can wisdom be found?" (Job 28:12).

7.1.1. Wisdom Is Found in Textual and Extratextual Worlds

The book of Proverb creates a textual world, which relates in some sense to the outside extratextual world of the reader. But in which world is true wisdom to be found? Many have suggested that Proverbs' epistemology is essentially empirical—it advocates seeking wisdom in the extratextual world.[1] Several passages give apparent descriptions of empiricism in practice (e.g., 6:6–11; 7:6–27; 24:30–34), and it is characteristic of the proverb genre to give straightforward observations of life.

However, the epistemology cannot be *simply* empiricism. The act-consequence proverbs, for example—so often violated by the realities of life—are unlikely to have been empirically derived. Von Rad has suggested that empiricism was essential to the book's formation but that in its current form it stands two steps removed. Proverbs are by genre the product of an empirical quest, "a rudimentary expression of man's search for knowledge," a means of discovering the world.[2] However, by formulating the worldly tangle of events into language, the interpreter moves herself a first step beyond them, asserting an order. Situations are observed, and captured in language, in tight proverbial bindings. Thereby, as Walther Zimmerli put it, "The things which are elusive, that seem to be so mobile that they cannot be grasped, are seized, stopped, established."[3] Through the textual world, the extratextual world is controlled. In a second step, von Rad suggests that the proverbs' form and goal were altered when incorporated into the biblical book: they were now oriented to the "cultivation of men" only.[4] The essential empiricism of the proverb was transformed when they became didactic.

Some have, in fact, challenged whether there is anything left of empiricism in the book. Fox argues instead that Proverbs operates with a "coherence theory" of truth.[5] It sets out a system of compatible beliefs, and no empirical insight can be accepted unless it is coherent with this system. Several scholars further argue that this constructed textual world "eclipses the tangible objective world."[6] It fills the reader's vision with a value system

---

1. In 2007, Fox could call this a "scholarly consensus." See Michael V. Fox, "The Epistemology of the Book of Proverbs," *JBL* 126 (2007): 669–84. E.g., James L. Crenshaw, *Education in Ancient Israel: Across the Deadening Silence*, ABRL (New York: Doubleday, 1998), 51–52; Frydrych, *Living under the Sun*, 53–57.

2. Von Rad, *Wisdom in Israel*, 30–32, quote from 30; von Rad, *Old Testament Theology*, 1:418–41; cf. Walther Zimmerli, "The Place and Limit of the Wisdom in the Framework of the Old Testament Theology," *SJT* 17 (1964): 146–58.

3. Zimmerli, "Place and Limit of Wisdom," 149–50, elaborating on von Rad's view.

4. Von Rad, *Old Testament Theology*, 1:432.

5. Fox, "Epistemology."

6. See, e.g., Sandoval, *Discourse of Wealth and Poverty*, 6; Viljoen, *Exploration of the Symbolic World*, 35. The language is taken from Ricoeur.

not to be questioned or changed, more valid and true than anything outside of itself.

I suggest that there is an important relationship between these worlds, but it is not one of eclipsing. The outside world retains some independent status. Along with listening to the book's instruction, personal observation *is* validated: "The hearing ear and the seeing eye, the Lord made them both" (Prov 20:12). The proverb genre cannot function unless embedded in real life. A proverb has only a partial meaning until applied to a situation (see §3.2), and its legitimacy depends upon finding genuine traction there. Spoken aptly, it emerges as the crystallization of an insight discovered in the world. The book does offer its own textual world, but this is open and not immutable. It is more a generalized framework, responsive to specific situations as they emerge.

7.1.2. Wisdom Is General and Specific

The textual world of Prov 10:1–22:16 is structured around regularities. Each proverb offers a succinct principle, a "breakthrough to the generally and universally valid."[7] Each recognizes a recurring type, a common category or pattern. Character categories (ch. 4) and act-consequence patterns (ch. 5) are paramount. Brought together into a didactic collection, these provide sound instruction for the whole of life. The principles are not neutral but value laden and morally charged, shaping a new vision for reality. But the outside world is not eclipsed by this vision; rather, it is seen through it. It offers a framework of general principles by which to understand and evaluate the specificities of life. This is not, however, absolute law. It is no closed inviolable system, but by virtue of its construction through *proverbs*, it remains essentially open.

The self-contained form and haphazard arrangement of the sayings means that no total system is reached. This mentality has been described as gnomic, rather than systematic.[8] As characterized by literary critic André Jolles, the individuality of each saying is paramount: "In the bonds, separation predominates; in the relatedness, juxtaposition remains; in the order,

---

7. Von Rad, *Old Testament Theology*, 1:420; cf. von Rad, *Wisdom in Israel*, 32.

8. See, e.g., Crenshaw, "Education in Ancient Israel," 116–17; von Rad, *Old Testament Theology*, 1:420–22; von Rad, *Wisdom in Israel*, 30; Williams, *Those Who Ponder Proverbs*.

the isolation of members exists."[9] Jolles influenced, for example, Hans-Jürgen Hermisson, who argued that the world of Proverbs progresses "in an abundance of single phenomena," and von Rad, for whom every individual phenomenon "stand[s] in its own particular character absolutely."[10] Each proverb provides only a shard of experience, a glistening fragment belonging to a mosaic whose overall construction is unknown.

This unsystematizing nature is particularly apparent in contradictory proverbs, which challenge any notion of a fully fledged coherence theory.[11] These occur in many cultures: "Absence makes the heart grow fonder," but also "Out of sight, out of mind"; in Proverbs, "Answer not a fool according to his folly," but also "Answer a fool according to his folly" (26:4–5; cf. also 17:27–28). In life, every rule admits of exceptions; experience is too unwieldy and variegated for rigid dogma. As didactic literature, wisdom can be generalized into time-tested principles, but as a proverb, it requires constant verification in the local and particular.

This further suggests that no single principle can apply to every situation. The external world has a reality unconstrained by the textual framework. Because of their generality, the proverbs are open to many circumstances, but there will always be those that do not fit. Several recent scholars have stressed this concern for fittingness, O'Dowd even calling it the "lost epistemology of aphoristic ... thinking."[12] This requires further nuance, however. It is not that the principle is a rigid crate into which only

---

9. "In den Bindungen überwiegt die Trennung, in den Bezogenheiten bleibt das Nebeneinander, in den Ordnungen die Sonderung der Glieder bestehen" (André Jolles, *Einfache Formen: Legende, Sage, Mythe, Rätsel, Spruch, Kasus, Memorabile, Märchen, Witz* [Tübingen: Niemeyer, 1930], 156, my translation; Jolles's work was recently translated into English as *Simple Forms*, trans. Peter J. Schwartz [New York: Verso, 2017]). Jolles distinguished seven "simple forms" in folk language, each tied to a particular form of thought.

10. Hermisson, *Studien zur israelitischen Spruchweisheit*, 140: "in einer Fülle von Einzelphänomenen." Von Rad, *Old Testament Theology*, 1:421; cf. von Rad, *Wisdom in Israel*, 113.

11. On contradiction, see, e.g., Jerry A. Gladson, "Retributive Paradoxes in Proverbs 10–29" (PhD diss., Vanderbilt University, 1978); Hatton, *Contradiction*; Yoder, "Forming 'Fearers of Yahweh.'"

12. Ryan O'Dowd, *The Wisdom of Torah: Epistemology in Deuteronomy and the Wisdom Literature*, FRLANT 225 (Göttingen: Vandenhoeck & Ruprecht, 2009), 136; cf. Bartholomew and O'Dowd, *Old Testament Wisdom Literature*, 91–95; van Leeuwen, *Context and Meaning*, 99–106.

certain situations will fit. Rather, the principle itself admits some flexibility and may be molded according to its contents. It is more like a bag than a box. Because of their openness—their ambiguity and fuzzy edges—we can nuance our understanding of the proverbial principles according to our experience of life.

7.1.3. Wisdom Is Moral and Intellectual

For didactic proverbs, then, wisdom is found in textual and extratextual worlds, in the general and the specific. It is also moral and intellectual. In chapter 4, we saw the close correlation between the "wise" and the "righteous," and the didactic concern for the development of moral character. In Proverbs' embodied epistemology, acquiring wisdom is not like receiving an object; it is like taking a medicine, effective over both mind and morals. It changes their decrepit state to one of health and vitality. Exploring the openness of proverbs and the world produces this character development. Exploration enlivens the moral senses and shapes the desires. True embodied wisdom must be manifested in practice. Wisdom is not a hypothetical construct of the textual world but a reality actualized by deeds in the extratextual world. Just as general principles are manifested in specific situations, character is borne out in action. This action-orientation is essential to the proverb genre.

But the wisdom of didactic proverbs does retain an intellectual aspect. As didactic texts, they instill a worldview, offering general principles for life. As proverbs, they evaluate specific situations according to these principles. Furthermore, they are intended to train the mind. Contrary to some scholarly views, the wisdom of this genre is neither naïve nor uncritical. The sayings encourage intellectual engagement as an avenue to wisdom. Akin to riddles and aphorisms, they are not always forthright in their meaning. Their polysemy, imagery, and parallelism must all be deciphered, requiring logic and imagination. Such skills for interpreting the text can then be deployed to interpret the world. Confronting contradictory proverbs trains the mind in how to approach contradictory realities. There must be a thoughtful negotiation between principle and situation, textual world and real world, not an uncritical superimposition. The principle must be both fleshed out and left flexible, open to reappraisal by an active mind.

Both the textual world and the real world are complex and sometimes deceptive. Sometimes neat causal structures, like the act-consequence connection, are violated (see ch. 5); sometimes social and moral categories, embodied in figures like the king, break down (see ch. 6). We will see below that even general teachings, specific situations, character, and intellect can deceive us, and they must be engaged with thoughtfully, scrutinized as well as trusted.

7.2. A Principle for Acquiring Wisdom: Trust and Scrutinize

In order to "get wisdom" (Prov 4:5, 7), I suggest that this stance can be adopted: trust and scrutinize. Proverbs' general didactic principles are safe and ordered, worthy of trust.[13] However, specific situations may display contradiction and ambiguity. An individual's actions are usually a guide to her overall character, but sometimes she may deceive. This necessitates scrutiny alongside trust, when interpreting both proverbs and the outside world. This is made possible by the openness of each.

In each section that follows (§§7.2.1, 7.2.2, 7.3), I will first outline the grounds for trust and scrutiny. I will then scrutinize a proverb that makes a comment on these issues, but whose position is ambiguous. By one interpretation, these proverbs advocate trust; by another they advise scrutiny. In their status as sagacious wisdom, they are to be trusted; by encapsulating the debate within themselves, they goad their readers to scrutinize.

7.2.1. Trusting and Scrutinizing Other People

7.2.1.1. Introduction

Wisdom is moral—embodied in general character and actualized in specific actions. It can be acquired by observing human behavior and evaluating it according to the sages' overall framework. Proverbs affirms the trustworthy simplicity of this process. Yet it also recognizes the art of deception; human character and behavior should be scrutinized.

In Proverbs, other people are central to wisdom acquisition; this is unsurprising given the community-centered ethos of the book. The implicit addressee is inextricably enmeshed in "a small, tightly-knit community, in which each individual's behaviour has a great impact on the life of everyone else."[14] He is advised on interpersonal relationships and

---

13. See esp. von Rad, *Wisdom in Israel*, 190–95.
14. Frydrych, *Living under the Sun*, 148.

lured by the great reward of social esteem.[15] In this interdependent society, he learns from his fellows. "Walk with the wise" galvanizes Prov 13:20, "and become wise."[16] In general, the behavior of others can be trusted to reveal the character behind it. Wisdom is embodied and lived, and character manifests itself in action. The righteous man is clearly distinguishable from the wicked, and observing his behavior brings a greater understanding of righteousness.

However, some proverbs problematize this principle. "Deceit" (מרמה) characterizes wrongdoers' schemes (12:5) and hearts (12:20), even the balances they use in the marketplace (11:1; 20:23; cf. 16:11; 20:10). We cannot trust appearances. A fool stands tight-lipped in Prov 17:28, fooling others into thinking he is wise. One pretends to be rich in 13:7 (perhaps to attain social esteem); another pretends to be poor (perhaps to avoid almsgiving).[17] We are onlookers in a court case in 18:17. When we read the first colon, we believe in the litigant's innocence—צדיק הראשון בריבו ("Righteous is the first man in his case!")—but our false impression is corrected in the second colon, when יבא־רעהו וחקרו ("His neighbor comes and examines him"). Like that neighbor, we must examine and scrutinize others before placing our trust in them, for acts and appearances are no fail-safe measures for evaluating true character or for true wisdom.

7.2.1.2. A Proverb under Didactic Scrutiny

20:11 גם במעלליו יתנכר־נער אם־זך ואם־ישר פעלו:

Indeed, in his deeds a young man reveals/disguises himself, whether his conduct is pure and upright.[18]

---

15. For the former, see, e.g., 10:12; 15:18; 16:28; 17:9, 14; 18:19, 24; 19:13; 20:3; 21:9; 22:10; for the latter, 12:4; 13:18; 15:33; 18:12; 19:26; 21:21; 22:4.

16. *Ketiv*. The *Qere* changes the imperatives to a participle and imperfect respectively.

17. Though the *hithpael/hithpolel* forms may be ambiguous (see above, §2.1.2.6).

18. I have taken גם to qualify the whole of the subsequent clause as a rhetorical heightener "indeed!" (GKC §153). It may, however, be left untranslated, following Muraoka's argument that sometimes גם is simply additive, and need not be ascribed emphatic force. Takamitsu Muraoka, *Emphatic Words and Structures in Biblical Hebrew* (Leiden: Brill, 1985), 143–46. Alternatively, it might belong with the adjacent element, "even in his deeds" (NASB; Barucq, *Le livre des Proverbes*; McKane, *Proverbs*; Fox, *Proverbs 10–31*). However, it is unclear why the "deeds" should be highlighted like this. Many commentators and translators give "even a child" or similar. גם does

Let us turn now to a proverb that, I suggest, embodies the tension between trust and scrutiny within itself. Proverbs 20:11 comments on the possibility of acquiring knowledge through observing the behavior of others (*a* colon) and interpreting it according to the sages' ethical framework (*b* colon). The key point of openness is the polysemy of יתנכר. Either the young man "reveals himself"—you can trust that his behavior manifests his character—or he "disguises himself"—you cannot trust his behavior at all.

7.2.1.2.1. "Reveals Himself"

First, then, יתנכר may mean "reveals himself." The root נכר occurs frequently in the *hiphil* meaning "to regard, recognize." The corresponding reflexive *hithpael* would be "make oneself recognized, known."[19] Although this would be a *hapax legomenon* in Biblical Hebrew, it is plausible, corresponding to its meaning in several branches of Aramaic.[20] The versions attest to this understanding, and it has been accepted by the majority of translations and commentators.[21] It ties in with the book's basic message:

---

not elsewhere qualify an element not immediately subsequent to it, so this interpretation must assume that גם applies to the whole sentence and then implicitly to its most pertinent element, נער (ESV, HCSB, NKJV, NIV, NRSV; Clifford, *Proverbs*; Delitzsch, *Biblical Commentary*; Heim, *Poetic Imagination*; Toy, *Critical and Exegetical Commentary*; Waltke, *Book of Proverbs 16–31*).

19. Waltke objects that *hithpael* should be related to *piel*, not *hiphil* (*Book of Proverbs 16–31*, 120 n. 26). However, two examples of the *piel*, "to recognize," do occur (Job 21:29; 34:19). Cf. also the distribution across binyanim in the semantically close √ידע ("to know"). *Hiphil* is very common, and *piel* only occurs once (Job 38:12). *Hithpael* ("make oneself known") is attested twice: Gen 45:1; Num 12:6.

20. The *ithpeel* meaning "to be recognized" occurs in Jewish Palestinian Aramaic, Jewish Babylonian Aramaic, and Christian Palestinian Aramaic. See Michael Sokoloff, *A Dictionary of Jewish Palestinian Aramaic* (Ramat-Gan: Bar Ilan University Press, 1990); Sokoloff, *A Dictionary of Jewish Babylonian Aramaic of the Talmudic and Geonic Periods* (Ramat-Gan: Bar Ilan University Press, 2002); Sokoloff, *A Dictionary of Christian Palestinian Aramaic* (Leuven: Peeters, 2014); Marcus Jastrow, *Dictionary of Targumim, Talmud and Midrashic Literature* (Peabody, MA: Hendrickson, 2005). Correspondences with Aramaic have been noted throughout Prov 10:1–22:16; see Fox, *Proverbs 10–31*, 504–5.

21. Pesh./Targ. have *mtydꜥ* ("makes himself known"), and Vulg. has *suis intellegitur* ("is known"). The LXX is widely divergent here, and so of little help, but Symm. has ἐπιγνωρισθήσεται ("come to be recognized") and Venet. γνωσθήσεται ("come to be known"), suggesting this meaning (cited in Delitzsch [1884]). Almost all modern

a person reveals himself through what he does. His character is made evident in each of "his deeds" (מֵעֲלָלָיו). To move from observing the latter to understanding the former, the deeds must be interpreted through the sages' ethical framework: can they be classed as "pure" (זַךְ) and "upright" (יָשָׁר)?[22] The general terms are fleshed out by specific instances, and the evaluative system is developed accordingly.[23]

"Conduct" (פֹּעַל) stands as the conceptual midpoint between individual deeds and overall self. Accordingly, the second colon may elaborate on either. The revelation is by his deeds (i.e., by whether his conduct is pure in each instant) or of his self (i.e., of whether his conduct is pure overall). Self, conduct, and deeds are intimately related; wisdom is embodied and enacted. Here, אִם has been interpreted as introducing an indirect question, "whether." But it may also precede a direct question: "Is his conduct pure? Is it upright?" (cf. Job 6:12 for this syntax).[24] The hearer is urged to observe and evaluate for himself. If the question is genuine, the answer may not be obvious; character is not always absolutely clear, and borderline cases can exist.

> Trusted as a proverb: A young man has just shown unexpected kindness. I wish to educate an onlooker, so I say to her, "Indeed, in his deeds a young man reveals himself. Is his conduct pure? Is it upright?" I call upon her to evaluate the man, fleshing out her ethical framework according to his deeds and thus acquiring wisdom.

> "Even in his childish deeds a youngster reveals himself," I say to a father, "whether his conduct is pure and upright." By stressing his youth, and the importance of this formative period for ethical development, I implicitly encourage the father to exercise discipline, ensuring his son is on the right course.

The נַעַר ("young man") is just the type to stand on the border. Like the פֶּתִי ("simple"), he is malleable, susceptible to both wise and foolish influence (Prov 1:4;

translations give this meaning (except JPS). So BDB, *HALOT*, and many critical commentators (e.g., Delitzsch, *Biblical Commentary*; Fox, *Proverbs 10–31*; McKane, *Proverbs*; Murphy, *Proverbs*; Toy, *Critical and Exegetical Commentary*).

22. This pair of terms occurs also in 21:8; cf. 16:2/21:2. Some think that an antithesis is preferable and so emend יָשָׁר ("upright") to רָשָׁע ("wicked") (Toy, *Critical and Exegetical Commentary*) or זַךְ ("pure") to זָר ("strange") (Ehrlich, *Randglossen*).

23. In previous chapters, I included a separate section on proverbial use. Here I intersperse it among the didactic explorations in order to reflect the dynamic relationship between didactic and proverbial uses.

24. So Heim, *Poetic Imagination*; Waltke, *Book of Proverbs 16–31*.

7:7). He must be disciplined (22:15; 23:13; 29:15), for the path he chooses in his youth may become his path throughout life (22:6).[25] The ethical categories that sum up character have already begun to ingrain themselves. And if already in the youth, how much more in the adult!

Possibly, מעלליו here refers not just to "deeds" but to "childish deeds, play," related to the noun עולל ("child").[26] This would be a *hapax legomenon*, and it is possible but speculative and unverifiable. More plausibly, there may be a soundplay here. Hearing √עלל combined with נער may bring to mind connotations of childishness without changing the basic meaning: "deeds."[27] Moral character is manifested in the most unremarkable, even frivolous, of activities.

Thus the youth reveals himself through what he does. His individual actions are transparent to inquiry and can be trusted. The onlooker may observe them, relate them to the taught categories for ethical character, and acquire wisdom accordingly.

7.2.1.2.2. "Disguises Himself"

However, another interpretation is also possible: יתנכר means not "reveals himself" but "disguises himself"—almost its polar opposite.[28] This meaning is attested elsewhere in Biblical Hebrew (Gen 42:7; 1 Kgs 14:5–6; Sir 4:17), and √נכר can be related to "foreignness," such as is embodied in the "strange woman" (נכריה) of Prov 1–9.[29] Some passages even play on

---

25. On the difficulties of this verse, see Ted Hildebrandt, "Proverbs 22:6a: Train Up a Child?," *Grace Theological Journal* 9 (1988): 3–19.

26. So Heinrich Ewald, *Die poëtischen Bücher des alten Bundes: Vierter Theil* (Göttingen: Vandenhoeck & Ruprecht, 1837), "Spiele." Also Me'am Lo'ez, cited in Fox, *Proverbs 10–31*. Hurovitz paraphrases it as מעשי ילדות ("deeds of childhood"; משלי, 412).

27. Fox, *Proverbs 10–31*.

28. Such "antagonymy" (one word with two opposite meanings) is attested in many languages (e.g., English "cleave"). In Arabic, it is known as ʿaḍḍād (see Barr, *Comparative Philology*, 173–77). Cf. √סתם/שתם, both "to shut up" (its usual sense) and "to open" (Num 24:3, 15); also √רפה, "to be weak," and √רפא, "to heal" (conflation of the roots occurs orthographically in Jer 8:15 and possibly semantically in Prov 14:30; 15:4). This interpretation is rare in English Bible translations (but see JPS, ESV margin), but more common among rabbinical commentators (see Ginsburg, *Mishlei*) and recent interpreters (Clifford, *Proverbs*; Heim, *Poetic Imagination*; Hurovitz, משלי; Waltke, *Book of Proverbs 16–31*; Yoder, *Proverbs*).

29. Prov 2:16; 5:20; 6:24; 7:5; 20:16 (Qere); 23:27; 27:13.

the antithetical senses of the root (as I suggest this proverb does): Joseph "recognized" (ויכרם, *hiphil*) his brothers and "disguised himself" (ויתנכר) before them (Gen 42:7); Ruth asks Boaz why he "recognizes" her (להכירני, *hiphil*), even though she is a "foreign woman" (נכריה; Ruth 2:10).

Acquiring wisdom, then, is not so easy as slotting behavior into neatly prescribed categories. People may dissemble and hide their true character; they must be scrutinized. Despite appearances, perhaps their methods are reckless and ill-founded; perhaps their motives are disingenuous.

The intermediary position of "conduct" between "self" and "deeds" again allows different interpretations of the second colon. The youth disguises whether his conduct (i.e., his character) is *really* pure and upright. Or he disguises himself even though his conduct (i.e., his acts) seems pure and upright.[30] In either case, זך and ישר designate what seems to be, not what is (cf. 16:2; 21:2). The reader must see through these words, much as he must see through the youth's disguises.

> Outwardly, my student seems to be doing everything right, but I sense deception. "Indeed, in his deeds, the child dissembles," I say to him gravely, "even if his conduct seems pure and upright." I thus warn him that wickedness will not go unnoticed and perhaps imply that consequences will follow.

Indeed, his acts may be understood as "wicked deeds" if a possible nuance of מעלליו is allowed to come to the fore. Etymologically, it may be from √עלל "to act wantonly" (BDB), or √מעל "to act unfaithfully" (*HALOT*), and elsewhere it primarily designates evil acts.[31] Despite appearances, the child is wicked. His character and action must be scrutinized accordingly.

These apparently contradictory interpretations cannot both be true in the same circumstances. Each situation must be approached individually to see which applies. Knowledge is acquired in fragments and never reaches a total system. Paradigmatically cast in proverbial form, truth is situation-specific. Confronted by the enigma of opposed interpretations, the reader is forced into deep reflection. We can possibly trust the young man's deeds, for he "reveals himself" through them. Or he dissembles and

---

30. Clifford, *Proverbs*; JPS. Concessive use of אם is used in Num 22:18; Isa 1:18; Amos 9:2–4; Joüon §171d.

31. There are thirty-six instances; the exceptions are when it refers to God's "deeds" (Mic 2:7; Pss 77:12; 78:7). Heim, *Poetic Imagination*; Hurovitz, משלי; Waltke, *Book of Proverbs 16–31*.

cannot be trusted. The debate is condensed into a single sentence here; the two ends of the spring are forced on top of one another, and the reader is trapped in the tension between. The immediate literary context of the proverb offers no resolution either, apparently affirming both poles. In verse 8 the king can distinguish the wicked (see §6.2.2, above), and in verse 12 God gives tools for discernment. So in verse 11 the child is revealed? But verse 9 concerns the pretense of purity, and verse 10 concerns economic deceit. So in verse 11 the child dissembles? The reading process begins to mirror the message, as the reader is unsure which interpretation to trust. He must scrutinize the proverb's openness as he seeks wisdom from it. Does it reveal itself to us, as the child might? Or is it at play, disguising its true nature?

7.2.2. Trusting and Scrutinizing Words

7.2.2.1. Introduction

In Proverbs, words are a fundamental means of mediating wisdom.[32] Teachings are expressed verbally: spoken as proverbs and written in didactic collections. Words structure the ethical framework through categorical character terms (e.g., רשע, צדיק, אויל, חכם). When carefully applied at the proper time (15:23; 25:11), they pin down situations in language, making them comprehensible, revealing their wisdom.

Just like the wisdom they convey, words in Proverbs are social and moral, not just intellectual. They are one of the greatest revealers of character.[33] They are also potent: "Life and death are in the power of the tongue" (18:21a). Wise words are as valuable as "choice silver" (10:20) and a "precious jewel" (20:15). They are like a fountain of life (10:11), healing (12:18) and feeding (10:21) many. Through their wisdom, the student herself becomes wise (13:10; 15:31, 32; 19:20). Paradigmatically, she accepts a wise proverb's evaluation and follows its direction, letting her worldview

---

32. On the importance of words/speech in Proverbs, see Walter Bühlmann, *Vom rechten Reden und Schweigen: Studien zu Proverbien 10–31*, OBO 12 (Fribourg: Universitätsverlag, 1976); William McKane, "Functions of Language and Objectives of Discourse According to Proverbs 10–31," in Gilbert, *Sagesse de l'Ancien Testament*, 166–85.

33. Wise/fool and righteous/wicked are often distinguished by their use of speech. See above, §§4.2.1, 4.3.2.

and character be shaped accordingly. The proverbs are self-referential here. They themselves are trustworthy words, brimming with wisdom.

Not all language, however, should be accepted so readily. Indeed, only the simple man "believes every word" (14:15). Aware of the destruction that bad speech can wreak, proverbs of all cultures advise restraint.[34] The fool babbles and blunders, causing havoc for himself and others (10:19; 12:23; 13:3; 18:2; 20:19). Men are known for their untrustworthy verbiage: the "liar" (איש כזב), the "whisperer" (נרגן), the "gossip" (הולך רכיל), and the "scoffer" (לץ).[35] Lying lips are heard throughout daily life. In the marketplace a buyer lies about an item's worth (20:14), and the sluggard fabricates tales to avoid work (22:13). They are particularly dangerous in the courtroom (e.g., 12:17; 14:5, 25), where one encounters the "false witness" (עד שקרים), who "breathes out lies" (יפיח כזבים), perverting justice. Such falsehoods are an "abomination to the Lord" (12:22). They are more than factual inaccuracies; they are morally perverse and socially destructive. A lie in Proverbs is "not a theoretical lie ... but a breach of faith, unreliability, lack of trustworthiness."[36] In short, "Lying is harmful to society."[37]

However, it is not always clear how to distinguish between true and false words. It is all too easy to consume the "delicious morsels" coming from the whisperer's lips (18:8; 26:22). Proverbs 1–9 is structured around

---

34. Bad speech can be like a bloody ambush (12:6), sword thrusts (12:18), or scorching fire (16:27), destructive (11:9) and violent (10:6, 11). On restraint, see Prov 10:14, 19; 11:12, 13; 12:23; 13:3; 15:2; 17:9, 27; 18:2; 20:19; 21:23. In English, "Children should be seen and not heard," "Think before you speak," "Silence is golden." The silent man/hothead was a key contrast in Egyptian didactic literature (see Lyu, *Righteousness*, 102–7). From cross-cultural proverb analysis, paremiologist Neal R. Norrick has derived a "folk linguistics." Its first major theme is "Take care with language," explained by the principles "Language is powerful" and "Language reveals thoughts, feelings," and provoking the advice "Use words carefully; avoid careless speech" and "Use gentle words; avoid aggressive speech." This is strikingly similar to what we find in Proverbs. See Norrick, "'Speech Is Silver': On the Proverbial View of Language," *Proverbium* 14 (1997): 277–87.

35. Richardson argues that this term refers to the babbler ("Some Notes on ליץ").

36. שקר "meint ... nicht eine theoretische Lüge ... sondern den Treuebruch, die Unzuverlässigkeit, die fehlende Vertrauenswürdigkeit." Martin A. Klopfenstein, *Die Lüge nach dem Alten Testament: Ihre Begriffe, ihre Bedeutung und ihre Beurteilung* (Zürich: Gotthelf, 1964), 26.

37. "*Lüge ist gemeinschaftswidrig*" (Klopfenstein, *Die Lüge*, 353, emphasis original).

speeches by key characters: the father and Lady Wisdom on the one hand, sinners and the strange woman on the other. All make verbal appeals for the student's allegiance, and he may well find the language of the wicked characters persuasive.[38] The lips of Lady Folly "drip honey" (5:3), and she is filled with "smooth words" (2:16; 7:5, 21). The reader must learn to ignore such allures, so as to distinguish between true and deceptive speech when both are persuasive. For this, he must carefully scrutinize words.

7.2.2.2. A Proverb under Scrutiny

18:4 מים עמקים דברי פי־איש נחל נבע מקור חכמה:
Deep waters, the words of a man's mouth, a flowing brook, a fountain of wisdom.

Both sides of the debate are encapsulated in Prov 18:4. The proverb may affirm the life-giving power of words: they impart wisdom and should be trusted. Or it may warn of their destructiveness: they must be scrutinized. No character term is given—the speaker is simply a "man" (איש)—allowing either interpretation. The openness is generated by a series of images, whose nuances and interrelationship are unclear: deep waters, a flowing brook, a fountain of wisdom. These invite the reader into their depths and train her imagination.

Deep waters. Commentators are divided about whether the "deep waters" (מים עמקים) are a positive or negative trope.[39] In human experience and biblical tradition, the image opens up an ocean of connotations, to be blended imaginatively with the target domain of a man's words. First, deep waters (and men's words) can bring life or death (cf. 18:21). The raging ocean caused great fear for the Israelites and is sometimes imagined through the primordial creation myth of the battle with the sea

---

38. It may be the rhetorical strategy of these chapters to make the words of the wicked genuinely appealing to the reader. So Stewart: Lady Folly's poem "allows the student to enter deeply into precisely the nefarious desire that the father warns against" (*Poetic Ethics*, 160). Cf. J. N. Aletti, "Séduction et Parole en Proverbes I–IX," *VT* 27 (1977): 129–44; Weeks, *Instruction and Imagery*, 79–82.

39. Suggesting it is primarily negative: Brown, "Pedagogy of Proverbs"; Delitzsch, *Biblical Commentary*; Waltke, *Book of Proverbs 16–31*. Suggesting it is positive: Fox, *Proverbs 10–31*; Hatton, *Contradiction*; McKane, *Proverbs*; Reymond, *Eau*; Toy, *Critical and Exegetical Commentary*. The ambiguity is recognized by Bühlmann, *Vom rechten Reden*; Murphy, *Proverbs*; Yoder, *Proverbs*.

monster.[40] The trope swells up in the psalms of lament: "I have come into deep waters [במעמקי־מים], and the flood sweeps over me!" (69:3[2]; cf. Pss 69:15[14]; 130:1). Overwhelming tides bring terror and destruction. So too may a man's words, through their false accusations, malicious threats, or twisted advice. But deep waters can also bring life. Deep beneath the earth flow fresh, unpolluted streams.[41] Like sagacious words, they hold out the hope of restoration to the thirsty wanderer. But, second, these underground waters of wisdom, released in a well, are difficult to access. They require a man of skill and understanding to laboriously draw them up (20:5). Words must be plumbed, carefully considered, scrutinized.

Third, deep words and waters are expansive and profound. Deep wisdom belongs to the King (Prov 25:3) and God: "How great are your works, O Lord! Your thoughts are very deep [מאד עמקו]!" (Ps 92:6[5]). Long-enduring and all-encompassing, such words (like the sages' own) provide much to ponder and explore. However, wisdom too profound becomes unfathomable (e.g., Job 11:7–9, Qoh 7:24), impressing upon the student the limits of her own mind. Those "deep of lip" (עמקי שפה; Isa 33:19; Ezek 3:5–6) speak a foreign, incomprehensible tongue.

Fourth, expansive waters may hide many things. Gems of wisdom may nestle in crevices beneath the surface. But in the darkness, wicked and unwelcome secrets may also lurk (Isa 29:15; Ps 64:7[6]). The hearer must scrutinize the words she is offered, for they may conceal as much as they show.

A flowing brook. Surging alongside the "deep waters" is a "flowing brook"—נחל נבע. A נחל is a wadi: a dry valley in the rainless summer, but a plentiful stream in winter, such as flows through the "good land" of idealized Canaan.[42] It can provide an abundant habitat, where fish live, plant life thrives, and the needy may freely drink.[43] Similarly, wise speech brings refreshment and vitality.

> Trusted as a proverb: A well-known wise woman pronounces an enigma of utter profundity. "The words of a person's mouth are deep waters," I sigh in admiration, evaluating the words' sagacity and preparing myself for extensive contemplation. I hold them to be as life-giving as "a flowing brook, a fountain of wisdom."

---

40. Remnants of this view are found in, e.g., Ps 89:10–11[9–10]; Job 26:12.

41. Fox, *Proverbs 10–31*; Toy, *Critical and Exegetical Commentary*.

42. Deut 8:7; cf. Gen 26:19; Isa 35:6; Jer 31:9.

43. Fish: Lev 11:9, 10; Ezek 47:9. Plants: Lev 23:40; 1 Kgs 18:5; Ezek 47:7, 12; Job 40:22; Cant 6:11. Drinking: 1 Kgs 17:4, 6; Ps 110:7.

> A friend has been deceived by wicked words and has suffered extensively. Sympathizing with her, I acknowledge that "the words of a man's mouth are like the depths, like raging torrents." Consolingly, I add (with reference to my own advice) that they may be "a fountain of wisdom" too.

However, a נחל could also be dangerous. In heavy rains, the channel might fill and overflow, its currents unstoppably gathering momentum. Such torrents are depicted as overwhelming woeful psalmists (Pss 124:4; 18:5[4] // 2 Sam 22:5) and wicked nations (Isa 30:28; Jer 47:2). Words too can wreak destruction when wicked men "pour out" (√נבע) evil speech (Prov 15:28; cf. Pss 59:8[7]; 94:4; Prov 15:2). True wisdom is cast in a few precious words, not in a relentless stream.

A fountain of wisdom. The only unambiguously positive image is the מקור חכמה "fountain of wisdom." A מקור is a fountain or spring, accessing the purest deep waters. It is reliable and life-sustaining when surface moisture dries up. Used figuratively, the fountain imagery suggests strength, fertility, and joy (e.g., Jer 51:36; Hos 13:15; Ps 68:27[26]; Prov 5:18). It may even become a מקור חיים ("fountain of life"), an image used in Proverbs to depict "the mouth of the righteous" (10:11) and "the instruction of the wise" (13:14; cf. 14:27; 16:22).[44] If searching for wisdom, the student must drink deeply of the sages' trustworthy well of words.

Overall. The syntax of the proverb overall is not entirely clear. Images are pressed together into a complex interplay of similarity and difference. "The words of a man's mouth" may be the target domain for all three images. "The words of a man's mouth are: deep waters, a flowing brook, a fountain of wisdom."[45] If each image is taken positively, they complement each other. If the מים ("waters") or נחל ("brook") is negative, contrasts emerge. Alternatively, the cola may be parallel, with the "foun-

> I speak this proverb to a student, before he has uttered any words. I intentionally leave the ambiguities open. "The words of a man's mouth may be..." I invite him to consider how his own speech will flow, as what sort of "deep waters, flowing stream"? I exhort him to make it as "a fountain of wisdom."

---

44. The LXX has "fountain of life" (πηγὴ ζωῆς) in this verse too, prompting Toy to emend (*Critical and Exegetical Commentary*). It is likely that the LXX is assimilating to the known idiom.

45. So Clifford, *Proverbs*; Delitzsch, *Biblical Commentary*; Fox, *Proverbs 10–31*; McKane, *Proverbs*; Toy, *Critical and Exegetical Commentary*.

tain of wisdom" providing a second target domain. "The words of a man's mouth are deep waters; the fountain of wisdom is a flowing brook."[46] In this case, the נחל is presumably positive. If the מים are also positive, then the cola are synonymous. If they are negative, the cola are antithetical.

This proverb may affirm the value of words or warn of their dangers. The reader must hold together the simultaneous truth of apparently contradictory realities. Words can be a deep source of knowledge and life, and trusting them is a primary way of acquiring wisdom. But in their dark expanse, much wickedness can also hide. The literary context here stresses the problematic side of words and so may favor this latter interpretation (cf. Prov 18:2, 6, 7, 8).

This proverb's images are alluring and concise, with no elaborations to curtail their openness. The reader immerses herself in the world they evoke and blends them imaginatively with the situations in her own life. The apparent contradictions suggest the situational specificity of truth. Some words, such as the sages' didactic dictums, bring life; others bring death. Accordingly, the reader must scrutinize all the words she meets, which (like open waters) might be concealing or difficult to fathom. The proverb becomes practice in the very lesson espoused. It offers itself as an example of "the words of a man's mouth," "deep waters" for exploration. By offering two interpretations, it demonstrates that words are not always what they seem. Scrutiny of this proverb does not prohibit ultimate trust. With due recognition of the ambiguity of life and words, it may become part of the trustworthy ethical framework mediating wisdom.

7.3. Trusting and Scrutinizing Ourselves: The Limits of Acquiring Wisdom

7.3.1. Introduction

Wisdom contains an intellectual component and thus requires its seekers to trust their own minds. Proverbs' basic position is to affirm students in their capacity for wisdom. It has an optimistic and high anthropology, and as didactic literature it confidently trains its readers "to know wisdom and instruction; to understand words of insight" (1:2).[47] Char-

---

46. So Heim, *Poetic Imagination*; Waltke, *Book of Proverbs 16–31*.
47. On "high anthropology," see Frydrych, *Living under the Sun*, 127–34.

acter formation is a real possibility; the student can progress toward the central ideal of the "wise man" (see chapter 4). As he does so, a centripetal effect may take hold, like a whirlpool sucking him further in. The wiser he is, the wiser he gets. He seeks wisdom more (15:14; 18:15), and wisdom becomes easier to find (14:6). He may confidently trust his capacities to acquire and use it.

7.3.1.1. The Limited Human

Despite this, however, true wisdom recognizes its limitations.[48] It is folly indeed to be "wise in your own eyes" (Prov 3:7; 12:15; 26:5, 12; 28:11). Everyone can benefit from didactic instruction and well-spoken proverbs, even the sagest of the sages (10:8; 12:15; 13:1; 15:31; 17:10). Such limitations may already be implicit in the genre, for proverbs make no totalizing claims.[49] Each is limited to giving a single comment, tied to some particular situation (§7.1.2 above). Similarly, the human mind, for all its attempts at transcendence, is bounded by the here and now. General principles may be loosely hung together, but no completed system is reached. Life and proverbs are scattered with contradictions, paradoxes, and ambiguities. Confronted with these, the student becomes aware of her limitations. The book orients her through life, but moments of disorientation save her from proudly assuming complete mastery.[50]

What is more, human beings, who can so readily deceive others through word and deed, are not immune to their own falsehood. They may deceive even themselves. "Those who plan evil" have "deceit [מרמה] in the heart" (12:20a), intending to swindle other people for their own benefit. But it is others who end up with "joy" (12:20b), not they. Their internalized

---

48. Expressed by Paul S. Fiddes as the simultaneous "confidence and caution of wisdom"; see Fiddes, *Seeing the World and Knowing God: Hebrew Wisdom and Christian Doctrine in Late-Modern Context* (Oxford: Oxford University Press, 2013), 96–98. For Fiddes, this is related to the elusiveness of the world, which is at once self-revealing and self-concealing (87–129).

49. Perhaps for this reason, the aphorism experienced a resurgence in postmodern thought, disillusioned with absolute, totalizing claims to knowledge. William A. Beardslee, *Literary Criticism of the New Testament*, GBS New Testament Series (Philadelphia: Fortress, 1970), 30; Williams, *Those Who Ponder Proverbs*, 14. Fiddes explores this tension between striving after the "whole" and thinking this quest futile, in conversation with Qoheleth and late-modern thought (*Seeing the World*, 299–323).

50. So Yoder, "Forming 'Fearers of Yahweh.'"

deception has festered into self-deception, and their hoped-for gains prove illusory.[51] The fool thinks he is forging a fruitful path, but this too proves a "deception" (מרמה; 14:8; cf. 12:15; 14:12=16:25).[52] In fact, any man may be deluded about his own way and its ethics (16:2; 21:2), and a persistent recognition of moral incapacity weighs upon Proverbs' optimism, for none can claim to have an entirely pure heart (20:9a). Intellect will suffer or prosper along with morality, for wisdom is born out of character. Accordingly, the human self in all its aspects must be thoroughly scrutinized if it is to be trusted. Only then can true wisdom be acquired.

7.3.1.2. The Limiting Lord

These limitations are rooted in the human being herself, but she is further limited by the inscrutable work of Yahweh.[53] We saw in chapter 5 how ruptures appear in the world order, which might otherwise have offered safe mechanisms for securing one's own fate.[54] Behind these ruptures stands the creator and overseer of the order: the inscrutable God. A fissure emerges between two modes of causality: the act-consequence connec-

---

51. McKane, *Proverbs*; Murphy, *Proverbs*; and Waltke, *Book of Proverbs 16–31* recognize self-deception in this proverb.

52. "There is a straight path before a man, but its end is the ways of death" (14:12 =16:25). Reading the first colon, the reader is tricked into believing the beneficial prospects of this path. The second colon forces him to rectify this and to acknowledge his mistaken impression. Individuals are in perpetual danger of misreading—misreading both proverbs and situations in the world. See Suzanna R. Millar, "When a Straight Road Becomes a Garden Path: The 'False Lead' as a Pedagogical Strategy in the Book of Proverbs," *JSOT* 43.1 (2018): 67–82.

53. Thus wisdom is oriented toward both "secular pragmatism" (human limitations based on human nature) and "piety" (human limitations based on divine nature) (Fiddes, *Seeing the World*, 108). McKane argues that Yahwistic proverbs are a theological reaction against the self-confidence of sages, in keeping with the prophetic critique of wisdom (*Proverbs*). They "represent an attempt to demonstrate that the empire of the mind which the *hakamim* have pegged out for themselves is illusory" (McKane, *Prophets and Wise Men*, 50). However, there is little reason to think that Yahwistic elements are late in Proverbs (see above, §5.1.3).

54. Note that this conception of a world order masterable by individuals is somewhat different from the *Weltordnung* of Schmid, which was hardened and cut off from people's lives (see above, §4.1.1). For Schmid, a rupture occurred between Proverbs and the "real world." For the scholars discussed here, ruptures occur *within* Proverbs, between the sayings reflecting non-Yahwistic and Yahwistic causalities.

tion, clear and useful for mastering life, and Yahweh's activity, incalculable and unmanipulable. The anthropocentric and the theocentric are unreconciled by the sages.[55] The emerging cognitive gap marks the borderline of the student's understanding, beyond which lies only divine mystery, fundamentally inaccessible.[56]

This has implications for the individual: "Many are the plans in the heart of a man, but it is the counsel of the Lord that will stand" (רבות מחשבות בלב־איש ועצת יהוה היא תקום; Prov 19:21). The variegated and unreliable concoctions of the human mind are contrasted with the single divine purpose, which intervenes before their execution.[57] While the individual has some control over his mental world, the material world remains the exclusive and unpredictable domain of God. And true wisdom is no mental construction, but a lived reality, with manifestations in the real world. True wisdom, then, is here denied from humanity. Compared with the many proverbs stressing human capability, this may suggest something radical: a "determinism, which shakes wisdom thought to its foundations."[58]

With similarly convulsing force, Prov 20:24 declares, "From the Lord are a man's steps; as for a person, how can he understand his way?" (מיהוה מצעדי־גבר ואדם מה־יבין דרכו:). God and humans are emphatically paralleled in frontal positions, stressing the unbreachable gap between them (cf. Prov 16:1, 9; 21:31 below). A man might trust his self-direction, but as he walks, Yahweh is already at work (unnoticed by the earthbound mind). Not only are the ways of the world barred from comprehension (cf. Prov 30:18–19), but even "one's own way" (דרכו) is. The ambiguous suffix here suggests that the way may not be "his" (i.e., the man's) any longer but "his" (i.e., the Lord's). And if so, the student cannot even "consider" and analyze his way (√בין, BDB 3), let alone "understand" it (√בין, BDB 2). He is denied even self-scrutiny, let alone self-trust.

---

55. Von Rad, *Wisdom in Israel*, 98.

56. Gese, *Lehre und Wirklichkeit*, 38–42.

57. Cf. the similar plural/singular contrasts in 16:1; 20:24. Skladny, *Die ältesten Spruchsammlungen*, 75.

58. "Determinismus … die das Weisheitsdenken in seinen Grundlagen erschüttert" (Gese, *Lehre und Wirklichkeit*, 46). Gese described this as a *Sondergut* of Israel compared with the rest of the ancient Near East.

7.3.1.3. Reactions to Limitations: Trusting the Inscrutable God

The recognition of human limitations might encourage students to seek God in the openness of proverbs and life, mediating the tension between wisdom's secular and religious manifestations. The proverbial form means that the worldview never becomes a closed system (see §7.1.2). We only see snapshots of Yahweh's activity, without access to any overall divine construction plan. The collection places strikingly different proverbs side by side, leveling insights about Yahweh and sluggards (10:26–27; 19:23–24; 22:12–14). So too in life, Yahweh emerges among the humdrum. The sublime and the ridiculous succeed one another, and wisdom can be found in both. The openness emerging between the disparate proverbs may be filled however the interpreter chooses. Yahweh may or may not be found in the gaps. Equally, the concision and openness of individual proverbs and situations mean that sometimes Yahweh's presence is not obvious. Both Yahwistic and non-Yahwistic interpretations are possible. Other times, he is clearly present, but the nature of his activity is unclear. He cannot be bound by human language or human wisdom.

This openness, emerging through the proverb form, can be harnessed for didactic ends. The sayings can train their student to search for the divine in the mundane. As the student's character develops, she become more and more the kind of person who would seek God. Emerging like proverbs, Yahweh's actions might be scattered seemingly at random through life. But in the didactic collection, they are clustered in 15:33–16:9. They are central, structurally and interpretively. In the book as a whole, the sayings are prefaced with a much more theological introduction (Prov 1–9), grounding our subsequent understanding.

Acknowledging Yahweh's ultimate supremacy and his own incapacity, it would be possible for a student to resign himself to despair. Thus Jeremiah's comment that "a man's way is not his own" (לֹא לְאִישׁ דַּרְכּוֹ; Jer 10:23) forms part of a lament on the hopeless incapacity of Judah in face of the divinely ordained Babylonian threat: "Woe to me!" (אוֹי לִי; 10:19). But the same recognition might also elicit hope. One psalmist rejoices that "a man's steps are established by the Lord" (מֵיהוָה מִצְעֲדֵי־גֶבֶר כּוֹנָנוּ; Ps 37:23), for this ensures him a safe path. Yahweh—and not the human mind—is the ultimate object of his trust (Ps 37:3, 5; cf. Prov 3:5; 14:26; 28:25; 29:25). This can provide comfort, relief, and even a sense of liberation, for Yahweh is not capricious or malicious but fundamentally trustworthy.[59] When deeds are committed to the Lord, divine and human activity can work hand in hand, and plans will be established (16:3).

Within this framework of trust, human wisdom is not redundant but finds its truest expression. Indeed, "The fear of the Lord is the beginning of knowledge" (1:7). Variations of this programmatic statement structure the book: the capstone of the preamble (1:7), indeed of the whole prologue (9:10), and the centerpoint of the Solomonic collection (15:33). In "the fear of the Lord" (יראת יהוה), the recognition of human limitedness has been given contrite religious orientation, entailing willing and obedient submission to divine superiority. It is the "beginning" (ראשית) of knowledge, its "best part," "first manifestation," and "prerequisite."[60] In this last sense, it becomes an epistemological principle; wisdom is ethical-religious to its foundations. True wisdom then is not acquired *despite* human limitations, but *through* acceptance of them, through trust in the inscrutable God.

7.3.2. Proverbs under Didactic Scrutiny

The tension between divine and human agency is not resolved in Proverbs. In some verses, the two work in partnership (16:3). In others, there is apparent conflict (19:21; 20:14). In between are a number of proverbs open to interpretation. These will be our focus here.

16:1 לאדם מערכי־לב ומיהוה מענה לשון:

To a man, the arrangements of the heart; from the Lord, the answer of the tongue.[61]

Paralleled in the first position, the tension between a "man" and the "Lord" here is palpable. A man's thought-world is his own, bubbling with arrange-

---

59. So von Rad, *Wisdom in Israel*, 101, 106.

60. See Zoltán Schwab, "Is Fear of the Lord the Source of Wisdom or Vice Versa?," *VT* 63 (2013): 652–62.

61. There are a number of ancient Near Eastern parallels to this proverb: Instruction of Amenemope 19.16–17, *AEL* 2:157: "The words men say are one thing, the deeds of a god are another." Instruction of Amenemope 20.5–6, *AEL* 2:158: "If a man's tongue is the boat's rudder, the Lord of All is yet its pilot." Instruction of Anchsheshonq 26.14, *AEL* 3:179: "The plans of the god are one thing, the thoughts of [men] are another." Instruction of Ahiqar 115 (saying 32): "If [a young man] is beloved of the gods, they will put in his mouth something good to say" (והן רחים אלהן הו ישימון טב בחנכה למאמר) (Lindenberger, *Aramaic Proverbs of Ahiqar*, 101).

ments and machinations. But bubbles burst. Even the best-laid plans he struggles to make real; without divine assistance, they cannot be actualized.[62] They cannot even be enunciated, for the "answer of the tongue" (מענה לשון) is directed by Yahweh. The "answer" is a powerful tool in Proverbs (15:1, 23, 28), and here it might stand as a metonymy for the broad sweep of human activity: all is "from the Lord."[63]

This proverb begins a cluster of Yahweh sayings that is similarly concluded in 16:9: "The heart of a man plans his way; the Lord establishes his step" (לב אדם יחשב דרכו ויהוה יכין צעדו). The journey is left not to human direction but to the divine navigator. The war march too has Yahweh at its head: "The horse is made ready for the day of battle; to the Lord belongs the victory" (סוס מוכן ליום מלחמה וליהוה התשועה; Prov 21:31). Even the most fearsome of human equipment cannot secure success.[64]

An openness arises in these proverbs. The cola may be synonymous ("and") or antithetical ("but").[65] If synonymous, the *a* cola are prerequisites of the *b* cola. Individuals have a responsibility to arrange their thoughts, to lay plans, to prepare equipment. "And" then the Lord will fulfill the human initiative, with an answer, a stride, a victory. The divine response validates human wisdom as trustworthy. If antithetical, God and humans are in conflict. Meticulous plans may be laid, "but" the Lord takes the last word and decisive step. Victory is his alone to grant. Human wisdom is ineffica-

---

62. מערכי here is a *hapax legomenon*. However, √ערך, "to arrange," suggests "'thought-through plans' or 'arguments,' not 'brainstorming' or 'half-baked ideas'" (Waltke, *Book of Proverbs 16–31*, 100).

63. So Clifford, *Proverbs*. McKane suggests that the "answer of the tongue" refers to what Yahweh says: "We are to think of Yahweh's creative word, which is the final answer and determines the shape of the future" (*Proverbs*, 496; sim. Murphy, *Proverbs*). However, nowhere else is Yahweh said to have a "tongue," while the human tongue is a common trope in Proverbs. Accordingly, it is probably the man's answer here.

64. In the ancient Near East, horses were a sign of power and strength and were a military innovation that gave a great advantage. Many texts caution against putting one's trust in warhorses (e.g., Deut 17:16; Isa 31:1; Mic 5:9[10]; Zech 9:10; Pss 20:8[7]; 33:17).

65. This ambiguity is noted in, e.g., Horst Dietrich Preuß, *Einführung in die alttestamentliche Weisheitsliteratur*, Urban-Taschenbücher Band 383 (Stuttgart: Kohlhammer, 1987); Waltke, *Book of Proverbs 16–31*; Yoder, *Proverbs*. The LXX does not include 16:1. MT 16:9 is reflected in LXX 15:29b (according to the numbering of Rahlfs, *Septuaginta*), where the relationship between the clauses is made causal (ἵνα). The LXX construes 21:31 as antithetical (δὲ).

cious (and therefore akin to untruth). People cannot trust themselves, but only fling themselves into despair, or into trust of the Lord.

Meticulously, and in the fear of the Lord, my neighbor is preparing for a new economic endeavor. "The heart of a man plans his way, so the Lord will establish his step," I say to him (16:9). I evaluate his care as commendable and direct him to further fastidiousness through the hope of success.	My son has been wrongly accused, and the matter is to be taken to court. He is aware of his own weakness and the strength of his accusers as they compile their lies about him. In encouragement, I comment, "The horse is made ready for the day of battle, but victory belongs to the Lord." Apparent human strength is to no avail.

21:30 אין חכמה ואין תבונה ואין עצה לנגד יהוה:
There is no wisdom, and no understanding, and no counsel before/against the Lord.

Heralding the warhorse of 21:31, Prov 21:30 can be read as a fervent denunciation of claims to wisdom, which dissolve to nonexistence "before" (לנגד) the Lord. As von Rad put it, the "vital art of mastering life is aware that it must halt at these frontiers—indeed, it even contrives to liquidate itself there."[66] Breaking the usual pattern of parallelism, the heavy repetition of the monosyllabic אין ("there is not") drums its point. But the message might be more temperate. Pesh. (=Targ.) interprets לנגד as "like/compared with" (hyk), or it could be taken in an adversative sense as "against": wisdom is specious only when it opposes the Lord.[67] When it trusts in him, it too can be trusted.

10:22 ברכת יהוה היא תעשיר ולא־יוסף עצב עמה:
The blessing of the Lord, that is what makes rich, and he adds no pain with it/and toil will not add to it.

This proverb affirms the Lord's prerogative to bestow riches (a colon). Concerning human efforts, it may be interpreted as remaining neutral

---

66. Von Rad, *Old Testament Theology*, 1:440.
67. See the adversative sense used in Dan 10:13; Neh 3:37[4:5]. So McKane, *Proverbs*: "to withstand Yahweh"; Clifford, *Proverbs*: "that prevails against Yahweh."

or as denigrating them (*b* colon). By the first interpretation, the Lord is the only active party in *b* (and the grammatical subject of יוסף). In his great beneficence, "he adds no pain [עצב]" (cf. Gen 3:16; Prov 15:1) with his blessing.[68] Treasures acquired by the wicked may prove fleeting and deathly (Prov 21:6; cf. 10:2; 13:11; 15:16), but Yahweh's favored ones will prosper pain-free. Human work is not mentioned; perhaps diligence was a basis for the blessing (cf. 10:4; 12:24; 13:4; 14:23; 21:5).

Alternatively, human "toil" (עצב; Prov 5:10; 14:23; Ps 127:2) makes a vain effort to exert its influence (cf. Prov 23:4).[69] Grammatically the subject of יוסף, it tries to "add" to what the Lord has given. But "no" (לא)—humans cannot effect or even affect their own blessing. A person's wisdom and work, by this interpretation, should not be trusted.

The concise form of these proverbs presents a fragmentary view of reality. No elaborations are offered to explain them or combine them into a system. Their ambiguities at once train the mind and expose its limits. Should people trust themselves? Do they have a vital role in beginning what Yahweh completes, or is their work irrelevant, overridden by the divine? The answer may be "It depends." Plans in line with Yahweh's are encouraged and will be fulfilled. Those that diverge must be overruled (cf. Ps 127:1). We are offered a situation-specific model of truth: different interpretations suit different people at different times.

20:27: נר יהוה נשמת אדם חפש כל־חדרי־בטן:
The lamp of the Lord—the breath of man, searching all the chambers of the belly.

Proverbs 20:27 addresses, through its corporeal-domestic imagery, scrutiny of the human self. What is unclear is *who* is scrutinizing: the "Lord" (יהוה) or the "man" (אדם)? The Lord's lamp and the man's breath are juxtaposed without explanation; the reader must discern the connection between disparate phenomena. The source domain is probably "the lamp," and the target is probably "the breath."[70] But both are rich images to be explored individually, before an imaginative blending.

---

68. So Boström, *God of the Sages*; McKane, *Proverbs*; Toy, *Critical and Exegetical Commentary*.

69. Clifford, *Proverbs*; Fox, *Proverbs 10–31*; Murphy, *Proverbs*; Preuß, *Einführung*; Scott, *Proverbs, Ecclesiastes*.

70. Murphy proposes the opposite in *Proverbs*.

The metaphor continues in the second colon by "searching" (חפש) through a corporeal house (cf. 1 Kgs 20:6). The expression "chambers of the belly" (חדרי־בטן) is found only in Proverbs, and it apparently depicts a locus of moral behavior.[71] As is common in character ethics, the focus is on internal disposition more than external actions. Elsewhere (Ps 64:7[6]), the "inward parts" (קרב) and "heart" (לב) are searched, and "injustices" (עולת) are revealed, but here the discovery is undisclosed. Good or ill may lurk in the shadowy recesses of human character, which evades straight-forward classification into "righteous" and "wicked." But the portable, illuminating "lamp" (נר; cf. Zeph 1:12) exposes all, casting its scrutinizing glare into the darkest corners.[72]

Reorienting the imagery, the instrument of the search is also desig-nated as "the breath of man" (נשמת אדם).[73] Usually, נשמה refers to physical breath. This verse alone assigns it a spiritual task: searching moral charac-

---

71. Cf. 20:30; 18:18=26:22, cf. use of בטן in 22:18. The phrase is apparently bor-rowed from Egyptian, where "the casket of the belly" is "a person's innermost soul"; see Nili Shupak, "The Instruction of Amenemope and Proverbs 22:17–24:22 from the Perspective of Contemporary Research," in Troxel, Friebel, and Magary *Seeking Out the Wisdom of the Ancients*, 210; cf. Shupak, *Where Can Wisdom Be Found?*, 291–97.

72. Some scholars take נֵר as a participle from √niר "to break up [ground], to till" (though נָר would be expected morphologically); see Samuel E. Loewenstamm, "Remarks on Proverbs XVII 12 and XX 27," *VT* 37 (1987): 221–24; M. Seidel, *Hiqre Lashon* (Linguistic Studies) (Jerusalem, 1932), 30; Torcszyner, משלי שלמה, 27–28. Yahweh "plows" a man's spirit, to see what lies under its surface. Loewenstamm also argues that חפש means "digs," to create a parallel. Another suggestion is to emend נר to נצר "the Lord guards" the man's breath before searching him; cf. Prov 24:12, where "he who guards your soul" (נצר נפשך) parallels "he who weighs hearts" (תכן לבות); see *BHS* [though not *BHQ*]; Ehrlich, *Randglossen*; Hans Walter Wolff, *Anthropology of the Old Testament* (London: SCM, 1974), 60. However, neither of these interpretations has textual support or gives a significantly improved reading. They destroy the congenial connection between "lamp" and "searches."

73. A few commentators suggest that נשמה here refers to a man's words, for they reveal his character. Klaus Koch suggests the targumic understanding of נשמה as "*Sprachgeist*"; see Koch, "Der Güter Gefährlichstes, die Sprache, dem Menschen gege-ben ... Überlegungen zu Gen 2,7," *BN* 48 (1989): 56. Waltke in *Book of Proverbs 16–31* compares Prov 1:23, where he argues that רוח (which can mean "breath") receives a similar metonymic extension to mean "words" (cf. also Ps 150:6; Job 26:4; 32:18). Cf. also the common phrase "breathes out lies" (יפיח כזבים; Prov 6:19; 14:5, 25; 19:5, 9). However, in all these examples, context *requires* some vocalic resonances to stretch the usual understanding of the breath, which is not the case here. Furthermore, here the נשמה "searches" character and does not "reveal" it (as Waltke suggests).

ter.[74] The unusual usage is best explained not by imposing new semantic content on the word but by considering its role in the metaphor. The ephemeral breath can be pervasive. It fills the belly, permeating each cavity and crevice. So scrutiny reaches each corner of character. While a person lives, there is always breath in her (cf. 1 Kgs 17:17). Accordingly, she is always examined. At each inhalation, she should remember the searchlight. Furthermore, the נשמה is the particular possession of both humanity and God. It is a person's life-breath; a basic and fundamental necessity of her existence. But it is always a gift of God. Human breath was from the beginning divinely breathed (Gen 2:7), and it never ceases to originate with the Creator (Isa 42:5; 57:16; Job 27:3; 32:8; 33:4). As Wolff put it, "Breath as the characteristic of life shows that man is indissolubly connected with Yahweh."[75]

This raises the questions of the relationship between the man and God and of the identity of the searcher. Perhaps the man examines his own character. His breath is a lamp: divinely bestowed, and therefore effective and reliable. His introspective capacities are trustworthy, and the proverb provides "a confident assertion that he need not be a victim of self-deceit."[76] Its implication becomes an exhortation elsewhere: "Let us search [נחפשה] and examine our ways!" (Lam 3:40). After such thorough self-scrutiny, the inner chambers can be cleaned, and character can be trusted accordingly.

> A conscientious and anxious friend is concerned to ensure that her course is ethical. I encourage her in the efficacy of her self-examination: "A person's breath is a lamp bestowed by the Lord, searching all the chambers of the belly."

Alternatively, perhaps the Lord examines the man, fully in control of the נשמה he created. It is a lamp not *from* the Lord, but *used by* the Lord. As a moral scrutineer, he elsewhere weighs (21:2) and tests (17:3)

---

74. Toy describes it here as man's "moral and intellectual being" (*Critical and Exegetical Commentary*, 396; cf. Delitzsch, *Biblical Commentary*; Murphy, *Proverbs*). Scholars highlight that the נשמה is sometimes a distinguishing feature between humans and animals and therefore may refer to man's higher faculties. So T. C. Mitchell, "The Old Testament Usage of Nešāmâ," *VT* 11 (1961): 186.

75. Wolff, *Anthropology of the Old Testament*, 60. Cf. H. Lamberty-Zielinkski, "נשמה," *TDOT* 10:65–70, 67.

76. McKane, *Proverbs*, 547; cf. Delitzsch, *Biblical Commentary*; Hausmann, *Studien zum Menschenbild*; Murphy, *Proverbs*; Toy, *Critical and Exegetical Commentary*.

hearts, which lie fully open to him (15:11). Men try "to hide iniquity in the bosom" (לטמון בחבי עוני; Job 31:33), in deep and dark places, challenging, "Who can see us?" (מי ראנו; Isa 29:15). This proverb's answer: the Lord can. His divine searchlight exposes all (cf. Ps 90:8).

> I warn the wicked man that his evil will be exposed, however deep he thinks he has buried it. "A man's life-breath is a lamp used by the Lord, searching all the chambers of the belly." I darkly hint the punishment to follow, directing him to change his course.

After searching, he will respond appropriately. Both נר and נשמה are powerful symbols of life, and in the imaginative blend, such connotations might be foregrounded.[77] A positive verdict allows the man to breathe easy, for "the light of the righteous will rejoice" (Prov 13:9a). But a guilty sentence may entail the breath leaving the body, for "the lamp of the wicked will be put out" (Prov 13:9b=24:20b). Such imagined implications train the reader to discern the consequence of character.

But something more alarming still may lurk in the recesses: perhaps the light exposes sins not hidden *by* the man but even hidden *from* the man. A man's own character may be unknown to him, for he does not wield the examination light. Indeed, "Who can discern his errors?" (Ps 19:13[12]); "Who can say 'I have made my heart pure, I am clean from my sin'?" (Prov 20:9). Attempts at self-scrutiny may ultimately be in vain.

Exploring this proverb trains the skills of imagination and discernment so important for navigating life. It may exhort self-scrutiny or deny its possibility, even as it coaxes scrutiny of its own words. Vacillating between interpretations, the reader recognizes the limits of his wisdom. He must exercise self-trust and self-scrutiny, yet both may evade him.

7.4. Conclusion

This chapter has endeavored to acquire wisdom about acquiring wisdom. The didactic proverb genre can explain and elucidate three dualities that scholars have discerned in Proverbs' view of wisdom (§7.1): wisdom is found in the textual and extratextual worlds, in general principles and specific instances, and in moral and intellectual forms. To these is added

---

77. נשמה is the vitalizing breath. נר is often used figuratively of prosperity and life (e.g., Prov 13:9; 20:20; 24:20).

a fourth (§7.3): in the religious and the secular. The openness of the proverbs allows wisdom to be mediated across these tensions. Exploring the openness of the textual world trains characters and intellects for the openness in the extratextual world. Interpreters can flesh out and adapt general principles for specific situations and learn to seek God through ambiguities.

To acquire this wisdom, students should trust and scrutinize—a hermeneutical principle for interpreting text and world. A text's meaning emerges from three interacting forces: the speaker/author, the text itself, and the reader/hearer. Each of these—other people (§7.2.1), words (§7.2.2), oneself (§7.3)—are basically trustworthy but can deceive and should be scrutinized. Scrutiny is possible because of the textual openness.

The openness of proverbs might allow some speakers to deploy them harmfully. Lady Folly can use Lady Wisdom's own words deceptively (Prov 9:4, 16), and fools can cause pain by misappropriating proverbs (26:9; cf. 26:7). Speakers may hide their true selves (20:11) and must be scrutinized. The words themselves must be scrutinized too, sometimes providing deep and open waters to explore (18:4). Their polysemy, imagery, and complex parallelism goad us to infer, imagine, reason and reflect. The hearer can trust her own powers of interpretation, but only after they too have been scrutinized. The words' openness can generate ambiguities and contradictions that force her to acknowledge her limitations. She must scrutinize her own mind—and yet this scrutiny too might evade her (20:27). Only Yahweh's lamp can fully illuminate it.

Yahweh's role is elusive: he emerges at once as the enabler and limiter of human wisdom. Recognizing these divinely set limitations, the reader may respond as she chooses. But Proverbs' didactic intention is to shape characters who would interpret Yahwisticly and trust in God. This object of trust is utterly *in*scrutable. A stance of trusting subordination to the divine orients students to the world, proverbs, and self and allows them to achieve their fundamental aim: "Get wisdom" (4:5).

Conclusion

Summary

Inspired by von Rad's suggestion that proverbs "do not circumscribe their range of possibilities of comprehension," I set out to explore the openness of the sayings in Prov 10:1–22:16.[1] I found this to be intimately tied to the question of genre, which I came to see as the didactic proverb. Accordingly, I set for myself three main aims: first, to justify this genre ascription; second, to show how openness contributes to didactic and proverbial functions; and third, to see how this interpretation strategy might influence some issues in Proverbs scholarship.

Chapter 1 was directed toward the first aim. I argued that the sayings in Prov 10:1–22:16 are best classed as didactic proverbs. This was based on their generic relations (didactic instructions and folk proverbs), social settings (court and family), media (written and oral), self-presentation (חידות and משלים), and form (aphorism and proverb, collection and individual saying).

The next goal was approached in the rest of part 1. I suggested in chapter 2 that openness occurs pervasively throughout Prov 10:1–22:16. On a literary level, it is generated in three main ways. Some proverbs are characterized by polysemy (grammatical and semantic ambiguities). Their parallelism may be open to interpretation as antithetical or synonymous or may contain an imbalance to be filled out. Their imagery opens up a world for exploration, which can be imaginatively applied to the situations in the proverb and in the reader's own life.

Chapter 3 began to show how openness contributes to the functions of didactic proverbs. In a didactic use, openness helps the student develop a broad yet flexible worldview. It also provides stimulation for intellectual

---

1. Von Rad, *Wisdom in Israel*, 32.

training and character development. In a proverbial use, openness allows the sayings to be applied in many different situations and functions (particularly to evaluate or direct).

In part 2, I demonstrated the importance of openness for didactic proverbs by exploring a sample of texts. This also contributed to my third aim: in each case this interpretive strategy cast new light on an important issue in scholarship. Chapter 4 considered the character categories so pervasive in Proverbs (e.g., wise and foolish, righteous and wicked). I suggested that these categories are open, and their structure is best understood through prototype theory. They are conceptualized around central cases, which provide ideal, prototypical characters for emulation. Without necessary and sufficient conditions for membership, categories can be fleshed out in various ways. They have graded centrality, permitting different degrees of morality and making character development possible, and they have fuzzy borders, allowing the foolish one to become wise.

In chapter 5, I considered the apparent act-consequence connection in Proverbs. Some of its imagery constructs metaphorical worlds where act and consequence are intrinsically related. For example, "the straight path" is at once morally correct and beneficial; "eating evil" energizes wicked activity and poisons the eater. Such connections can be applied to the real world too, where the link between act and consequence is often predicable. However, the connection is not inviolable, and some proverbs use polysemy to problematize the principle. The agent behind the connection is often left open: perhaps it is Yahweh, society, or an intrinsic causality. This keeps the attention firmly on the actor and his responsibility. The proverbs are primarily intended not to explain causality but to motivate good behavior and character development. If they are not an absolute reflection of real life, this may be not a detriment but a motivational heightener.

In chapter 6, I considered the depiction of the king. The kingship proverbs may have been used in the actual royal court, but they are not restricted to these environs. Indeed, the king and the courtier provide examples of general principles. When their positive qualities are forefronted (e.g., the king's beneficent favor and righteous judgment), they can function pedagogically as paradigms for emulation or standards for evaluation. However, there are also darker undertones; the proverbs provide no naïve or sycophantic idealization. The king offers an example of human character in its irreducible complexity.

The final chapter (ch. 7) suggested that the didactic proverb genre can explain and elucidate various dualities in Proverbs' view of wisdom:

wisdom is found in the textual and extratextual worlds, the general and specific, the moral and intellectual, and the religious and secular. To acquire this wisdom, a principle can be applied to the proverbs and the world: trust and scrutinize. It is the openness of each that permits this. The world is generally trustworthy; people's behavior and words provide reliable wisdom. However, they may also deceive and should be scrutinized. Our own minds have great capacities, but they cannot be relied on fully, for human character and intellect are limited by the inscrutable work of Yahweh. Only by trusting him is wisdom validated and can we trust ourselves.

As well as addressing these scholarly debates (my third aim), part 2 sought to fulfill my first and second aims through practice—that is, to interpret the sayings as didactic proverbs and to explore the contribution of openness. Here, I will draw together my findings about proverbial and didactic functions.

Use as Proverbs

Throughout this investigation, I have shown how the sayings might be used as proverbs—that is, in specific situations with specific purposes. Such insights have hitherto been largely absent from Proverbs scholarship. If a saying has multiple base meanings—that is, it is polysemous—each meaning may be spoken into a different circumstance. If it employs generality or metaphor, how this is specified may vary: the images of paths and dining (ch. 5), lions and rains (ch. 6), or waters and lamps (ch. 7) might be applied to many different concrete referents. Furthermore, the speaker might give various opinions about the situation through the same proverb. Does she, for example, intend to glorify or to condemn the king (ch. 6)?

The proverbs could have a positive or a negative relation to context, describing the current situation or its opposite. I can say "A righteous man hates lies" (13:5a; ch. 5) positively of the truthful man, affirming him, or negatively of the liar, in condemnation. Further, different correlations of person are possible between the characters in the proverb and the people using the proverb. A proverb about a child might address the child himself, his parent, an onlooker, or someone else (20:11; ch. 7). A proverb about the king's legal judgment could be directed to the defendant, the plaintiff, or the king (ch. 6). Equally, it could be spoken in different temporal orientations; in this case, before the crime, between the crime and the verdict, or after the verdict.

In each different situation, a proverb might take a different function. In the last three chapters, we have seen them used, for example, to comfort, encourage, and celebrate; to lament, rage, and complain; to glorify and extol; and to condemn and rebuke. The most important functions are evaluation and direction. A proverb offers the correct way to evaluate a situation. Character terms in particular provide broad categories for making sense of the world (ch. 4) and developing an ethical framework. A proverb also directs its hearer. It often uses consequence terms for their strong motivational force, prompting the hearer to immediate action. Proverbs that combine character and consequence are particularly suited for a dual evaluative-directive function (ch. 5). From a long-term perspective, evaluation can provide stimulus for a worldview and direction for character development, moving the sayings from a proverbial to a didactic use.

Didactic Use: Intellectual Training

As well as instilling worldview and developing character, the didactic sayings aim to train their reader's mind. A primary way they do this is by encouraging him to explore their openness. He thereby learns modes of thought essential to life. Some proverbs are riddle-like, goading deep reflection and scrutiny. They may bring moments of psychological disorientation, and as the reader seeks reorientation, he himself is formed.

For proverb interpretation, skills of logic are required. The reader must work out implications and connotations. He must offer analysis and synthesis, striving for internal consistency and relevance. He must reason and deduce, calculate and surmise. In particular, he learns to infer the connection between acts and consequences (ch. 5). Such a skill set will benefit him throughout life.

The proverbs also train the (no less essential) skills of imagination. Particularly through metaphor, the reader is taught to see things anew and to forge connections between what had seemed incommensurable. Phenomena are reconceptualized, recategorized, and reimagined. Worlds are opened up, full of paths (ch. 5), streams (ch. 6), and deep waters (ch. 7) ready for exploration. The reader may take his own mental lamp through the chambers of these worlds, exploring, narrating, and imagining possibilities. His prize discoveries may then be brought home into the real world.

More than one interpretation may arise, and the reader learns to adjudicate between competing opinions, in proverbs as he must in life. Some implications may lie deep beneath the surface. The reader must attend to these nondominant voices and interpret courageously, evaluating for himself, weighing the possibilities. In the proverbs about the king, for example (ch. 6), there are some subtle subversions among the glorifications, for those who would give ear. But words can be deceitful (ch. 7). Not all voices are valid, though all voices must be heard.

Sometimes, the voices might be irreconcilable, but the reader holds them as simultaneously true. He is forced into an interpretive tension that he feels compelled to loosen. We saw this first in the problematizing polysemies of chapter 5, and even more in subsequent chapters. Just like the world, proverbs contain complexity, paradox, and enigma. Perhaps situational specificity provides a solution: each interpretation for a different place and time. But sometimes, the reader must simply accept the irresolvability, hold his preliminary interpretation lightly, and acknowledge his limitations (ch. 7).

Didactic Use: Character Development

Proverbs is a didactic book of character-based ethics. It makes human characters central, presented in ideal, prototypical types (e.g., righteous and wicked, wise and foolish [ch. 4]). These can be fleshed out into a moral framework and provide paradigms for emulation. The types suggest stable dispositions, which determine both acts and consequences (ch. 5). The overall course of moral conduct is paramount—the whole life path. Within holistic human character, the qualities that direct behavior are internalized. Those found appealing are consumed like a meal, energizing action and fulfilling the appetite. Proverbs knows the importance of appetite and desire for character, and it attempts to shape its readers' cravings through its appeals.

Character is usually revealed through action (ch. 7). Students can observe people's behavior and fit it into their ethical framework. Some people may be close to Proverbs' ideals, and they can be emulated. The king, for example, might be a paradigm of justice, generosity, and piety (ch. 6). However, fitting prototypes to the real world can prove problematic. People are not wholly righteous or wicked. The king himself contains both light and shade. The value of some characteristics—like a king's anger or a woman's grace (11:16; ch. 5)—may depend on how they are used. Furthermore, people can hide their true character (20:11; ch. 7), even from themselves (20:27). Self-scrutiny is essential, for dark shadows may lurk in our own hearts.

This inevitable nonperfection makes character development essential. Character-consequence rhetoric offers strong motivation to this end (ch. 5). Overall, Proverbs is optimistic in this endeavor. Folly can be overcome, and wise character achieved. Life is a path, a journey toward proper character. But the destination is never quite reached; for all their striving, no one is ever entirely righteous or wise (ch. 7).

Indeed, some proverbs suggest that your own character is not fully under your control. Just as consequences can be affected by society, external forces, and Yahweh (ch. 5), so, too, can character. Character can be formed by wise guides (§5.3.1), or disintegrated by wrongdoers. Sometimes, wickedness can take hold like a poison (§5.3.2), ingraining patterns of sin. Yahweh has ultimate control of a person's steps (§7.3); how then can she understand or control her way?

The Role of Yahweh

Yahweh has had a subtle but recurrent presence in the sayings I have examined. In Prov 10:1–22:16, he only appears explicitly in a selection of verses around a few themes. He is sometimes conspicuously absent from places we might expect him, such as the act-consequence connection (ch. 5). However, this may not be a denial of his activity. Rather, it keeps the focus squarely on the human, so as to stress personal responsibility. What is more, there are hints of Yahweh's activity under the surface; he may infuse the sayings and world without need for dramatic intervention. Along the path, perhaps he is "the one who preserves your life" (16:17); perhaps he sends his divine messengers to meet you (14:22).

As in these instances, language that ordinarily speaks of God is sometimes employed in the proverbs without explicit reference to him. In chapter 6 we saw imagery that conventionally depicts the deity being transferred to the monarch. How to interpret this is not obvious. At one extreme, perhaps the king has usurped Yahweh's authority. It is not the Lord whose face will shine (16:15) or whose roar will resound (19:12; 20:2). All power over life and death belongs instead to the king (16:14–15). At the other extreme, perhaps Yahweh has complete authority, and the king has none at all. It is God who ultimately winnows the wicked (20:8, 26) and who provides rain and dew (16:15; 19:12). The monarch is but a puppet in his hand (21:1). The proverbs could be spoken from either side of the debate. But we should probably avoid both extremes: Yahweh's activity is not all or nothing but is subtle, complex, and mysterious.

This came out more fully in the similar debates of chapter 7. What are the extent and limits of human wisdom and agency? Does Yahweh allow the individual her own authority and empower her, helping to complete what she begins? Or does he take away all autonomy, overpower her, and enforce his own desires instead? Again, no simple resolution can be found. And perhaps such a solution would not be desirable. Proverbs does not want us to comprehend his activity, for this would be an attempt to usurp his control. Yahweh is utterly inscrutable, and he must remain so. The elusive manner in which the proverbs refer to him perhaps reflects his elusive activity in the world. In proverbs, as in life, tantalizing glimpses are caught, shimmering reflections, of the divine presence. But grasping them is like grasping oil in the hand. And yet Proverbs teaches us to look. The book's pedagogy goads us to search beneath the surface, to scrutinize proverbs and the world. And sometimes Yahweh may be found there. As she searches, the reader might find her character and intellect formed, in humility and trust of the Lord. "It is the glory of God to conceal a thing, but the glory of kings to search a thing out" (Prov 25:2).

Appendix: Tables Showing Different Types of Openness

Table 1: Semantic Ambiguities Occurring in the Proverbs Discussed

For a discussion of the different types of semantic openness, see §2.1.1. The proverbs are listed in the order they occur in the book; for explanations of each instance, see the discussion of the proverb in question.

Prov	Pages	Polysemy: conceptually distant	close	Connotations	Vague/general	Soundplay	Metonymy?	Metaphor?
					Chapter 5			
13:5	120–21					יבאש		
10:8	121–23							
10:14	121–23			יצבר				
10:16	123–25				חטאת			חטאת, מעלה
16:17	131–33	נפשׁ	שׁמר, נצר		דרך			
14:22	134–35				רע, טוב			
10:17	135–37							

Prov	Pages	Polysemy: conceptually distant	close	Connotations	Vague/general	Soundplay	Metonymy?	Metaphor?
11:5	137–38					ברשעתו		
19:28	140–41		און					
12:21	141–43				רע			
13:2	143–45	נפש						
20:17	145–46							לחם
11:24	149–51				מפזר		יש	
11:16	151–54			חן, עריצים				
Chapter 6								
20:8	168–72	מזרה					לב	
20:26	168–72	מזרה		קסם				
16:10	172–74	ממשלת						
16:15	177–79							
21:1	179–81				לב		לב	
19:12	181–85							
20:2	185–87	חוטא	נפש					
16:14	187–89	מלאכי						מלאכי

Prov	Pages	Polysemy: conceptually distant	close	Connotations	Vague/general	Soundplay	Metonymy?	Metaphor?
					Chapter 7			
20:11	197–202	יזכור		מעלליו		מעלליו		
18:4	204–7							
16:1	212–14						מענה	
16:9	212–14							
21:31	212–14							סוס, במלחמה
21:30	214							
10:22	214–15		עצב					
20:27	215–18							

Table 2: Grammatical Ambiguities, Ambiguous Parallelisms, and Open Imagery Discussed

For discussions of the phenomena, see §§2.1.2, 2.2, and 2.3, respectively. For explanations of each instance, see the discussion of the proverb in question.

Prov	Pages	Grammatical ambiguities						Parallelism		Imagery
		Ambiguous modifier	Subj.-obj. ambiguity	Juxtaposition of nominals	Construct state	Preposition/ conjunction	Binyan	Antithetical/ synonymous	Unbalanced	
							Chapter 5			
13:5	120–21						יַחְפִּיר, יַבְאִישׁ		x	Stinking
10:8	121–23								x	
10:14	121–23								x	
10:16	123–25								x	
16:17	131–33		סוּר							Path
14:22	134–35			b colon						Path
10:17	135–37			a colon			מתעה			Path
11:5	137–38					ה				Path
19:28	140–41									Dining
12:21	141–43								x	Dining

Prov	Pages	Ambiguous modifier	Subj.-obj. ambiguity	Juxtaposition of nominals	Construct state	Preposition/ conjunction	Binyan	Antithetical/ synonymous	Unbalanced	Imagery
		Grammatical ambiguities						Parallelism		
13:2	143–45		אכל	b colon					x	Dining
20:17	145–46				לחם שקר					Dining
11:24	149–51					מן				Scattering
11:16	151–54							x		Scattering
				Chapter 6						
20:8	168–72	בעיניו				ה				Throne, winnowing
20:26	168–72									Winnowing, threshing
16:10	172–74		ימעל			ה				Oracle
16:15	177–79									Cloud, rain
21:1	179–81									Stream, hand, heart
19:12	181–85							x		Lion, dew
20:2	185–87			a colon	חוטא נפשו					Lion
16:14	187–89									Messengers

Chapter 7

Prov	Pages	Grammatical ambiguities						Parallelism		Imagery
		Ambiguous modifier	Subj.-obj. ambiguity	Juxtaposition of nominals	Construct state	Preposition/ conjunction	Binyan	Antithetical/ synonymous	Unbalanced	
20:11	197–202	גַּם				גַּם				
18:4	204–7			both cola				x		Waters
16:1	212–14							x		
16:9	212–14							x		
21:31	212–14							x		Horse, war
21:30	214					לַיהוה				
10:22	214–15		יוֹסִף							
20:27	215–18				נֵר יְהוָה					Lamp, breath, belly

Bibliography

Aasland, Erik. "Two Heads Are Better Than One: Using Conceptual Mapping to Analyze Proverb Meaning." *Proverbium* 26 (2009): 1–18.

Abrahams, Roger D. "Introductory Remarks to a Rhetorical Theory of Folklore." *JAF* 81.320 (1968): 143–58.

Ackroyd, P. R. "A Note on the Hebrew Roots באש and בוש." *JTS* 43 (1942): 160–61.

Adams, S. L. *Wisdom in Transition: Act and Consequence in Second Temple Instructions.* JSJSup 125. Leiden: Brill, 2008.

Albright, W. F. "Some Canaanite-Phoenician Sources of Hebrew Wisdom." Pages 1–15 in *Wisdom in Israel and in the Ancient Near East.* Edited by Martin Noth and David Winton Thomas. Leiden: Brill, 1955.

Aletti, J. N. "Séduction et parole en Proverbes I–IX." *VT* 27 (1977): 129–44.

Alonso Schökel, Luis. *A Manual of Hebrew Poetics.* SubBi 11. Rome: Editrice Pontificio Instituto Biblico, 1988.

———. *Proverbios.* Nueva Biblia Española, Sapienciales 1. Madrid: Cristiandad, 1984.

———. "ישר." *TDOT* 6:463–72.

Alster, Bendt. "Literary Aspects of Sumerian and Akkadian Proverbs." Pages 1–21 in *Mesopotamian Poetic Language: Sumerian and Akkadian.* Edited by Marianna E. Vogelzang and H. L. J. Vanstiphout. Groningen: Styx, 1996.

———. "Proverbs from Ancient Mesopotamia: Their History and Social Implications." *Proverbium* 10 (1993): 1–19.

Alt, Albrecht. "The Origins of Israelite Law." Pages 101–71 in *Essays on Old Testament History and Religion.* Oxford: Blackwell, 1966.

Alter, Robert. *The Art of Biblical Poetry.* New York: Basic Books, 2011.

Amzallag, Nissim G., and Shamir Yona, "The Meaning of ʿÔpan in Proverbs 20.16." *BT* 67 (2016): 292–302.

Anbar, M. "'Laire à l'entrée de la porte de Samarie' (1 R. XXII 10)." *VT* 50 (2000): 121–23.

Andersson, Daniel. "Understanding Figurative Proverbs: A Model Based on Conceptual Blending." *Folklore* 124 (2013): 28–44.

Ansberry, C. B. *Be Wise, My Son, and Make My Heart Glad: An Exploration of the Courtly Nature of the Book of Proverbs.* BZAW 422. Berlin: de Gruyter, 2011.

———. "What Does Jerusalem Have to Do with Athens? The Moral Vision of the Book of Proverbs and Aristotle's *Nicomachean Ethics.*" *HS* 51 (2010): 157–73.

Assmann, Jan. *Ma'at: Gerechtigkeit und Unsterblichkeit im alten Ägypten.* München: Beck, 1990.

Audet, J. P. "Origines comparées de la double tradition de la loi et de la Sagesse dans le Proche-Orient ancien." Pages 352–57 in *Twenty-Fifth International Congress of Orientalists.* Moscow: n.p., 1960.

Austin, J. L. *How to Do Things with Words: The William James Lectures Delivered at Harvest University in 1955.* Oxford: Clarendon, 1975.

Bacon, Francis. *The New Organon.* Edited by Lisa Jardine and Michael Silverthorne. Cambridge Texts in the History of Philosophy. Cambridge: Cambridge University Press, 2000.

Barkay, Gabriel, Andrew G. Vaughn, Marilyn J. Lundberg, and Bruce Zuckerman. "The Amulets from Ketef Hinom: A New Edition and Evaluation." *BASOR* 334 (2004): 41–71.

Barley, Nigel. "A Structural Approach to the Proverb and the Maxim with Special Reference to the Anglo-Saxon Corpus." *Proverbium* 20 (1972): 737–50.

Barr, James. *Comparative Philology and the Text of the Old Testament.* Oxford: Oxford University Press, 1968.

———. *The Semantics of Biblical Language.* Oxford: Oxford University Press, 1961.

Barthes, Roland. "La Rochefoucauld: Réflexions ou sentences et maximes." Pages 69–88 in *Le degré zero de l'écriture: Suivi de nouveaux essais critiques.* Paris: Éditions du Seuil, 1972.

Bartholomew, Craig G. *Ecclesiastes.* Grand Rapids: Baker Academic, 2009.

Bartholomew, Craig G., and Ryan P. O'Dowd. *Old Testament Wisdom Literature: A Theological Introduction.* Downers Grove, IL: InterVarsity Press, 2011.

Barton, John. *Ethics in Ancient Israel.* Oxford: Oxford University Press, 2014.

———. "Natural Law and Poetic Justice in the Old Testament." *JTS* 30 (1979): 1–14.

———. *Understanding Old Testament Ethics: Approaches and Explorations.* London: Westminster John Knox, 2003.

Barucq, André. *Le livre des Proverbs.* Sb. Paris: Gabalda, 1964.

———. "Proverbes (Livre des)." Columns 1395–476 in vol. 8 of *Supplement au dictionnaire de la Bible.* Edited by L. Pirot, André Robert, Jacques Briend, and Édouard Cothenet. Paris: Letouzey & Ané, 1972.

Basson, Alec. "The Path Image Schema as Underlying Structure for the Metaphor 'Moral Life Is a Journey' in Psalm 25." *OTE* 24 (2011): 19–29.

Baudry, Gérard-Henry. *La voie de la vie: Étude sur la catéchèse des Pères de l'Église.* ThH 110. Paris: Beauchesne, 1999.

Beardslee, William A. *Literary Criticism of the New Testament.* GBS New Testament Series. Philadelphia: Fortress, 1970.

Becker, Joachim. *Gottesfurcht im Alten Testament.* AnBib 25. Rome: Pontifical Biblical Institute, 1965.

Berlin, Adele. *The Dynamics of Biblical Parallelism.* Biblical Resource Series. Grand Rapids: Eerdmans, 2008.

Binder, Katherine S. "Sentential and Discourse Topic Effects on Lexical Ambiguity Processing: An Eye Movement Examination." *Memory and Cognition* 31 (2003): 690–702.

Birch, Bruce C. *Let Justice Roll Down: The Old Testament, Ethics, and Christian Life.* Louisville: Westminster John Knox, 1991.

Bitzer, Lloyd. "The Rhetorical Situation." *Philosophy and Rhetoric* 1 (1968): 1–14.

Black, Edwin. *Rhetorical Criticism: A Study in Method.* New York: MacMillian, 1965.

Black, Jeremy, Graham Cunningham, Eleanor Robson, and Gabor Zolyomi. *The Literature of Ancient Sumer.* Oxford: Oxford University Press, 2006.

Black, Max. *Models and Metaphors: Studies in Language and Philosophy.* New York: Cornell University Press, 1962.

Bland, Dave. "The Formation of Character in the Book of Proverbs." *ResQ* 40 (1998): 221–37.

———. *Proverbs and the Formation of Character.* Eugene, OR: Wipf & Stock, 2015.

———. "A Rhetorical Perspective on the Sentence Sayings of the Book of Proverbs." PhD diss., University of Washington, 1994.

Blenkinsopp, Joseph. *Wisdom and the Law in the Old Testament: The Ordering of Life in Israel and Early Judaism.* Oxford: Oxford University Press, 1983.

Blum, Erhard. "Formgeschichte—A Misleading Category? Some Critical Remarks." Pages 32–45 in *The Changing Face of Form Criticism for the Twenty-First Century*. Edited by Marvin A. Sweeney and Ehud Ben Zvi. Grand Rapids: Eerdmans, 2003.

Bodner, Keith. "Layers of Ambiguity in 2 Samuel 11,1." *ETL* 80 (2004): 102–11.

Boecker, Hans Jochen. *Law and the Administration of Justice in the Old Testament and Ancient East*. London: SPCK, 1980.

Borowski, Oded. *Agriculture in Iron Age Israel*. Winona Lake, IN: Eisenbrauns, 1987.

———. "Irrigation." Pages 181–84 in vol. 3 of *The Oxford Encyclopedia of Archaeology in the Near East*. Edited by Eric M. Meyers. Oxford: Oxford University Press, 1997.

Boström, Gustav. *Paronomasi i den äldre hebreiska maschallitteraturen med särskild hänsyn till proverbia*. Luå 1.23.8. Lund: Håkan Ohlssons Boktryckeri, 1928.

Boström, Lennart. *The God of the Sages: The Portrayal of God in the Book of Proverbs*. ConBOT 29. Stockholm: Almqvist & Wiksell, 1990.

Bricker, Daniel P. "The Doctrine of the 'Two Ways' in Proverbs." *JETS* 38 (1995): 501–17.

Brown, William P. *Character in Crisis: A Fresh Approach to the Wisdom Literature of the Old Testament*. Grand Rapids: Eerdmans, 1996.

———. *Character and Scripture: Moral Formation, Community, and Biblical Interpretation*. Grand Rapids: Eerdmans, 2002.

———. "The Didactic Power of Metaphor in the Aphoristic Sayings of Proverbs." *JSOT* 29 (2004): 133–54.

———. "The Pedagogy of Proverbs 10:1–31:9." Pages 150–82 in *Character and Scripture: Moral Formation, Community, and Biblical Interpretation*. Edited by William P. Brown. Grand Rapids: Eerdmans, 2002.

———. *Seeing the Psalms: A Theology of Metaphor*. Louisville: Westminster John Knox, 2002.

———. *Wisdom's Wonder: Character, Creation, and Crisis in the Bible's Wisdom Literature*. Grand Rapids: Eerdmans, 2014.

Bruins, Hendrik J. "Runoff Terraces in the Negev Highlands during the Iron Age: Nomads Settling Down or Farmers Living in the Desert?" Pages 37–43 in *On the Fringe of Society: Archaeological and Ethnoarchaeological Perspectives on Pastoral and Agricultural Societies*. Edited by Benjamin A. Saidel and Eveline J. van der Steen. Oxford: Archaeopress, 2007.

Brunner, Hellmut. "Der freie Wille Gottes in der ägyptischen Weisheit." Pages 103–20 in *Les sagesses du Proche-Orient Ancien: Colloque de Strasbourg 17–19 Mai 1962*. Paris: Presses Universitaires de France, 1963.

Bryce, Glendon E. *A Legacy of Wisdom: The Egyptian Contribution to the Wisdom of Israel*. Lewisburg: Bucknell University Press, 1979.

Bühlmann, Walter. *Vom rechten Reden und Schweigen: Studien zu Proverbien 10–31*. OBO 12. Fribourg: Universitätsverlag, 1976.

Buljan, Gabrijela, and Tanja Gradečak-Erdeljić. "Where Cognitive Linguistics Meets Paremiology: A Cognitive-Contrastive View of Selected English and Croatian Proverbs." *Explorations in English Language and Linguistics* 1 (2013): 63–83.

Buss, Martin J. *Biblical Form Criticism in Its Context*. JSOTSup 274. Sheffield: Sheffield Academic, 1999.

Byargeon, Rick W. "The Significance of Ambiguity in Ecclesiastes 2,24–26." Pages 367–72 in *Qohelet in the Context of Wisdom*. Edited by A. Schoors. Leuven: Leuven University Press, 1998.

Camp, Claudia. "Proverbs and the Problems of the Moral Self." *JSOT* 40 (2015): 25–42.

———. *Wisdom and the Feminine in the Book of Proverbs*. Sheffield: Almond Press, 1985.

———. "The Wise Women of 2 Samuel: A Role Model for Women in Early Israel?" *CBQ* 43 (1981): 14–29.

Camp, Claudia, and Carole R. Fontaine. "The Words of the Wise and Their Riddles." Pages 127–52 in *Text and Tradition: The Bible and Folklore*. Edited by Susan Niditch. Atlanta: Society of Biblical Literature, 1990.

Carr, David M. *The Formation of the Hebrew Bible*. Oxford: Oxford University Press, 2011.

———. *Writing on the Tablet of the Heart: Origins of Scripture and Literature*. Oxford: Oxford University Press, 2005.

Carroll R., M. Daniel, and Jacqueline E. Lapsley, eds. *Character Ethics and the Old Testament: Moral Dimensions of Scripture*. London: Westminster John Knox, 2007.

Černak, F. "Reason and Thought: Pillars of Intellectual Behaviour in Proverbs." Pages 149–60 in *Tenth Interdisciplinary Colloquium on Proverbs*. Edited by Rui Soares and Outi Lauhakangas. Tavira: AIP-IAP, 2017.

Cervantes, Miguel de. *The History of Don Quixote de la Mancha*. Great Books of the Western World 29. Chicago: University of Chicago Press, 1952.

Cheetham, L. "Thresh and Winnowing: An Ethnographic Study." *Antiquity* 56.217 (1982): 127–30.

Clifford, Richard J. "Observations on the Text and Versions of Proverbs." Pages 47–61 in *Wisdom, You Are My Sister: Studies in Honor of Roland E. Murphy, O.Carm., on the Occasion of His Eightieth Birthday.* Edited by Michael L. Barré. Washington, DC: Catholic Biblical Association of America, 1997.

——. *Proverbs: A Commentary.* OTL. Louisville: Westminster John Knox, 1999.

Clines, David J. A. "The Parallelism of Greater Precision." Pages 77–100 in *Directions in Biblical Hebrew Poetry.* Edited by Elaine R. Follis. Sheffield: Sheffield Academic, 1987.

Collins, Terence. *Line-Forms in Hebrew Poetry: A Grammatical Approach to the Stylistic Study of the Hebrew Prophets.* Studia Pohl, Series Maior 7. Rome: Biblical Institute Press, 1978.

Cook, Johann A. "Genericity, Tense, and Verbal Patterns in the Sentence Literature of Proverbs." Pages 117–33 in *Seeking Out the Wisdom of the Ancients: Essays Offered to Honor Michael V. Fox on the Occasion of His Sixty-Fifth Birthday.* Edited by Ronald L. Troxel, Kelvin G. Friebel, and Dennis R. Magary. Winona Lake, IN: Eisenbrauns, 2005.

——. *The Septuagint of Proverbs: Jewish and/or Hellenistic Proverbs; Concerning the Hellenistic Colouring of LXX Proverbs.* VTSup 69. Leiden: Brill, 1997.

Cornelius, I. "The Lion in the Art of the Ancient Near East: A Study of Selected Motifs." *JNSL* 15 (1989): 53–89.

Crenshaw, James L. "Clanging Symbols." Pages 51–64 in *Justice and the Holy: Essays in Honor of Walter Harrelson.* Edited by Douglas A. Knight and Peter J. Paris. Atlanta: Scholars Press, 1989.

——. "Education in Ancient Israel." *JBL* 104 (1985): 601–15.

——. *Education in Ancient Israel: Across the Deadening Silence.* ABRL. New York: Doubleday, 1998.

——. "Wisdom." Pages 225–64 in *Old Testament Form Criticism.* Edited by John H. Hayes. San Antonio, TX: Trinity University Press, 1974.

Croft, William, and D. Alan Cruse. *Cognitive Linguistics.* Cambridge Textbooks in Linguistics. Cambridge: Cambridge University Press, 2004.

Cuppi, Lorenzo. "Long Doublets in the Septuagint of the Book of Proverbs with a History of Research on the Greek Translations." PhD diss., Durham University, 2011.

Dahood, Mitchell J. *Proverbs and Northwest Semitic Philology.* Scripta Pontificii Instituti Biblici 113. Rome: Pontifical Biblical Institute, 1963.

Davies, Eryl W. "The Meaning of Qesem in Prv 16,10." *Bib* 61 (1980): 554–56.

Davis, Ellen F. *Proverbs, Ecclesiastes, and the Song of Songs.* Westminster Bible Companion. Louisville: Westminster John Knox, 2000.

———. "Surprised by Wisdom: Preaching Proverbs." *Int* 63 (2009): 264–77.

Davison Hunter, James. *The Death of Character: Moral Education in an Age without Good or Evil.* New York: Basic Books, 2000.

Day, John. "Foreign Semitic Influence on the Wisdom of Israel and Its Appropriation in the Book of Proverbs." Pages 55–70 in *Wisdom in Israel: Essays in Honour of J. A. Emerton.* Edited by John Day, Robert P. Gordon, and H. G. M. Williamson. Cambridge: Cambridge University Press, 1998.

Delitzsch, Franz. *Biblical Commentary on the Proverbs of Solomon.* Clark's Foreign Theological Library 4/45. Edinburgh: Clark, 1884.

Delkurt, Holger. *Ethische Einsichten in der Alttestamentlichen Spruchweisheit.* Biblisch-Theol. Studien 21. Neukirchen-Vluyn: Neukirchener Verlag, 1993.

Dell, Katharine J. *The Book of Job as Sceptical Literature.* BZAW 197. Berlin: de Gruyter, 1991.

———. *The Book of Proverbs in Social and Theological Context.* Cambridge: Cambridge University Press, 2006.

———. "Deciding the Boundaries of 'Wisdom': Applying the Concept of Family Resemblance." Pages 145–60 in *Was There a Wisdom Tradition? New Prospects in Israelite Wisdom Studies.* Edited by Mark R. Sneed. Atlanta: SBL Press, 2015.

———. "How Much Wisdom Literature Has Its Roots in the Pre-exilic Period?" Pages 251–71 in *In Search of Pre-exilic Israel: Proceedings of the Oxford Old Testament Seminar.* Edited by John Day. London: T&T Clark, 2004.

———. "The King in the Wisdom Literature." Pages 163–86 in *King and Messiah in Israel and the Ancient Near East: Proceedings of the Oxford Old Testament Seminar.* Edited by John Day. London: Bloomsbury T&T Clark, 2013.

Dever, William G. *What Did the Biblical Writers Know and When Did They Know It? What Archaeology Can Tell Us about the Reality of Ancient Israel.* Grand Rapids: Eerdmans, 2001.

Di Lella, Alexander A. *Proverbs, Wisdom, Qohelet, Song of Songs.* Fasc. 5.2 of *The Old Testament in Syriac: According to the Peshitta Version.* Leiden: Brill, 1979.

Dobbs-Allsopp, F. W. *On Biblical Poetry.* New York: Oxford University Press, 2015.

Donald, Trevor. "The Semantic Field of 'Folly' in Proverbs, Job, Psalms, and Ecclesiastes." *VT* 13 (1963): 285–92.

Dorsey, David A. *The Roads and Highways of Ancient Israel.* ASOR Library of Biblical and Near Eastern Archaeology. Baltimore: Johns Hopkins University Press, 1991.

Driver, G. R. "Hebrew Notes on Prophets and Proverbs." *JTS* 41 (1940): 162–75.

———. "Problems and Solutions." *VT* 4 (1954): 225–45.

———. "Problems in the Hebrew Text of Proverbs." *Bib* 32 (1951): 173–97.

Dundes, Alan. "On the Structure of the Proverb." *Proverbium* 25 (1975): 961–73.

Ehrlich, Arnold B. *Randglossen zur hebräischen Bibel: Textkritisches, sprachliches und sachliches.* 7 vols. Leipzig: Hinrichs, 1908.

Eichrodt, Walther. *Theology of the Old Testament.* 2 vols. London: SCM, 1961.

Eißfeldt, Otto. *Der Maschal im Alten Testament: Eine wortgeschichtliche Untersuchung nebst einer literargeschichtlichen Untersuchung der genannten Gattungen "Volkssprichwort" und "Spottlied."* BZAW 24. Giezen: Töpelmann, 1913.

Emerton, J. A. "The Meaning of Proverbs XIII.2." *JTS* 35 (1984): 91–95.

———. "The Teaching of Amenemope and Proverbs XXII 17–XXIV 22: Further Reflections on a Long-Standing Problem." *VT* 51 (2001): 431–65.

Engelken, Karen. "Erziehungsziel Gewaltlosigkeit? Überlegungen zum Thema 'physische Gewalt' im Buch Proverbien.'" *BN* 45 (1988): 12–18.

Erman, Adolf. "Eine ägyptische Quelle der 'Sprüche Salomos.'" Pages 86–93 in *Sitzungberichte der preussischen Akademie der Wissenschaften, Sitzung der philosophisch-historischen Klasse.* Berlin: de Gruyter, 1924.

Ewald, Heinrich. *Die poëtischen Bücher des alten Bundes: Vierter Theil.* Göttingen: Vandenhoeck & Ruprecht, 1837.

Fahlgren, Karl Hj. "Die Gegensätze von sedaqa im Alten Testament." Pages 87–129 in *Um das Prinzip der Vergeltung in Religion und Recht des Alten Testaments.* Edited by Klaus Koch. Darmstadt: Wissenschaftliche Buchgesellschaft, 1972.

Fauconnier, Gilles, and Mark Turner. "Conceptual Integration Networks." *Cognitive Science* 22 (1998): 133–87.

Fauconnier, Gilles, and Lakoff, George. "On Metaphor and Blending." *Cognitive Semiotics* 5 (2009): 393–99.

Fichtner, Johannes. *Die altorientalische Weisheit in ihrer israelitisch-jüdischen Ausprägung: Eine Studie zur Nationalisierung der Weisheit in Israel.* Giessen: Töpelman, 1933.

Fiddes, Paul S. *Seeing the World and Knowing God: Hebrew Wisdom and Christian Doctrine in Late-Modern Context.* Oxford: Oxford University Press, 2013.

Fillmore, Charles J. "An Alternative to Checklist Theories of Meaning." Pages 123–31 in *Proceedings of the First Annual Meeting of the Berkeley Linguistics Society.* California: University of California Press, 1975.

———. "Towards a Descriptive Framework for Spatial Deixis." Pages 31–59 in *Speech, Place, and Action.* Edited by R. J. Jarvella and Wolfgang Klein. London: John Wiley, 1982.

Fischer, Bonifatius, and Robert Weber. *Biblia sacra: Iuxta Vulgatam versionem.* Stuttgart: Württembergische Bibelanstalt, 1969.

Fishelov, David. *Metaphors of Genre: The Role of Analogies in Genre Theory.* University Park: Pennsylvania State University Press, 1993.

Flatto, David C. "The King and I: The Separation of Powers in Early Hebraic Political Theory." *Yale Journal of Law and the Humanities* 20 (2008): 61–110.

Fokkelman, Jan P. *Reading Biblical Poetry: An Introductory Guide.* London: Westminster John Knox, 2001.

Fontaine, Carole R. *Traditional Sayings in the Old Testament.* Sheffield: Almond Press, 1982.

Forti, Torva L. *Animal Imagery in the Book of Proverbs.* VTSup 118. Leiden: Brill, 2008.

———. "Bee's Honey—From Reali to Metaphor in Biblical Wisdom Literature." *VT* 56 (2006): 327–41.

Fowler, Alastair. "Genre." Pages 215–17 in vol. 2 of *International Encyclopedia of Communications.* Edited by Erik Barnouw et al. Oxford: Oxford University Press, 1989.

Fox, Michael V. "Ancient Near Eastern Wisdom Literature (Didactic)." *RC* 5 (2011): 1–11.

———. "Aspects of the Religion of the Book of Proverbs." *HUCA* 39 (1968): 55–69.

———. "The Epistemology of the Book of Proverbs." *JBL* 126 (2007): 669–84.

———. "How the Peshitta of Proverbs Uses the Septuagint." *JNSL* 39.2 (2013): 37–56.

———. "The Pedagogy of Proverbs 2." *JBL* 113 (1994): 233–43.

———. "A Profile of the Septuagint Proverbs." Pages 3–17 in *Wisdom for Life: Essays in Honour of Maurice Gilbert*. Edited by Nuria Calduch-Benages. Berlin: de Gruyter, 2014.

———. *Proverbs 1–9: A New Translation With Introduction and Commentary*. AB 18A. New York: Doubleday, 2000.

———. *Proverbs 10–31*. AB 18B. New Haven: Yale University Press, 2009.

———. *Proverbs: An Eclectic Edition With Introduction and Textual Commentary*. Hebrew Bible Critical Edition. Atlanta: Society of Biblical Literature, 2015.

———. "The Rhetoric of Disjointed Proverbs." *JSOT* 29 (2004): 165–77.

———. "The Social Location of the Book of Proverbs." Pages 227–39 in *Texts, Temples, and Traditions: A Tribute to Menahem Haran*. Edited by Michael V. Fox, Victor Avigdor Hurowitz, Avi M. Hurvitz, Michael L. Klein, Baruch J. Schwartz, and Nili Shupak. Winona Lake, IN: Eisenbrauns, 1996.

———. "Three These on Wisdom." Pages 69–86 in *Was There a Wisdom Tradition? New Prospects in Israelite Wisdom Studies*. Edited by Mark R. Sneed. AIL 23. Atlanta: SBL Press, 2015.

———. *A Time to Tear Down and a Time to Build Up: A Rereading of Ecclesiastes*. Grand Rapids: Eerdmans, 1999.

———. "Who Can Learn? A Dispute in Ancient Pedagogy." Pages 62–77 in *Wisdom, You Are My Sister: Studied in Honor of Roland E. Murphy, O. Carm., on the Occasion of His Eightieth Birthday*. Edited by Michael L. Barré. Washington, DC: Catholic Biblical Association of America, 1997.

———. "Wisdom and the Self-Presentation of Wisdom Literature." Pages 153–72 in *Reading from Right to Left: Essays on the Hebrew Bible in Honour of David J. A. Clines*. Edited by Jo Cheryl Exum and H. G. M. Williamson. Sheffield: Sheffield Academic, 2003.

———. "World Order and Maʿat: A Crooked Parallel." *JANESCU* 23 (1995): 37–48.

Franzmann, Majella. "The Wheel in Proverbs XX 26 and Ode of Solomon XXIII 11–16." *VT* 41 (1991): 121–23.

Frazier, Lyn, Katy Carlson, and Charles Clifton Jr. "Prosodic Phrasing Is Central to Language Comprehension." *Trends in Cognitive Sciences* 10 (2006): 244–49.

Freadman, Anne. "Anyone for Tennis?" Pages 37–56 in *Genre and the New Rhetoric*. Edited by Aviva Freedman and Peter Medway. Bristol: Taylor & Francis, 1994.

Freuling, Georg. *"Wer eine Grube gräbt..."*: *Der Tun-Ergehen-Zusammenhang und sein Wandel in der alttestamentlichen Weisheitsliteratur*. WMANT 102. Neukirchen-Vluyn: Neukirchener Verlag, 2004.

Fritsch, Charles T. "The Treatment of the Hexaplaric Signs in the Syro-Hexaplar of Proverbs." *JBL* 72 (1953): 169–81.

Frydrych, Tomáš. *Living under the Sun: Examination of Proverbs and Qoheleth*. VTSup 90. Leiden: Brill, 2002.

Geary, James. *The World in a Phrase: A Brief History of the Aphorism*. New York: Bloomsbury, 2005.

Geeraerts, Dirk *Theories of Lexical Semantics*. Oxford: Oxford University Press, 2009.

Geller, Stephen A. *Parallelism in Early Biblical Poetry*. HSM 20. Missoula, MT: Scholars Press, 1979.

Gemser, Berend. "The Importance of the Motive Clause in Old Testament Law." Pages 50–66 in *Congress Volume Copenhagen 1953*. Leiden: Brill, 1953.

———. "The Instructions of 'Onchsheshonqy and Biblical Wisdom Literature." Pages 102–28 in *Congress Volume Oxford 1959*. Edited by G. W. Anderson et al. Leiden: Brill, 1960.

———. *Sprüche Salomos*. HAT 1.16. Tübingen: Mohr Siebeck, 1963.

Gerstenberger, E. *Wesen und Herkunft des "apodiktischen Rechts."* WMANT 20. Neukirchen-Vluyn: Neukirchener Verlag, 1965.

Gese, Hartmut. *Lehre und Wirklichkeit in der alten Weisheit*. Tübingen: Mohr Siebeck, 1958.

Gibbs, Rayond W., Jr. "Multiple Constraints in Theories of Metaphor." *Discourse Processes* 48 (2011): 575–84.

Gilead, M., and N. Rosenan. "Ten Years of Dew Observation in Israel." *IEJ* 4 (1958): 120–23.

Gillon, Brendan S. "Ambiguity, Indeterminacy, Deixis, and Vagueness." Pages 157–87 in *Semantics: A Reader*. Edited by Steven Davis and Brendan S. Gillon. Oxford: Oxford University Press, 2004.

Ginsberg, H. L. "Baal's Two Messengers." *BASOR* 95 (1944): 25–30.

Ginsburg, Eliezer. *Mishlei: A New Translation with a Commentary Anthologized from Talmudic, Midrashic, and Rabbinic Sources.* Artscroll Tanach Series. New York: Mesorah, 1998.

Giora, Rachel. *On Our Mind: Salience, Context, and Figurative Language.* Oxford: Oxford University Press, 2003.

Gladson, Jerry A. "Retributive Paradoxes in Proverbs 10–29." PhD diss., Vanderbilt University, 1978.

Goering, Greg Schmidt. "Honey and Wormwood: Taste and the Embodiment of Wisdom in the Book of Proverbs." *HBAI* 5 (2016): 23–41.

Golka, Friedemann. *The Leopard's Spots: Biblical and African Wisdom in Proverbs.* Edinburgh: T&T Clark, 1993.

Gordon, Edmund I. *Sumerian Proverbs: Glimpses of Everyday Life in Ancient Mesopotamia.* Philadelphia: University Museum, University of Pennsylvania, 1959.

Gray, Alison Ruth. *Psalm 18 in Words and Pictures: A Reading through Metaphor.* BibInt 127. Leiden: Brill, 2014.

Green, Thomas, and William Pepicello. "The Proverb and Riddle as Folk Enthymemes." *Proverbium* 3 (1986): 33–46.

Greenstein, Edward L. "How Does Parallelism Mean?" Pages 41–70 in *A Sense of Text: The Art of Language in the Study of Biblical Literature.* Edited by Stephen A. Geller. Winona Lake, IN: Eisenbrauns, 1982.

Grice, Herbert Paul. "Logic and Conversation." Pages 41–58 in vol. 3 of *Syntax and Semantics.* Edited by Peter Cole and Jerry L. Morgan. New York: Academic Press, 1975.

Gros, André. *Je suis la route: Le thème de la route dans la Bible.* Thèmes Bibliques. Paris: Desclée de Brouwer, 1961.

Grzybek, Peter. "Semiotic and Semantic Aspects of the Proverb." Pages 68–111 in *Introduction to Paremiology: A Comprehensive Guide to Proverb Studies.* Edited by Hrisztalina Hrisztova-Gotthardt and Melita Aleksa Varga. Berlin: de Gruyter, 2015.

Gunkel, Hermann. *Genesis.* Göttingen: Vandenhoeck & Ruprecht, 1901.

———. *Die Psalmen.* Göttingen: Vandenhoeck & Ruprecht, 1926.

Habel, Norman C. "The Symbolism of Wisdom in Proverbs 1–9." *Int* 26 (1972): 131–57.

Hamilton, Mark W. "Riddles and Parables, Traditions and Texts: Ezekielian Perspectives on Israelite Wisdom Tradition." Pages 241–64 in *Was There a Wisdom Tradition? New Prospects in Israelite Wisdom Studies.* Edited by Mark R. Sneed. Atlanta: SBL Press, 2015.

Handelman, Don. "Traps of Trans-formation: Theoretical Convergences between Riddle and Ritual." Pages 37–61 in *Untying the Knot: On Riddles and Other Enigmatic Modes*. Edited by Galit Hasan-Rokem and David Shulman. Oxford: Oxford University Press, 1996.

Harnish, Robert M. "Communicating With Proverbs." Pages 163–84 in *Cognition, Comprehension and Communication: A Decade of North American Proverb Studies (1990–2000)*. Edited by Wolfgang Mieder. Baltmannsweiler: Schneider-Verlag Hohengehren, 2003.

Hasan-Rokem, Galit. "And God Created the Proverb … Inter-generic and Inter-textual Aspects of Biblical Paremiology—Or the Longest Way to the Shortest Text." Pages 107–20 in *Text and Tradition: The Hebrew Bible and Folklore*. Edited by Susan Niditch. Atlanta: Society of Biblical Literature, 1990.

Hasan-Rokem, Galit, and David Shulman. Introduction to *Untying the Knot: On Riddles and Other Enigmatic Modes*. Edited by Galit Hasan-Rokem and David Shulman. Oxford: Oxford University Press, 1996.

Hatton, Peter. *Contradiction in the Book of Proverbs: The Deep Waters of Counsel*. SOTSMS. Aldershot: Ashgate, 2008.

Hausmann, J. *Studien zum Menschenbild der älteren Weisheit (Spr 10ff.)*. FAT 7. Tübingen: Mohr Siebeck, 1995.

Healey, John F. "The Targum of Proverbs." In *The Targum of Job, the Targum of Proverbs, the Targum of Qohelet*. Edited by Céline Mangan, John F. Healey, and Peter S. Knobel. Edinburgh: T&T Clark, 1991.

Heerden, Willie van. "The Rhetoric of Using Proverbs in Conflict Situations: The Cases of a Biblical Text and an African Proverb." *OTE* 16 (2003): 731–44.

Heim, Knut M. *Like Grapes of Gold Set in Silver: An Interpretation of Proverbial Clusters in Proverbs 10:1–22:16*. BZAW 273. Berlin: de Gruyter, 2001.

———. *Poetic Imagination in Proverbs: Variant Repetitions and the Nature of Proverbs*. BBRSup 4. Winona Lake, IN: Eisenbrauns, 2013.

Hempel, Johannes. *Die althebräische Literatur in ihr hellenistisch-jüdisches Nachleben*. Wildpark-Potsdam: Athenaion, 1930.

Herbert, Arthur Stanley. "The 'Parable' (*Māšāl*) in the Old Testament." *SJT* 7 (1954): 180–96.

Hermisson, Hans-Jürgen. *Studien zur israelitischen Spruchweisheit*. WMANT 28. Neukirchen-Vluyn: Neukirchener Verlag, 1968.

Hess, Richard S. "Questions of Reading and Writing in Ancient Israel." *BBR* 19 (2009): 1–9.

Hildebrandt, Ted. "Motivation and Antithetical Parallelism in Proverbs 10–15." *JETS* 35 (1992): 433–44.

———. "The Proverb: An Interdisciplinary Approach to a Biblical Genre." (2005): https://tinyurl.com/SBL2642a.

———. "Proverbs 22:6a: Train Up a Child?" *Grace Theological Journal* 9 (1988): 3–19.

———. "Proverbial Strings: Cohesion in Proverbs 10." *Grace Theological Journal* 11 (1990): 171–85.

Hind, M. "Teaching for Responsibility: Confirmation and the Book of Proverbs." *RelEd* 93 (1998): 207–24.

Hirsch, E. D. *The Aims of Interpretation*. Chicago: University of Chicago Press, 1976.

Hoad, T. F. *The Concise Oxford Dictionary of English Etymology*. Oxford: Oxford University Press, 1996.

Holmstedt, Robert D. "Word Order in the Book of Proverbs." Pages 135–54 in *Seeking Out the Wisdom of the Ancients: Essays Offered to Honor Michael V. Fox on the Occasion of His Sixty-Fifth Birthday*. Edited by Ronald L. Troxel, Kelvin G. Friebel, and Dennis R. Magary. Winona Lake, IN: Eisenbrauns, 2005.

Huettig, Falk, Joost Rommers, and Antje S. Meyer. "Using the Visual World Paradigm to Study Language Processing: A Review and Critical Examination." *Acta Psychologica* 137 (2011): 151–71.

Humphreys, W. Lee. "The Motif of the Wise Courtier in the Book of Proverbs." Pages 177–90 in *Israelite Wisdom: Theological and Literary Essays in Honor of Samul Terrien*. Edited by John G. Gammie et al. Missoula, MT: Scholars Press, 1978.

Hurovitz, Victor Avigdor. "Unsavoury Personalities in the Book of Proverbs in Light of Mesopotamian Writings." *HS* 54 (2013): 93–106.

Huwiler, Elizabeth Faith. "Control of Reality in Israelite Wisdom." PhD diss., Duke University, 1988.

Ijzerman, Hans, and Sander L. Koole. "From Perceptual Rags to Metaphoric Riches—Bodily Constraints on Sociocognitive Metaphors: Comment on Landau, Meier, and Keefer." *Psychological Bulletin* 137 (2011): 355–61.

Ingram, Doug. *Ambiguity in Ecclesiastes*. LHBOTS 431. New York: T&T Clark, 2006.

Iser, Wolfgang. "Indeterminacy and the Reader's Response in Prose Fiction." Pages 1–45 in *Aspects of Narrative: Selected Papers from the Eng-*

lish Institute. Edited by J. Hillis Miller. New York: Columbia University Press, 1971.

Jäkel, Olaf. "How Can Mortal Man Understand the Road He Travels? Prospects and Problems of the Cognitive Approach to Religious Metaphor.'" Pages 55–86 in *The Bible through Metaphor and Translation: A Cognitive Semantics Perspective.* Edited by Kurt Feyaerts. Bern: Lang, 2003.

Jameson, Frederic. "Magical Narratives: On the Dialectical Use of Genre Criticism." Pages 103–50 in *The Political Unconscious: Narrative as a Socially Symbolic Act.* New York: Cornell University Press, 1982.

Janowski, Bernd. "Die Tat kehrt zum Täter zurück: Offene Fragen im Umkreis des 'Tun-Ergehen-Zusammenhangs.'" *ZTK* 91 (1994): 247–71.

Janzen, Waldemar. *Old Testament Ethics: A Paradigmatic Approach.* Louisville: Westminster John Knox, 1994.

Jason, Heda. "Proverbs in Society: The Problem of Meaning and Function." *Proverbium* 17 (1971): 617–23.

Jastrow, Marcus. *Dictionary of Targumim, Talmud and Midrashic Literature.* Peabody, MA: Hendrickson, 2005.

Jeremias, Joachim. *The Parables of Jesus.* NTL. London: SCM, 1963.

Johansen, J. D. "When the Cat's Away, the Mice Will Play: On Proverbs, Metaphors, and the Pragmatics of Blending." Pages 61–76 in *Semiotic Rotations: Modes of Meanings in Cultural Worlds.* Edited by Sunhee Kim Gertz, Jaan Valsiner, and Jean-Paul Breaux. Greenwich, CT: Information Age, 2007.

Johnson, A. R. "משל." Pages 162–69 in *Wisdom in Israel and the Ancient Near East: Presented to Professor Harold Henry Rowley.* Edited by Martin Noth and David Winton Thomas. VTSup 3. Leiden: Brill, 1955.

Johnson, Mark. *Moral Imagination: Implications of Cognitive Science for Ethics.* Chicago: University of Chicago Press, 1994.

Jolles, André. *Einfache Formen: Legende, Sage, Mythe, Rätsel, Spruch, Kasus, Memorabile, Märchen, Witz.* Tübingen: Niemeyer, 1930.

———. *Simple Forms.* New York: Verso, 2017.

Kamtekar, Rachana. "Ancient Virtue Ethics: An Overview With an Emphasis on Practical Wisdom." Pages 29–48 in *Cambridge Companion to Virtue Ethics.* Edited by Daniel C. Russell. Cambridge: Cambridge University Press, 2013.

Katz, Jerrold J., and Jerry A. Fodor. "The Structure of a Semantic Theory." *Language* 39 (1963): 170–210.

Kavusa, Kivatsi Jonathan. "The Life-Giving and Life-Threatening Potential of Water and Water-Related Phenomena in the Old Testament Wisdom Literature: An Eco-theological Exploration." PhD diss., University of South Africa Press, 2015.

Kayatz, Christa. *Studien zu Proverbien 1–9: Eine form- und motivgeschichtliche Untersuchung unter Einbeziehung ägyptischen Vergleichsmaterials.* WMANT 22. Neukirchen-Vluyn: Neukirchener Verlag, 1966.

Keel, Othmar. "Eine Diskussion um die Bedeutung polarer Begriffspaare in den Lebenslehren." Pages 225–34 in *Studien zu altägyptischen Lebenslehren.* Edited by Erik Hornung and Othmar Keel. Göttingen: Vandenhoeck & Ruprecht, 1979.

———. *The Symbolism of the Biblical World: Ancient Near Eastern Iconography and the Book of Psalms.* New York: Seabury, 1978.

Keller, Carl-Albert. "Zum sogenannten Vergeltungsglauben im Proverbienbuch." Pages 223–38 in *Beiträge zur alttestamentlichen Theologie: Festschrift für Walther Zimmerli zum 70. Geburtstag.* Edited by Herbert Donner, Rudolf Hanhart, and Robert Smend. Göttingen: Vandenhoeck & Ruprecht, 1977.

Kennedy, Christopher. "Ambiguity and Vagueness: An Overview." Pages 507–33 in vol. 1 of *Semantics: An International Handbook of Natural Language Meaning.* Edited by Claudia Maienborn, Klaus von Heusinger, and Paul Portner. Berlin: de Gruyter, 2011.

Kern-Ulmer, Brigitte. "Consistency and Change in Rabbinic Literature as Reflected in the Terms Rain and Dew." *JSJ* 26 (1995): 55–75.

Kim, Hee Suk. "Yhwh Sayings and King Sayings in Proverbs: 10:1–22:16." *Korean Journal of Christian Studies* 75 (2011): 83–104.

Kimilike, Lechion Peter. *Poverty in the Book of Proverbs: An African Transformational Hermeneutic of Proverbs on Poverty.* Bible and Theology in Africa 7. New York: Lang, 2008.

King, Phil D. *Surrounded by Bitterness: Image Schemas and Metaphor for Conceptualizing Distress in Classical Hebrew.* Eugene, OR: Pickwick, 2012.

Kirshenblatt-Gimblett, Barbara. "Towards a Theory of Proverb Meaning." Pages 111–21 in *The Wisdom of Many: Essays of the Proverb.* Edited by Wolfgang Mieder and Alan Dundes. New Yorks: Garland, 1981.

Kitchen, Kenneth A. "The Basic Literary Forms and Formulations of Ancient Instructional Writings in Egypt and Western Asia." Pages 235–82 in *Studien zu altägyptischen Lebenslehren.* Edited by Erik Hornung and Othmar Keel. Göttingen: Vandenhoeck & Ruprecht, 1979.

Klopfenstein, Martin A. *Die Lüge nach dem Alten Testament: Ihre Begriffe, ihre Bedeutung und ihre Beurteilung.* Zürich: Gotthelf, 1964.

Klostermann, August. "Schulwesen im alten Israel." Pages 193–232 in *Theologische Studien: Theodor Zahn zum 10. Oktober 1908 Dargebracht.* Edited by Gottlieb Nathanael Bonwetsch and Theodor Zahn. Leipzig: Deichert, 1908.

Knierim, Rolf. *Die Hauptbegriffe für Sünde im Alten Testament.* Gütersloh: Gütersloher Verlagshaus, 1965.

Koch, Klaus. "דרך." *TDOT* 3:270–93.

———. "Der Güter Gefährlichstes, die Sprache, dem Menschen gegeben … Überlegungen zu Gen 2,7." *BN* 48 (1989): 50–60.

———. "Gibt es ein Vergeltungsdogma im Alten Testament?" Pages 130–80 in *Um das Prinzip der Vergeltung in Religion und Recht des Alten Testaments.* Edited by Klaus Koch. Darmstadt: Wissenschaftliche Buchgesellschaft, 1972.

———. "Is There a Doctrine of Retribution in the Old Testament?" Pages 57–87 in *Theodicy in the Old Testament.* Edited by James L. Crenshaw. London: SPCK, 1983.

Krašovec, Joze. *Antithetical Structure in Biblical Hebrew Poetry.* VTSup 35. Leiden: Brill, 1984.

Krikmann, Arvo. *Some Additional Aspects of Semantic Indefiniteness of Proverbs: Remarks on Proverb Semantics 2.* Tallinn: Academy of Sciences of the Estonian SSR, 1974.

Krüger, Thomas. "Meaningful Ambiguities in the Book of Qoheleth." Pages 63–74 in *The Language of Qohelet in Its Context: Essays in Honour of Prof. A. Schoors on the Occasion of His Seventieth Birthday.* Edited by Angelika Berlejung and Pierre van Hecke. Leuven: Uitgeverij Peeters, 2007.

Kugel, James. *The Idea of Biblical Poetry: Parallelism and Its History.* New Haven: Yale University Press, 1981.

Kynes, Will. "The Modern Scholarly Wisdom Tradition and the Threat of Pan-sapientialism: A Case Report." Pages 11–38 in *Was There a Wisdom Tradition? New Prospects in Israelite Wisdom Studies.* Edited by Mark R. Sneed. Atlanta: SBL Press, 2015.

Lakoff, George. *Women, Fire, and Dangerous Things: What Categories Reveal about the Mind.* Chicago: University of Chicago Press, 1987.

Lakoff, George, and Mark Johnson. *Metaphors We Live By.* Chicago: University of Chicago Press, 1980.

Lakoff, George, and Mark Turner. *More Than Cool Reason: A Field Guide to Poetic Metaphor.* Chicago: University of Chicago Press, 1989.

Lam, Joseph. *Patterns of Sin in the Hebrew Bible: Metaphor, Culture, and the Making of a Religious Concept.* Oxford: Oxford University Press, 2015.

Lambert, Wilfred G. *Babylonian Wisdom Literature.* Oxford: Clarendon, 1960.

Lamberty-Zielinkski, H. "נשמה." *TDOT* 10:65–70.

Landes, George M. "Jonah: A *Māšāl*?" Pages 137–58 in *Israelite Wisdom: Theological and Literary Essays in Honor of Samuel Terrien.* Edited by John G. Gammie. New York: Scholars Press, 1978.

Lang, Bernhard. "Schule und Unterricht im alten Israel." Pages 186–201 in *La sagesse de l'Ancien Testament.* Edited by Maurice Gilbert. Leuven: Leuven University Press, 1979.

Lapsley, Jacqueline E. *Can These Bones Live? The Problem of the Moral Self in the Book of Ezekiel.* Berlin: de Gruyter, 2000.

Lauhakangas, Outi. "Proverbs in Social Interaction: Questions Aroused by the Multi-functionality of Proverbial Speech." *Proverbium* 24 (2007): 204–28.

Lagarde, Paul de. "Anmerkungen zur griechischen Übersetzung der Proverbien." Pages 19–26 in vol. 1 of *Mittheilungen.* Göttingen: Dieterich, 1884.

———. *Hagiographa Chaldaice.* 4 vols. Leipzig, 1873.

Leeuwen, Raymond C. van. *Context and Meaning in Proverbs 25–27.* SBLDS 96. Atlanta: Scholars Press, 1988.

———. "Proverbs." Pages 256–67 in *A Complete Literary Guide to the Bible.* Edited by Leland Ryken and Tremper Longmann III. Grand Rapids: Zondervan, 1993.

———. "Wealth and Poverty: System and Contradiction in Proverbs." *HS* 33 (1992): 25–36.

Lemaire, André. *Écoles et la formation de la Bible dans l'ancien Israël.* OBO 39. Fribourg: Universitätsverlag; Göttingen: Vandenhoeck & Ruprecht, 1981.

Lewandowska-Tomaszczyk, Barbara. "Polysemy, Prototypes, and Radial Categories." Pages 139–69 in *The Oxford Handbook of Cognitive Linguistics.* Edited by Dirk Geeraerts and Hubert Cuyckens. Oxford: Oxford University Press, 2010.

Lichtheim, Miriam. "Didactic Literature." Pages 243–62 in *Ancient Egyptian Literature: History and Forms.* Edited by Antonio Lopriendo. Leiden: Brill, 1996.

———. *Maat in Egyptian Autobiographies and Related Studies.* OBO 120. Fribourg: Universitätsverlag; Göttingen: Vandenhoeck & Ruprecht, 1992.

———. *Moral Values in Ancient Egypt.* OBO 155. Fribourg: Universitätsverlag; Göttingen: Vandenhoeck & Ruprecht, 1997.

———. "Observations on Papyrus Insinger." Pages 283–306 in *Studien zu altägyptischen Lebenslehren.* Edited by Erik Hornung and Othmar Keel. Göttingen: Vandenhoeck & Ruprecht, 1979.

Lieber, Michael D. "Analogic Ambiguity: A Paradox of Proverb Usage." *JAF* 97.386 (1984): 423–41.

Lindenberger, J. M. *The Aramaic Proverbs of Ahiqar.* Baltimore: Johns Hopkins University Press, 1983.

Loader, James Alfred. "The Problem of Money in the Hand of a Fool." *HvTSt* 68 (2012): 1–9.

Loewenstamm, Samuel E. "Remarks on Proverbs XVII 12 and XX 27." *VT* 37 (1987): 221–24.

Longman, Tremper, III. *The Book of Ecclesiastes.* NICOT. Grand Rapids: Eerdmans, 1998.

Lowth, Robert. *Isaiah: A New Translation; With a Preliminary Dissertation, and Notes, Critical, Philological, and Explanatory.* Boston: Hillard, 1834.

———. *Lectures on the Sacred Poetry of the Hebrews.* Andover: Codman, 1829.

Lund, Øystein. *Way Metaphors and Way Topics in Isaiah 40–55.* FAT 2/28. Tübingen: Mohr Siebeck, 2007.

Lyu, Sun Myung. *Righteousness in the Book of Proverbs.* FAT 2/55. Tübingen: Mohr Siebeck, 2012.

Maier, Christl M. *Die "fremde Frau" in Proverbien 1–9: Eine exegetische und sozialgeschichtliche Studie.* Göttingen: Vandenhoeck & Ruprecht, 1995.

Malchow, Bruce V. "A Manual for Future Monarchs." *CBQ* 47 (1985): 238–45.

Margolis, Eric, and Stephen M. Laurence. *Concepts: Core Readings.* Cambridge: MIT Press, 1999.

Mason, Robert A., and Marcel Adam Just. "Lexical Ambiguity in Sentence Comprehension." *Brain Research* 1146 (2007): 115–27.

McCawley, James D. *Everything That Linguistics Have Always Wanted to Know about Logic but Were Ashamed to Ask.* Chicago: University of Chicago Press, 1981.

McCreesh, Thomas P. *Biblical Sound and Sense: Poetic Sound Patterns in Proverbs 10–29.* JSOTSup 128. Sheffield: JSOT Press, 1991.

McKane, William. "Functions of Language and Objectives of Discourse according to Proverbs 10–31." Pages 166–85 in *La sagesse de l'Ancien Testament.* Edited by Maurice Gilbert. Leuven: Leuven University Press, 1979.

———. *Prophets and Wise Men.* SBT 44. London: SCM, 1965.

———. *Proverbs: A New Approach.* OTL. London: SCM, 1970.

McKeating, Henry. *Studying the Old Testament.* London: Epworth, 1979.

Mervis, Carolyn B., and Eleanor Rosch. "Categorization of Natural Objects." *Annual Review of Psychology* 32 (1981): 89–115.

Meynet, Roland. *Rhetorical Analysis: An Introduction to Biblical Rhetoric.* JSOTSup 256. Sheffield: Sheffield Academic, 1998.

Mieder, Wolfgang. "The Essence of Literary Proverb Studies." *Proverbium* 23 (1974): 888–94.

Millar, Suzanna R. "The Path Metaphor and the Construction of a *Schicksalwirkende Tatsphäre* in Proverbs 10:1–22:16." *VT* 69 (2019): 95–108.

———. "When a Straight Road Becomes a Garden Path: The 'False Lead' as a Pedagogical Strategy in the Book of Proverbs." *JSOT* 43.1 (2018): 67–82.

Millard, Alan R. "Writing, Writing Materials and Literacy in the Ancient Near East." Pages 1003–11 in *Dictionary of the Old Testament: Historical Books.* Edited by Bill T. Arnold and H. G. M. Williamson. Downers Grove, IL: InterVarsity Press, 2005.

Miller, Cynthia L. "A Linguistic Approach to Ellipsis in Biblical Poetry." *BBR* 13 (2003): 251–70.

Miller, Patrick D., Jr. *Sin and Judgment in the Prophets: A Stylistic and Theological Analysis.* SBLMS 27. Chicago: Scholars Press, 1982.

Milner, G. B. "Quadripartite Structures." *Proverbium* 14 (1969): 379–83.

Mitchell, T. C. "The Old Testament Usage of Nešāmâ." *VT* 11 (1961): 177–87.

Mouser, William E. "Filling in the Blank: Asymmetrical Antithetical Parallelism." Pages 137–50 in *Learning from the Sages: Selected Studies of the Book of Proverbs.* Edited by Roy B. Zuck. Grand Rapids: Baker, 1995.

Mowinckel, Sigmund. *The Psalms in Israel's Worship.* Oxford: Blackwell, 1962.

Muraoka, Takamitsu. *Emphatic Words and Structures in Biblical Hebrew.* Leiden: Brill, 1985.

Murphy, Roland E. *Proverbs.* WBC. Nashville: T. Nelson, 1998.

Nahkola, Aulikki. "Orality and the Sage: A Word (Proverb) to the Wise Suffices." Pages 56–82 in *Perspectives on Israelite Wisdom: Proceedings of the Oxford Old Testament Seminar.* Edited by John Jarick. Oxford: Bloomsbury T&T Clark, 2016.

Naré, Laurent. *Proverbes salomoniens et proverbes mossi: Etude comparative à partir d'une nouvelle analyse de Pr 25–29.* Bern: Lang, 1986.

Nel, Philip J. "Juxtaposition and Logic in the Wisdom Sayings." *JNSL* 24 (1998): 115–27.

Newsom, Carol A. *The Book of Job: A Contest of Moral Imaginations.* Oxford: Oxford University Press, 2003.

———. "Spying Out the Land: A Report from Genology." Pages 437–50 in *Seeking Out the Wisdom of the Ancients: Essays Offered to Honor Michael V. Fox on the Occasion of His Sixty-Fifth Birthday.* Edited by Ronald L. Troxel, Kelvin G. Friebel, and Dennis R. Magary. Winona Lake, IN: Eisenbrauns, 2005.

Nicol, George G. "The Alleged Rape of Bathsheba: Some Observations on Ambiguity in Biblical Narrative." *JSOT* 73 (1997): 43–54.

Niditch, Susan. *Folklore and the Hebrew Bible.* GBS. Minneapolis: Fortress, 1993.

———. *Oral World and Written Word: Ancient Israelite Literature.* LAI. Louisville: Westminster John Knox, 1996.

Nietzsche, Friedrich. *Beyond Good and Evil.* New York: Modern Library, 1917.

Nöldeke, Theodor. "Das Targum zu den Sprüchen von der Peschita abhängig." *Archiv für wissenschaftliches Erforschung des Alten Testaments* 2 (1871): 246–49.

Norrick, Neal R. "'Speech Is Silver': On the Proverbial View of Language." *Proverbium* 14 (1997): 277–87.

———. "Subject Area, Terminology, Proverb Definitions, Proverb Features." Pages 7–27 in *Introduction to Paremiology: A Comprehensive Guide to Proverb Studies.* Edited by Hrisztalina Hrisztova-Gotthardt and Melita Aleksa Varga. Berlin: de Gruyter, 2015.

Nötscher, Friedrich. *Gotteswege und Menschenwege in der Bibel und in Qumran.* BBB 15. Bonn: Hanstein, 1958.

Nyika, Hillary. "The Traditional Israelite Legal Settings: Social Contexts in Proverbs." Pages 34–55 in *Wisdom, Science, and the Scriptures: Essays in Honor of Ernest Lucas.* Edited by Stephen Finamore and John Weaker. Wipf & Stock, 2015.

O'Connor, Michael. *Hebrew Verse Structure*. Winona Lake, IN: Eisenbrauns, 1980.

O'Dowd, Ryan. *The Wisdom of Torah: Epistemology in Deuteronomy and the Wisdom Literature*. FRLANT 225. Göttingen: Vandenhoeck & Ruprecht, 2009.

Oesterley, W. O. E. *The Book of Proverbs*. London: Methuen, 1929.

Pagliaro, Harold E. "Paradox in the Aphorisms of La Rochefoucauld and Some Representative English Followers." *PMLA* 79 (1964): 42–50.

Pardee, Dennis. *Ugaritic and Hebrew Poetic Parallelism: A Trial Cut (ʿnt 1 and Proverbs 2)*. VTSup 39. Leiden: Brill, 1988.

———. "YPḤ 'Witness' in Hebrew and Ugaritic." *VT* 28 (1978): 204–13.

Parkhurst, John. *Hebrew Lexicon and Grammar*. London: Sherwood, Neely & Jones, 1821.

Paterson, John. *The Book That Is Alive: Studies in Old Testament Life and Thought as Set Forth by the Hebrew Sages*. New York: Scribner's Sons, 1954.

Payne, Geoffrey. "Parallelism in Biblical Hebrew Verse." *SJOT* 8.1 (1994): 126–40.

Pedersen, Johannes. *Israel: Its Life and Culture*. 2 vols. Copenhagen: S. L. Møller, 1926.

Penfield, Joyce, and Mary Duru, "Proverbs: Metaphors That Teach." *Anthropological Quarterly* 61.3 (1988): 119–28.

Perdue, Leo G. "Liminality as a Social Setting for Wisdom Instructions." *ZAW* 93 (1981): 114–26.

———. *Proverbs*. IBC. Lewisville: John Knox, 2000.

———. "The Riddles of Psalm 49." *JBL* 93 (1974): 533–42.

———. *The Sword and the Stylus: An Introduction to Wisdom in the Age of Empires*. Grand Rapids: Eerdmans, 2008.

———. *Wisdom Literature: A Theological History*. Louisville: Westminster John Knox, 2007.

Perry, Theodore A. "Quadripartite Wisdom Sayings and the Structure of Proverbs." *Proverbium* 4 (1987): 187–210.

———. *Wisdom Literature and the Structure of Proverbs*. University Park: Pennsylvania State University Press, 1993.

Pilch, John J. "Proverbs in Middle East North Africa (Mena*) Cultural Context." *BTB* 45 (2015): 202–14.

Polk, Timothy. "Paradigms, Parables, and *Měšālîm*: On Reading the *Māšāl* in Scripture." *CBQ* 45 (1983): 563–84.

Preuß, Horst Dietrich. *Einführung in die alttestamentliche Weisheitslitera-tur*. Urban-Taschenbücher Band 383. Stuttgart: Kohlhammer, 1987.

Quack, J. F. *Die Lehren des Ani: Ein neuägyptischer Weisheitstext in seinem kulturellen Umfeld*. OBO 141. Fribourg: Universitätsverlag; Göttingen: Vandenhoeck & Ruprecht, 1995.

Rad, Gerhard von. *Old Testament Theology*. 2 vols. Edinburgh: Oliver & Boyd, 1962.

———. *Wisdom in Israel*. London: SCM, 1972.

Rayner, Keith, Anne E. Cook, Barbara J. Juhasz, and Lyn Frazier. "Imme-diate Disambiguation of Lexically Ambiguous Words during Read-ing: Evidence from Eye Movements." *British Journal of Psychology* 97 (2006): 467–82.

Reider, Joseph. "Etymological Studies in Biblical Hebrew." *VT* 4 (1954): 276–95.

Rendsburg, Gary A. "Literary and Linguistic Matters in the Book of Prov-erbs." Pages 111–47 in *Perspectives on Israelite Wisdom: Proceedings of the Oxford Old Testament Seminar*. Edited by John Jarick. Oxford: Bloomsbury T&T Clark, 2016.

Reventlow, Henning G. "Sein Blut komme über sein Haupt." *VT* 10 (1960): 311–27.

Reymond, Philippe. *L'eau, sa vie, et sa signification dans l'Ancien Testa-ment*. VTSup 6. Leiden: Brill, 1958.

Richards, I. A. *The Philosophy of Rhetoric*. Mary Flexner Lectures on the Humanities 3. Oxford: Oxford University Press, 1936.

Richardson, H. Neil. "Some Notes on ליץ and Its Derivatives." *VT* 5 (1955): 163–79.

Ringgren, Helmer, Artur Weiser, and Walther Zimmerli. *Sprüche/Prediger; Das Hohe Lied/Klagelieder; Das Buch Esther*. ATD 16. Göttingen: Van-denhoeck & Ruprecht, 1962.

Robert, André. "Les attaches litteraires bibliques de Prov. I–IX." *RB* 43 (1934): 42–68, 172–204, 374–84.

———. "Les attaches litteraires bibliques de Prov. I–IX (Suite)." *RB* 44 (1935): 344–65, 502–25.

Rodd, Cyril S. *Glimpses of a Strange Land: Studies in Old Testament Ethics*. OTS. Edinburgh: T&T Clark, 2001.

Rogland, Max. *Alleged Non-past Uses of* Qatal *in Classical Hebrew*. Studia Semitic Neerlandica 44. Assen: Royal Van Gorcum, 2003.

Rollston, Christopher A. *Writing and Literacy in the World of Ancient Israel: Epigraphic Evidence from the Iron Age.* Atlanta: Society of Biblical Literature, 2010.

Rosch, Eleanor. "Cognitive Reference Points." *Cognitive Psychology* 7 (1975): 532–47.

———. "Cognitive Representations of Semantic Categories." *Journal of Experimental Psychology* 104 (1975): 192–233.

———. "Natural Categories." *Cognitive Psychology* 4 (1973): 328–250.

———. "Principles of Categorization." Pages 27–48 in *Cognition and Categorization.* Edited by Eleanor Rosch and Barbara B. Lloyd. Hillsdae, NJ: Lawrence Erlbaum, 1978.

Roth, Martha T., ed. *The Assyrian Dictionary.* Vol. 12. Chicago: Oriental Institute of the University of Chicago, 2005.

Roth, Wolfgang M. W., ed. *Numerical Sayings in the Old Testament: A Form-Critical Study.* VTSup 13. Leiden: Brill, 1965.

Russell, Daniel C. "Virtue Ethics in Modern Moral Philosophy." Pages 1–6 in *The Cambridge Companion to Virtue Ethics.* Edited by Daniel C. Russell. Cambridge: Cambridge University Press, 2013.

Sanders, Seth L. *The Invention of Hebrew.* Chicago: University of Illinois Press, 2009.

Sandoval, Timothy J. *The Discourse of Wealth and Poverty in the Book of Proverbs.* Leiden: Brill, 2006.

Scharbert, Josef. "Šlm im Alten Testament." Pages 300–24 in *Um das Prinzip der Vergeltung in Religion und Recht des Alten Testaments.* Edited by Klaus Koch. Darmstadt: Wissenschaftliche Buchgesellschaft, 1972.

Schipper, Bernd U. *Hermeneutik der Tora: Studien zur Traditionsgeschichte von Prov 2 und zur Komposition von Prov 1–9.* Berlin: de Gruyter, 2012.

Schmid, Hans Heinrich. *Gerechtigkeit als Weltordnung: Hintergrund und Geschichte des alttestamentlichen Gerechtigkeitsbegriffes.* BHT 40. Tübingen: Mohr Siebeck, 1968.

———. *Wesen und Geschichte der Weisheit: Eine Untersuchung zur altorientalischen und israelitischen Weisheitsliteratur.* Berlin: Töpelmann, 1966.

Schmid, Hans-Jörg. "Entrenchment, Salience, and Basic Levels." Pages 117–38 in *The Oxford Handbook of Cognitive Linguistics.* Edited by Dirk Geeraerts and Hubert Cuckens. Oxford: Oxford University Press, 2007.

Schneider, Théo R. *The Sharpening of Wisdom: Old Testament Proverbs in Translation.* OTESup 1. Pretoria: OTSSA, 1992.

Schniedewind, William M. *How the Bible Became a Book: The Textualization of Ancient Israel.* Cambridge: Cambridge University Press, 2004.

Schwab, Zoltán. "Is Fear of the Lord the Source of Wisdom or Vice Versa?" *VT* 63 (2013): 652–62.

———. "Mind the Gap: The Impact of Wolfgang Iser's Reader-Response Criticism on Biblical Studies—A Critical Assessment." *Literature and Theology* 17 (2003): 170–81.

———. "The Sayings Clusters in Proverbs: Towards an Associative Reading Strategy." *JSOT* 38 (2013): 59–79.

Scoralick, Ruth. *Einzelspruch und Sammlung: Komposition im Buch der Sprichwörter Kapitel 10–15.* BZAW 232. Berlin: de Gruyter, 1995.

Scott, R. B. Y. "Meteorological Phenomena and Terminology in the Old Testament." *ZAW* 64 (1952): 11–25.

———. *Proverbs, Ecclesiastes.* AB 18. New York: Doubleday, 1965.

———. "Wise and Foolish, Righteous and Wicked." Pages 146–65 in *Studies in Religion of Ancient Israel.* Edited by Gary W. Anderson et al. Leiden: Brill, 1972.

Searle, John R. *Speech Acts: An Essay in the Philosophy of Language.* Cambridge: Cambridge University Press, 1970.

Seeligmann, Isac Leo. "Voraussetzungen der Midraschexegese." Pages 150–81 in *Congress Volume Copenhagen 1953.* Edited by G. W. Anderson et al. Leiden: Brill, 1953.

Seidel, M. *Hiqre Lashon* (Linguistic Studies). Jerusalem, 1932.

Seitel, Peter. "Proverbs: A Social Use of Metaphor." *Genre* 2 (1969): 143–61.

Seow, C. L. *Ecclesiastes: A New Translation with Introduction and Commentary.* AB 18C. New York: Doubleday, 1994.

Seybold, Klaus. "Anmerkung zum Parallelismus Membrorum in der hebräische Poesie.'" Pages 105–16 in *Parallelismus Membrorum.* Edited by Andreas Wagner. Göttingen: Vandenhoeck & Ruprecht, 2007.

Shupak, Nili. "The Instruction of Amenemope and Proverbs 22:17–24:22 from the Perspective of Contemporary Research." Pages 203–20 in *Seeking Out the Wisdom of the Ancients: Essays Offered to Honor Michael V. Fox on the Occasion of His Sixty-Fifth Birthday.* Edited by Ronald L. Troxel, Kelvin G. Friebel, and Dennis R. Magary. Winona Lake, IN: Eisenbrauns, 2005.

———. "Learning Methods in Ancient Israel." *VT* 53 (2003): 416–26.

———. "Positive and Negative Human Types in the Egyptian Wisdom Literature." Pages 245–60 in *Homeland and Exile: Biblical and Ancient*

Near Eastern Studies in Honour of Bustenay Oded. Edited by Gershon Galil, Mark Geller, and Alan Millard. Leiden: Brill, 2009.

———. *Where Can Wisdom Be Found? The Sage's Language in the Bible and in Ancient Egyptian Literature.* OBO 130. Fribourg: Universitätsverlag; Göttingen: Vandenhoeck & Ruprecht, 1993.

Skehan, Patrick W. "A Single Editor for the Whole Book of Proverbs." Pages 329–40 in *Studies in Ancient Israelite Wisdom.* Edited by James L. Crenshaw. New York: Ktav, 1976.

Skehan, Patrick W., and Eugene Ulrich. "Proverbs." Pages 181–86 in *Qumran Cave 4: XI: Psalms to Chronicles.* Edited by Eugene Ulrich, Frank Moore Cross, and Joseph A. Fitzmyer. DJD 16. Oxford: Clarendon, 2000.

Skladny, Udo. *Die ältesten Spruchsammlungen in Israel.* Göttingen: Vandenhoeck & Ruprecht, 1962.

Smith, Sidney. "The Threshing Floor at the City Gate." *PEJ* 78 (1946): 5–14.

Snedeker, Jesse, and John C. Trueswell. "Using Prosody to Avoid Ambiguity: Effects of Speaker Awareness and Referential Context." *Journal of Memory and Language* 48 (2003): 103–30.

Sneed, Mark R. "'Grasping after the Wind': The Elusive Attempt to Define and Delimit Wisdom." Pages 39–68 in *Was There a Wisdom Tradition? New Prospects in Israelite Wisdom Studies.* Edited by Mark R. Sneed. Atlanta: SBL Press, 2015.

———. "Is the 'Wisdom Tradition' a Tradition?" *CBQ* 73 (2011): 50–71.

———, ed. *Was There a Wisdom Tradition? New Prospects in Israelite Wisdom Studies.* AIL 23. Atlanta: SBL Press, 2015.

Snell, Daniel C. "The Relation between the Targum and the Peshitta of Proverbs." *ZAW* 110 (1998): 72–74.

———. *Twice-Told Proverbs and the Composition of the Book of Proverbs.* Winona Lake, IN: Eisenbrauns, 1993.

———. "The Wheel in Proverbs XX 26." *VT* 39 (1989): 503–7.

Sokoloff, Michael. *A Dictionary of Christian Palestinian Aramaic.* Leuven: Peeters, 2014.

———. *A Dictionary of Jewish Palestinian Aramaic.* Ramat-Gan: Bar Ilan University Press, 1990.

———. *A Dictionary of Jewish Babylonian Aramaic of the Talmudic and Geonic Periods.* Ramat-Gan: Bar Ilan University Press, 2002.

Spivey, M. J., M. K. Tanenhaus, K. M. Eberhard, and J. C. Sedivy. "Eye Movements and Spoken Language Comprehension: Effects of Visual

Context on Syntactic Ambiguity Resolution." *Cognitive Psychology* 45 (2002): 447–81.

Sternberg, Meir. *The Poetics of Biblical Narrative: Ideological Literature and the Drama of Reading.* Indiana Literary Biblical Series. Bloomington: Indiana University Press, 1985.

Stewart, Anne W. *Poetic Ethics in Proverbs: Wisdom Literature and the Shaping of the Moral Self.* Cambridge: Cambridge University Press, 2016.

———. "Wisdom's Imagination: Moral Reasoning and the Book of Proverbs." *JSOT* 40 (2016): 351–72.

Strawn, Brent A. *What Is Stronger Than a Lion? Leonine Imagery and Metaphor in the Hebrew Bible and the Ancient Near East.* OBO. Fribourg: Academic Press; Göttingen: Vandenhoeck & Ruprecht, 2005.

Sullivan, Karen, and Eve Sweetser. "Is 'Generic is Specific' a Metaphor." Pages 309–28 in *Meaning, Form, and Body.* Edited by Fey Parrill, Vera Tobin, and Mark Turner. Stanford, CA: CSLI, 2010.

Suter, David W. "*Māšāl* in the Similitudes of Enoch." *JBL* 100 (1981): 193–212.

Tamás, K. "Paremiography: Proverb Collections." Pages 229–42 in *Introduction to Paremiology: A Comprehensive Guide to Proverb Studies.* Edited by Hrisztalina Hrisztova-Gotthardt and Melita Aleksa Varga. Berlin: de Gruyter, 2015.

Tauberschmidt, Gerhard. *Secondary Parallelism: A Study of the Translation Technique in LXX Proverbs.* AcBib 15. Atlanta: Society of Biblical Literature, 2004.

Taylor, Archer. *The Proverb.* Cambridge: Harvard University Press, 1931.

Taylor, Barry. "Medieval Proverb Collections: The West European Tradition." *Journal of the Warburg and Courtauld Institutes* 55 (1992): 19–25.

Taylor, J. "The Sumerian Proverb Collections." *RA* 99 (2005): 13–38.

Tidwell, N. L. "No Highway! The Outline of a Semantic Description of Mesillâ." *VT* 45 (1995): 251–69.

Tobolwsky, Andrew. "Where Doom Is Spoken: Threshing Floors as Places of Decision and Communication in Biblical Literature." *JANER* 16 (2016): 95–120.

Torcszyner, Harry. משלי שלמה. [Proverbs of Solomon] Tel Aviv: Yavneh, 1947.

———. "The Riddle in the Bible." *HUCA* 1 (1924): 125–49.

Tov, Emanuel. "Recensional Differences between the Masoretic Text and the Septuagint of Proverbs." Pages 43–56 in *Of Scribes and Scrolls:*

Studies on the Hebrew Bible, Intertestamental Judaism, and Christian Origins Presented to John Strugnell on the Occasion of His Sixtieth Birthday. Edited by Harold W. Attridge, John J. Collins and Thomas H. Tobin. Lanham, MD: University Press of America, 1990.

Toy, Crawford Howell. *A Critical and Exegetical Commentary on the Book of Proverbs.* ICC. Edinburgh: T&T Clark, 1899.

Traxler, Matthew J. *Introduction to Psycholinguistics: Understanding Language Science.* Chichester: Wiley-Blackwell, 2012.

Tribushinina, Elena. *Cognitive Reference Points: Semantics beyond the Prototypes in Adjectives of Space and Colour.* Utrecht: LOT, 2008.

Tucker, Gene M. "Sin and 'Judgment' in the Prophets." Pages 373–88 in *Problems in Biblical Theology: Essays in Honor of Rolf Knierim.* Edited by Henry T. C. Sun and Keith L. Eades. Grand Rapids: Eerdmans, 1997.

Tuggy, David. "Ambiguity, Polysemy, and Vagueness." *Cognitive Linguistics* 4 (1993): 273–90.

Veldhuis, Niek. "Sumerian Proverbs in Their Curricular Context." *JAOS* 120 (2000): 383–99.

Viljoen, Anneke. "An Exploration of the Symbolic World of Proverbs 10:1–15:33 with Specific Reference to 'the Fear of the Lord.'" PhD, University of Pretoria, 2013.

Vittmann, Günter. *Altägyptische Wegmetaphorik.* Beiträge zur Ägyptologie 15. Wein: Afro-Pub, 1999.

Waard, Jan de. "4QProv and Textual Criticism." *Text* 19 (1998): 87–96.

Wagner, A. "Der Parallelismus Membrorum zwischen poetischer Form und Denkfigur." Pages 1–28 in *Parallelismus Membrorum.* Edited by Andreas Wagner. Göttingen: Vandenhoeck & Ruprecht, 2007.

Waltke, Bruce K. *The Book of Proverbs: Chapters 1–15.* NICOT. Grand Rapids: Eerdmans, 2004.

———. *The Book of Proverbs: Chapters 16–31.* NICOT. Grand Rapids: Eerdmans, 2005.

Washington, Harold C. *Wealth and Poverty in the Instruction of Amenemope and the Hebrew Proverbs.* SBLDS 142. Atlanta: Scholars Press, 1994.

Waters, Jaime L. *Threshing Floors in Ancient Israel: Their Ritual and Symbolic Significance.* Minneapolis: Fortress, 2015.

Watson, Wilfred G. E. *Classical Hebrew Poetry: A Guide to Its Techniques.* JSOTSup 26. Sheffield: JSOT Press, 1984.

———. *Traditional Techniques in Classical Hebrew Verse.* Sheffield: JSOT Press, 1994.

Weeks, Stuart. *Early Israelite Wisdom.* Oxford Theological Monographs. Oxford: Oxford University Press, 1994.

———. *An Introduction to the Study of Wisdom Literature.* T&T Clark Approaches to Biblical Studies. London: T&T Clark, 2010.

———. *Instruction and Imagery in Proverbs 1–9.* Oxford: Oxford University Press, 2007.

———. "The Limits of Form Criticism in the Study of Literature, with Reflections of Psalm 34." Pages 15–25 in *Biblical Interpretation and Method: Essays in Honour of John Barton.* Edited by Katharine J. Dell and Paul M. Joyce. Oxford: Oxford University Press, 2013.

———. "Wisdom, Form, and Genre." Pages 161–80 in *Was There a Wisdom Tradition? New Prospects in Israelite Wisdom Studies.* Edited by Mark R. Sneed. Atlanta: SBL Press, 2015.

Westermann, Claus. *Roots of Wisdom: The Oldest Proverbs of Israel and Other Peoples.* Louisville: Westminster John Knox, 1995.

Whitelam, Keith W. *The Just King: Monarchical Judicial Authority in Ancient Israel.* JSOTSup 12. Sheffield: JSOT Press, 1979.

Whybray, R. N. *The Composition of the Book of Proverbs.* Sheffield: JSOT Press, 1994.

———. *Wealth and Poverty in the Book of Proverbs.* JSOTSup 99. Sheffield: JSOT Press, 1990.

———. "Yahweh-Sayings and Their Context in Proverbs 10:1–22:16." Pages 153–65 in *La sagesse de l'Ancien Testament.* Edited by Maurice Gilbert. Leuven: Leuven University Press, 1979.

Whybray, R. N., and Robert Morgan, eds. *The Book of Proverbs: A Survey of Modern Study.* History of Biblical Interpretation Series 1. Leiden: Brill, 1995.

Widbäck, Anders. "Summary: Proverbs in Play; Usage of Proverbs in Drama Dialogue." Pages 160–69 in *Ordspråk i bruk: Användning av ordspråk i dramadialog.* Uppsala: Uppsala Universitet, 2015.

Williams, James G. "The Power of Form: A Study of Biblical Proverbs." *Semeia* 17 (1980): 35–58.

———. "Proverbs and Ecclesiastes." Pages 263–82 in *The Literary Guide to the Bible.* Edited by Robert Alter and Frank Kermode. London: Collins, 1987.

———. *Those Who Ponder Proverbs: Aphoristic Thinking and Biblical Literature.* Sheffield: Almond, 1981.

Williams, Ronald J. *Williams' Hebrew Syntax.* Revised and expanded by John C. Beckman. 3rd ed. Toronto: University of Toronto Press, 2007.

Wilson, Lindsay. "Artful Ambiguity in Ecclesiastes 1,1–11." Pages 357–66 in *Qohelet in the Context of Wisdom.* Edited by Anton Schoors. Leuven: Leuven University Press, 1998.

Wilson, Robert R. "Israel's Judicial System in the Preexilic Period." *JQR* 74 (1983): 229–48.

Wimsatt, W. K., and Monroe C. Beardsley. "The Intentional Fallacy." *Sewanee Review* 54 (1946): 468–88.

Winton Thomas, D. "Proverbs XX 26." *JJS* 15 (1964): 155–56.

———. "The Meaning of חטאת in Proverbs X.16." *JTS* 15 (1964): 295–96.

Wittgenstein, Ludwig. *Philosophical Investigations.* Oxford: Blackwell, 1958.

Wolde, Ellen José van. *Reframing Biblical Studies: When Language and Text Meet Culture, Cognition, and Context.* Winona Lake, IN: Eisenbrauns, 2009.

Wolff, Hans Walter. *Anthropology of the Old Testament.* London: SCM, 1974.

Wolters, Albert M. "Proverbs XXXI 10–31 as Heroic Hymn: A Form-Critical Analysis." *VT* 38 (1988): 446–57.

Wong, Ka Leung. *The Idea of Retribution in the Book of Ezekiel.* VTSup 87. Leiden: Brill, 2001.

Yee, Gale A., "'Fraught with Background' Literary Ambiguity in Ii Samuel 11." *Int* 42 (1988): 240–53.

Yoder, Christine Roy. "Forming 'Fearers of Yahweh': Repetition and Contradiction as Pedagogy in Proverbs." Pages 167–83 in *Seeking Out the Wisdom of the Ancients: Essays Offered in Honor of Michael V. Fox on the Occasion of His Sixty-Fifth Birthday.* Edited by Ronald L. Troxel, Kelvin G. Friebel, and Dennis R. Magary. Winona Lake, IN: Eisenbrauns, 2005.

———. *Proverbs.* AOTC. Nashville: Abingdon, 2009.

———. *Wisdom as a Woman of Substance: A Socioeconomic Reading of Proverbs 1–9 and 31:10–31.* Berlin: de Gruyter, 2001.

Zabán, Bálint Károly. *The Pillar Function of the Speeches of Wisdom: Proverbs 1:20–33, 8:1–36 and 9:1–6 in the Structural Framework of Proverbs 1–9.* BZAW 429. Berlin: de Gruyter, 2012.

Zadeh, Lotfi A. "Fuzzy Sets." *Information and Control* 8 (1965): 338–53.

Zehnder, Markus Philipp. *Wegmetaphorik im Alten Testament: Eine semantische Untersuchung der alttestamentlichen und altorientlischen*

Weg-Lexeme mit besonderer Berücksichtigung ihrer metaphorischen Verwendung. BZAW 268. Berlin: de Gruyter, 1999.

Zempleni, M.-Z., R. Renken, J. C. J. Hoeks, J. M. Hoogduin, and L. A. Stowe. "Semantic Ambiguity Processing in Sentence Contexts: Evidence from Event-Related Fmri." *NeuroImage* 34 (2007): 1270–79.

Zer Kavod, Mordechai. "חידות בספר משלי" [Riddles in the Book of Proverbs]. *Beit Mikra* 64 (1975): 7–11.

Zerafa, P. "Retribution in the Old Testament." *Angelicum* 50 (1973): 464–94.

Zhang, Qiao. "Fuzziness—Vagueness—Generality—Ambiguity." *Journal of Pragmatics* 29 (1998): 13–31.

Zimmerli, Walther. "The Place and Limit of the Wisdom in the Framework of the Old Testament Theology." *SJT* 17 (1964): 146–58.

Ancient Sources Index

Modern Authors Index

Lightning Source UK Ltd.
Milton Keynes UK
UKHW010621140520
363168UK00006B/1826